Insurgent Citizenship

 *Series*

Series Editor
Paul Rabinow

A list of titles in the series appears at the back of the book

Insurgent Citizenship

Disjunctions of Democracy and Modernity in Brazil

James Holston

PRINCETON UNIVERSITY PRESS
PRINCETON AND OXFORD

Copyright © 2008 by Princeton University Press

Published by Princeton University Press,
41 William Street, Princeton, New Jersey 08540

In the United Kingdom: Princeton University Press,
3 Market Place, Woodstock, Oxfordshire OX20 1SY

Library of Congress Cataloging-in-Publication Data

Holston, James.
    Insurgent citizenship : disjunctions of democracy and modernity in Brazil / James
Holston.
        p. cm. — (In-formation series)
    Includes bibliographical references and index.
    ISBN 978-0-691-13021-7 (hardcover : alk. paper)   1. Sociology, Urban—Brazil.
2. Urban anthropology—Brazil.   3. Citizenship—Brazil.   4. Democracy—Brazil.
5. Law—Political aspects—Brazil.   6. Land tenure—Brazil.   7. Cities and
towns—Brazil.   8. Urban poor—Brazil.   9. Urban policy—Brazil.   10. Squatter
settlements—Brazil.   11. São Paulo (Brazil)—Social conditions.   I. Title.
    HT129.B7H65 2008
    307.760981—dc22   2007015458

British Library Cataloging-in-Publication Data is available

This book has been composed in Sabon with Futura display.

Printed on acid-free paper. ∞

press.princeton.edu

Printed in the United States of America

10 9 8 7 6 5 4 3 2 1

For Teresa

Contents

PART FOUR DISJUNCTIONS

Illustrations and Tables

Figures

Maps

Tables

I might not have studied citizenship if Brazilians had not insisted on its importance. My interest developed with theirs. Their concern with democratic citizenship (and not just certain rights) grew from incidental to overwhelming in the twenty years I have worked and lived in Brazil. Along the way, "citizenship" became a ubiquitous word in Brazilian everyday life, its use more evocative of alternative futures than in the United States, where I also work and live. As a political anthropologist, I studied citizenship because Brazilians considered it critical. That is the right word—critical—for their considerations of citizenship changed from something static, already given, and even alienating into something insurgent and indispensable, yet also deficient and risky. As Brazilians led me to examine their citizenship, moreover, I put my American citizenship under new scrutiny. With their critical sense my own developed. Studying both citizenships gave me a comparative appreciation. It not only made me grasp the fundamental significance of citizenship in defining what it means to be a member of modern society and state in much of the world. In the crucible of fieldwork, I also discovered that many of my assumptions about American citizenship crumbled in light of both the democratic innovations of Brazilian citizenship and its history of inequality and violence. In effect, each citizenship made the other strange, a defamiliarization that let me to see both as being at critical moments in their histories, as simultaneously expanding and eroding their democracies.

This book was researched and written in two places I call home, São Paulo and California. I write about São Paulo in these pages, therefore, as one of its residents, not as a detached observer—which is to say, my concerns as a resident with a home, family, neighborhood, friends, and colleagues are not divorced from my subject of study. I consider that engagement fortunate. Through it, I am connected to the city's life. I see my work as part of a project of social transformation, one of democratic citizenship, that I want for myself. As an anthropologist, I want my work to affect the city and its society, not to leave them untouched. Thus I engage São Paulo and its insurgent citizenship not only to understand them as a scholar but also to contribute to the great social change that is underway and that will change my own future.

Anthropological bookmaking takes a long time and depends on lots of people and institutions. I have therefore incurred many debts of gratitude. My research in Brazil spans two decades and has involved many projects. The principal fieldwork for this book occurred in two periods, 1995–1997 and 2001–2002. During the first, I was privileged to be a visiting professor in the Department of Sociology at the University of São Paulo, supported by fellowships for research and teaching from the extraordinary state funding institution Fapesp (Fundação de Amparo à Pesquisa do Estado de São Paulo). I thank all my colleagues and students in the department and especially Maria Arminda Arruda, then head of the graduate program, for sponsoring my affiliation and for sharing their engagements in the intellectual agitations of the university and the city. The second period of intense fieldwork was generously supported by an eighteen-month Fulbright-Hays Faculty Research Fellowship from the U.S. Department of Education. Without such dedicated funding to support senior faculty, I would never have had the freedom to commit myself solely to the discoveries of fieldwork. I also received a grant from the National Endowment for the Humanities to focus on legal aspects of my study, an award from the Graham Foundation for Advancement in the Arts to investigate house building and architecture among the working classes of São Paulo, and a number of summer research grants from the Academic Senate of the University of California at San Diego that allowed me to be in São Paulo for several months each year between major funding.

The long periods of concentration necessary to think and write about the material gathered in fieldwork were provided by the International Center for Advanced Studies at New York University and by the Maison des Sciences de l'Homme in Paris. Ignacy Sachs and Michel Wieviorka welcomed me into the lively centers they direct in Paris where we worked to triangulate American, Brazilian, and French discussions of citizenship, a mapping that became essential to the historical analysis of this book. I especially thank Thomas Bender, director of ICAS, for a magical year at the center, in which he created perfect conditions for his fellows to be creative, and for his generous and spirited friendship ever since. I have to say that my colleagues in the Department of Anthropology at UCSD have been valiant in defending the kinds of schedules that allow faculty concentrated time to write during the year, amid the often overwhelming additional responsibilities we have. To all these people and institutions, I gratefully give my thanks for their support.

I can hardly begin to acknowledge here the contributions of the residents of the two neighborhoods in São Paulo in which I focused my fieldwork, Jardim das Camélias and Lar Nacional. I have been collaborating with many of them for more than fifteen years. Without their insistence that I understand their struggles with poverty and inequality, their achievements in building their homes and neighborhoods—indeed, the city itself—and their frustrations and tragedies, my research would have amounted to very little. Although media pundits bombard us with images of "third world" destitution and predictions of catastrophe, these pioneering residents of what were once very poor outlying neighborhoods have taught me to reject the language of chaos, crisis, and disease. They have shown me that amid the gargantuan urbanizations of our times, they have accomplished extraordinary things as new citizens and city builders in just a few decades. Publicizing their story is something they have worked to help me do. I can only hope that when I give them this book, they feel that it does so with some justice.

I would like to acknowledge a few individuals in each neighborhood whose collaboration has been indispensable. In Jardim das Camélias, there is José and Vera Nogueira Souza, Sérgio and Ana Santos Melo and their children, and João and Yolanda Vieira dos Santos. I must also mention Hilda, Josefa, Manoel, Milton, Paulo, and Tereza. In Lar Nacional, there is Arlete and Aléssio Silvestre and their son Fábio, José Conceição de Aguiar, and Pedro Pastor Avalo, as well as Adriana, Antônio, Eugenia, Galeati, José Raimundo, Luiz, and Ondina. In the following pages, José Nogueira, Arlete, and Aguiar—each gifted with remarkable abilities, energies, and knowledges to articulate the struggles of residents for citizen rights and dignity—appear as leaders of their neighborhood associations. I have been fortunate to count on their steadfast friendship and guidance, as well as that of the attorney-at-law for the associations in both neighborhoods, Antônio Benedito Margarido. Without their counsel, I would not have made much sense of either the dramas or the intricacies of land conflicts in the settlement of the urban peripheries. I met Margarido when we were both emerging from graduate school. His dedication ever since to defending the poor against eviction and to resolving their interminable property disputes with innovations in legal strategy is exemplary.

In Brazil, research for this book benefited enormously from my associations with the Department of Sociology, the Núcleo de Estudos da Violência, and the Law School of the University of São Paulo. I am particularly indebted to Sérgio Adorno of the first two and José Reinaldo de Lima Lopes of the last. I have been able to rely on both to ambush my assumptions and on the adventures of Zé Reinaldo's legal reasoning to find alternatives. I thank them both for helping over the years to arrange various kinds of appointments, lectures, and courses that have given me the privilege of working with a new set of colleagues and students. My research inside the tribunals of São Paulo would not have gone very far without the support, insight, and friendship of Judge Luiz Mário Galbetti, who generously let me begin my ethnography of the adjudication of land conflicts in his court. I have been broadly inspired by a senior generation of engaged intellectuals in São Paulo, whom I got to know while affiliated with Cebrap (the Centro Brasileiro de Análise e Planejamento), and who remain important interlocutors for me about the prospects of combining scholarship, public debate, and politics, including Ruth Cardoso, José Arthur Giannotti, Juarez Rubens Brandão Lopes, Guillermo O'Donnell (a guide at several important moments), Pedro Paulo Poppovic, and Roberto Schwarz. Many other colleagues and friends in São Paulo discussed aspects of this book with me and generously shared their insights. I thank especially Danielle Ardaillon, Leonardo Avritzer, Guita Debert, Esther Hamburger, Maria Célia Paoli, Paulo Sérgio Pinheiro and Jorge Wilheim. In my Brazilian family, Jorge Alberto, Jorge, and Marina Caldeira have been special allies in developing this research, as has my friend architect Sérgio Kipnis.

My colleagues in anthropology at the University of California both engaged the substance of this book and shared a vision for transforming American anthropology into a discipline of the modern world in ways that have kept academe vital for me. Especially important on both counts are Nancy Scheper-Hughes, Paul Rabinow, Aihwa Ong, Laura Nader, and Michael Meeker. Many more friends have helped me struggle through the writing of my arguments. They have been crucial and generous, and I thank especially Arjun Appadurai, Etienne Balibar, Charles Briggs, Marco Cenzatti, Jean and John Comaroff, Fernando Coronil, Margaret Crawford, James Ferguson, Daniel Herwitz, George Marcus, Nancy Postero, Michael Storper, Edward Telles, and Li Zhang. My students at UCSD have often suffered through my ideas first. In particular, I could count on João H. Costa Vargas and J. Cody Petterson to return me to my senses. I thank both Paul Rabinow and my editor, Fred Appel, for their strong support at Princeton University Press.

I wish that my father, Marc, had lived to see this book. He was a designer of things, from factories and furniture to books and evening gowns. I think he would have liked this one. My mother, Ruth, who still sends me recipes for meals "quick and delicious," has been a wonderful grandmother too.

Teresa Caldeira has been my companion on every page of this book. I hear our voices go back and forth as I write, arguing, making up, making better. She opened her world of São Paulo to me, and although we each had a prior foothold in the other's camp, we have managed to create one home in two places. To be able to say that she is my fellow anthropologist, co-explorer of the ideas and their cities in this book and other projects, is my great fortune.

Olivia came into our lives between the two rounds of fieldwork for this study. Sometimes I wonder whether she has seen me mostly as a man with the scowl of writing a book on his face. Yet there is hope. For last Father's Day, she wrote from second grade: "One day, my dad was writing a fantastic book that everybody in his class liked. But it wasn't finished. So that night he went to his office and continued to write. My dad was so surprised that he finally finished his long book. Then, the next day he went to his class and yelled 'I'm Finished With My Book!' All the coleeges cheered and everybody was happy."

PART ONE

DISRUPTIONS

Chapter 1
Citizenship Made Strange

All nation-states struggle to manage the social differences they distinguish among their inhabitants. Some measures they take are drastic, like slavery, forced migration, and genocide. But most administer differences according to formulations of equality and inequality that define their citizenships. Democracies have held particular promise for more egalitarian citizenships and thus for greater justice and dignity in the organization of differences. In practice, however, most democracies experience tremendous conflict among citizens, as principle collides with prejudice over the terms of national membership and the distribution of rights. Indeed, citizen conflicts have increased significantly with the extraordinary democratization and urbanization of the twentieth century. Thus, the worldwide insurgence of democratic citizenships in recent decades has disrupted established formulas of rule and privilege in the most diverse societies. The result is an entanglement of democracy with its counters, in which new kinds of citizens arise to expand democratic citizenship and new forms of violence and exclusion simultaneously erode it. Moreover, if cities have historically been the locus of citizenship's development, global urbanization creates especially volatile conditions, as cities become crowded with marginalized citizens and noncitizens who contest their exclusions. In these contexts, citizenship is unsettled and unsettling.

This book studies the engagements of a particular citizenship with such processes of change. It takes the case of Brazil as paradigmatic of a type of citizenship that all nations have at one time or another developed and one that remains among the most common: a citizenship that manages social differences by legalizing them in ways that legitimate and reproduce inequality. Brazilian citizenship is typical, moreover, in the resilience of its regime of legalized privileges and legitimated inequalities. It has persisted under colonial, imperial, and republican rule, thriving under monarchy, dictatorship, and democracy. Yet this book also demonstrates that the most entrenched regimes of inegalitarian citizenship can be undone by insurgent citizen movements. It shows that in the peripheries of Brazilian cities, since the 1970s, the working classes have formulated an insurgent citizenship that destabilizes the entrenched. It argues that their experience of these peripheries—particularly the hardships of illegal residence, house building, and land conflict—became both the context and substance of a new urban citizenship. Contrary to so much nineteenth and twentieth century social theory about the working classes, members of those classes became new citizens not primarily through the struggles of labor but through those of the city—a process prevalent, I suggest, throughout the global south. This book is thus about the persistence of inequality and its contestation. However, it presents no linear progression. Rather, it shows that the dominant historical formulations of citizenship both produce and limit possible counterformulations. As a result, the insurgent and the entrenched remain conjoined in dangerous and corrosive entanglements.

When I first went to Brazil in 1980, I rarely heard the words citizen or citizenship in everyday conversation. Certainly, people spoke about having particular rights. But they did so without an apparent connection with citizenship. Rights seemed to exist apart, conferred by statuses other than citizen, such as worker. When I noticed the use of "citizen" (*cidadão*), it mostly had a different sense among Brazilians of all classes. It meant someone with whom the speaker had no relation of any significance, an anonymous other, a John Doe—a person, in fact, without rights. When I asked directly, people described themselves as Brazilian citizens and suggested how their citizenship (*cidadania*) had changed under Brazil's military dictatorship (1964–1985). Occasionally in our conversations, people also used the words as a status of respect, for example, to complain that they were "not being treated as citizens but as marginals" by public officials. But at the same time, among themselves, they generally used "citizen" to refer to the insignificant existence of someone in the world, usually in an unfortunate or devalued circumstance. People said "that guy is a *cidadão qualquer*" to mean "a nobody." They said it to make clear that the person was not family, friend, neighbor, acquaintance, colleague, competitor, or anyone else with a familiar identity—to establish, in short, not only the absence of a personal relation but also the rejection of a commensurable one that would entail social norms applied in common. "Citizen" indicated distance, anonymity, and uncommon ground.

In this formulation, citizenship is a measure of differences and a means of distancing people from one another. It reminds people of what they are not—even though, paradoxically, they are themselves citizens—and defines citizens as others. I call this formulation a differentiated citizenship because it is a based on differentiating and not equating kinds of citizens. Moreover, it considers that what such others deserve is the law—not in the sense of law as rights but of law as disadvantage and humiliation, a sense perfectly expressed in the Brazilian maxim "for friends, everything; for enemies, the law." To people like myself accustomed to a rhetoric of liberal democracy that emphasizes the centrality of law-as-rights and citizenship in social relations, this expression presented a radically different articulation of what is near and far in the social order. I found it hard to understand, and the aphorism, which made immediate sense to Brazilians I asked, became emblematic during fieldwork of my attempts to chart an unfamiliar territory of social taken-for-granteds.

Twenty years after this initial disorientation, I was in São Paulo for the victorious presidential campaign of Luiz Inácio Lula da Silva, of the Workers' Party (PT). It was a massive, ecstatic victory, under red banners of "citizenship," "democracy," and "social justice." I realized that Brazilians voted for Lula not only to demand future change but also to acclaim as emblematically theirs a life story about what has already changed: a story of industrialization, urban migration, city transformation, and citizen struggle that has remade Brazil in the last fifty years. It is a history that Lula personifies charismatically. In 1952, at age seven, he migrated from a dirt-poor region of Brazil's Northeast, traveling two thousand miles in the back of a truck to São Paulo. Although he remained poor, the urban conditions of poverty were not stagnant: he became both a factory worker and an urban pioneer, as he and legions of other migrants powered São Paulo's industrial boom and transformed its hinterland by turning the shacks they had to build for themselves into masonry homes and urbanizing their neighborhoods. Through their labor, they became modern industrial workers in urban peripheries they constructed out of "bush." By 1980, they had defied military rule to mobilize factories and founded a political party of their own, the PT, that organized the periphery's neighborhoods through a mix of leftist politics and popular Catholicism. After three failed presidential bids, Lula and the PT won, with more than 60% of the national vote, by pledging to forge a "social pact" for all citizens and a "social justice" for the poor.

Brazilians voted for Lula not only to celebrate an ascension story as his opponent, José Serra, overcame a lower-class childhood to become an elite professional. Rather, they were finally willing to elect to highest office a man who campaigned explicitly as a nonelite—not merely as "the Brazilian equal to you," which had been the slogan of Lula's first

5

failed campaign against the elite Fernando Collor de Mello, but as a man who had triumphed without becoming elite, who had succeeded through his experience of the common, and who presented his individual success as expressly collective.[1] Lula won because Brazilians recognized in this common aspect of achievement the best possibility for remaking a nation rotted by the convergence of great wealth and grotesque inequality. In that recognition, Lula's story touched the deeply messianic nerve of Brazilian popular imagination. What impressed me on election night in October 2002 was how many people, mostly working-class, I saw openly weep on the streets of São Paulo after Lula's victory. And they cried on national television over the next days when asked to recall the Lula they once knew as a worker and common Brazilian. They cried when trying to explain what that experience of commonality was and what it meant to them that such a man could become president. The tears of tough working-class men and women sprang from their painful, passionate longing for Brazil to *dar certo*, to "succeed and become right," as much as from their own suffering. There is such frustration among laboring Brazilians. They long for their nation to make good after so many misses, for their work to be valued, accomplishments recognized, and injustices righted. They long for a just share in their country's immense resources, forever monopolized by a habitually disparaging, pampered, and immune elite who always seem relentlessly in control of Brazil's destiny.

Lula represents this laboring Brazil precisely because he comes from the "autoconstructed" peripheries—from the kind of impoverished urban periphery in which a majority of Brazilians now live and in which they build, through a process called autoconstruction (*autoconstrução*), their own houses, neighborhoods, and urban life. In that struggle, they also construct a new realm of participation, rights, and citizenship. Lula embodies, in other words, not only the individual self-making of an immigrant and industrious São Paulo. He also exemplifies the collective experience of the city making of peripheries and their citizenry throughout Brazil. That Lula's administration is today sunk in profound corruption, having apparently traded its project of social justice for one of mere power, is another matter—if a tragic one—I consider later. On that October night, his election affirmed the body and spirit of this complex autoconstruction, synthesizing the unprecedented national force the peripheries had become. In just a few decades, the urban working classes had constructed a civic force capable of striking hard at that still-dominant Brazil in which the historical norm of citizenship fosters exclusion, inequality, illegality, violence, and the social logics of privilege and deference as the ground of national belonging. The development of the autoconstructed urban peripheries had thus produced a confrontation between two citizenships, one insurgent and the other entrenched.

This book investigates their entanglement. It does so by making three sorts of arguments. The first analyzes the historical trajectory of Brazilian citizenship as a combination of two considerations. One is formal membership, based on principles of incorporation into the nation-state; the other is the substantive distribution of the rights, meanings, institutions, and practices that membership entails to those deemed citizens. This combination produced a distinctive formulation, distinguishing Brazil from other nations on the world stage of eighteenth and nineteenth century nation building: it generated a national citizenship that was from the beginning universally inclusive in membership and massively inegalitarian in distribution. This inclusively inegalitarian citizenship has been remarkably consistent in maintaining its principles of both incorporation and distribution since the inception of the Brazilian nation-state almost two hundred years ago.

This formulation of citizenship uses social differences that are *not* the basis of national membership—primarily differences of education, property, race, gender, and occupation—to distribute different treatment to different categories of citizens. It thereby generates a gradation of rights among them, in which most rights are available only to particular kinds of citizens and exercised as the privilege of particular social categories. I describe it, therefore, as a differentiated citizenship that uses such social qualifications to organize its political, civil, and social dimensions and to regulate its distribution of powers. This scheme of citizenship is, in short, a mechanism to distribute inequality. Citizenships do not directly create most of the differences they use. Rather, they are foundational means by which nation-states recognize and manage some differences as systematically salient by legitimating or equalizing them for various purposes. Typically, a regime of citizenship does both simultaneously, and its particular combinations give it historical character. The Brazilian formulation equalizes social differences for national membership but legalizes some as the basis for differentially distributing rights and privileges among citizens. Thus, at the beginning of the republic, it denied education as a citizen right and used literacy and gender to restrict political citizenship. In legalizing such differences, it consolidates their inequalities and perpetuates them in other forms throughout society.

Due to this perpetuation, most Brazilians have been denied political rights, limited in property ownership, forced into segregated and often illegal conditions of residence, estranged from the law, and funneled into labor as servile workers. These discriminations result not from the exclusion of Brazilians from citizenship itself. If that were the case, it would be difficult to explain their sense of belonging to the nation. Rather, these Brazilians are discriminated against because they are certain kinds of citizens. The question I ask, therefore, is what kinds they are and how the application of a particular type of citizenship generates their discriminations. The difference-specific citizenship I identify is not an archaic embodiment of backland Brazil. I stress that it remains a dominant aspect of Brazilian modernity. Indeed, one of my objectives is to account for the persistence of its inequalities.

My second argument is that since the 1970s, Brazil's working classes have articulated a different formulation of citizenship, as they moved to cities and built the urban peripheries. This urbanization transformed them. They were drawn to Brazil's industrializing cities to become the new labor force of a modern urban economy and society. Yet as nationalizing elites redeveloped city centers to become the modernized capitals of this new Brazil (figure 1.1), they expelled the working poor and forced them to reside in undeveloped hinterlands. There, they lived in precarious and typically illegal conditions (figures 1.2 and 1.4). They had to construct their own houses, organize to gain basic services, and struggle to retain their house lots in often-violent conflicts over landownership. Nevertheless, within decades, they had urbanized their neighborhoods and improved their living conditions remarkably (figures 1.3 and 1.5). Moreover, as residents spent decades transforming shacks into finished, furnished, and decorated masonry homes, this autoconstruction became a domain of symbolic elaboration. It expresses both collective and equalizing narratives of settling the peripheries and individual ones of unequal achievements (figures 1.6 and 1.7). Thus autoconstruction turned the peripheries into a space of alternative futures, produced in the experiences of becoming propertied, organizing social movements, participating in consumer markets, and making aesthetic judgments about house transformations.

Figures 1.1 to 1.7 register the force of these conditions in shaping the city of São Paulo. They compare the principal ethnographic sites I investigate in studying the entanglements of Brazilian citizenship: São Paulo's center and its peripheries, the latter typified by the neighborhoods Jardim das Camélias and Lar Nacional. These comparisons suggest that the city is not merely the context of citizenship struggles. Its wraps of asphalt, concrete, and stucco, its infrastructure of electricity and plumbing also provide the substance. The peripheries constitute a space of city builders and their pioneering citizenship. Through autoconstruction, the working classes transformed the unoccupied hinterlands of 1940 into the densely populated, socially organized, and urbanized peripheries of 1990 in all major Brazilian cities. They made them not only their principal residential space within Brazil's city-regions but also a new kind of political and symbolic space within Brazil's social geography. In particular, residential illegality galvanized a new civic participation and practice of rights: the conditions it created mobilized residents to demand full membership in

FIGURE 1.1. Center of São Paulo, c. 1955. Photo by Francisco Albuquerque/ MIS-SP/Acervo Instituto Moreira Salles.

the legal city that had expelled them through the legalization of their property claims and the provision of urban services.

Thus I argue that in the development of the autoconstructed peripheries, the very same historical sites of differentiation—political rights, access to land, illegality, servility—fueled the irruption of an insurgent citizenship that destabilizes the differentiated. Although these elements continue to sustain the regime of differentiated citizenship, they are also the conditions of its subversion, as the urban poor gained political rights, became landowners, made law an asset, created new public spheres of participation, achieved rights to the city, and became modern consumers. In such ways, the lived experiences of the peripheries became both the context and the substance of a new urban citizenship. In turn, this insurgence of the local transformed national democratization.

I do not study these developments, as some theorists and activists do by separating civil society and state. Nor do I view the mobilization of social movements as the resistance of the former and their demobilization as cooptation by the latter. I avoid such dichotomies by focusing on citizenship as a relation of state and society, and I study its processes to reveal the entanglements of the two that motivate social movements

Figure 1.2. Jardim das Camélias being autoconstructed in the eastern periphery of São Paulo, 1980. Photo by Teresa Caldeira.

Figure 1.3. Jardim das Camélias, approximately the same view as in figure 1.2 after ten more years of autoconstruction and urbanization, 1990.
Photo by James Holston.

FIGURE 1.4. Lar Nacional at the beginning, 1973.
Photo by Ezequiel V. dos Reis Filho.

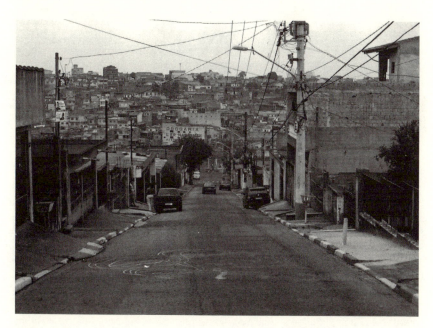

FIGURE 1.5. Lar Nacional thirty-three years later, 2006. Photo by James Holston.

11

FIGURE 1.6. Lar Nacional, José Raimundo's house: original model of attached housing, modified only with gate and carport, 1996.
Photo by James Holston/Teresa Caldeira.

FIGURE 1.7. Lar Nacional, Antonio's house next door: identical house type transformed through autoconstruction, 1996. Photo by James Holston/Teresa Caldeira.

to emerge and subside. I examine these processes as they appear in the practices of citizens. That is, I emphasize the experiences of citizens with the elements—such as property, illegality, courts, associations, and ideologies—that constitute the discursive and contextual construction of relations called citizenship and that indicate not only particular attributes of belonging in society but also the political imagination that both produces and disrupts that citizenship. But because what counts as experience is never self-evident, I try not to naturalize or essentialize it. Rather, I interrogate experience: when I use it to indicate, in terms of what people say and do, the efficacies of categories, rules, and constructions of citizenship, I simultaneously develop a historical investigation (in Foucault's sense, a genealogy) of them to account for the production of citizenship's experience, that is, to interpret both its perpetuation and its transformation as experience.[2]

Hence, the agency of citizens this book investigates is not only one of resistance. I have learned, especially from feminist theory, to see that human agency also produces entrenchment, persistence, and inertia. Thus citizens actively perpetuate the entrenched regime of citizenship, even as some also resist it. Accordingly, I do not reduce the concept of agency to one or the other. Moreover, taking clues from the subaltern historian Ranajit Guha (1983), I do not situate possibilities of entrenchment, insurgence, persistence, and resistance as something in the consciousness of individual agents. Though they may be there, I emphasize their location in the historical structuring of a paradigm of citizenship around sets of social relations, resources, and concepts—around access to land, labor, urban services, and rights, for example, and around supposed antinomies like illegal/legal, political/domestic, and public/private. That is, I consider these possibilities as inherent in structures of power and their practices. This focus shows that the insurgent undoubtedly perpetuates attributes of the historically dominant citizenship, like the significance of property ownership, the practice of legalizing the illegal, and the norm of special treatment rights. Yet it also shows that rather than merely nourish new versions of the hegemonic, the insurgent disrupts: it remains conjoined with the entrenched, but in an unbalanced and corrosive entanglement that unsettles both state and society.

Under the political democracy that Brazilians achieved in 1985, this corrosion became perverse: as the working classes democratized urban space and its public, new kinds of violence, injustice, and impunity increased dramatically. Brazilian cities experienced a generalized climate of fear, criminalization of the poor, support for police violence, abandonment of public space, and fortification of residences. The judiciary and the police became even more discredited. My third argument considers this entanglement of democracy and its counters and the erosions of citizenship it causes. I contend that because the old formulas of differentiated citizenship persist, the confrontation between the insurgent and the differentiated creates inherently unstable and dangerous spaces of citizenship in contemporary Brazil. The new democracy disrupts established formulas of rule and their hierarchies of place and privilege. If not, it would be inconsequential. Democracy is not the only force of destabilization, and it gets tangled with others, such as urbanization and privatization. But, undeniably, democracy erodes taken-for-granted categories of domination and deference that gave the everyday its sense of order and security. Such destabilization provokes violent reactions, some to restore old paradigms of order and others to express outrage that their elements—now more visible because disrupted—persist. I conclude that although Brazil's democratization has not been able to overcome these problems, neither have the counterconfigurations of violence and injustice been able to prevent the development of significant measures of democratic innovation. Above all, they have not prevented the widespread legitimation of an insurgent democratic citizenship.

Such disjunctions of government and citizenship are in fact found in many electoral democracies that have emerged beyond the North Atlantic since the mid-1970s. I describe Brazil's case in these terms not to brand it as pathological or deviant from some supposed norm. This kind of evaluation thrives among both Brazilian and international critics because all too often they understand citizenship, democracy, rule of law, and modernity itself as original formulations of European or North American experience. In that register, these notions can only seem incomplete, pathetic, derivative, or failed when grafted onto countries with different histories and cultures. To the contrary, my work in Brazil leads me to see them as assemblages of the modern that have circulated around the world for centuries and that people engage with variously depending on their circumstances, so that any one current of social time and place is always a mosaic of superimposed engagements. In this view, contradictions between forms of government and practices of citizens, simultaneous expansions and erosions of rights, and other contradictions characterize modern citizenship everywhere.

Therefore, the problem in this book is not an incomplete modernity, dysfunctional citizenship, ineffective law, deficient nationality, or failed democracy, but the particularity of Brazil's engagement. From this perspective, North Atlantic formulations appear as particulars as well, though ones often presented as universals. Thus, the disparity between the form of government and the substance of citizenship I analyze in Brazil suggests that all democracies—emerging and established—are normally disjunctive in their realization of citizenship. It indicates not only that the timing and substance of citizenship's development vary in different historical and national contexts but also that this development is never cumulative, linear, or evenly distributed. Rather, citizenship always simultaneously expands and erodes in uneven ways.

This book considers, therefore, the insurgence of democratic citizenship in Brazil's urban peripheries, its engagement with the dominant historical regime of citizenship, and its contradiction in violence and injustice under political democracy. To analyze these processes of differentiation, domination, insurgence, and disjunction, I divide the whole into four parts. Part 1 develops a framework to consider the unsettling of citizenship. Part 2 establishes the historical foundations and premises of Brazil's differentiated regime and accounts for the persistence of its inequality. Part 3 focuses on the insurgence of new citizenship in the urban peripheries of São Paulo. Part 4 considers disjunctions that violate this citizenship under electoral democracy and that make citizenship an unstable sphere of social change.

Although grand national events, like Lula's election, certainly put citizenship into practice, most of its performances involve commonplace public encounters. This chapter continues with an example of the latter to illustrate an everyday confrontation between the entrenched and the insurgent formulations of citizenship in São Paulo. I then use it to structure a discussion about the terms of my analysis—about the formal and substantive study of particular citizenships, the importance of the city, the problem of equality and inequality, and my use of history as an argument about the present.

Public Standing and Everyday Citizenship

As I investigated the formulations of citizenship and law that Brazilians took for granted, I began to see them at work in everyday public encounters. I realized, for example, that standing in line for services is a privileged site for studying performances of citizenship, because it entails encounters between anonymous others in public space that require the negotiation of powers, rights, and vulnerabilities. Surely, such encounters are mundane. But trafficking in public space is a realm of modern society in which city residents most frequently and predictably experience the state of their citizenship.[3] The quality of such mundane interaction may in fact be more significant to people's sense of themselves in society than the occasional heroic experiences of citizenship like soldiering and demonstrating or the emblematic ones like voting and jury duty. Everyday citizenship entails performances that turn people, however else related, into fellow citizens related by measures specific to citizenship. These may be empowering or debilitating, equalizing or differentiating; but, in that

15

manner, they become evident. Moreover, although they reproduce authority, they typically relate citizens directly to each other through mutual self-regulation without its explicit vigilance. Rather, they depend on the internalization of assumptions that get expressed in the performance. Let me give an example.

Like most other interactions with bureaucracy in Brazil, bank lines are notorious for humiliating the poor and the unprivileged. Lines are long because all bills (from utility charges to installment payments to state fees) are paid at banks and because most people pay them in person. However, privileged customers do not wait in line. Those who have so-called special accounts get preferential treatment from bank managers. Others employ errand "boys" to pay bills. A few other categories of people are privileged as well. Pregnant women, seniors, and the physically challenged have the right to cut the line or go to a special window. The rest wait. In my experience, unfortunately extensive in this regard, people in line do not complain, at least publicly. When I asked fellow line sufferers to explain why the preference, privilege, or right of some and on what basis, they would shrug off the special treatment by saying "that's the way it is for them" (the rich), or "it's the law," or "the bank authorizes it" (for certain people), pointing to a sign saying as much hung above a teller's window. Sometimes, they would explain that these kinds of people deserve special treatment and the authorities recognize that. In other words, those I asked raised issues of authority and the authorization of privilege, different rights for different categories of persons, relative public standing and worth, need and compensation, and resignation to the reinforcement of social inequality in everyday public interactions. They did not raise issues of fair treatment, accountability, or other aspects of equal worth.

These submissive responses to everyday negotiations of public standing occur when citizenship disempowers citizens, strange as that might seem. Empowerment happens when a citizen's sense of an objective source of right in citizenship entails a corresponding sense of subjective power—power to change existing arrangements (legal and other), exact compliance, compel behavior. In turn, such citizen power establishes the liability of others to it. However, when some people lack citizen power in relation to other people, the latter benefit from an immunity, an absence of liability. The one is powerless, the other immune. These relations of powerlessness for most and immunity for some precisely characterize the public realm of Brazilian citizenship I describe.[4]

In general terms, such relations of right establish the compact of citizenship as a specific distribution of various kinds of power in society (political, economic, repressive, sovereign, legal, and so forth). Moreover, the subjective aspect of these relations nourishes a self-interest in fortifying the objective conditions that are their source and justification, namely, the premises of citizenship. Hence, people practice everyday citizenship because it is in their self-interest, because it gives them rights, powers, and privileges. This sort of egoism is not, however, solipsistic or isolating. Rather, it requires social relations and thus public performances to establish its objective and subjective claims. This framework of negotiating public standing lets us appreciate the following confrontation between entrenched and insurgent formulations of citizenship.

I was standing in line at a bank in São Paulo in the mid-1990s. I recognized ahead of me a manicurist who works in a beauty salon near my home. I could imagine the occupations of others in line: domestic workers, clerks, errand boys, drivers, store attendants, many of them people of color. Nearer the front was a decidedly more middle-class-looking man, dressed in a tie and jacket. Suddenly, a teenager cut the line in front of this man. He was dressed in a recognizably middle-class style for his age. Neither the man nor the teenager said a word to each other or exchanged a glance that I could see. At that point, the manicurist stepped forward and objected: "You can't cut the line." Others nodded, and someone added: "You can't; your place is at the back." The teenager said nothing and remained at the front. Then, the man in the tie and jacket turned to the manicurist and announced: "I authorize it." If the man had said, "he's my son," "he's my friend," or even "he's with me," that would surely have been a satisfactory explanation. But regardless of whether the two even knew each other, which was not clear, the man had used the language, tone, and gesture of power and privilege. His was a predictable response to achieve what he assumed would be the predictable outcome of this classic encounter of Brazilian social identities in public space. Without retreating a step, however, the manicurist turned this world of assumptions upside-down: "This is a public space," she asserted, "and I have my rights. Here, you don't authorize anything. You don't rule [*mandar*]. You only rule in your kitchen and over your wife." She replied with such assurance that the man turned around without a word, and the teenager went to the back of the line.

Leaving aside for the moment the issue of "kitchens and wives," the manicurist's performance indicates the force of a new conviction about citizenship among the working classes. Her demand for respect and equality; assertion of rights in public and to the public; and realignment of class, gender, and race in the calculations of public standing are evidence not only of being fed up with the old formula of civic assumptions. They also articulate essential premises of a new formulation. They establish a radically common measure among Brazilians who are anonymous to each other—neither friends nor enemies, but citizens who, for some purposes, are equal. This performance of a new civility has not, I stress, replaced the historic one of citizen privilege for some and degradation for many—as

17

the higher-class man assumed and tried to enact. Rather, the two formulations coexist, unhappily and dangerously, creating the mix of contradictory elements that constitutes Brazilian public space today. Nevertheless, an insurgent form of citizenship has arisen, and its rising threatens many long-term and deeply entrenched assumptions about the compact of Brazilian society. Even at banks, waiting in line has changed as a result. Within a decade of the manicurist's protest, banks massively installed automated teller machines that offer equal access to most banking services.

Particular Citizenships

To be sure, many forms of protest have had significant consequences throughout Brazilian history. These include millenarian movements, slave rebellions, popular insurrections, social banditry, urban mobs, agrarian revolts, and organized land seizures. There have been countless factory-based strikes and labor agitations, and many since the 1930s have been based on rights specifically authorized for workers. Moreover, during the nineteenth and twentieth centuries, several periods of broad and vibrant public debate engaged fundamental questions of membership in Brazilian society. As subsequent chapters discuss, these debates galvanized segments of all classes to consider access to political citizenship and land (mid-nineteenth century), socioeconomic rights (1920–1940), and democracy (from 1970). Of more spontaneous and individual reactions, I have also seen Brazilians burn buses in anger over fare increases and demonstrate against violence, both police and criminal. Without doubt, a strong sense of injustice and outrage at the betrayal of values (especially familial and religious) drives many of these protests. Sometimes, anger over the state's abuse of power or failure of responsibility sparks them. Thus, members of the Brazilian lower classes have consistently struggled for dignity, resources, and at times rights, both collectively and individually, even though they also maintain an attitude of deference and accommodation with respect to established powers.

Nevertheless, if we consider the course of five centuries, it is a standard of Brazilian history that popular protest gets crushed. Occasionally, it is co-opted. But, until recently, it has met its end in the police bullet, henchman's truncheon, and army cannon. Almost always, the vibrant public spheres of debate have been shut down by those at the top of society who do not tolerate any underlying erosion of their position.[5] Thus, Brazilian elites have typically and mercilessly responded to popular mobilization with repression, and the force of protest has rarely been sufficient to avoid destruction. In this relation, the masses have been deeply vulnerable to the power of elites while elites have been broadly immune to their force.

18

This relation of vulnerability and immunity is one of the hard kernels of Brazilian society that has resisted change for centuries.[6]

In this persistence, the elite construction and application of law has been a significant factor. Far from "having no law" or a law the "doesn't work," as one frequently hears from Brazilians and foreigners alike, I demonstrate in later chapters that elites have used law brilliantly—particularly land law—to sustain conflicts and illegalities in their favor, force disputes into extralegal resolution where other forms of power triumph, maintain their privilege and immunity, and deny most Brazilians access to basic social and economic resources. This use of law not only sabotaged universal application but also estranged most Brazilians from the institution of law itself as an ally of their citizenship. Rather, it became what I call a misrule of law: a system of stratagem and bureaucratic complication deployed by both state and subject to obfuscate problems, neutralize opponents, and, above all, legalize the illegal. This law has little to do with justice, and obeying it reduces people to a category of low esteem. Thus, for friends, everything; for enemies, citizens, the poor, squatters, marginals, migrants, inferiors, communists, strikers, and other others, the law. For them, law means humiliation, vulnerability, and bureaucratic nightmare.

When this legal system is played to advantage, Brazilians have generally viewed rights as providing special treatment to particular categories of citizens that the state differentiates, regulates, and rewards. Rights have not referred to citizenship per se, unconditionally, but to statuses that only some citizens have for reasons that do not determine their citizenship. For example, registered workers (a small minority) have the right to employment benefits others do not, women can retire five years earlier than men, military police have the right to be tried in military courts, the educated get a special jail cell, and only the literate could vote between 1881 and 1985. As rights have generally meant special treatment, and people seek them on that basis, citizenship itself became formulated as a means to distribute rights to some citizens and deny them to others. The social groups targeted for such rights view them as their privilege—privilege in the Hohfeldian (1978) sense of a freedom from the claims of others and therefore an absence of duty. For them, different treatment for different categories of citizen, called citizenship, means privilege and immunity. For most, however, differentiated citizenship is harsh: it means a lack of rights and powers and, as a result, vulnerability.

In a brilliant essay, Roberto DaMatta (1991) advances a different view of law in Brazil. He argues that Brazilian society establishes a powerful dichotomy between individual and person that opposes the former as the seat of universal law, equality, anonymity, impersonal relations, and citizenship to the latter as the domain of special treatment, social differences, known identities, hierarchical personal relations, and clientelism.

In DaMatta's analysis, Brazilians always promote the person at the expense of the individual. Thus the person demands that the law be bent especially for him, that he obtain a singular application of law. This special pleading based on personal circumstances often happens, I agree. I am this and that sort of person, so the law should apply this way and not that. But this pleading for special treatment occurs in every society, including the United States, which is DaMatta's contrasting case. I argue against this kind of dichotomization, using a historical and not a structuralist analysis. In my view, Brazilian law is already personalized, developing since colonial times with personalization. No special pleading is required. The individual is the seat of rights that are distributed to him or her because s/he is a certain kind of social person. The law does not divide individual from person. Rather, it unites them in the paradigm of differentiated citizenship explicitly, legally, and without special pleading. Certainly, as I show later, Brazilian law is often formed as a compendium of particularisms (individual acts tailored for specific people or personal statuses). However, the key point is that far from opposing the individual and the person, it treats all individuals equally according to personal distinctions that are legalized—such treatment is precisely what the principle of "equality before the law" means in Brazil, as I discuss in the next section.[7]

I hasten to add that all national citizenships I know of have, at one time or another, assigned most categories of rights differentially. Typically, they use differences in property, education, race, gender, and religion to discriminate. Furthermore, such qualification tends to be more significant early in the development of national citizenships. The next chapter considers this comparative history to show that during the first part of the nineteenth century, Brazil is not that different in matters of citizenship from most European countries. In fact, in some aspects, it is more generous. Both use similar criteria to restrict the exercise of citizenship among citizens. I do not refer here to the obvious difference that Brazil had slavery, but only to the treatment of citizens. However, as part 2 demonstrates, Brazilian citizenship becomes even more restrictive during the course of the nineteenth century, while European and American citizenships expanded dramatically on the basis of struggles for inclusion, equality, and uniform legal treatment. To be sure, there are a host of problems, hypocrisies, and failures in these expansions. But there can be no doubt that in Europe and North America equalization becomes a driving force of citizenship, while in Brazil it does not. Moreover, in many cases, local and national elites support significant aspects of an egalitarian citizenship, whereas in Brazil they resolutely oppose it.

The question this book examines, therefore, is not Brazil's singularity in developing a difference-based citizenship. Most if not all nation-states have done so. Rather, the important historical problem is Brazil's particular development, which permitted an overwhelming persistence of inequality. Thus, the next four chapters consider why and how Brazilian citizenship remained inclusively inegalitarian, while other citizenships—especially those of nations with which Brazilians have consistently engaged in dialogue about issues of modernity, primarily France and the United States—moved toward significantly greater formal and substantive equality for their citizens during the last two centuries.

To reveal the course of particular citizenships is, therefore, to study them within a framework capable of sustaining comparisons in time and space. The case of citizenship is especially challenging because it both constitutes fundamental structures of modern society and unsettles them. Since the eighteenth century, one of the defining marks of modernity has been the use of citizenship to establish such structures of social membership. Citizenship, rather than subjectship, kinship, or cultship, has defined the prerogatives and encumbrances of that membership, and the nation-state, rather than the neighborhood, village, city, or region, established its scope. To a significant degree in many areas of the world, people came to comprehend their standing as members of society in terms of their standing as national citizens. Correlatively, national governments came to rely on citizenship as a basic means and rationality for organizing their nation-states, imposing it on populations within their borders through specific programs, policies, plans, and works.

The peculiarity of this modern citizenship is that although it is one of many associational identities people normally assume, the state that defines it is like no other association. Although the state is part of society, it also frames it. Although the state is an association, it is also an association of associations that establishes the rules of other associations and regulates their membership. Therefore, as the primary identity of state association, citizenship is like no other status. Its conditions have greater effect because it articulates the other statuses in terms of the nation-state's particular framework of law, institutions, demands, and sentiments. Accordingly, where the modern state came to compete with and dominate other forms of union, national citizenship became a trump status, managing the differences of other identities.

Viewed comparatively on the world stage of nation-states, however, the development of this citizenship has been anything but homogeneous. Rather, as a means of organizing society, citizenship has been both subversive and reactionary, inclusionary and exclusionary, a project of equalization and one of maintaining inequality. Moreover, these modes usually occur simultaneously in the same society. On the one hand, for persons deemed eligible, many nation-states have promoted citizenship as an identity that subordinates all other identities to a framework of common

21

standards of justice and dignity. Overwhelming other titles with a universal one, such citizenships erode local hierarchies, privileges, and statuses in favor of supralocal jurisdictions, equal rights, and respect for anonymous others. In these ways, they may advance a project of democratic equality among citizens who think of themselves as commensurable. On the other, most national societies have also used citizenship as a means to exclude and discriminate on the basis of selected differences among citizens. Through laws, institutions, and social performances, this differentiating citizenship produces and maintains inequality. Nations have typically employed this kind of citizenship to modernize long-standing regimes of social difference and prejudice by rearticulating them in terms of the modern language of rights and powers of state. Indeed, citizens often hold these contrary conceptions of their status simultaneously, as I suggested in my opening observation: "citizen" may be both a status of privilege, opposed to "marginal," and "a nobody." Citizenship is therefore much more than a formal political institution. Its lived history develops in the tensions between conflicting productions of social life as it both motivates struggles for inclusion and equality and sustains deep and common desires for exclusion.

To investigate this lived history in Brazil in ways capable of sustaining comparison, I focus on the engagements between projects of government and practices of people that give both the formal and the substantive aspects of citizenship their vitality. By formal, I refer to membership in the political community, based in modern times on national belonging. It establishes who is and who is not a citizen, whether citizenship has degrees (inclusive or restrictive), and who owes allegiance to the community and is owed protection by it. By substantive, I refer to the distribution of rights, duties, and resources this formal status entails and people actually exercise. Part 2 analyzes how both aspects combine to produce and sustain the Brazilian regime of an inclusively inegalitarian citizenship. Part 3 demonstrates how the urbanization of the working classes created conditions that undermine this particular combination.

The experience of the city is, therefore, critical to the insurgence of a new formulation of citizenship. This urban unsettling of national citizenship is comparatively significant because for most of the modern era, in Brazil and elsewhere, the nation and not the city has been the principal domain of citizenship. Indeed, one of the fundamental projects of modern nation building has been to dismantle the classic primacy of urban citizenship and replace it with the national. Nevertheless, as I have argued elsewhere in greater detail, cities remain strategic arenas for the development of citizenship. Far from dematerializing their importance, today's globalizations of capital, industry, migration, communication, and democracy render cities more strategic: by inscribing these global forces into the spaces and relations of daily life, contemporary cities make them manifest for unprecedented numbers of people. City streets combine new identities of territory, contract, and education with ascribed ones of race, religion, culture, and gender. Their crowds catalyze these new combinations into the active ingredients of political movements that develop new sources of rights and agendas of citizenship concerning the very conditions of city life. This chemistry in turn transforms the meanings and practices of national belonging. Thus cities provide the dense articulation of global and local forces in response to which people think and act themselves into politics, becoming new kinds of citizens. In the process, cities become both the site and the substance not only of the uncertainties of modern citizenship but also of its emergent forms.[8]

The third part of this book analyzes how the urban peripheries of São Paulo became such an arena. It shows that residents generated new kinds of public participation, conceptions of rights, and uses of law to redress the inequities of their residential conditions, primarily as they struggled to develop and legalize their housing stakes. I consider such new publics to constitute an urban citizenship when they develop under four conditions: when urban residence is the basis of mobilization, right claims addressing urban experience compose their agenda, the city is the primary political community of reference for these developments, and residents legitimate this agenda of rights and participatory practices on the basis of their contributions to the city itself. In the case of São Paulo, I show that the working classes developed a new sense of citizenship in terms of their contributions to the city's construction through house and neighborhood building, to its government through paying taxes, and to its economy through consumption. Thus, in building the urban peripheries, São Paulo's workers became property owners, taxpayers, and modern consumers. Through the development of these unprecedented identities, they came to see themselves as contributor-citizens entitled to stakeholder rights in the city.

To understand both the articulations and the limitations of this change, I study it at the intersection of two historical perspectives. One is the promotion by state agencies and elite organizations of projects to turn the urban poor into a modern, productive, and disciplined labor force—projects of urban development, land-tenure reform, and public works. The other is the working-class engagement of these projects, which inevitably refashions them. Thus, in the 1930s, promoters of Brazilian modernization advocated home ownership as the means to "rationalize" workers around values of property and single-family residence. Yet when public and private developers opened the hinterlands for working-class residence, the urban segregation they created politicized workers who settled there—producing a new rationality, but not the one promoters anticipated.

23

I consider especially three ways that formal qualifications and substantive distributions combine in these engagements of project and practice to produce a specific historical confrontation of citizenships: I focus on relations of illegality and legality, meanings of inequality and equality, and citizen performances. The first refers to the consistent and reliable use in Brazil of law to legalize illegalities and thus of illegality itself (and its accomplices of bureaucratic complication and legislative manipulation) as a mode of constituting legitimate power. The legal and the illegal maintain, in other words, a porous intimacy. If citizenship establishes complex relations of legal right between individuals, groups, and the state, then the conditions of illegality that also bind them produce a very different rationality of citizenship and law than T. H. Marshall, the doyen of modern citizenship studies, imagined when he described citizenship as "a direct sense of community membership based on loyalty to a civilization which is a common possession" (1977: 101). To consider this array of legal and illegal relations, I use the three "elements" into which Marshall divided the whole of citizenship—namely, the political, civil, and social (or socioeconomic).[9] I find this typology useful because it expands the legal conception of citizenship beyond the narrowly political, suggests how citizenship mediates state and society, and helps to distinguish the practices as well as the institutions and bureaucracies through which citizenship becomes substantive. However, I jettison Marshall's progressive, cumulative, and law-abiding historical scheme in favor of one that emphasizes admixture, assemblage, simultaneous expansion and erosion, disjunction, unevenness, and illegality.[10]

Hence, chapter 3 examines the exclusion of most Brazilians from political citizenship from 1881 to 1985. Chapter 4 considers the limited legal access to landed property that the vast majority of Brazilians experienced, which forced many into some form of illegal residence and which had dire consequences for their civil citizenship. Chapter 5 analyzes the development of social rights in the 1930s and 1940s as special entitlements available only to certain kinds of urban citizens, as well as the urban segregation that organized the peripheries for the settlement of an industrial workforce.

In mapping the historical form and substance of Brazilian citizenship, I give particular attention therefore to their expression in legislation, bureaucracy, and practices associated with each. Without doubt, this perspective has limitations. The gap between legislated text and social practice is usually wide enough to accommodate the passage of history itself. But this passage is also of the law's making. Its distribution of rights and duties, powers and liabilities, and statuses and procedures establishes not only the formal requirements for the assumption of citizenship but also the means of its practice. Even when other factors animate the

24

performance of citizenship, their efficacy is in some fashion grounded in its legal framework. Moreover, legislation represents the social order to the nation, especially elite conceptions of it. This representation submits specific cases to general principles and therefore allows us to interrogate particular social facts as part of larger projects. Furthermore, people craft legislation and exploit its complications as strategies, or stratagems, of social action. Especially important in my analysis is that Brazilians have massively used the strategies of law to legitimate illicit appropriations of land—to legalize the illegal as I describe it—to the extent that illegality became a general condition of settlement and the distinction between legal and illegal porous. Even in its violation, law establishes the terms if not the means of conflict.

By making available strategies of action and argument, law also motivates the development of specific types of citizens to enact citizenship. It creates a cast of dramatis personae who mold their characters to citizenship's specificities: not only the voters, soldiers, taxpayers, and nationals but also the bosses, swindlers, thugs, and residents who come into conflict around its possibilities and who therefore populate the pages of this book. Thus, although law is only part of the story, it structures what I am after in the following chapters: the self-understanding of particular citizenships as it emerges at the intersection of the assignments of general membership, the distributions of rights, and the performances of citizens.

Treating the Unequal Unequally

The formal qualifications and substantive distributions of citizenship that define a particular formulation ultimately depend on the meanings of equality and inequality they embody. All citizenships manage the social differences of citizens according to these underlying meanings. As Aristotle (1962: 119) observed long ago in the *Nicomachean Ethics*, different types of citizens agree that those considered equal deserve the same "just share" but disagree on the criterion by which people should be considered deserving: "Democrats say it is free birth, oligarchs that it is wealth or noble birth, and aristocrats that it is excellence." The French *Declaration of the Rights of Man and Citizen* (1789) promotes the first standard. This revolutionary charter is important to my story because it was selectively copied into Brazil's independence constitution of 1824. The *Declaration*'s famous initial article proposes that "Men are born and remain free and equal in rights." It proposes, in other words, that the natural condition of people's freedom (by virtue of birth) is sufficient to determine a universal equality among them. Furthermore, this equality is substantive, an equality *in* rights, meaning that people deemed equal

(i.e., by nature, everyone) must have the same distribution of rights regardless of other differences. Article 2 specifies what these rights are:
"The aim of every political association is the preservation of the natural
and imprescriptible rights of man," which are "liberty, property, security,
and resistance to oppression." Although equality itself does not appear
among these fundamental rights, it is an enabling condition, as Article 6
establishes that all citizens have an equal right to participate in making
the law itself, "personally or by their representatives"—to participate,
therefore, in the constitution of the political association that safeguards
the egalitarian distribution of rights. The *Declaration*'s first principle of
natural and substantive equality is radical indeed. It is a theory of origins
intended to ground a new type of polity by countering the ancient and
then-dominant concept of rule that political power derives from the inherently hierarchical inequality of people.[11]

However, this principle of fundamental equality is immediately conjoined to another concept of equality in the first article with which it is
in deep and lasting tension: "Social distinctions can be based only upon
public utility." This second principle means that a political association
may make legal social distinctions if they are useful to it, but only those
founded on that utility. The latter part of Article 6 specifies the criteria
of such distinctions: "All citizens being equal in its [the law's] eyes, are
equally eligible to all public dignities, places, and employments, according to their capacities, and without other distinction than that of their
virtues and their talents." Thus, under the new French citizenship, the
law may legalize social distinctions if they are publicly useful and based
on individual merit. This principle establishes that everyone must submit
to the same rules of individual qualification in obtaining public positions
and resources, as evaluated by uniform criteria rather than by ascribed
social categories such as family origin.

Both of these principles concern a radical equality, but of different
sorts. The first is about indefeasible substantive equality, as indicated by
the distribution of fundamental rights; the second, about formal or procedural equality, "equality before the law." The latter is a measure meant
to eliminate the legal privileges of nobility, against which the French had
rebelled. It abolishes the private jurisdictions and legal spheres to which
feudal society assigned individuals on the basis of their ascribed group
status, rank, and family, rather than individual achievement. Its new
equality of merit also establishes that the state's law binds all its subjects
equally because all equally belong to the state. On both accounts, it too
is a radical measure, nullifying the previous legal order.

The problem is that these two revolutionary standards of citizenship
contradict essential aspects of each other. The principle of equality before
the law contradicts the principle of equality in rights, because it allows

group differences to flourish as long as they are reducible to individual capacities and based on legislators' assessment of public utility. Hence, it permits capacity qualifications of citizenship that produce an unequal distribution of rights, based, for example, on the wealth of individuals. It permits the first French Constitution (1791), a few chapters after the *Declaration* that introduces it, to divide the citizenry into active and passive citizens and to deny the latter political rights. This provision thus contradicts the first part of Article 6 of the *Declaration* by denying the right to make the law to some 3 million Frenchmen, about 39% of voting-age males (Soboul 1974: 180). The same principle allowed the Assembly to make constitutional distinctions between men and women based on supposed differences in their capacities, refuse workers the right to strike as a contravention of public utility, and yet permit the wealthy to form employer associations based on individual affinities.

Therefore, the standard of equality before the law permits the legal distribution of greater citizen powers to some individuals. What it prohibits is that general laws apply to some citizens but not to others and that laws tailored for legally distinguished groups apply selectively among members of that group or to other groups. Thus, the laws of French political citizenship required that all citizens submit to the classifications active and passive and that those for active citizens not apply to passive and vice versa. In these ways, the principle of procedural equality establishes that all citizens are formally equal in terms of whatever classifications and distinctions may legally apply. In deep contradiction with the principle of equality in rights, it allows that this formal equality may generate new substantive inequalities.

Brazil's Imperial Constitution (1824), the nation's independence charter, imports the French *Declaration* to construct its article on citizen rights (Art. 179), much of it translated verbatim. However, it leaves out the first half of the *Declaration*'s first article. That is, it stipulates equality before the law but omits equality in rights. Brazil's Republican Constitution (1891) follows suit. The imperial charter mentions the word equality only once in the thirty-five sections of Article 179. Section 13 copies from the French (Art. 6) "The Law will be equal for all, whether it protects or punishes," adding "and will recompense in proportion to the merits of each one."[12] The republican charter uses equality in paragraph 2 of Article 72 to guarantee to citizens and resident foreigners that "all are equal before the law." The next paragraphs in each article make clear that for both constitutions, equality before the law means the elimination of the private legal spheres that characterized aristocratic privileges at law and thus signifies the equalization of ascribed status. Hence, the Republican Constitution abolishes the legal privileges of nobility, including all titles, honorific orders, special courts, and exemptions. The Imperial Constitution says nothing about the titles and privileges of nobility outside the law but abolishes aristocratic privileges at law. In addition, it stresses the compensatory function of law, but bases it on individual merit and "public utility" rather than ascribed status. Hence, copying the French, it declares that "All citizens can be admitted to Civic, Political, and Military Public office, without other difference, except for those of talents and virtues" (Art. 179, sec. 14). What is missing, however, in both the Imperial and the Republican legal orders is precisely a concept of fundamental substantive equality.

Sometime near the end of the Empire (1822-1889), the politician, lawyer, abolitionist, republican, and advocate of public education Rui Barbosa is credited with coining a maxim that encapsulates this Brazilian formulation of equality and that has become a mantra for law students ever since: "Justice consists in treating the equal equally and the unequal unequally according to the measure of their inequality." I have not been able to locate the exact reference in Barbosa's writings, and perhaps the attribution is folkloric. In any case, if the phrase is his, he was reiterating a view usually traced to Aristotle.[13] As it has become a fixture of legal education in Brazil, I researched its significance by consulting legal textbooks and questioning law students, professors, and judges in São Paulo. Both sources gave essentially the same assessment. Everyone I asked took the phrase to mean that unequal treatment is a just means to produce equality by leveling or adjusting preexisting inequalities. In this sense, justice is clearly compensatory. Nearly all also provided the same example, the same one commonly found in standard Brazilian law books (e.g., Silva 1992: 199): The law permits women to retire five years earlier than men. This discrimination is just because over the course of a normal life, working women "have more service" than working men in that, in addition to work outside the home, they have to do the housework and childcare with which they are little aided by their husbands. "Thus," renowned law professor and scholar Silva concludes, "she has an overload of services that is just to compensate by allowing her to retire with less time of service and less age." The solution for the social facts of inequality in this case—that working women are unequal because they work more—is not to propose to change the social relations of gender and work. Rather, it is to produce more inequality, in the form of the compensatory legal privilege of earlier retirement.

None of the legal professionals I asked or textbooks I consulted questioned this solution. None discussed the fact that regardless of whether its compensatory function is actually realized, this kind of justice not only legalizes new inequality but also reinforces existing social inequalities by rewarding them. None suggested that it uses the legal system to distribute unequal treatment throughout society. None observed, furthermore, that in Barbosa's maxim the unequal may also be the elite who, because of their individual education, wealth, or achievement, deserve to be treated differently. Does not the maxim justify their different standing at law and different recompense, on the basis of different individual capacities, from that of the illiterate and the poor? For example, by this legal reasoning—as standard today as it was in the nineteenth century—it is not unjust to treat a slave differently from her owner, but only to treat the one as the other or to treat the members of each group differently among themselves. Until recently (1985), the same compensatory logic legitimated the right of literates to monopolize political citizenship and continues to justify the right of university graduates (and other "dignitaries") to a private jail cell. In these examples, the preexisting measures of elite inequality justify their unequal treatment, even though it amounts to privilege.[14]

Rui Barbosa's justice may be a means of compensating an inequality of disprivilege by legalizing privilege. But it may also compensate an inequality of privilege by legalizing more privilege. In either case, it reproduces privilege throughout the social and legal system. It is, moreover, a static concept of justice. It does not contest inequality. Rather, it accepts that social inequalities exist as prior conditions of either disprivilege or privilege and treats them differently by distributing resources accordingly. Thus, the justice system in which Barbosa's maxim is a taken-for-granted standard enforces a differentiated citizenship: it maintains a society of social differences by organizing it according to legalized privileges and disprivileges.

Brazilian elites formulated this notion of justice out of Greek and French elements because it made sense to them as a foundation of citizenship during the nineteenth century and, indeed, throughout the twentieth. Like other nationalizing elites, Brazil's founders faced the problem of how to construct a national citizenship to regulate the vast social differences of inhabitants. They recognized that the conflicts over equality that the French Revolution ignited determined the outcome of this construction. For that reason, the terms of the French debate became a central preoccupation in the development of many new nation-states. Brazilians selectively appropriated these terms for their own purposes because they perceived, in the rhetoric of the day, that the French constitution had entangled a liberal understanding of equality with a democratic one they wanted to avoid. The liberal emphasized equality only in the formal sense—an equality before the law—establishing that individuals were the seat of rights and were equally free to pursue their differences in the market. But it entailed no responsibility of state or society to insure substantive rights that would equalize opportunity or realize a measure of social justice among citizens. The democratic emphasized precisely such substantive equality in rights and resources regardless of citizen differences. It created a principle of indivisible national membership that equated prior differences for purposes of citizenship.[15]

Where these principles of equality became conjoined in a single national charter—as in both the French and the American cases Brazilians studied—they observed that tremendous conflict, instability, and violence resulted over the management of social differences. Principle collided with prejudice in pitched battles over the terms of incorporation into the polity and the distribution of rights to those admitted. As I examine in the next chapter, these conflicts were largely absent from the development of Brazil's national citizenship. They did not occur because the principles of universal equality that drove French and Americans to fight each other over citizenship never became either the core or leading edge of the citizenship Brazilians constructed. I am by no means holding up French or American citizenships as democratic standards. I present them rather as specific historical regimes that Brazilians studied and criticized in formulating a regime that excluded these principles. Rather, dominant elites devised an inclusively inegalitarian national citizenship, fundamentally antithetical to the French and American because the kind of liberalism they aimed to create had no compromise with democracy. It was liberal only in the sense that individuated rights depended on the formal equality of individuals before the law without substantive equality or justice. This type of liberalism reigned among elites in many Latin American countries during the nineteenth and twentieth centuries, where it neither required nor engaged democratic projects of citizenship. Instead, elites governed by combining economic liberalism and authoritarian rule with regimes of differentiated citizenship. Thus they managed the enormous social differences of these nations with a politics of difference.

In contemporary debates about citizenship, the politics of difference is not usually presented in this context. Rather, it is offered as an alternative to a liberal regime of citizenship based on supposedly difference-neutral rights, of which the French and the American are seen as prime examples. The politics of difference—also called identity politics and multiculturalism—accuses this liberal citizenship of disrespecting the salient differences of the many peoples and cultures that constitute modern nation-states. It contends that this liberalism uses putatively difference-blind principles to homogenize differences into common denominators that are little more than reflections of the particular interests of a dominant culture. For cultural minorities, liberal equality, where it means the mold of sameness, is not neutral at all. The politics of difference rejects this equality-as-sameness with the charge that homogenization disrespects and impoverishes while creating a norm of assimilation that in fact discriminates. Instead, it demands a new principle of equality that respects salient differences. This demand becomes especially unsettling when minority groups become convinced that the relegation of their cultural differences and convictions to the private sphere under difference-blind liberal citizenship not only belittles their dignity but also threatens their survival. At that point, they demand explicit public and legalized support for the differences that they define as essential to their identity.[16]

While defenders of supposedly difference-blind citizenship often recognize the validity of these criticisms, they counter that a compelling account of a different notion of equality remains elusive and that current experiments in legalized multiculturalism do not give cause for enthusiasm.[17] How does one decide which differences are salient in a society and worth distinguishing as such in law? If public debate is the answer, how does one avoid majority tyranny or the terror of a Jacobin citizenship obsessed with its own virtues? How does the law avoid discrimination if it legalizes particular differences for some, without common standards that privilege none? If the legal system gives full expression to cultural differences, will it not create a honeycomb of jurisdictions in which there are as many kinds of law as kinds of citizens? What would justice mean in such a configuration of nonuniform memberships? What constitutes a culture, and which cultures are authentic, autochthonous, and original, all notoriously slippery categories of past and discriminating precedent? What is to prevent majority populations from using a politics of difference to give explicit legal mandate to their cultural values (e.g., language) and thereby overwhelm minorities? Despite the enormous difficulties of these questions, barely broached in detail in most cases, the politics of a difference-specific citizenship remains the most popular focus of debate about new forms of citizenship in both emerging and established democracies. The sum of these challenges has profoundly unsettled the assumptions of many national citizenships. While not providing many solutions, the challenges indicate nevertheless that a basic change is underway in the historical role of citizenship as most modern societies have used it to regulate difference.

My intension is not to review these debates, some of which I discuss elsewhere. It is rather to make two points. First, Brazil's differentiated citizenship is a case of a centuries-persistent politics of legalized differences. It has thrived under every major type of regime, including monarchy, military dictatorship, and electoral democracy. If we want to understand the possibilities and problems of this politics, if we want to have reasonable answers to the questions above, it is critical to investigate this kind of case. Second, the study of this persistence suggests that when citizenships are viewed historically, the dichotomy of difference-neutral and difference-specific that structures many of the debates is false. From the perspective of their particular histories, all citizenships struggle in managing the differences they distinguish among their citizens and between citizens

31

and noncitizens. Although this regulation is an overarching purpose of citizenship, it generates chronic conflict. In assessing differences, citizens confront each other in making decisions about their significance, assembling regulations for their management, and realizing them in practice. In these assessments, they calculate the consequences of legalizing differences to legitimate inequality or denying them by means of principles of abstract equality. A specific right may be legislated to ignore social differences—and in that way be considered difference-neutral—but the citizenship that makes it meaningful had to problematize these differences to produce it. All citizenships engage this calculation of differences and equalities and, furthermore, are forced to reevaluate it periodically. Thus they must be studied historically.

Rather than categorizing citizenships ahistorically as difference-blind or difference-specific, therefore, the important question is to investigate how a citizenship problematizes the legalization and equalization of differences and struggles with the problems of justice that result. Some so-called difference-neutral citizenships have consistently generated extraordinary turmoil in structuring the differences and equalities of their citizens.[18] Other citizenships have managed differences by legalizing them in ways that consistently legitimate and reproduce inequality. Thus, American citizenship has set armies of people against each other and erected libraries of legal opinion to figure out how both to equalize and to legalize differences—for example, whether to admit free blacks as full citizens or preemptively exclude them and whether to give special treatment to veterans (on civil service exams), farmers (crop subsidies), and minorities (admission to university). The last two questions remain passionately debated. Thus, American citizenship combines problems of equalization and differentiation in matters of both incorporation and distribution, and it struggles with the legitimacy of each combination.[19] By contrast, Brazil's citizenship has managed the differences of Brazilians—no less great than those of Americans—in very different ways. While Americans fought over inclusion, Brazilians opted for universal membership. But by denying the expectation of equality in distribution, Brazilian citizenship became an entrenched regime of legalized privileges and legitimated inequalities.

Most of the world's citizenships beyond the North Atlantic are decidedly more like Brazil's. Yet their chronic reproduction of inequality is rarely studied and more rarely compared—a persistence not revealed in institutional history alone, but in studies that also analyze citizenship as a development of processes, mechanisms, categories, and practices. When democratization destabilizes these differentiated citizenships, their reimagination should be based no more on a shallow critique of liberal citizenship than on a naive advocacy of a politics of difference. The study of

Brazilian citizenship I undertake in this book demonstrates that the most inegalitarian politics of difference can be unsettled by insurgent-citizen movements. It suggests, moreover, that new differences do not necessarily become a basis for new privileges. But it also shows that entrenched regimes of legalized inequality remain the ground, boglike and treacherous, in which new democracies and their citizenships must take root.

History as an Argument about the Present

This book combines ethnography and history to study this entanglement of citizenships. It began with fieldwork on land disputes that mobilized residents in the urban peripheries of São Paulo. My objective was to use ethnography to register these conflicts with depth and precision. But the mappings of fieldwork have always suggested to me that a particular social problem encountered in the field takes on a specific articulation because its historical formulation continues to structure its present possibilities. Thus I realized that the use of law to legalize illegal land seizures in the contemporary peripheries makes sense as a strategy only in relation to the centuries of land occupation in Brazil that made illegal settlement the norm of residence. In this case, moreover, the historical accounting was also ethnographic: I soon discovered that all parties in these neighborhood land conflicts struggled over the meaning of history. They searched for origins to justify their claims to land, following the disputes back in time, typically to the nineteenth century and often to the sixteenth, to construct their genealogies of right. Whether and to what extent people use this history are significant contemporary ethnographic and political issues. But they are important precisely because what structures and sustains these conflicts are various installments of a relation between land and law first developed in Portuguese land policy as an instrument of colonization, refashioned in imperial and republican attempts to use land reform to bring free European immigrants to Brazil to replace slaves, and later reiterated in the development of segregated urban peripheries to house an industrial workforce. This history is not past. It continues to structure the present.

Contemporary citizenships develop as assemblages of entrenched and insurgent forms, in tense and often dangerous relation, because dominant historical formulations simultaneously produce and limit possible counterformulations. The insurgent predictably irrupts at the very same sites that sustain the entrenched, but under changed circumstances. In the case at hand, the same factors that fragmented and dominated the rural poor—restricted access to political rights and land, residential illegality, misrule of law—mobilized workers in the urban peripheries. Insurgent citizenship

33

is inevitably bogged downed by this past because it is shaped and constrained by the terms these factors assume, even as it unsettles them.

The sense of "insurgent" I use to investigate this entanglement is not normative. It has no inherent moral or political value. Insurgent citizenships are not necessarily democratic or just, socialist or populist. Each case must be evaluated. Nazism surely launched an insurgent movement of citizenship in Germany, as did the American fundamentalist right in the United States. Rather, insurgence describes a process that is an acting counter, a counterpolitics, that destabilizes the present and renders it fragile, defamiliarizing the coherence with which it usually presents itself. Insurgence is not a top-down imposition of an already scripted future. It bubbles up from the past in places where present circumstances seem propitious for an irruption. In this view, the present is like a bog: leaky, full of holes, gaps, contradictions, and misunderstandings. These exist just beneath all the taken-for-granted assumptions that give the present its apparent consistency. I study this ethnographic present historically not to give a historian's complete account. Rather, I use historical investigation to show how the past always leaks through the present, breaking it up into heterogeneous elements, and permitting it to be recomposed and transformed. I use history to make an argument about the present.

Most Brazilians who live in the peripheries understand them as a process of transformation because they have built them, turning their hinterlands into urbanized neighborhoods. But most who do not reside there have only a presentist view of their formation and significance. They do not consider them a work in the making. In fact, they often see them as little more than "crime-infested favelas," committing the flagrant mistake of assuming that all their residents are squatters. Instead, they think of the peripheries as something to be acted upon from the outside. As they look down on them from airplanes, view them on television, and drive past them on highways, they may see them as targets of assorted political and economic proposals for a different future in Brazil. This bird's-eye view of history is, paradoxically, dehistoricizing because it works backward from an imagined future to a proposal for the present as its precondition. As it hovers outside and above, it does not recognize the peripheries as a place where Brazil's past and present disrupt each other, much less does it consider this disruption an important agent in constructing a different future. If my ethnography of the peripheries remained in such a dehistoricized present, or if it proposed historical baselines of before-and-after change but neglected historical process, it would be complicit with this kind of reductive dismissal. To avoid it, this book works in the opposite direction by historicizing the present.

In doing so, it aims to produce not only a work of scholarship but also one of critical research. By critique, I do not mean pronouncing what is right or wrong with the way things are, judging them by some external measure. Rather, I mean pointing out the ways that thoughts and actions rest on taken-for-granted, unexamined assumptions and the consequences that both the unexamination of the familiar and its defamiliarization have for the construction of the way things are. Thus, in the course of my study, I use ethnography and history to debunk a number of professional policies, practices, and presuppositions: to expose practices of urban planning that segregate; to doubt distinctions between the illegal and the legal that ground the profession of law and the constitution of political power; to demonstrate how land reform policies have predictably promoted conflict because they set the terms by which encroachments are reliably legalized; to argue that political definitions alone are inadequate to evaluate democratic development and that political democracies do not necessarily produce a democratic rule of law. In addition, I investigate the ethnographic and historical sites of insurgent citizenship to open up the present to their possibilities. Their study not only makes them evident. It also indicates opportunities for further change that are not based on utopian impositions but grounded in a defamiliarized, messy ethnographic present, where projects that I value—of social democracy, justice, and equality—have a better chance to flourish.

PART TWO

INEQUALITIES

Chapter 2
In/Divisible Nations

I have suggested that Brazilian citizenship has been remarkably consistent in maintaining a regime of inclusive membership and inegalitarian distribution for the last two centuries. Brazilians made differences based on various kinds of social standing paramount in citizenship's organization and, in turn, used citizenship to legalize social inequalities and distribute rights selectively. In these ways, national citizenship in Brazil consolidated a deeply hierarchical social structure. I also claimed that for much of the nineteenth century, postcolonial Brazil was similar to most economically but not democratically liberal European nations in the use of qualifications to limit the exercise of citizenship. However, by the end of that century, the development of Brazilian citizenship diverged significantly: sustained by violence and corruption, it became even more differentiating and exclusionary for Brazilian citizens while other world citizenships became more universal, egalitarian, and indivisible with the spread of mass democracy. Like poison in the soil, this different development subverted not the liberal model of state many Brazilians espoused, but whatever democratic aspects it may have had. Few have described this Brazilian liberalism more scornfully than the great novelist Machado de Assis: in an allegory about fakery written in 1878, he observed that in Brazil "political science finds a limit in the hard head of the hired gun" (1944: 12).

The next four chapters present my case. They demonstrate the premises and persistence of Brazil's differentiated citizenship by analyzing key aspects of its historical development. My point is to show that throughout

Brazilian history, the difference-based formulation of citizenship over-whelms. It persists as a system of unequal and differential access to rights, privileges, and powers from the colonial period (1500–1822), to the imperial (1822–1889), and through the republican (1889–present), thriving under monarchy, both civilian and military dictatorships, and electoral democracy. I show the enormous historical weight of this formulation of citizenship to stress that it has only begun to change significantly in recent decades, precisely with the development of the autoconstructed urban peripheries and their insurgent citizen movements.

During fieldwork in these peripheries, residents made clear to me that without doubt they considered themselves fully Brazilian, no less so than any other member of the nation-state. However, they also thought of themselves as discriminated-against citizens and, in that sénse, as second-rate members. Rather than conclude that these considerations were in contradiction, I realized that they distinguish two dimensions of citizenship. One is national incorporation, a formal status of membership based on criteria of national belonging. The other is the substantive distribution of the bundle of rights, obligations, and practices that membership entails to those deemed national members. Both dimensions, the formal and the substantive, define the historical trajectories of particular citizenships.

With regard to the first, nation-states everywhere use principles of *ius soli* (birthplace) and *ius sanguinis* (descent) to determine national belonging, either exclusively or in combination, and often conditioned by such qualifications as residence, race, and religion. These criteria establish the rules of general admission to membership in the nation-state. They admit some people as citizens and exclude others as noncitizens, thus regulating the permeability of national identity. As a result, they determine the conditions of closure and boundary, the terms of entry and exit, and the rules of who is in and out of the national body. Citizenship as national incorporation therefore creates a national people by bounding people: it marks and maintains a boundary as fundamental to the constitution of the nation-state and its particular type of belonging as its territorial borders. Exactly because national states are states of specifically bounded people, the rules of including some as citizens and excluding others as noncitizens reveal basic conceptions of state sovereignty.

In feeling fully national but second-class, Brazilians were describing a citizenship that is both universally inclusive and generally inegalitarian. These are two different though related considerations. To sort them out is to understand how they combine to produce the Brazilian formulation of an inclusively inegalitarian citizenship, one that is expansive but differentiated at the same time. To do so, I concentrate in this part of the book on the historical framing of these twin aspects of citizenship. This chapter analyzes the development of Brazilian national incorporation. It focuses on the incorporation at independence (1822) of those people considered most problematic for the new nation-state, namely, those groups of native-born residents who did not fit majority assumptions of membership: Indians, slaves, and freeborn and freed blacks. The terms of their incorporation grounded the development of an arsenal of ideologies of inclusion that Brazilians in power have used ever since—including race mixing, urban populism, and state modernism—to produce universally inclusive identifications with the nation-state that effectively blur, in that universality, the inegalitarian distributions of resources. This chapter examines the foundation of this strategy of inclusion, one only recently rendered less effective by the insurgence of democratic citizenship. The next three chapters concentrate on the restricted distribution of political, civil, and social rights among national citizens, the last in the context of segregating the city of São Paulo.

Comparative Formulations

Brazilians did not articulate their national sovereignty and citizenship in isolation. They acted on a world stage of nineteenth-century nation building, making direct reference to other national experiences. These modernities are thus co-occurring. Just as colonialism shaped capitalism and "the rest" returns to unsettle "the west," so too were Brazilians shadowed by other national experiences in making their own. To establish the specificity of the formulation Brazilians developed, therefore, it is necessary to understand the comparisons they made, many explicit and some spectral. Thus, this chapter first analyzes conflicts of inclusion that were decisive for the two new national citizenships with which Brazilians were most in dialogue throughout the nineteenth century: the French and the American. I then turn to Brazil's formulation. These comparisons demonstrate that the relation between citizenship incorporation and distribution varies distinctively among nation-states and over time: at national foundation, France may be described as inclusively egalitarian, the United States as restrictively egalitarian, and Brazil as inclusively inegalitarian. This comparative study avoids rendering the Brazilian case—its citizenship, society, modernity, democracy—as either exotic or pathological. It demonstrates that through comparison the particularities of each case become evident.

From its first stirrings, both proponents and opponents of Brazilian independence were passionately engrossed in the course of the revolutions in France and the United States.[1] They understood that these upheavals

41

had consolidated an ideal of the modern nation-state by inventing its institution in national citizenship. They knew that this was not an ex ni-hilo creation but rather the culmination of several centuries of European statecraft in the development of national peoples and territories. Yet, like colonials elsewhere in Latin America, they grasped that both revolutions had established benchmarks of national development against which other nations would now be measured and had, in that sense, given the world an image of its own future. At the same time, Brazilians perceived clearly that it was a radical image—radical because American and French revolutionaries had attacked old regimes of privilege by defining national citizenship as a singular, indivisible, and individual status of membership. They had created an "all or nothing" membership that in principle admitted no degrees or ranks among citizens.

It was readily evident to Brazilians, however, that this principle was compromised at the outset by the exclusion of pariah groups in France and America—though the absence of any Brazilian discussion that I can find of the denial of political rights to women in both is so complete as to suggest its utter naturalization. Moreover, it was equally clear that although a radical idea of citizenship had been established with extensive institutional and popular powers in both countries, many of its consequences were much more than merely unanticipated. As observers soon discovered, they were also unacceptable to many French and American citizens who found that the revolutionary principle of indivisible citizenship clashed with deep-seated prejudices about who should belong to the nation and by what terms. It took many decades, even centuries, on both sides of the North Atlantic to struggle through the conflicts that the principle of citizen equality provoked.

As Brazilian elites constructed their own nation-state, they analyzed each and every turn of these conflicts. I cannot stress enough how well versed they were in the developments of French and American national experience. Throughout the nineteenth century, the formulators of Brazilian citizenship published works crammed with detailed discussions of their history, law, politics, and economy. When Congressman Francisco Belisário de Souza published his reform of the Brazilian electoral system in 1872, for example, he included a detailed analysis of the electoral provisions of each French constitution to date and debated the role of suffrage with Tocqueville, J. S. Mill, Locke, and other French, American, and British authors. Another deputy, A. C. Tavares Bastos, published a work in 1867 on problems of Brazilian immigration, in which he analyzes the impact of the U.S. Homestead Act of 1862 on the price of land and of that price on immigration. In the introduction to his 1873 book on parliamentary and judicial reform in Brazil, he writes of the impact of the French Revolution: "We were very close to 1789; and for the disciples whom the great revolution disseminated everywhere and who initiated here [Brazil] the movement of insurrection and liberty, 'the people' were not only the rich bourgeois, the happy merchant, the high official; the people were the entire nation, all who maintain the state, contributing with taxes and blood" (1939: 181–82).

Among nineteenth-century nation builders everywhere, French and American citizenships circulated as case studies. Nevertheless, knowing full well of these alternatives, Brazilians formulated an understanding of national membership (both under imperial and republican regimes) antithetical to these models in important ways. Several conflicts over French and American national inclusion were particularly revealing to Brazilians of the basic principles and problems of these citizenships. In what follows, I discuss these conflicts to contextualize the different formulation Brazilians developed. My aim is to present the repertoire of ideas, cases, methods, and techniques on which these formulators drew, which is to say, the intellectual theater in which they were immersed. Only a misinformed opinion could imagine that Brazilians were isolated in developing their society and culture. To the contrary, their comparative engagements with this repertoire, their dialogue with other moderns, formed an important part of the cultural matrix in which Brazilian citizenship developed and to which its contemporary conflicts still respond. I need not, however, present the French and American cases by citing Brazilian accounts of them. That would be too cumbersome, as the cases are well known. Rather, I need to specify the fundamental issues of citizenship that crystallized in the French and American experience, and thus became evident on the world stage of national development during the nineteenth century as Brazilians articulated their own formulation.

The conflicts of French and American citizenship on which I focus are of two sorts in each case. The first concerns the national incorporation of resident groups of native-born people who, for reasons of prejudice, do not fit majority assumptions of membership. The conflicts surrounding such pariah groups reveal many of those assumptions. Thus I am less concerned with the incorporation of candidates considered uncontroversially appropriate for national membership—Northern European immigrants in the American case, for example—than with those judged problematic. The second sort concerns the legally and institutionally defined distribution of citizenship rights among those deemed citizens—not, I emphasize, the actual realization of rights in specific cases, which is a related but different matter. In both cases, these conflicts over inclusion of candidates and distribution among citizens engaged fundamental and at times irreconcilable differences over the definition of national belonging and the parameters of citizen equality.

French Indivisibility

The first case involves French citizenship for Jews at the time of the Revolution. About forty thousand Sephardic and Ashkenazi Jews resided in France at the end of the eighteenth century. They were ghettoized and demonized. They could not own land, join guilds, work in most trades and professions, marry freely, or reside legally in many places. They were frequently the victims of violence, special taxes, and other forms of extortion. Although they had contractual grants from local authorities to perform various activities, these could be withdrawn at whim because Jews had no inalienable rights. By medieval arrangement, they had corporate autonomy that enabled them to live in self-governing communities but that also forced them into isolation. Although this reviled group constituted only a fraction of the national population (0.16%), the issue of Jewish membership in the new nation-state was the subject of more than thirty sessions of the National Constituent Assembly between August 1789 and September 1791 (Jaher 2002: 3). The Jewish question was so intensely debated because it synthesized a fundamental dilemma for the Revolution: Could a despised and marginalized group of people become citizens? And could they become full citizens, equal in their rights and duties with the French? Or were they destined to remain a separate nation within a nation, at best of second-rate membership? In that case, what indeed did the Revolution's proclamation of universal equality mean?

Most deputies to the Assembly agreed that the Jews were debased. The question was whether degradation was an inherent consequence of their culture or the result of their persecution, which would disappear with citizenship. Those opposed to Jewish citizenship argued that civil and political equality would never overcome Jewish separatism because Jews were inherently aloof and disloyal. Those in favor based their argument not on Jewish character or culture but on the logic of national citizenship. The most memorable declaration of this position in the debate of 1789 came from Deputy Clermont-Tonnerre:

> The Jews should be denied everything as a nation, but granted everything as individuals. They must be citizens . . . they cannot be a nation within another nation. . . . It is intolerable that the Jews should become a separate political formation or class in the country. Every one of them must individually become a citizen; if they do not want this, they must inform us and we shall then be compelled to expel them. The existence of a nation within a nation is unacceptable to our country. (cited in Jaher 2002: 67)

On the same day that the Assembly granted Protestants full citizenship for these very reasons, it denied the measure for Jewish emancipation. Nevertheless, the debate continued. The Sephardic Jews were considered separately from the more disliked Ashkenazim of Alsace and, a year later, were granted full-citizen status. In the next year, the Assembly passed the revolutionary constitution of 3 September 1791 that guaranteed freedom of religion. It also permitted the Assembly to make special grants of citizenship requiring only that petitioners reside in France and take a civic oath (Title II, Art. 4). Now, with clear constitutional support for equal rights, the deputies again took up the question of full Jewish citizenship. Opening the debate, Deputy Du Port declared "I believe that freedom of religion does not permit a single distinction to be made between the political rights of citizens by reason of their beliefs." With near unanimity and a specific provision for Jewish emancipation, the Assembly passed his resolution that "conditions necessary to be a French citizen, and to become an active citizen, are fixed by the Constitution, and that all men who, satisfying the stated conditions, render the civic oath, and engage themselves to satisfy all the responsibilities that the Constitution imposes, have the right to *all* the advantages that it assures" (cited in Jaher 2002: 75, italics added).

The Assembly had granted Jews formal national citizenship as an individual status, with the same full bundle of rights as other French citizens. In doing so, it consolidated and institutionalized the principle of national citizenship as an individual, indivisible, ungraded status, one unmediated by any group attribute, consideration, or privilege. Accordingly, in exchange for legal equality, it stripped the Jews of their corporate identity ("a renunciation of all privilege," as Du Port's measure put it). Nevertheless, French Jews continued to experience not only de facto persecution but also de jure discrimination. In addition to suffering pogroms, Jews were often harassed by local authorities who prevented them from taking the civic oath, voting, and purchasing nationalized property; levied special taxes on them; refused to register their marriages; and so forth. Although such local persecution defied national law, Paris did little about it.[2]

Jews were not the only people whose citizenship was problematic for the Revolution. Indeed, all manner of prejudice collided directly with the promise of an all-embracing and fully equal citizenship. Such collisions unleashed tremendous turmoil and yielded an astonishing register of instability: within eight decades of the Revolution, France experienced ten constitutions (five in the first thirteen years), organized terror, restoration of monarchy, insurrection, coups, autocracy, and democracy. Conflicts over the meaning and organization of citizenship, especially its inclusiveness, were central to this extraordinary turbulence. Two strategies of discrimination resulted, already evident in the case of the Jews.

I call them preemptive exclusion and selective disqualification. The first aimed to keep those deemed unworthy of national membership excluded altogether, since admission required full rights. This was the strategy plotted against the Jews, and it was deployed against other stigmatized groups, including those in the colonies.[3] During these tumultuous decades, preemptive exclusion secured the gate to French national identity, precisely because the principle that all French citizens have equal civil rights was one feature of the Revolution that endured. For this reason, when universal citizenship proved untenable in the colonies, the French state preemptively reinstituted slavery in 1802, after having abolished it in 1794 throughout the empire and incorporated ex-slaves as full citizens.[4]

The case of foreigners residing in France was somewhat different. Technically, they enjoyed civil rights only to the extent that the French state had reciprocal agreements with foreign states. But sociopolitically, the more important problem immigrants presented was the possibility of assimilation to the status of French citizen. Therefore, it became essential to the organization of nation and state to specify who was French and who foreign. In effect, the resident Jews were a special case of this broader problem.

The first revolutionary constitution of 1791 combined principles of birthplace (*ius soli*), descent (*ius sanguinis*), residence, and participation to determine membership. What is distinctive and original about this combination is the way in which the first two are conditioned by the last two. To be a citizen, those born in France of a foreign father must have fixed residence in the country, and those born in a foreign country of a French father must have both established residence in France and taken the civic oath (Art. II). The swearing of the latter established, in performative fashion, the petitioner's allegiance to and participation in *la patrie* as an act of individual volition. Citizenship was also extended to those born abroad but descended in any degree from French ancestors who had been expelled from France on account of religion. Citizenship was unconditional for only one group, albeit that of the vast majority: those born in France of a French father.

Given the possible combinations, it is clear that both *ius soli* and *ius sanguinis* are conditioned by the same feature: attachment to France.[5] This refers to a socialization into French values, broadly understood as the development of abiding connections to republican ideals, cultural habits, family mores, and a national "civilizing mission." This attachment is only presumed self-evident for one group, those born in France of French fathers. But this presumption is not based on descent alone— hence restrictions on foreign-born descendents. Rather, it is presumed for this group because their socialization is all but guaranteed. For the rest, attachment must be proved by evidence of the desire to be French, either by residence (for the native-born of foreign fathers) or by residence and oath (for the foreign-born of French fathers or ancestors). Denied is unconditional *ius soli* or *sanguinis*, to guard against attributing citizenship either to those of "accidental" French birth who have no intention of becoming French or to those of "mere" French blood who are raised elsewhere. Such people were undesirable as citizens because their attachments were presumed to be weak. They were therefore preemptively excluded. For others, the Constitution put forward a reasonably expansive definition of French nationality.

We need only note three changes to this conceptualization. Subsequent revolutionary constitutions dropped the use of citizenship in this sense of national membership. Rather, they retained the term to refer to political participation only. In this way, they more accurately expressed the Revolution's conceptual division of the nation-state into a political society comprised of citizens and a civil society of private individuals.[6] Citizenship as general national membership became the concern of ordinary civil law, after Napoleon Bonaparte imposed the Civil Code of 1804 (which became a model for all Latin America). The Civil Code contained two important changes to the understanding of national citizenship.[7] First, the Code adopted as the basic principle of French identity unconditional *ius sanguinis*, that is, transmission by descent from father to child regardless of birthplace. Second, it reconditioned the acquisition of citizenship by *ius soli*. Children born in France of foreign parents and of fixed residence were no longer attributed citizenship. Rather, they had the right to claim citizenship at majority by declaring their intention to reside permanently in France.

Within a few decades, another sort of problem emerged. Few people in this situation used their right of election. Most foreign men declined and thereby escaped military service. Most foreign women followed the men. Needless to say, French citizens resented the inequality that allowed these native-born foreign residents to advance their lives while citizens had to sacrifice theirs to universal military conscription. The issue peaked after the Revolution of 1848. The government responded by denying naturalization and its benefits to those born in France who refused citizenship at majority. To prevent draft evasion, it also imposed *ius soli* citizenship at majority on third-generation (1851) and then second-generation (1889) immigrants born in France of foreign parents, though it allowed them to renounce citizenship.

These extensions of conditional *ius soli* and the resulting expansiveness of French citizenship derived from a second concern for equality: the continued rejection of the development of different nations within the French nation. The political standard of "a nation unified and indivisible," first argued in the case of the Jews, led the French to convert immigrants into citizens individually rather than let them remain foreign collectively. As a result, both at home and in the colonies, Europeans (Italians and Portuguese primarily) and colonials (Algerians, Senegalese, and Vietnamese, in particular) were assimilated to French nationality as a matter of political principle. Deep ethnic, racial, and religious antipathies remained, however, and, if anything, increased in France during the century with the development of "scientific racism," defeat in the Franco-Prussian War (1871), economic crisis (1880s), and the Dreyfus Affair (1894–1906). Nevertheless, over the ebbs and flows of exclusionism, racism, and xenophobia, a politics of assimilation crystallized during the nineteenth century as the dominant conception of national citizenship. It sustained the republican ideal that anyone could become legally French because they could become socially French with proper exposure to the greatness of French institutions, language, and civilization. With roots in the revolutionary principles of indivisibility and equality, this politics legitimated the *ius soli* expansion of citizenship.

By midcentury, therefore, the basic formulation of French national membership was firmly established: unconditional *ius sanguinis* complemented by conditional *ius soli*, with the latter accounting for the eventual but automatic incorporation of resident immigrants. Despite several major revisions in the twentieth century and serious bouts with xenophobic exclusionism (the Vichy Regime in 1940 and the National Front in the 1980s), this conception endures to this day.

The second strategy of discrimination that developed in conflicts of citizenship principle and prejudice was the selective disqualification of citizens from specific rights. With regard to *civil* rights, localized discrimination against the poor and the detested remained a problem, as in most systems of citizenship. But officially sanctioned disqualification was rare, as it contravened a raison d'etre of the Revolution.[8] Rather, it was in the realm of political citizenship that the French tried disqualification and debated it intensely for sixty years. The Revolution profoundly altered the concept of political representation: it transformed its basic unit from that of separate corporate estates (e.g., of the clergy, nobility, and commoners) to that of the individual citizen, represented in a single unified national assembly of legislators. The question that took sixty years to resolve, however, was what sort of citizen would have the right to contribute to the formation of the state and its legal authority. The principal doubts that it should not be all citizens revolved around issues of gender, wealth, and capacity. Until the French settled these concerns, the formula they instituted for national association remained egalitarian civil rights with differentiated political citizenship.

Although French women were citizens in the general sense of the term, the first National Assembly categorically excluded them from the political process. Indeed, it was moved to derision upon the publication in 1791 of Olympe de Gouges' *Declaration of the Rights of Woman and Citizen*, in which she uses the reasoning of the Revolution to make a case for the political citizenship of women.[9] When the Jacobins took power two years later, they even denied French *citoyennes* the right to associate to discuss public affairs. Using conventional notions of gender difference, the Jacobins argued that the sole duty of women to the Revolution lay in the domestic sphere, where they were responsible for the preparation of male virtue. If by nature women were incapable of governing, then they should not form political associations either—though the Assembly admitted that women could attend political meetings to listen as a means to prepare them for motherhood.

The total exclusion of women from politics was an extreme consequence of a belief common among revolutionaries that active participation in the formation of the state and its laws required specific qualifications not held by all citizens. Enough deputies agreed with this view that they imposed restrictions on the political rights of French men as well. In relation to the past, the Constitution of 1791 was without doubt revolutionary in allowing all male citizens over twenty-five the possibility of suffrage (Sec. II, Arts. 1–7). However, it distinguished between "active and passive citizens," restricting political participation in primary assemblies to the former and limiting the active to those who had established a domicile for over a year, were not dependents of any kind, and had paid the equivalent of three days of labor in taxes. To participate in electoral assemblies and to hold elected office, the qualifications became even more restrictive.

These concerns expressed two distinctions of central importance in the eighteenth-century discourse of revolution, which also became fundamental to the subsequent development of citizenship throughout Latin America. The first contrasts the terms "subject" (*sujet*) and "citizen" (*citoyen/citoyenne*), a distinction invoked by the complete replacement of the former by the latter in revolutionary usage. As famously distinguished in Rousseau's *The Social Contract*, for example, the term "subject" epitomized the old regime. It denoted not only subjection to the person of the king but also to the laws of state that resulted from his arbitrary will. Furthermore, submission was not uniform among subjects. Rather, it differentiated subjects according to the multitude of private and ranked relations that characterized the corporate structure of the regime. In contrast, the term "citizen" signified the active and sovereign participation of members of the nation-state in the business of rule, above all in the formulation of and uniform submission to laws that expressed "the general will." Hence, the use of "citizen" as the universal term of address and political reference became a central symbol, if not performative, of the Revolution's unifying objectives: the transformation of passive subjects into active citizens and of differentiated subjectship into egalitarian citizenship.

The second significant contrast is that between active and passive citizen (*citoyen actif/passif*). The latter is something of a contradiction in terms, insofar as what distinguishes citizens from subjects is specifically their active participation in public affairs. But the designation "citizen" always retained a second meaning of general membership, commonly used to indicate a distinctive affiliation with a city or nation-state rather than mere residence. For the Revolution, this distinction was minimally one of uniform relation to the state in terms of equality before the law and civil standing. Many revolutionaries used the term "passive citizen" to refer to those people who enjoyed these attributes of general membership but who, they argued, should not be responsible for its political constitution. A passive citizen is a citizen, therefore, in the general but not the specific sense of the word. Sewell (1988: 106–7) observes that this distinction frames the Abbé Sieyès' draft of the *Declaration of the Rights of Man and Citizen*. In the expository section, he distinguishes between passive and active rights, the former being "natural and civil" and the latter "political." In Sieyès' words, passive rights are "those for the maintenance of which society is formed . . . and political rights those by which society is formed." It thus follows that all who enjoy passive rights—in particular the "protection of their person, property, and liberty"—are deemed "passive citizens" and that all members of the nation have these rights. But "all do not have the right to take an active part in the formation of public powers." Those who do are the "active citizens."[10]

What qualifies some citizens to be active? Sieyès set out the basic concepts in his draft declaration: "All can enjoy the advantages of society, but only those who contribute to the public establishment are as the true stockholders of the great social enterprise. Only those are the veritable active citizens." What kind of contributions qualify? Those that distinguish "citizens who have for the public good, interest with capacity" (cited in Sewell 1988: 107). Applying these notions, Sieyès concluded that active citizens must be adult male nationals, make some contribution to public expenses, and be independent of the will of others. The key qualities from which the last two derive are interest and capacity. Sieyès and his supporters insisted that only those citizens who have a financial interest in the state should make the laws, because only those who support the state financially, through the production of wealth and especially the payment of taxes, sustain the institutions that guarantee the laws and thereby demonstrate a real shareholder stake in the constitution of society. Although legislators debated the amount of financial interest necessary, they agreed to establish a minimum tax payment to qualify as voter and a minimum annual income to qualify as elector/representative. Albeit with a significant twist, the concept of stakeholder citizen will become central to the insurgence of new citizenship I investigate in the urban peripheries of São Paulo.

Active citizens must also have the capacity to make decisions that rely on their own judgment. Thus, they must have an independence of both means and mind to formulate just laws. Those who depend either financially or intellectually on the will of others cannot be entrusted with this responsibility and can only be passive citizens. It is the presumed lack of this capacity for exercising independent will that accounts for the greatest denial of political rights. The disqualifications of gender and age result from the assumption that women and minors are by nature dependents of male heads of households and thus naturally passive. Employees are also dependent on their employers, but by contract. Hence, either by nature or by contract, the wills of these citizens are not their own and they are therefore unfit for active citizenship. As introduced with the French Revolution, such capacity qualification would become the most widespread type of restriction on modern citizenship. It has taken many forms, from age requirements to gender exclusion, from tax payment to independence of household, from basic literacy to advanced education, from minimum income to significant wealth. It characterizes the formulation of citizenship whenever a presumed inequality of means or mind is considered significant for its exercise.

To be sure, these restrictions of interest and capacity disenfranchised many citizens. That they seemed a flagrant contradiction of the ideals of the Revolution was not lost on the more radically democratic deputies, such as Robespierre, who protested with accusations of hypocrisy and betrayal. However, several considerations put these accusations in perspective. First, the electorate created by the Constitution of 1791 numbered over 4.4 million, about 17% of the total population and 61% of men over twenty-five (Applewhite 1993: 50). In these terms, it was by far the most extensive experiment in electoral representation by direct vote ever attempted. Second, Robespierre's arguments triumphed one year later. During the insurrection of August 1792, which led to the overthrow of the monarchy and the creation of a republic, many Parisian electoral assemblies invited passive citizens to join their deliberations. The revised constitution they drafted in 1793 created a nearly universal manhood suffrage, dropping the distinction between active and passive, lowering the voting age to twenty-one, and even allowing paupers to vote if they met a six-month residency requirement (Arts. 4 and 11).

Nevertheless, the opinion that the poor and the dependent are not qualified to decide political matters became entrenched. Although the term "passive citizen" never reappeared, a new constitution two years later reintroduced tax qualifications for participating in electoral assemblies. The next two constitutions, imposed by Napoleon, further limited male suffrage. Then, in 1814, the Bourbon Restoration radically restricted political rights: its charter increased the voting age to thirty and required the payment of high direct taxes. The results were dramatic: the number of voters dropped to 0.3% of the population (Anderson 1908: 513) and remained under 1% until the explosion of the Revolution of 1848. A new constitution in that year finally gave universal suffrage to all Frenchmen over twenty-one. For men, political citizenship had become as egalitarian as civil citizenship. From that moment on, universal suffrage remained the standard of French citizenship, though only a fraternal one until women gained the franchise in 1944.[11]

In sum, after sixty years of intense conflict, the French finally consolidated an enduring version of the principles of indivisible national membership and universal citizen equality with which their revolution began: the formula of unconditional *ius sanguinis* complemented by conditional *ius soli* defined national membership, and that of egalitarian civil and political citizenship (the latter for men only) defined the distribution of its rights.

It remains the case, however, that for many French citizens these formulas are unacceptable. As a result, some persist in trying to repudiate them. Hence, the Vichy regime stripped French Jews of their naturalization, delivering them to the Nazis as foreigners. In the same tradition, the xenophobic National Front proposes to eliminate every trace of *ius soli* from French citizenship. These efforts mean not, however, that the principles are frauds, but rather the contrary: the exclusionists persist because they are never entirely successful in subverting them. They fail because enough French condemn the attempts by adopting some form of Clermont-Tonnerre's argument that both the preemptive exclusion of resident immigrants and the partial disqualification of citizens contradict the founding conception: that the French nation-state is a politically constructed unity that assimilates differences to its republican ideal on the basis of equality and indivisibility, and not a solidarity that divides itself from others by ethnocultural means. Such censure does not excise the prejudice, but it is uncompromising because halfway measures of disqualification remain "intolerable." The only alternative this formulation leaves, one embraced passionately by some French at various times, is either to transform the entire model of national membership for the sake of prejudice or to expel pariahs entirely from the body politic (a "final solution").

American Restriction

In nineteenth-century America, equally ferocious battles raged to keep certain groups that resided permanently in the United States from becoming American citizens. As in France, the preferred strategy was preemptive exclusion and for the same reasons. However, the problem of national membership that provoked preemption was not religious affiliation. From initial colonization, religious freedom was fundamental to the developing conception of American nationhood. It matured, for example, into Article VI of the U.S. Constitution, which requires all who hold "office or public trust" to swear by oath to support the Constitution, but which explicitly prohibits any religious test as a qualification. Moreover, it emphasizes that none "shall ever be required." With this one phrase, the Constitution eliminated the primary obstruction widely used in Europe and in some American colonies to keep non-Christian minorities from participating in the political process, namely, a public oath affirming Christian faith. Even though anti-Semitism was hardly less ardent in the United States than in France, Jews enjoyed full American citizenship from the outset. They may not have been elected to office, but they suffered no attempts to repudiate or qualify their membership.

The decisive problem for American membership at the founding of the nation was not the bigotry of religion but that of race. This prejudice relied primarily on preemptive exclusion but also utilized selective disqualification to deny American citizenship to three resident groups that had reasonable claims to it: Indians, slaves, and freeborn blacks.[12] The dilemmas of national belonging derived from the central assumption of birthright citizenship that all born in the American republic automatically acquired American membership. Although this assumption seemed secure with regard to whites, profound constitutional uncertainties over the entailments of membership complicated it for others.[13] Not only was there no definition of citizenship in the U.S. Constitution for nearly a century after its ratification in 1789—until the passage of the Fourteenth Amendment (1868)—but many provisions contained ambiguities about the exact relationship between state and national citizenships. These uncertainties plagued every debate about membership and provided exclusionists with much ammunition. The exclusion of Indians and slaves presented lesser contradictions because it could be rationalized within a framework of ideas that most American citizens and their courts accepted, at least for a time. But for freeborn blacks, no compromise between principle and prejudice seemed possible.[14]

After the consolidation of government in 1789, most Indians were barred from citizenship by virtue of federal naturalization laws that restricted admission to free white "aliens." Considered aliens, Indians were thus excluded by race.[15] But what kind of aliens were these native-born peoples? That question soon became a dilemma for the courts—for if they were not aliens, then why were they not citizens? Two justifications combined. The first was that Indians required wardship, not citizenship, because— as various courts in the nineteenth century wrote (cited in Kettner 1978:

293–300)—they were "incapacitated, by their mental debasement" from dealing with whites as equals. Instead, these "unfortunate children of the public" needed the federal government's protection against the "superior intelligence" and "cupidity" of whites. However, unlike white children, who were citizens nonetheless, Indians became permanently dependent wards, "an inferior race of people, without the privileges of citizens, and under the protection of the government."

The second argument concerned tribal organization, and it became the main justification for denying American citizenship. Indians could be considered aliens because they were born under the jurisdiction of their tribes and tribes considered nations of some sovereignty within the territorial United States because they demanded allegiance from their members and provided protection. As Chief Justice John Marshall put it in *Cherokee Nation v. Georgia* (1831), with a set of phrases that framed debate for a century, the Indian tribes were "domestic-dependent nations" in a "state of pupilage" in relation to the United States, "resembl[ing] that of a ward to a guardian." Although the Court disagreed as to whether tribes should be considered "foreign" or "domestic-dependent," it unanimously held that they were separate nations. Thus, it ratified a multinational formulation of nationhood for the United States, based on the assumption of Indian tribal sovereignty and cultural autonomy—precisely the concept of "nations within a nation" the French rejected. This sanction gave legal foundation to the federal government's long-standing policy of considering the tribes sovereign for purposes of concluding treaties, many motivated by the goal of removing Indians to lands in the western territories and thereby freeing vast areas for white settlement in the East.[16]

Tribal Indians were in a double bind as a result of this multinationalism, the logic of which was not unimpeachable but functional enough to facilitate their removal to the West and to deny them citizenship pre-emptively. To the extent that tribes were separate nations into whose allegiance its members were born, Indians who retained tribal identity (as most did) could not claim American citizenship by birthright. However, because these sovereign nations were not considered fully foreign, their members could not demand access to the federal courts (as citizens of foreign states have the right to do) and therefore could not apply for citizenship via ordinary naturalization. Even if individual Indians managed to expatriate themselves from tribal jurisdiction, they were still barred from naturalization because of its race restriction and from citizenship without a specific act of government. As long as the tribes were "domestic" and "dependent," they fell under U.S. law and white control. As long as they were viewed as separate nations, their members were aliens and denied the full protection of that law.

After the Civil War, however, the priority of preemptive exclusion for Indians changed. Congress ended its assumption of multinationalism and set out to destroy tribal sovereignty by drawing Indians out of tribal membership and assimilating them as individuals to U.S. citizenship. However, it was to a citizenship diminished by selective disqualification, and it turned them into an oxymoron: citizen wards of the federal government. For many in Congress, the policy of assimilation was driven by the objective of allowing white appropriation of Indian lands as much as ending the "savagery" rooted in tribal autonomy. The policy proposed to "civilize" Indians into ways of life that would, coincidentally, need less land and to extinguish tribal land titles. The main method of breaking up tribal estates was compulsory allotment, which assumed a standard pattern in the 1850s. With the General Allotment Act of 1887, it became the comprehensive framework for the policy of assimilation. Typically, allotment declared tribal holdings in part or whole abolished, surveyed them into lots, assigned these lots to individual Indians, and held them in inalienable federal trust for twenty-five years or longer. In exchange, allottees received U.S. citizenship and guarantees of federal protection. The latter turned these new citizens into wards by establishing federal control over key aspects of their lives.[17]

However, Indian citizenship ignited tremendous debate precisely because its reduction by wardship contradicted the principle of indivisibility, assumed fundamental for white citizens. Could American citizenship be legally diminished by selective disqualification? Could Indian adults be both citizens and wards? Even though the Allotment Act explicitly granted immediate citizenship to Indian allottees, "with all the rights, privileges, and immunities" (sec. 6), many lawmakers continued to treat them as wards, exploiting every uncertainty to deny them full benefit of the Fourteenth Amendment. For example, although one representative declared in congressional debate in 1897 that "it is utterly impossible for [Indian allottees] to be citizens and pupils of the United States at the same time," a federal judge concluded the opposite in the case that justified prohibiting liquor sales to Indians (*Farrell v. U.S.*, 1901): "the government [may] confer all the privileges and immunities of citizenship upon its wards, and yet retain its power . . . to protect them against their appetites, passions, and incapacity" (Wilkins 1997: 120–21). Battered by contradictory judicial and legislative initiatives, the question of the indivisibility of Indian citizenship remained unresolved for decades.[18] It was not until the Citizenship Act of 1924—after wide recognition of Indian contributions to U.S. forces in World War I—that all Indians born within the territorial United States were finally and fully admitted to citizenship. Yet special treatment for Indian citizens, whether restrictively or affirmatively deployed, in such matters as fishing rights, land use, alcohol consumption, cigarette taxes, and gambling, continues to vex American citizenship.

The strategy of preemptive exclusion also functioned to deny citizenship to native-born black slaves. There is ample evidence that between the ratification of the Constitution and the passage of its Thirteenth Amendment in 1865, many judges and legislators personally viewed slavery as an abomination and were moved to outlaw it. Nonetheless, until the Civil War, more in Southern slave states than in Northern free ones, American courts consistently reduced slaves to the status of property. Generally, they did so by recognizing the primacy of local laws that sanctioned slavery. As long as slaves were considered commodities, they were neither aliens nor citizens, and judges could avoid fitting them into one category or another.

However, the denial of citizenship to freeborn blacks was a different matter altogether, which no attribution of autonomy could justify as in the case of Indians. Indeed, no justification seemed theoretically consistent with the accepted foundations of American citizenship and its acquisition. Its principle of unconditional birthright *ius soli* made it contradictory to deny that freeborn blacks were citizens. Nevertheless, many white Americans refused to accept them as such, and certainly not as equal citizens.[19] Instead, they attempted to diminish free black citizenship, both preemptively and selectively. In effect, they made *ius soli* conditional on race. Congress engaged this apparently insoluble contradiction between principle and prejudice during debates on Missouri's admission to statehood in 1820. Southern representatives pressed to add a provision to its constitution that prevented free blacks from entering the state. Other congressmen objected that the proposed clause violated the constitutional rights of free blacks because they were citizens by virtue of the indivisible and unconditional logic of birthright citizenship: since free blacks were "not aliens or slaves, . . . [they] were of consequence free citizens," concluded a senator from Massachusetts (Kettner 1978: 312). When proponents of the provision denied that they were, the lines of conflict were drawn.

In the decades prior to the Civil War, courts throughout the South began to develop a new vocabulary of membership to identify a category of American citizens with diminished rights. Freeborn blacks were called "subjects, denizens, alien strangers, wards, quasi citizens, degraded persons, and a third class," to list examples from court decisions in six southern states from 1820 to 1860 (cited in Kettner 1978: 319–20). This vocabulary invoked the British system of separate legally ranked categories of membership, which included denizen, naturalized subject, and natural-born subject, in addition to various kinds of aliens, each with different privileges and liabilities. In appealing to the British system, many Americans had no doubt that these maneuvers to institute new and lesser categories of membership constituted an organized effort to create a differentiated American citizenship. They violated precisely what had distinguished revolutionary American citizenship from British subjectship: the principle of indivisibility.

This principle developed over time as American colonists rejected British discriminations and opened their New World communities to different kinds of people seeking membership based on opportunity and work. It became consolidated as a vital force by the Revolution in the ideology of "one nation, indivisible." By the time the Constitution was ratified, it had matured into a legal doctrine that got refined through subsequent congressional debates about naturalization, dual citizenship in nation and state, and expatriation. Consider the first. Although the Constitution did not define citizenship, the principle of indivisible membership in the nation is clearly expressed in the discussion of its acquisition by naturalization. Article I, section 8, gives Congress the sole authority "to establish a *uniform* rule of naturalization" (italics added). In congressional debates on the first two naturalization acts (1790 and 1795), this principle of uniform admission to citizenship prevailed over proposals to institute ranked, sliding, or progressive acquisition. In response to one such proposal, a congressman from Virginia denied that Congress had the constitutional power to admit aliens as citizens with some rights and not others because the Constitution had already defined the rights of citizens for all citizens. Based on this indivisible, all-or-nothing principle of American citizenship, he articulated the only logical alternatives: "Foreigners must, therefore, be refused the privilege of becoming citizens altogether, or admitted to the rights of citizens" (cited in Kettner 1978: 245).

The attempt by Southern courts to introduce differentiated categories of membership amounted, therefore, to a direct assault on core assumptions about the meaning of American citizenship. As Kettner (1978: 322–23) argues, it brought Americans into conflict over three central tenets of citizenship with regard to the status of freeborn blacks. The first was the assumption of birthright citizenship. The second was the principle that American citizenship was indivisible for fundamental rights, a status without differentiated classes. The third was the presumption that American citizenship normally involved a dual membership in the nation and in a constituent state, and that national allegiance entailed certain obligations for state allegiance. These tenets developed in American law before the status of free blacks became publicly debated, and they seemed uncontroversial when applied to white men. However, these same principles became obstacles to those who wished to deny or diminish black citizenship when that problem became a national issue. The indivisibility and mutual exclusivity of the categories "alien, citizen, and slave" limited their options to exclude.

Attempts to circumvent these limitations by inventing new categories of membership for freeborn blacks or by selectively disqualifying them from particular rights collided so blatantly with these tenets that the Supreme Court was finally forced, after much evasion, to consider the exclusion of blacks from citizenship. If selective disqualification at the level of general membership was untenable because it fragmented what Congress had held on numerous occasions to be uniform and indivisible, then the Supreme Court adopted the only other strategy available to maintain blacks outside the framework of the Constitution: preemptive exclusion. In the infamous *Dred Scott* case (1857), a divided court ruled that blacks could not be American citizens within the meaning of the Constitution. It excluded them categorically. The majority opinion accepted the proposition that there existed a legitimate separation between individual state and national citizenships. It held that the latter did not derive automatically from birth within the jurisdiction of the national government. Rather, it ruled that national citizenship was a closed community, restricted to those who founded the Union in 1789, their descendants, and aliens transformed by the process of naturalization. As blacks were none of these, according to the Court, they could not be national citizens.

The ruling did little, however, to resolve the conflict. Instead, by challenging the assumption of unconditional birthright citizenship and stressing the ambiguities of dual membership, it underscored the uncertain constitutional meaning of American citizenship. As a result, disputes about the nature of membership in the Union intensified without resolution. Arguments exhausted, the North and the South engaged the issue in civil war within four years of the Supreme Court ruling. It was only after the war, with the passage of the Thirteenth, Fourteenth, and Fifteenth Amendments, that the basic formulation of American citizenship attained a real measure of constitutional clarity. When the Fourteenth Amendment defined citizenship inclusively and unconditionally in terms of either birth or naturalization in the United States, it voided the strategy of preemptive exclusion for freeborn blacks.

Nevertheless, exclusionists continued to find and exploit sufficient constitutional ambiguities about citizenship to sustain their efforts to limit black membership. One strategy they developed was the fiction of "separate but equal" to justify the so-called Jim Crow segregation—a devious attempt to exclude black citizens preemptively from the world of white citizens. Another strategy involved supposed constitutional ambiguities about political rights. Citizens of the United States were eligible for federal office by virtue of the federal constitution. But their right to vote depended upon state laws, because the Constitution allowed the states to determine and regulate the franchise (Arts. I and II). Indeed, throughout much American history, political rights have seemed less absolutely inherent in the status of citizen and more subject to qualification, even among the white citizenry, than many other rights. Hence, having lost the battle for the outright denial of citizenship to blacks, exclusionists turned to manipulating the franchise as their principal strategy. During the nineteenth century and much of the twentieth, in some states, they successfully resisted the federalization of suffrage as an automatic corollary of national citizenship. Instead, they defended the right of states to regulate suffrage, including the use of qualifications to identify citizens entitled to vote.[20]

The result was the use of state law to deny black Americans the franchise. In reviewing such legislation, state supreme courts often maintained ambivalent policies toward their free black populations. Although many ruled that free blacks were citizens under the existing principles of American citizenship, some drew a distinction between the political rights of voting and holding office and other rights of citizenship, and used this distinction to deny black citizens the right to political participation. As a result, free blacks could vote in only six of the thirty-four states in the union in 1860.[21]

Even after the Civil War amendments, many southern states persistently claimed to find enough constitutional ambiguity in the meaning of citizenship to justify the continued use of local qualifications to deny black Americans equal political rights. As these measures were designed to circumvent the federally mandated equality of the Fourteenth and Fifteenth Amendments, they were evasions. They included grandfather clauses, white-only primary elections, poll taxes, and literacy tests. Given that they were obvious deceits, intended to exclude blacks, their longevity was shameful: it took the Supreme Court and Congress almost fifty years to strike down the grandfather clause, eighty years to prohibit white primaries, and one hundred years to remove the last vestiges of local franchise taxes and tests. In other words, it took another century of struggle *after* the Civil War, culminating in the civil rights movement of the 1960s, to eliminate the local disqualification of political rights that contradicted the principles of general membership.

■ ■ ■

We can now identify what Brazilians perceived as they surveyed the development of French and American citizenships during the nineteenth century. Foremost, they beheld conflict and instability: a terrifying perspective of revolution, civil war, mass democracy, mob rule, and despotism. They saw societal relations shaken to their foundations: the end of aristocracy, violence over slavery, erosion of landed estates. They understood as well that these conflicts derived directly from the interaction of radical first premises of incorporation.[22] These principles inspired both the French and the American Revolutions with the vision of a national membership that would be uniform, individually based, and indivisible for those considered eligible, and that would entitle members to an egalitarian distribution of citizen rights. Once admitted, citizens received the full bundle. This all-or-nothing principle of civic incorporation served well the interests of many, for whom it equated prior differences for purposes of citizenship. It proved intolerable, however, for members with strong religious, racial, and gender prejudices. Hence, the crucial battles over membership in both cases were fought at the point of entry, as exclusionists used strategies of preemption to deny initial access to residents they deemed unfit.

Consequently, both French and American citizenships were initially formulated as restrictive statuses of membership with regard to religious, racial, and gender ascriptions. However, in the French case, the early resolution of the admission of Jews consolidated the argument that national membership should be inclusive of such groups and uncompromisingly indivisible. On this basis, French citizenship quickly developed into a relatively inclusive civic incorporation. Although its premise changed after 1804 to unconditional *ius sanguinis*, which by itself is restrictive, the complement of conditional *ius soli* made French citizenship expansive. From the first, furthermore, French constitutions distributed rights among citizens with extensive, if not complete, equality. The main exception was suffrage, which varied for men from nearly universal to extremely restricted until 1848, and which excluded women entirely for another century.

Membership in the American nation remained far more ascriptively restrictive. It excluded native-born resident groups preemptively on the basis of race. Unlike France, this preemption made America a multinational society. Although the rhetoric of national self-understanding was for many Americans one of inclusion by means of unconditional *ius soli*, in fact the attribute of race *formally* conditioned this principle for most of the nineteenth century and much longer in many cases. Only for a core minority of American residents, white men, was American citizenship fully egalitarian. For the rest, it was ascriptively inegalitarian; that is, around the core, most other adults encountered an array of legally and ascriptively defined inequalities. Nevertheless, the idealized white core of American citizenship proved responsive to popular pressures for expansion. After the Civil War, American national membership became fully inclusive in legal terms for the native born, on the basis of unconditional *ius soli* citizenship—with the exception of about one-third of American Indians with tribal affiliations. For them, exclusion lasted until 1924.

Among American citizens, the legally defined distribution of rights became egalitarian for men, in both civil and political aspects, as soon as suffrage became universal—in many states by 1820 and in most by 1850. Women citizens achieved civil equality by midcentury, with changes in property law, and political equality in 1920. However, for the one group whose unconditional *ius soli* membership had been the most problematic—American blacks—political citizenship remained differentiated until 1965 in a handful of states. These used selective disqualification to deny blacks political rights in an effort to evade the constitutional equalities established after 1865. For American blacks and other nonwhites, moreover, discriminatory social and economic practices made the subsequent formal equality of their citizenship difficult to realize.

At midcentury, therefore, it became evident that citizenships based on principles of indivisibility were more likely to exclude people altogether than to exclude them partially. These principles led exclusionists to favor strategies of preemption because they rendered strategies of selective disqualification among citizens ultimately indefensible. Although this consequence is one of logic, it was nevertheless a powerful weapon in struggles for full and equal rights. When disqualification among citizens occurred, the discriminated against were able to argue their case as a contradiction of principle, forcing exclusionists to make a difficult choice: either maintain prejudice and sacrifice the principle or maintain the principle and readjust prejudice. Indeed, in the history of these violent citizenships, the argument from principle has mobilized powerful rights movements, with considerable, though by no means complete, success in reducing the legal effects of prejudice.

At the core of this argument is a radical ideal of legal equality. The French and American Revolutions established this ideal as the cutting edge of national citizenship, as the means to excise prerevolutionary privilege based on private law and corporate immunities and replace it with an undifferentiated individual membership based on common rights. In 1789, the arch-rationalist Abbé Sieyès penned a geometric image of this unmediated legal equality: "I picture the law as being at the center of a huge globe; all citizens, without exception, stand equidistant from it on the surface and occupy equal positions there; all are equally dependent on the law, all present it with their liberty and their property to be protected; and this is what I call the *common rights* of citizens, the rights in respect of which they are all alike" (cited in Brubaker 1992: 39–40).

At the beginning of the nineteenth century, such circles of full and equal citizens were indeed small in most countries. However, in European and North American nations they expanded steadily and at times dramatically throughout the century, precisely in the terms Sieyès imagined: although the results are by no means progressively cumulative, although there is backsliding and erosion, their citizenship struggles generally focused on the proposition that the legal equality and dignity of citizens should advance at the expense of the legal protection of inequality. Especially in the realm of civil citizenship, the locus of this concern for equality became the individual citizen, the seat of equal fundamental rights. Formal civil rights expanded to include illegitimate children and minorities, and women increasingly gained full control of their bodies and property. With the spread of movements for mass representative democracy, political rights also became ever more individualized, universalized, and extended to poor men and eventually to all women. The principle of legal equality helped end hereditary servitude, curb the extent of paternal power, and balance the statuses of husband and wife.

Nonetheless, as Bendix (1977: 74–104) observes, legal equality initially benefited only those whose socioeconomic standing enabled them to take advantage of their rights. Legal equality produced, in other words, new kinds of inequalities. To counter them, new institutions emerged to help equalize the capacity of all citizens to access their formal rights. By the mid-twentieth century, these means were widely consolidated in legislation. Principal among them were the right to free elementary education, the institution of public defenders as a means to secure the right to justice, the development of socioeconomic rights to guarantee minimal citizen well-being, and the legalization of trade unions to represent the economic interests of the working poor on the basis of their civil right to associate.

Yet it was much earlier, during the first part of the previous century, that equality had become the vanguard of European and North American citizenships, their leading edge, cutting away at privilege and delegitimating legalized exclusion and disqualification. Certainly, this citizenship equality was simultaneously advanced to some and denied to others. Certainly, its very expansion produced new inequalities of power, types of violence, and kinds of hypocrisy. Certainly, the poor and the nonwhite were much less able to realize their paper rights. But just as certainly, the extraordinary conflicts of the first seventy-five years of French and American citizenships demonstrated that a defining horizon of modern national experience had been established: once set down and rooted, the development of an indivisible and equalizing citizenship was as difficult to escape as to abide.

Brazilian Inclusion

Brazilians struggled no less than the French and the Americans with the difficulty of constructing a new nation out of an assortment of already-resident populations. However, at the time of Brazil's independence from Portugal in 1822, their formulation of the problem was distinctly different. Unlike American citizenship, which remained constitutionally undefined for almost one hundred years, or French citizenship, the definition of which twisted and turned through ten constitutions during the same period, Brazilian citizenship was clearly specified at the inception of nationhood in a constitution in 1824 that lasted through the century: "Brazilian citizens are those born in Brazil, either freeborn or freed, even if the father is a foreigner, . . . and the children of a Brazilian father, and the illegitimate children of a Brazilian mother, born in a foreign country, who come to establish residence in the Empire" (Art. 6). Thus, the constitution formulated national membership in terms of unconditional *ius soli* and conditional *ius sanguinis*. Established in 1824, this formulation of citizenship remains essentially unchanged to this day.[23]

The Brazilian consideration of *ius soli* differed significantly from its American counterpart as the basis for general membership. In the United States, conditions of race and slavery restricted *ius soli* preemptively. In Brazil, no less a slave society, with enormous numbers of black, Indian, and mixed-race people in various states of emancipation, it was only conditioned by freedom—and even then, not absolutely. Rather, *ius soli* citizenship was inclusive and unrestricted for all free people in Brazil regardless of racial profile. Given this basis for membership, the Portuguese/Brazilians did not treat Indians as alien nations, as did the English/Americans in North America, but as vassals and nationals.[24] Nor was there any doubt that freeborn blacks were national citizens. If freed, moreover, Brazil-born slaves not only immediately became citizens, but they also voted, regularly and without challenge if they qualified for political rights in the same manner as other citizens. In Brazil, neither the denial of national citizenship for racial or religious reasons nor the imposition of local definitions of membership on national citizenship ever occurred. Just as remarkable by comparison, Brazilian law encouraged rather than prohibited "race mixing." Hence, the conflicts that racked the United States about the formal status of citizenship—about belonging to the national body—were absent from Brazilian law and practice. Whereas Americans ascriptively restricted citizenship for significant groups of native-born residents, Brazilians included all such free people in their national identity.[25]

Although an inclusive status, however, Brazilian national citizenship was not an egalitarian one. From the beginning, inclusion mattered less than the kind and quality of included citizen. All free native-born residents may have been Brazilian national citizens, but not all citizens had legally equal and uniform rights. Rather, the principles of equality that drove Americans and French to fight each other and to try to restrict citizenship—principles of the uniform, indivisible, individual, all-or-nothing distribution of rights—never became either the core or leading edge of Brazilian citizenship. They were absent from its articulation because equality was not an expectation of citizenship. Indeed, the word *equality* does not appear in the 1824 Constitution, with the single exception discussed in the previous chapter. It is notably absent from Article 179, which defines citizen rights by copying, in most other aspects, the French *Declaration of the Rights of Man and Citizen*. However, the *Declaration*'s famous first article—"Men are born and remain free and equal in rights"—is left out. Instead, the Brazilian state formulated citizenship, and Brazilians practiced it, as a system for the differential distribution of rights. On the basis of social distinctions not inherent to the definition of national membership, the state discriminated citizens into different categories of unequal rights, privileges, immunities, and powers.

In what manner did Brazilians justify the formulation of an inclusive but differentiated citizenship, of what I call an inclusively inegalitarian national membership? How did they construct a broadly inclusive national identity that nonetheless uses citizenship to consolidate a deeply hierarchical social structure? Let us first consider the conditions of territory, sovereignty, and population that Brazilians encountered at independence and that were fundamental elements of this construction.

The Brazilian nation-state inherited from the Portuguese crown a continent-sized territory almost identical to current national boundaries. Except for the addition of the territory of Acre in the north in the twentieth century and for a few adjustments along the southern border with Uruguay, these borders were set in 1750 by the Treaty of Madrid (see Reis 1968; Boxer 1962). In these negotiations, the Crown persuaded Spain to recognize that the Line of Tordesillas, established in 1494 to divide their respective holdings in the New World, had been irrevocably overrun by subsequent Portuguese explorations. Both sides agreed to redraw the boundaries of their lands on the basis of the principle *uti possidetis*, de facto possession. However, the Brazil that emerged from the Treaty of Madrid was one delineated not primarily by the activities of productive settlers, but by those of adventurers who had pushed far into the interior in search of gold, slaves, and souls: expeditions of Paulista *bandeirantes* in the southwest, *sertanistas* in the northeast, missionaries in the north and south, and military units warring against natives far from the coast. Thus, the Brazilian nation was born full-size. However, the state that created it confronted an overwhelmingly remote, mostly empty, and largely unconsolidated territory to administer.

A comparison with the United States is again revealing. The American state consolidated its nationhood over a segment of its current territory—the Atlantic seaboard—and then expanded west. Moreover, by 1808, the

U.S. Congress had completed the National Land Survey, begun in 1787, whereby it divided the national territory into an extendable and almost infinite number of square-mile units, each abstractly but precisely known and equal. Jefferson and others justified the imposition of this grid as an efficient and democratic way not only to organize individual landholdings but also to manage space for purposes of administration, settlement, and commercial development.

In Brazil, by contrast, the nation began with a continental extension of sovereignty, inclusive and overarching, but one throughout which the state was unable to extend either its authority or knowledge. Simply put, the national state was nonexistent in the greater part of the national territory, just as the colonial administration before it. Part of the problem was that the nation-state based its model of administration on that of the colony: all authorities—judges, prosecutors, aldermen, and so forth—were concentrated in settlements that had urban status as seats of municipal councils and districts. If a settlement had this status, all authorities were present; if not, there was none. Authorities were supposed to travel regularly through the country, but that happened rarely, given its remoteness. Therefore, as urban seats were few and far between, most of Brazil lacked public authority. As a result, the state found that local interests and unruliness regularly undermined its powers. This incapacity to consolidate itself nationally characterized the state during the entire imperial period and outlasted the inception of the Republic. While it is unwarranted to reduce this problem solely to matters of geography, the state's inability to administer large areas of the country forced it into sustaining certain arrangements and habits that had important consequences for the development of citizenship.

The first to note is that the new national government depended heavily on local elites—primarily large landholders—to exercise powers of state. Many aspects of this arrangement lasted into the 1930s. One manifestation was the creation of the National Guard in 1831 to defend the interests of the state in the absence of a professional military and police. The central government recruited local elites to command units of the Guard, giving them commissions as colonels and captains. However, their authority did not extend beyond their residential districts and they did not form a unified national military corporation. In turn, these officers recruited and maintained their own forces. Thus, the Guard units constituted private militias, often no more than a gathering of thugs in the employ of a local "colonel." Although they may have at times carried out the state's bidding, they did so therefore in a way that held the national government hostage to local and private structures of power. Furthermore, although they represented "the law," this representation was thoroughly conflated with private interests and their application through thuggery.

This alliance between public power and private local powers, between law and private force—commonly known as *coronelismo*—amounted to a nationwide privatization of the public. Henceforth, this appropriation of the res publica becomes a taken-for-granted norm of the public sphere in Brazil, one in which privatization and violent misrule of law corrode all dimensions of citizenship.[26]

The central government found recompense for its inabilities to exercise authority locally by investing in what it could accomplish in the capital: pass legislation, issue decrees, and establish bureaucratic regulations to oversee its always suspect agents. In this manner, the Brazilian state perpetuated another habit of Portuguese colonial administration, namely, an obsessive reliance on bureaucratic and statutory rule making as a means to solve problems in distant places and to tranquilize its distrust of its own representatives.[27] Moreover, one is struck both by the sheer volume of colonial and imperial legislation and also by its repetition. With regard to volume, a tremendous amount is of narrow application, concerning idiosyncratic cases. It is tempting to claim that this kind of particularism henceforth becomes an enduring element—indeed, a strategy—of the misrule of law: universal application is systematically avoided as a goal of legislative acts, governmental edicts, and judicial decisions. Instead, narrowly construed, these acts provide such little continuity and generality that each new case must be negotiated from scratch. The resulting legal complication, uncertainty, and inertia favor not merely the status quo but also fait accompli usurpations that eventually get legitimated through political and not judicial action. Under such conditions, usurpation becomes an excellent bet, a minimal risk with predictably high return for those with political power.

The repetition of similar legislation appears as another attribute of this misrule of law: it indicates not only that the substance of a ruling is repeatedly ignored but also that the perceived solution to disobedience is to issue it again. Thus, over the course of several centuries, the Indians are "freed" many times in legislation because they continue to be illegally enslaved. Furthermore, just as the state gives itself substance primarily in the copious production of documents, so its paper formalism requires voluminous documentation, duly signed, stamped, and registered, from citizens who wish to make claims on its offices. In short, based on well-founded distrust between government and citizen, ruler and functionary, and state and nation, a culture of stamps, ribbons, and sealing wax arose to give the state a compensatory sense of grandeur in the absence of control.

How did this hobbled state produce a national body of citizens out of Brazil's preexisting populations? At independence, approximately 4.4 million people resided in Brazil. Using an estimate calculated in 1819, this total comprised 2,488,743 free people; 1,107,389 slaves; and a "non-domesticated" indigenous population of approximately 800,000 (IBGE 1990: 32). Of the "domesticated" population, therefore, about 31% were slaves, approximately one for every two free persons. The majority were Africans and their descendants, but Indians captured in "just wars" could also be enslaved. Although census data of the period does not indicate the "color" composition of the free population per se, narrative accounts describe many as racially miscegenated. They emphasize the rapid growth of this mixed population during the nineteenth century, from approximately 10%–20% at the beginning to 40% and more, depending on the region, at the end. For these people, Brazilians created a menagerie of terms to specify particular combinations of "white, red, and black blood" in the offspring of mixed-race unions, including *caboclo* (Indian + white, with straight hair), *cabra* (mulatto + black, light-skinned), *cafuzo* (black + Indian, with dark skin and smooth hair), *mameluco* (Indian + white), and *mulato* (black + white).

Also among the free were foreign-born residents (mostly Portuguese concentrated in commerce and government), manumitted slaves (*libertos*), and emancipated village Indians who were, nevertheless, generally pressed into servile labor. At the time of independence, the nondomesticated Indians (*bravos*, wild) were either subject to enslavement for periods of ten to fifteen years if captured in warfare or, if not at war with the state, considered free but deemed "orphans" under state tutelage.

Without drawing any distinctions of race, the imperial constitution considered all these free people member-citizens of the nation-state, including the "orphan Indians" who, like minors, had their membership reduced to wardship. Race was not relevant to this consideration. Rather, the constitution established only birthplace (Brazil) and civil status (free) as the fundamental criteria of membership. With the exception of wards and slaves conditionally manumitted, the native freeborn and freed people of color in Brazil were fully Brazilian nationals. Moreover, many nineteenth-century Brazilians thought that slavery should normally lead to manumission. Thus to the extent that slaves were viewed as freeable, and freedom as a process of assimilation, they were also considered inevitably Brazilian.

To describe the free as full members does not mean, however, that they had equal access to a full set of rights. Although nationalizing elites rejected, like the French and unlike the American, a multinational structure for Brazil, they also rejected uniform citizenship. As a result, all Brazilians were full members of the nation-state, but they were not equal citizens. As we shall see, most free Brazilian citizens suffered a wide range of civil and political limitations on their citizenship, for which race, gender, and religion were occasionally specified as disabling criteria. To describe

Brazilian national citizenship as inclusive is thus to emphasize that no one was excluded ascriptively on racial or religious grounds from general membership in the nation. To the contrary, Brazilian elites may have harbored grave and racist doubts about the capacities of freeborn blacks and Indians to contribute to national development; they may have therefore restricted their participation and share of rights; but they had no doubts about their being Brazilian.

In considering all these free peoples as compatriots, as making up a single colonial and then a national body, Brazilian intellectuals and state builders never developed policies based on the absoluteness of racial differences. Certainly, they believed in the superiority of "white Christian civilization." But in denying absolute racial differences, they are perhaps unique in the development of the Americas—or, if similar to the French, then opposite the Americans and distinct from the Spanish. Unlike the latter, they neither established a colonial regime of legally separate "republics," one European and the other Indian, nor, when that had broken down, a legal regime of pure and mixed-blood casts based on theories of the inherent degeneracy of miscegenation and the absolute superiority of whiteness. Unlike Americans, Brazilians did not adopt the one-drop rule, which categorically condemned any trace of "bad blood," nor did they exclude such racially constituted categories from national membership. Rather, Brazilians consistently viewed race as a malleable and indeterminate feature of human development, though they did so within a racist framework of white superiority.[28]

Thus both colonial and national social policy in Brazil considered that the white ("European, civilized, our people") race would assimilate and "perfect" the inferior races, extinguishing their racially marked inferiorities through the application of "proper methods of civilization." As the most effective method of such "integration," Brazilians consistently promoted biological and spatial "race mixing." At independence, this proposal was best expressed by the statesman, writer, scientist, and Minister of Empire (in effect, prime minister) José Bonifácio de Andrada e Silva. In 1823, he submitted a project to the constitutional assembly on the policies necessary for the "civilization of the wild Indians of the Brazilian Empire," from which the above phrases in quotation are taken. Bonifácio proposed that the Indians were legitimate members of the new nation and should be integrated peacefully by "Christianizing and civilizing" them. The prime way to do so is "to favor by all possible means marriage between Indians and whites and mulattos, who should therefore settle in the [Indian] villages, taking precaution however to avoid that by their dealings and bad habits they do not ruin these same Indians" (2002: 190). What is the objective of this race mixing? Bonifácio clearly states it: "to make of them all one sole body of the nation, stronger, better educated, and more entrepreneurial" (198). Though original, Bonifácio's project articulated ideas, sentiments, and methods of national consolidation that were of long-term standing and circulation in Brazil. Indeed, his proposals were familiar enough that the project received favorable evaluation in congressional committee and final approval by the full assembly. Today, Bonifácio is consecrated as "the patriarch of independence" and "father of the nation."[29]

It may be claimed that, given their thoroughly miscegenated population, Brazilian state builders had little choice but to reject European and American notions of the irredeemable degeneracy of race mixing. How else could they escape a fate of second-rate nationhood other than by denying the determinacy of race? Whatever the underlying perception, these Brazilians consistently advocated race mixing as the way to perfect the inferior races and achieve national unity out of Brazil's disparate peoples. Without doubt, where practiced, this integration-through-assimilation resulted in the theft of Indian lands and the impoverishment of Indians and blacks. Yet identical results occurred in Spanish and English America without such policies or practices of mixing. To be sure, by the nineteenth century, theories of whitening the population through race mixing had become popular in other Latin American nations, especially Columbia, Mexico, and Venezuela. But in Brazil, the encouragement of integration through mixed-race settlement and marriage had been official, legislated policy since colonial times. Thus, there remains something distinctive about Brazil's use of race mixing to create a national body that includes all residents regardless of racial profile as Brazilian or, in the case of slaves, as potentially Brazilian.

At least three related forms of this project of integration appeared over the centuries, occurring in various combinations during colonial, imperial, and republican periods. One encourages race mixing as a thinly veiled strategy for the appropriation of Indian lands and the destruction of any autonomous Indian or African identity in Brazil. This version is associated, for example, with a set of important policies established in 1757 in the so-called Directory of Indians. A second became prevalent at the end of the nineteenth century and reflects the influence on Brazilian intellectuals of European "scientific racism" and Social Darwinism. In this form, race mixing explicitly constitutes a process of genetically based whitening (essentially because white genes are thought stronger) that will result in the eventual erasure of blackness and Indianness from the nation. "The whiter the better" had always been a dominant cultural orientation in Brazil. Between 1880 and 1920, it became a process with scientific validity.[30]

Both strategies of miscegenation are especially directed at the "pure" forms of the nonwhite races, considered the greatest obstacles to national development. Mixing thus means whitewashing the other colors to pro-duce people who are on the way to becoming both phenotypically and culturally white. In both versions, it also means redefining race in sociocul-tural terms: miscegenation creates intermediate and ambiguous categories that provide a kind of sanctuary for people who are not obviously white in a phenotypic sense but who may negotiate their whiteness on the basis of personal success. However, such ambiguity also transformed whiteness. As Mattoso (1986: 199) observes, although elite Bahian society in the nineteenth century wished to remain closed and white, it "never managed to find a way to refuse the new blood constantly offered by a social group whose only ambition was to disappear [into whiteness]: the mulattoes."[31]

A third version hints at the superiority of the hybrid and is often asso-ciated with the arguments of Bonifácio. In submerging racial differences "to make of them all one sole body of the nation," it views miscegenation as a means to improve the white race as well as the others. National in-clusion by this method benefits everyone. However, this version is no less racist, as it disparages blacks, Indians, Asians, and even whites in racial terms in advocating miscegenation as a means of national development. Thus, in his congressional project, Bonifácio (2002) calls the "wild" In-dians "vagabonds, lazy, like animals, vengeful, brutal, stupid, without ambition, lacking calculation, given to immediate gratification," and so forth. However, he generally assigns the causes of these attributes to en-vironmental conditions and social practices. Hence, he argues that by changing those factors, race mixing and Christian education will trans-form the "brute" into the "civilized." The resulting miscegenated national body, he suggests, will be better for all.

With somewhat different coloration, these three strategies of national consolidation are thus inclusionist and racist simultaneously. This (per-haps) oxymoronic construction, this racist inclusionism, has remained an enduring feature of Brazil's nationhood. Although the genetic theory of whitening has long since lost both scientific and popular credibility, race mixing continues to be a source of Brazilian pride and a key attribute of Brazil's self-understanding as an inclusive nation. In addition, more current versions of Brazilian inclusionism, such as the claim of "racial democracy" popularized by Gilberto Freyre and the modernist theory of *antropofagia*, perpetuate ideas of mixing, assimilation, and tutelage developed as methods of inclusion at independence and earlier. These methods applied especially to two groups of people for whom the edges of Brazilian national membership remained unusually if ambiguously po-rous, namely, Indians and freed slaves. Let us look at the inclusion of each to understand the general principles.

At the beginning of the colonial period (1500), the Indians of Brazil numbered about five million. By its end (1800), there were eight hundred thousand. A century later, at the close of the Empire, only four hundred thousand survived. The fate of the natives of both Brazil and the United States is thus similar: extermination of vast numbers of people, destruction of whole societies, theft of lands. However, the national frameworks of these terrible histories are very different. The American state treated tribal members as "aliens," excluded them as "domestic dependent nationals," separated the races, and maintained boundaries in every sense. The Brazilian state consistently refused to recognize the sovereign standing of Indian societies.[32] It refused to allow the existence of nations within the nation. Rather, it considered tribal specificity and indeed Indianness itself a temporary condition, one that would pass as Indians became "civilized" and fully Brazilian. From first contact, the Crown generally viewed Indians as subjects of the king, vassals on their own lands—lands which the Crown claimed, although the nature of this claim has always been subject to dispute. Hence, the Brazilian state (both colonial and national) saw itself as the proprietor of the land on behalf of the Indians. It was the owner, the Indians usufruct holders, and the lands a public good—precisely the kind of good that was prize picking for private appropriation by non-Indian settlers and speculators.

Therefore, although I call Brazilian policy toward the Indians inclusionary, there should be no mistaking that it was one of total domination. Brazilian inclusion allowed the Indians no existence apart from the Brazilian nation, no autonomous culture, settlement, or even biology. In this sense, inclusion entailed domination to the point of extinction—even without wars of extermination—as Indianness was to "pass" through race mixing.

A second crucial distinction between American and Brazilian states in their treatment of Indians involves the extraction of labor. The Brazilians relied heavily on Indian labor, forcing Indians into slavery and other compulsory-work regimes on a massive scale not found in the United States. Even after it became generally acknowledged that Indians did not make "good slaves" and they were replaced by Africans, the extractive economy of the Amazon and several other regions remained dependent on native labor. Hence, from the first regulation in 1548, much of the heap of legislation about Indians concerns the conditions of their labor and its allocation. Framed by the twin ideological pillars of the Portuguese/Brazilian empire, Christianization and colonization, "to civilize" the Indians means to submit them (for their own good) to the yoke of European law and the discipline of European work. The laws administer this submission with a combination of ambivalence and deceit. They regulate Indian subjection by "just warfare" and their "descent" into mission villages for domestication. At times they revoke their captivity and at other times they renew it, alternately declaring their freedom and accepting their enslavement.

All the while, they distribute their labor to the missions, public projects, and private individuals. Summarizing this legislative tangle, Gomes (2000: 59) writes that "all legal texts that set out to clarify the issue of freedom versus slavery consistently left loopholes for the persecution, captivity, dispossession, and reallocation of Indians."

As long as the Indian question remained primarily one of labor extraction, the state organized the submission/assimilation of Indians into a two-step process: one of domestication through village-based wardship and one of enslavement or extermination in "just wars." "Wild Indians" who submitted "peacefully" were "descended" to controlled villages (*aldeias*), usually near Luzo-Brazilian settlements. By the mid-seventeenth century, the Jesuit order controlled both the deportation and the villages. The mission of village directors was to prepare the Indians for eventual "emancipation" from wardship and assimilation into Brazilian society through a combination of religious instruction and disciplined work. Thus, in the villages, Indians would be Christianized, civilized, relieved thereby of their Indianness, and turned into Brazilians. All the while, they would also be funneled into labor service. Those Indians who did not submit peacefully to this Brazilianization became the targets of "just wars," authorized by the pope and licensed by the king, in which captives could be legitimately killed or enslaved for fixed periods of time. Both steps were but phases, therefore, of the overarching process of assimilating the Indians—that is, of causing them to disappear as an autonomous population: both the "deinfestation" of the backlands and the "reduction" to controlled villages "freed" Indian land and labor for Brazilian consumption, thus incorporating them into the expanding body of Brazil.

By the mid-eighteenth century, however, the Jesuits had shipwrecked their Society on the shoals of conflicting colonial interests. With varying motives, the Crown, colonial administrators, and local settlers accused them of devious enrichment, hoarding native labor, isolating the Indians, and thereby inhibiting their integration into the Empire. These conflicts led to the expulsion of the Jesuits from the villages in 1757 and from the Empire altogether two years later. In their place, the Portuguese instituted a new ordinance concerning the Indians, the License of 3 May 1757 (called the Directory of Indians). Among other things, it created incentives for the settlement of non-Indians in the Indian villages, where it encouraged mixed marriages and mandated the use of Portuguese. To further the elimination of autonomous Indian identity, it transformed these miscegenated villages into towns and districts of normal Portuguese administration and place names. The Indians remained wards of the new administrators, "as long as they lack the capacity to govern themselves" (cited in Cunha 1992: 24). So comprehensive was this legislation in reformulating the Indian question that within a few years of its application, many Indian villages had been abandoned or privatized. As Jesuit holdings were auctioned off or usurped by settlers and as village lands became private estates, Indians found that the law had transformed them into squatters on what had once been their own lands.

This legislation was effective because by independence the Indian question had largely shifted from one of extracting labor to one of extracting land. In most places, African slaves had replaced Indian labor. At the same time, the Brazilian expansion of agriculture, mining, and ranching brought many new Indian lands within range. Brazilian strategy changed accordingly. Part of the problem was legal. Though a matter of disputed interpretation through the centuries, the state recognized that Indians had primordial claims to the lands they occupied—whether as "legitimate owners [*senhores*], because God gave them [the lands]," as Bonifácio (2002: 190) argued, or as legitimate users of God's lands as others argued. In either terms, the Indians had to be dispossessed legally. The solution was to bifurcate Indian policy. In frontier areas, "wild Indians" continued to be "descended" to new villages, thus "liberating" vast areas of territory. The innovation came in 1808 when Prince Regent and later King João VI declared that lands conquered in "just wars" were *devoluta* (devolved, Carta Régia, 2 December 1808). By that, he meant either returned to the Crown as the original owner by right of "discovery and conquest" or empty. *Devoluta* was used in both ways. In either case, the lands could be legally reassigned as a result of this legal maneuver to those who would "erect mining operations and agricultural works on these lands newly restored." Settlers were then obligated to legalize their possession (*posse)* by "procuring a legitimate title of *sesmaria* [a royal land grant]".[33]

In areas of established settlements, however, where Indians were already domesticated and miscegenated, the strategy became the contrary: that of dismantling and extinguishing the villages, thereby freeing the land for non-Indian settlers. As the misdealings of Indian village lands become fundamental in the next century to the settlement of São Paulo's urban peripheries and their citizenship conflicts, it is worthwhile at this point to relate their fate. The villages created to receive Indian deportees were given royal concessions of land. It is plausible to claim that the Crown intended these Indian villages to have inalienable rights to the land thus granted which, therefore, could never be considered devolved—though this claim is endlessly debated. However, it was never doubted that village lands could be legally leased to non-Indians, rents from which were to be used to support the "civilization" of Indian wards. These leases (*aforamentos*) established usufructary rights to the land that were both alienable and inheritable. As they were far easier to arrange than royal grants—in principle not available for Indian village land but occasionally granted anyway—they initiated a private market in land rights.

Consequently, they enabled the state to dispose quickly and legally of Indian lands once villages were abandoned, declared extinct, or otherwise dissolved. Such disposal began in 1832 when the central government legislated the public sale of land in two villages (Decree of 6 July 1832, Art. 7). As Cunha (1992: 20) points out, this sale initiated a century-long rush on Indian village lands, as well as exceedingly complex disputes between municipal, provincial, and central governments, and between them and private parties, over ownership of the spoils. Many of these disputes remain unresolved to this day.

Twenty years later, the state intervened decisively to permit the large-scale appropriation of Indian lands, which it justified in terms of the assimilation produced by race mixing. Just after the passage of comprehensive Land Law 601 that created a national land market, the state issued Decision 92 (21 October 1850). This act "incorporated into the National Assets the lands of Indians who no longer live in villages, but are rather dispersed and mixed into the mass of the civilized population" (head note). It also declared unoccupied lands in Indian villages to be devolved, in apparent contradiction of earlier legislation. Thus, after a century of encouraging both the settlement of non-Indians in Indian villages and mixed marriages, the state pronounces its policy of assimilation a success: in many settlements, Indians are no longer distinguishable from the general population. Where this assimilation has occurred, the reservation of land exclusively for Indians loses its original object, the Indian, and hence can be terminated. Immediately, local governments in various states extinguished Indian villages and appropriated their lands, claiming that identifiable Indians no longer existed.

Apparent assimilation had legitimated apparent land theft. I say "apparent" theft because the legislation that four years later regulated Land Law 601 declared in no uncertain terms that "lands reserved for the colonization of natives, and to them distributed . . . cannot be alienated until such time as the Imperial Government, by special act, has not conferred on them full possession of them [the lands], as permitted by their state of civilization" (Art. 75 of Decree 1318, 30 January 1854).[34] However, as the century progressed, local governments successfully ignored this legislation in usurping control over the lands of extinct villages. As a result, they freely leased, sold, and otherwise incorporated them. When the Empire fell in 1889, these (perhaps) illegal practices became, in any case, faits accomplis: the new republican constitution (1891) assigned the lands of extinct villages to the patrimony of local states. There remained, however, many jurists who insisted that these lands belonged to the patrimony of the federal government. Indeed, their arguments prevailed in the next constitution (1934). Retaining their passion for this dispute to this day, both sides regularly intervene to claim ownership when a conflict arises, thereby rendering it practically insoluble—as we shall see in the case of the peripheries of São Paulo. However, as local, state, and federal interests dispute each other, one thing is certain. The Indian claim has all but vanished.

In sum, the inclusion of Indians into the national body through race mixing led, step by step, deceit by deceit, contradiction by contradiction, to the nearly total *legalized* usurpation of their land by the end of the nineteenth century: "liberated" from their tribal territories, the Indians are concentrated into villages, in which non-Indians are encouraged to settle, marry, and lease land; the villages are then abolished because the Indians are declared no longer identifiable within the miscegenated population that results; instead of belonging to the Indians and their descendents, the lands of these extinct villages revert to either central or local administrations that sell or grant them to non-Indians for new purposes. When the dust settles on the nineteenth century, the Indian lands are practically gone.

Wardship is the accomplice of this project of national inclusion and its deceit. In 1798, wardship is redefined by royal charter into a paternalistic master-servant relation. The charter abolishes the Directory and declares that Indians should act "as servants to their masters," who should treat them "as orphans" (cited in Gomes 2002: 69). This "promotion" to the condition of orphan becomes the basis for future Indian policies. It accompanies the shift in strategy with regard to Indian land. The royal charter of 1798 permits the free settlement of whites on Indian lands. After this date, the crown emancipates Indians in established and now miscegenated villages from their wardship and makes them equivalent to non-Indians in the labor market. Hence, these Indians may be declared to have been assimilated and their village reserves extinguished.

However, undomesticated tribal Indians descended to new settlements, those recently freed from slavery, and those directly "contracted for services" by individuals are legally deemed orphans. The "privilege" of this new status is that the orphans now have contractual rights with regard to their new masters: the latter assume legal responsibility for the education, well-being, and baptism of their Indian wards, in a tutelary relation overseen by the Court of Orphans. The Crown thought judicial oversight necessary because it considered the uncivilized Indians as children whose innocence and ignorance whites would easily exploit. It therefore required judges to monitor their work relations to make certain that free workers were not being enslaved. It also allowed these judges to distribute the "orphans" as laborers. One does not know whether to laugh or cry at this arrangement. In either case, as managers of free labor—of both Indians and manumitted slaves—judges of the Orphan Court often became notoriously rich.[35]

Henceforth, major legislation concerning Indians in Brazil reiterates this concept of tutelage: the Indian is defined as an orphan of "relative capacity, both mentally and judicially" and therefore under guardianship of the state (Law of 27 October 1831). This law established orphan status for the duration of the Empire. Although there is some ambiguity in its wording as to whether it declared all Indians orphans, it especially applied to Indians recently freed from compulsory labor. That is, in general terms, tutelage applied to Indians still readily identifiable as such, to "pure" Indians not yet assimilated. Although the state considered such Indians Brazilian citizens, it circumscribed their civil and political rights as legal minors under paternalistic tutelage. The Civil Code of 1916 reaffirmed this status for the Republic, as does the current Statute of the Indian of 1973 as the condition under which Indians are included in the Brazilian nation.

A ruling from the Province of Minas Gerais in 1858 illustrates these relations perfectly.[36] An official of a local electoral board received an inquiry as to whether two individuals, one born of an Indian mother and the other a manumitted African slave, could be included in the list of qualified voters. Both had met the income requirement for eligibility, but each was possibly disqualified for different reasons. Without ever calling the first an Indian, the official describes the doubt: can the petitioner vote if "Indians are reputed incapable of administering their assets"? He then rules favorably for two reasons: first, "as the individual [in question] . . . cannot cease to be considered a Brazilian Citizen, he should be included in the general list of voters," as long as he has met the qualifications required of other citizens for political rights. Second, as the petitioner is the child of a father "who is not Indian . . . although the mother is Indian," the orphan status of the "1831 law cannot be applied to him." That is, the official considers the mixed-race offspring an adult citizen, fully Brazilian, and emancipated from the tutelage his mother suffered as an Indian. To what extent legally adult Brazilians are full and equal citizens is another matter. The point here is that race mixing as a policy-mandated means of inclusion extinguished the legal liability of Indianness and thus the status of minor orphan-citizen. This case also demonstrates that race mixing as policy reached even remote regions of the Empire.

The petition of the freed African slave is similarly revealing. The official does not rule on it specifically but sets out the principle for the registrar of voters to apply. The freed African has amassed the income necessary to qualify as a voter. The doubt is whether he can be considered a Brazilian citizen because of his foreign birth and not, I stress, because of his race. The question hinges on which section applies of the article that defines Brazilian citizenship in the 1824 Constitution. This doubt in turn depends on the date of manumission. If the African was freed before independence, then section 4 of Article 6 applies. This section awards Brazilian citizenship to those born in Portugal or its possessions who resided freely in Brazil at independence. If that is the case, then the African is a citizen and, meeting other qualifications, is entitled to vote. However, "if he was manumitted after independence, he cannot be considered a Brazilian Citizen," because then section 1 of Article 6 applies. That section awards citizenship to the freeborn and freed alike, but only if they have been born in Brazil. If the manumitted are foreign born, and if they received their freedom after independence, they can only be citizens by virtue of naturalization, the same process available to any foreigner wishing to become Brazilian (Art. 6, sec. 5). Not being citizens, they cannot vote.

These cases bring into correlation the two variables that formally determine national citizenship, freedom and *ius soli*, and several assumptions that condition it: that miscegenation attenuates legal disability and that manumission under a regime of national citizenship constitutes a change in civil status of new significance. The latter indicates the impact of national citizenship on the miscegenated social relations of colonial Brazil. Portuguese colonial legislation discriminated against blacks as such and often against blacks and mulattoes together, ignoring any distinction between the free and the enslaved. What mattered in this legislation was African descent, as demonstrated by skin color. Thus, regardless of civil status, both blacks and mulattoes were at various times during Portuguese rule prohibited by law from carrying weapons, serving in backland expeditions, being goldsmiths, and holding high public offices. Among the most notorious prohibition directed at both was the sumptuary regulations of the Royal Proclamation of 24 May 1749. It forbade the wearing of fine clothing and jewelry for "blacks and mulattoes, the children of blacks or mulattoes . . . regardless of sex, and even if they have been freed, or were born free" (cited in Conrad 1983: 248). Ecclesiastical law as well discriminated against blacks and mulattoes regardless of civil status, excluding them from the priesthood.

Colonial historians generally conclude, however, that local conditions of race mixing rendered these discriminatory laws unenforceable. Degler (1971: 213–22) argues convincingly that, unlike in the United States, where legal discriminations of color were effectively applied, they were "overrun" in Brazil by the widespread practices of miscegenation. Nevertheless, as he also argues, failed policy still indicates intention. The discriminatory laws demonstrate that the Portuguese Crown attempted to impose legal distinctions based on ascriptive categories of color as a means to regulate Brazilian colonial society (see also Boxer 1962: 300–301). By independence, however, it is clear that race mixing has overrun even this intention. Hence, Bonifácio is able to imagine a Brazilian national society in which racial difference has ceased to exist. It is this imagination of "one body" that informs the new constitution of 1824 and explains why its formal act of creating the nation makes no mention of race but only of civil status and birthplace in assigning membership. Although slavery is not abolished for another sixty-four years, a crucial change has already occurred with the constitution that transforms its meaning in national society: slavery becomes a civil status, not a natural destiny. For the purposes of national organization, distinctions of African ancestry, race, and ethnicity have been replaced by that of freedom, a civil status.

This transubstantiation informs the central argument of a famous treatise on slavery published in the 1860s by the conservative slave owner and passionate abolitionist Perdigão Malheiro. He described the denial of citizenship as a strictly legal consequence of the loss of freedom. "Reduced to a condition of *thing*, subject to the *power* and *dominion* or property of another," those enslaved were "taken to be *dead*, deprived of *all rights*, and without *any representation*" (cited in Chalhoub 1990: 36). As Chalhoub observes, Perdigão Malheiro's point was to demonstrate that slavery was a legal institution and not a natural, normal, or moral condition of human social relations. Based on positive statute and not nature, it could be changed through both personal and political action. To describe slaves as things is thus to emphasize that as legal statuses, "slave" and "citizen" are in fact joined by legal procedure, namely, manumission and, ultimately, abolition.[37]

Moreover, to call slaves noncitizens during this period of national slavery does not mean that they had no privileges or differentiated statuses. Rather, it stresses that such privileges referred to a civil status that deprived slaves of their own legal personality and were, therefore, wholly the master's prerogative.[38] It is well documented that slaves could seek remedy in Brazilian courts against masters for excessive cruelty, forced prostitution, and, after 1869, separation by sale from spouse. However, to bring suit, slaves needed a *curador* (a trustee and sponsor) who was a citizen, because they lacked the legal personality that comes with freedom and therefore the legal representation necessary to access the law. To describe slaves as legally things, therefore, emphasizes the problem of incorporation that necessarily follows from the moment that manumission seems possible, from the change that brings legal personhood and resurrects the slave from legal death.

Thus, between Brazil-born slaves (*crioulos*) and freeborn citizens existed a middle passage, the transitional category of *libertos*. It consisted of slaves who had typically obtained a charter or letter of freedom (*alforria*). *Crioulos* fully freed immediately became full-fledged member-citizens. Those conditionally freed became minor member-citizens, like children and "orphan Indians." Although most manumission was conditional, it amounted to a long process for all: many years generally passed from the first hint of being freeable through wardship (for most) to final emancipation. Even after full manumission, however, the freed constituted a liminal category. Their former masters both exploited them as ex-slaves and patronized them as "still brutes." For most Brazilians, the stain of slavery on the manumitted could only lessen after several generations, after the attenuations of race mixing, whitening, and other processes of assimilation had a chance to work.

Moreover, the citizenship of even fully freed slaves was limited in the new nation-state. To be sure, they gained a series of important rights: to own property without restriction, maintain a family, inherit and bequeath, be a legal guardian, and represent themselves at court and before the state. However, full *libertos* suffered restrictions. For example, they could vote but only in primary elections, serve in the armed forces but only at the lowest rank, and not hold elected office. As these restrictions applied to anyone who had been a slave, they made civil status the explicit basis for the selective disqualification of citizens. They also made race an implicit basis as slaves were people of African and Indian ancestry. Nevertheless, compared with the preemptive exclusion from citizenship most freed slaves suffered in the United States, they constituted a set of relatively few conditions placed on the assumption of Brazilian citizenship that manumission initiated.

Thus, with independence, manumission became a legal procedure that transformed slaves into national citizens. However, it was usually both a capricious and conditional process. Although several laws appeared just before abolition freeing entire categories of slaves—with generally perverse effects[39]—for most of the nearly four centuries of Brazilian slavery, manumissions were individual and private acts, entirely at the master's discretion. As such, they were typically ambiguous procedures.[40] Manumission could be granted formally or informally, verbally or in writing, conditionally or unconditionally, by the living or the dead. Overwhelmingly, slaves purchased their own freedom for their market worth. Gathering this sum typically required slaves to negotiate with their masters, usually by agreeing to a series of installments and continued service that conditioned their freedom for years. In fact, manumission letters show that slaves frequently received full freedom only upon their owner's death, decades after the grant of conditional manumission. Moreover, many conditionally freed slaves had to serve the master's family after the latter's death for a specified period. It is not difficult to conclude that many slaves granted conditional freedom at middle age remained in servitude until death.

From the slave's perspective, therefore, the passage to freedom and citizenship required continued obedience, humility, and submission; from the master's, it depended on the production of continued dependence and the generation of new kinds of dependents. Even for fully emancipated slaves, the status of their freedom remained uncertain and the worth of their citizenship equivocal, though universally recognized. For the majority of *libertos*, however, their freedom was explicitly conditional and their social status more certain: they were legal minors. They had a recognized measure of legal personality and citizenship, but one reduced by wardship. Indeed, like "orphan Indians," conditionally freed slaves were placed under the jurisdiction and protection of the Orphan Courts. Thus, against those who argued that conditional freedom was freedom suspended altogether until the conditions were satisfied, Perdigão Malheiro argued in the 1860s more persuasively: upon receipt of conditional manumission, the slave "immediately . . . had his natural condition of humanity and personality restored." His full liberty was nevertheless restricted, not because he remained a thing, but because he was like a minor "who depends on certain facts or time to enter, emancipated, into the enjoyment of his rights and the acts of civil life" (cited in Chalhoub 1990: 130).

The conditional status of *libertos* and "orphan Indians" gave Brazilian national society a distinctively porous enclosure. Their incorporation at its edges expressed the founding concept of a "single body" that is inclusive of different kinds and qualities of citizens, of a membership that comprehends separate categories of citizenship. Thus, Brazilian national belonging is expansive and generous, a tent that gathers everyone. But it does so in rank and file as a body in which each member has a publicly acknowledged place. In short, its belonging is inclusively inegalitarian, a sort of contradiction in terms that describes a condition both brutally clear in its differentiation and effectively ambiguous in its incorporation. It is a single body divisible into unequal parts.

The inclusion of freed slaves and "orphan Indians" embodies this contradiction. It derives from a national commitment to social and cultural "processes of perfectibility," which, as the patriarch Bonifácio wrote in his 1823 congressional project for the gradual abolition of slavery, "converts immoral brutes [slaves] into useful, active, and well-behaved citizens . . . [slaves] who today have no country and who could become our brothers and our compatriots . . . one day our equals in rights" (2002: 208–9). Yet that day was so far off and so obscured by worldly conditions that most of these "brothers" reached its promised land only after last rites. For the *libertos*, to be freed was also not to be free, for as Mattoso observes (1986: 183), "it is as if Brazilian society, which used manumission much more freely than other slave societies in the New World, did so in full awareness, even certainty, that the distinction between slave and freed man was in the end a sham, a matter of semantics." Surely, Mattoso hyperbolizes, for if freedom were entirely hollow slaves would not seek it.

Yet, in substantive terms, freedom brought little to most *libertos* and only little more to their descendents.

Inclusive and perfectible, Brazilian incorporation was at the same time based on dependency, deference, and deceit, as well as their correlates of exploitation, paternalism, and ambiguity. It is not as if the two other national incorporations examined in this chapter did not have their hypocrisies and deceptions. It is rather that, in comparison, Brazil's nation builders created a formulation distinctively their own. With this understanding of Brazilian inclusion, we now turn to the nature of its inequalities.

Chapter 3
Limiting Political Citizenship

The next three chapters examine the substantive distribution of Brazilian citizenship in relation to its formal qualifications by analyzing the historical development of its political, civil, and social components. In this chapter, I focus on the exclusion of most Brazilians from political citizenship that remained in effect from 1881 to 1985, that is, for nearly the entire history of the Brazilian Republic. The next chapter considers the limited access to landownership the vast majority of Brazilians experienced and its dire consequences for citizenship until the growth of the urban peripheries after the 1940s. The final chapter in this part analyzes the paradigm of urban segregation that produced these peripheries for the settlement of an industrial workforce. It then considers the development of social rights in the 1930s and 1940s as special entitlements available only to certain kinds of urban workers. The combination of these political, civil, social, and spatial exclusions turned Brazil's universalizing national membership into a highly differentiated citizenship.

In evaluating political exclusion, I focus on the size and composition of the Brazilian electorate—the body of citizens with suffrage—as a measure of the distribution of political rights. I emphasize the electorate because it indicates this distribution better than the number of those who actually vote in a given election. This difference is especially significant when voting is voluntary, as was the case in Brazil between 1881 and 1932. When both registering to vote and voting are compulsory—in imperial Brazil before 1881 and republican Brazil after 1932—the number of those registered to vote is a good indication of the number of Brazilians with political citizenship. However, it is not a perfect one because some eligible citizens neither register nor vote. Thus, whether citizens exercise their political citizenship is another matter, however important, from whether they have those rights in the first place. Moreover, the relation between the number of those with the right to vote (the electorate) and the number of those potentially eligible by age to vote (adults) is an especially good indicator of political differentiation, because age is a qualification of citizen suffrage universally used as the first cut to define the largest population pool for political citizenship. Thus, the higher the percentage the greater is the extension of political citizenship among citizens. In my consideration of electoral data, therefore, I give the size of the electorate as a percentage of both the total and the adult populations when the information is available.

Before 1932, the responsibility for voter registration, election returns, and electoral data was decentralized and frequently corrupt. As a result, there is some confusion about the statistics that Brazilian historians and social scientists use for this period, as the numbers often differ somewhat even where they cite the same and similar sources. It is also sometimes not clear whether their citations refer to registered voters or ballots cast, and, if the latter, whether they include null and blank votes. Furthermore, rather than the electorate, Brazilian studies generally use the number of votes cast as a percentage either of the total population or of the number of those registered. The latter relation can be misleading with regard to the distribution of political citizenship. For example, in 1933, the size of the electorate was miniscule (3.7%), but the number of voters among them high (83%). For greater consistency in assessing the extent of political citizenship, therefore, I have tried to work with original sources wherever possible and determine the size of the electorate in addition to the number of voters.

The Surprisingly Broad Colonial Franchise

Before the period of independence, colonial Brazil held elections only at the municipal level. These were regulated by Portuguese legal codes, especially the Ordenações Filipinas of 1603, that aimed to make municipal government in the colonies a local instance of imperial authority—an objective "always contrary to the autonomous spirit of Anglo-Saxon self-government," as Raymundo Faoro (1975: 183) concluded in his well-known political history of Brazil. This legislation established two features of colonial elections that would characterize Brazilian political citizenship for centuries: the use of requisites of social and economic standing to exclude most Brazilians and a bureaucratic qualification of voters.

83

The colonists elected local officials every three years to constitute municipal councils (*câmaras*), including councilmen, prosecutors, scribes, treasurers, inspectors, and judges. These officials administered municipal affairs without much separation of executive, judicial, or legislative powers. Elections were indirect and two-step. Each voter selected six "electors" in secret balloting. In turn, the six most-voted electors, in pairs, secretly drew up three signed lists of people to fill the available posts for a period of three years. Legislation required that the lists be sealed in balls of wax, placed in a sack, and stored in a safe with three locks, the keys to which were held separately by three outgoing councilmen. At a predetermined date, the safe would be opened at a public assembly, the lists removed from the sack "by a boy not older than seven," and the winners announced.[1] Such curiously complicated bureaucratic choreography would also become a perduring feature of Brazilian elections (and legal affairs generally). If the aim of this bureaucratic complication was to prevent fraud, its efficacy in important elections was dubious, as the results always had to be confirmed by higher royal authority.

Who could vote and in turn be elected? Electoral laws effectively limited the electorate to those considered *homens bons*, literally "good men," men of substance. This title is ancient in the Portuguese world and has ambiguous meaning in both social practice and law. Generally, it is a loose cover term for certain elites. When it refers to nobles, it means the most respected of them, as usually determined by performance at assembly or council. But it can also refer to nonnobles. When it does, it signifies those who had inherited property free and clear. Initially, this qualification was limited to property in land, but later came to include commercial assets as well. This evolution allowed merchants to assume the title and its privileges. Hence, signifying a certain quality in men, the appellation has two senses, that of character and that of wealth, perhaps conjoined in one individual and perhaps not.

However, for electoral purposes, the term *homens bons* had a specifically bureaucratic qualification: a ruling of 10 May 1640 determined that only those could vote who were qualified in "notebooks" (*cadernos*) where their "qualities . . . and talents to serve well in the offices of government" would be recorded in the margins next to their names (in Jobim and Costa Porto 1996: 22). Guarded in council chambers, these notebooks were called the Books of Nobility, which designation refers to both the aristocratic and the illustrious. Excluded from the possibility of electoral qualification were those who labored manually or whose parents had done so, those banished, those who had "any race whatsoever" (i.e., those considered nonwhites, including Jews and Arabs), and women (22).[2] By reason of specific identity or status, in other words, most people in the colonies could not have their names written in the qualifying books and were therefore denied political rights. Significantly, however, illiterates were not excluded—an important point as they constituted most of the population (85% in the first national census of 1872). An electoral provision of the Ordinações (Title 67) allowed that an illiterate *homen bom* could be assigned a literate one who would write down his vote and swear under oath not to divulge its content. Thus, electoral policy permitted illiterate *homens bons* to vote who succeeded in getting their names recorded in the Books.

In Brazil, therefore, the category *homens bons* referred to people of noble lineage or particular kinds of property who had, in either case, "clean blood"—a phrase used throughout the Americas to signify racial whiteness. However, for political purposes, its more decisive meaning was that of a textual status, that is, one produced by a bureaucratic text. Those who managed to get their names in the Books, by whatever means and on whatever grounds, inserted themselves and their descendents into the political and administrative machinery of the colony and later the empire. In this way, the bureaucratic qualification of voters was a means of social ascension during the colonial period for those who had the means to achieve "an aristocracy of resemblance" (Faoro 1975: 185). But it was also, and primarily, a way to exclude most people from political citizenship and assure the manipulation of elections by those who controlled the bureaucracy and its books.

The first general elections in Brazil were held in 1821, a year before independence. They are remarkable because they allowed nearly universal male suffrage—a realization of citizenship not repeated for more than a century and a half. These elections derived directly from the revolutionary conflicts of economic and political liberalism that roiled Europe at the beginning of the nineteenth century. When Napoleon's troops invaded the Iberian Peninsula in 1808, the Portuguese Court fled to Rio de Janeiro. The installation of the imperial government in the colony fundamentally changed colonial relations, especially after Brazil became a kingdom united with Portugal in 1815. Overnight, Rio became the capital of a world empire, its ports open to all nations, its streets crowded with a new population of Portuguese and international elites, its cityscape transformed by innumerable new buildings constructed to house the institutions of empire. Of all the new measures that seemed to benefit Brazil to the detriment of Portugal, none was more contentious than the adoption of free-trade policies ending the commercial monopolies that the Portuguese had enjoyed. Within a decade of the royal hegira, the lines were clearly drawn: one side of the Atlantic demanded a reinstatement of mercantile privileges as well as the king's return to Lisbon, and the other side an even greater commitment to free trade and Brazilian autonomy.

The conflict came to a head with a constitutionalist revolution in Portugal in 1820 that exacted both the king's return and a constitutional form of government based on liberal principles of rule. The revolutionaries adopted as their blueprint the Spanish Constitution of Cadiz (1812), itself the fruit of a liberal revolution in Spain and modeled on the revolutionary French constitutions of 1791 and 1793. On that basis, they convoked assemblies (*cortes*) to prepare, among other things, a Portuguese constitution that would subordinate the throne to a new legislature.[3] In Brazil, street demonstrations in early 1821 forced King João VI to accept the demands of the Lisbon Assemblies by swearing allegiance to the yet-to-be-written Portuguese constitution and temporarily adopting the Spanish one. He announced his intention to return to Portugal and leave his son, Pedro, in Brazil as prince regent. In the same proclamation (7 March 1821), he issued a decree calling for the election of Brazilian representatives to the Constitutional Assemblies in Lisbon. The decree determined that the elections would be held "according to the method established in the Spanish Constitution and adopted by the United Kingdom of Portugal, Brazil, and Algarves" (preamble, in Jobim and Costa Porto 1996: 25–33), namely, in accordance the liberal Constitution of Cadiz.

Although the adoption of the Spanish Constitution was revoked one day later, its electoral instructions remained in force. These established a four-step indirect election of representatives, in which those elected at one level would vote for electors at the next. The last elected became deputies. The size of the electorate diminished with each step. At the first level, the important one for our purposes, "all citizens domiciled and residing in the territory of their respective parish" could vote for electors (Art. 35) and none could be "excused . . . for whatever motive or pretext" (Art. 55). The convocation of "all citizens" notwithstanding, Article 50 established that an electoral board in each parish would judge "the requisite qualities to be able to vote" of those citizens present on election day. As stated in the preamble, the boards would do so by "the method" of the Spanish Constitution (its Article 25). Accordingly, the following citizens were denied suffrage: those considered by judicial order physically or morally incapacitated; bankrupt debtors; debtors of public patrimony; domestic servants; criminals; and the idle, vagrant, and unemployed. In addition, men younger than twenty-five (unless married) and all women were excluded. To be elected deputy, a candidate had to be more than twenty-five years old, a resident of his province for more than seven years if not a native, and not a member of a religious order or an employee of the royal household. Thus, it is evident that for the parish-level franchise, the exclusions were relatively few—with the exception of women, to which I will return. Significantly, the electorate included illiterate citizens. This inclusion followed the Spanish Constitution but was, in any case, a longstanding Brazilian practice. Surprisingly, moreover, the Brazilian decree suspended the annual income qualification for election to office that the Spanish charter imposed.[4]

Thus, the legislation for Brazil's first national elections in 1821 permitted a significant number—perhaps most—of adult male citizens of all classes to vote, including many denied suffrage in municipal elections. Given the absence of statistical data for this period, however, it is impossible to estimate precisely the size of the electorate. A guess of around 15%–20% of the total population and 45%–50% of free adults would not be unreasonable. Although the law excluded many Brazilians, the important comparative point is that it did not deny the vote to all male citizens from the lower classes on principle. Notably missing from the criteria of exclusion are those of literacy and wealth that would have done just that. Thus, inspired by the first constitutions of the French revolution, the concept of manhood suffrage governing these Brazilian elections was far more universal than that employed at the time in France, which had reduced the electorate to a mere fraction. Indeed, it was among the most inclusive in the world.[5]

Brazil's exclusion of women was not, however, remarkable. In no country in Europe or the Americas were adult female citizens allowed to vote. Yet I was surprised to discover that their exclusion is not specifically stated, much less justified, in any of the Brazilian, French, and American constitutions or electoral instructions I examined. Even in those with long lists of qualifications and exclusions, that of gender is not named. In Brazil, women are not expressly excluded from any of the many Brazilian electoral laws or several constitutions promulgated before they gained the franchise with the Constitution of 1934. Moreover, gender qualification is not given direct legal reference or discussion in any of the nineteenth-century studies I consulted. I can only conclude that legislators and writers of the time must have thought the exclusion of women from political citizenship so completely obvious and natural that it needed no mention.

The impact of democratic liberalism on electoral policy was, in any case, ephemeral in the formation of Brazilian citizenship. The future emperor of Brazil, Prince Pedro, and the ministers of his regency soon demonstrated that they did not support democracy. In the decade to come, their strategy would become clear: they were interested in maintaining the social and economic structures of the ancien régime, but in the context of an independent Brazil in which the advantages of free trade accrued to Brazilian planter elites. They were, in short, liberal in some ways and republican in others, but not democratic. Characteristically, José Bonifácio, the prince's chief minister, wrote "I never was, and never will be, a pure Royalist, but not for this will I ever enlist under the ragged banners of the dirty and chaotic Democracy. My constitution is not theirs; and I will always be what they want, as long as that is not what they are: neither *corcunda* [popular name for members of the king's absolutist party] nor *descamizado* [popular characterization of partisans of democratic political movements]" (cited in Neiva 1938: 249). When the conflict with Portugal peaked in 1822, the Lisbon Assemblies ordered the prince to return and sent troops to Brazil. In turn, the prince prohibited these troops from landing, ordered the naval squadron sent to collect him to return, declared that no ruling of the Assemblies could be enforced without his authorization, accepted the title offered him by the Municipal Council of Rio de Janeiro as "Perpetual Defender of Brazil," and called for the convocation of a Brazilian national assembly. Initially, the objective of this Constituent and Legislative General Assembly was to counterbalance the Lisbon Assemblies with a single centralized power in Brazil. But after Pedro declared Brazilian independence on 7 September 1822, it became charged with drafting the first constitution of an independent and imperial new nation.

Restrictions with Independence

The instructions for electing representatives to the Constituent Assembly set the basic structure of political citizenship for most of the Empire. As signed by the chief minister, José Bonifácio, Instruction No. 57 of 19 June 1822 established indirect elections in two steps, in which "voters" at the parish level elected "electors" who then elected "deputies" (in Campanhole and Campanhole 2000: 814–20). Voting was obligatory. For the first step, the ruling granted the right to vote to all married male citizens and to all single male citizens over twenty who were not living with their parents. However, in addition to women, criminals, slaves, and resident members of religious orders, it denied the ballot to all wage workers and all receiving military pay—with the exception of commercial bookkeepers and clerks, employees of the royal household, and administrators of rural plantations and factories. Those eligible to become electors had to meet the requirements of the first step and, in addition, be twenty-five or older, "virtuous and honorable, of good judgment, without a hint of being hostile to the Cause of Brazil, and have decent subsistence by means of employment, industry, or property." Finally, to be elected representative, a candidate had to meet the requirements for being both a voter and an elector and, moreover, "have superior education, recognized virtues, true patriotism, and decided zeal for the Cause of Brazil," in addition to various other requirements of birth and residence (Chap. 2, sec. 6). No doubt, some of these qualifications were deliberately vague and open to broad interpretation. Nevertheless, by eliminating nearly all wage laborers, the overall intent of these eligibility requirements could not be clearer: to locate political power entirely among the various classes of *homens bons* and deprive the mass of Brazilian citizens the right both to vote and to be elected.

As promulgated by the Emperor (and not the Assembly, which he had previously dissolved) and ratified by municipal councils, the Imperial Constitution of 1824 retained, in Articles 90 to 97, most of the electoral criteria and procedures of Instruction No. 57. In addition to women, criminals, slaves, and cloistered clerics, the Constitution excluded from voting citizens younger than twenty-five (with the exceptions noted below) and household dependents, disqualifying domestic servants and dependent adult children (except those holding public office). It also eliminated the criteria open to qualitative interpretation, substituting more objective restrictions.[6]

The most important change was to modify the blanket elimination of all wage workers by establishing net annual-income requirements for participation in the two-step indirect election for the national assembly: 100 mil-réis to qualify as a voter in the parish primaries to select electors and 200 mil-réis to qualify as an elector to select deputies and senators. The first amount was about half the average price of a slave (Mattoso 1986: 79). An elector needed an annual income of 400 mil-réis to be elected deputy and 800 mil-réis for senator. The last were elected to a list of three, one of whom the emperor appointed for life according to his preference. At the local level, citizens elected municipal council members and justices of the peace directly after 1828, in one-step elections, using the same qualifications specified for national elections—except that all voters could be elected to council. The Constitution eliminated age restrictions for citizens with university degrees and for noncloistered clergy, allowed married men and military officers older than twenty-one to vote, and specified that freed slaves could be voters but not electors. It also eliminated residency requirements for the offices of deputy and senator but excluded from their election naturalized foreigners and "those who did not profess the Religion of the State [Roman Catholicism]" (Art. 95, sec. 3). Thus, it denied non-Catholics a significant part of their political citizenship.[7]

Supplementary legislation substituted an electoral board for the Books of Nobility that had listed qualified voters, assigning to it the responsibility of producing on election day a list of citizens eligible to vote. However, in line with previous instructions, the Constitution did not condition eligibility on literacy. Although legislation required voters to sign their ballots, it also allowed qualified citizens who were illiterate to let the secretary of the electoral board record their vote. The illiterate voter then signed his ballot "with a cross," which the secretary declared to be

89

his mark (Instruction No. 57, Chap. 2, sec. 5). The number of illiterate voters during the empire was significant. For example, a study of voter lists from 1876 shows that 25% of registered voters were illiterate in eight parishes of the city of Rio de Janeiro and more than 50% in rural parishes (Nicolau 2002: 11).[8] Surprisingly, the Imperial Constitution also gave all citizens the right to free primary education (Art. 179, sec. 32), thereby instituting in Brazil a foundational element of modern citizenship. Thus, it not only allowed illiterates to vote but also obliged the state to educate citizens to be competent voters. Although the imperial state failed utterly to meet this obligation, it set a formal precedent that later regimes would renounce.

With its qualifications for political rights, the Imperial Constitution established the conceptual framework of a differentiated citizenship that held for most of the nineteenth century and, in several aspects, the twentieth. It organized Brazil's population into sets of opposed categories. The most basic differentiated "free" from "slave" and "citizen" from "alien." Only citizens were members of the nation, and only the free could be citizens (Arts. 1 and 6). Then, the Constitution divided the category "citizen" into distinct classes, mixing six sorts of restriction to limit suffrage among adults: gender, income, household dependence, residence, religion, and birthright. Significantly, it did not use qualifications typically considered indicative of the capacity of citizens to be competent voters, namely, literacy, formal education, and appointment to certain positions (e.g., public and military office). Rather it only used such capacity restrictions to allow exceptions to exclusions from political rights. Thus, male citizens with university diplomas were exempt from the age limitations applied to others. Similarly, bookkeepers, employees of the royal household, and plantation administrators were exempt from the exclusion of domestic employees.

The six types of qualification differentiated adult Brazilian citizens into a branching scheme of superior and inferior classes by eligibility to vote and be elected. The first differentiation divided citizens into what the Constitution called, following the French, "active" and "passive" categories. Active citizens were those who had political rights, because they qualified to vote in primary elections as determined in Articles 90 to 93. They constituted a minority of citizens. Passive citizens were all the others, who were disqualified to vote in these terms, barred as a result from holding elected office, and thus denied political citizenship. They constituted the vast majority of citizens, including adult men with annual income of less than 100 mil-réis, most domestic servants and employees, all underage citizens, and all women. The first three members of this inferior category of citizen might eventually qualify to be voters and active citizens. However, women were permanently disqualified.

The Constitution further differentiated the category "active citizen" into various classes of eligibility. In all cases except the last, some members of the inferior category of citizen might become members of the superior, while other members were permanently barred. The first differentiation was between voters eligible to be "electors" and those not. "Nonelectors" were voters who could not participate in the electoral process beyond the primary stage, including those with an annual income of less than 200 mil-réis and all freed slaves. The second division of active citizens differentiated electors into "representatives" and "nonrepresentatives." The latter were not eligible for election as deputy or senator, and included those who did not meet the income requirements, all non-Catholics, and all naturalized foreigners. The third differentiation divided the category "representative" into "senator" and "deputy," the latter comprising those who did not have the income to qualify for the former. Finally, the Constitution differentiated the category "senator" into "prince-senators" and "other senators," the former being the princes of the royal house who automatically became senators upon reaching the age of twenty-five. The latter had to be elected to a triple list of candidates. In sum, the Imperial Constitution created five grades of political citizenship, each with a superior and inferior degree of citizen, for a total of ten classes.

How many Brazilians had the right to vote under this scheme of differentiated citizenship? How did it determine the size and composition of the electorate? Given the precarious quality of demographic data for most of the nineteenth century in Brazil, it is only with the first national census in 1872 that it becomes possible to estimate the Brazilian franchise with some confidence. Based on that census and a report of the Imperial Ministry in 1870—cited in Francisco Belisário Soares de Souza's contemporary analysis of the electoral system (1979: 133)—it is likely that approximately 10% of the total population, 12% of the free population, and 24% of the adult population were registered to vote in 1872.[9] In other words, about 1.06 million Brazilian citizens were active (*votantes* and *eleitores*) and the remaining 7.4 million were passive, disqualified from voting for one reason or another. Of the active citizens, approximately twenty thousand were electors, amounting to 0.2% of the total population and 0.5% of the adult. These numbers are good indications of the size of the electorate and the effects of differentiation on political citizenship during the third quarter of the nineteenth century, as well as reasonable approximations for earlier years. Table 3.1 presents these electoral data comparatively.[10]

Some scholars argue that the income qualifications of imperial Brazil were primarily responsible for excluding the majority of citizens from political rights. However, others argue, more persuasively, that these income limitations were not of great significance.[11] Carvalho (2001: 30) writes

Table 3.1
Right to Vote: Population, Electorate, and Voters, Brazil, 1821–2002

Year	Population[a]	Electorate[b]				Voters[b]			Must Register & Vote	Election
		Total	% Total	% Adult	% Change	Total	% Total	% Adult		
1821[c]	4,396,132 total 2,488,743 *free*	Universal male suffrage	15–20?	45–50?	–	–	–	–	Yes	Deputies for Lisbon Assemblies
1872[d]	10,112,061 total 4,332,223 *adult*	1,039,659 voters 20,006 electors	10.3 0.2	24.0 0.5	–	–	–	–	Yes	Deputies & senators for General Assembly
1881	12,039,327 total	145,296	1.2	–	–86.0	96,411	0.8	–	No	General Assembly
1886[e]	13,264,549 total 5,682,160 *adult*	–	–	–	–	117,022	0.9	2.1	No	General Assembly
1894	15,460,502 total 7,033,862 *adult*	–	–	–	–	331,046	2.1	4.7	No	President
1922	32,089,922 total 13,339,365 *adult*	–	–	–	–	785,240	2.5	5.9	No	President

Year	Population		%	% adult			%	% adult		Office
1930	37,625,436 total	–	–	–	–	1,834,748	4.9	–	No	President
1933	39,939,154 total	1,466,700	3.7	–	–	1,222,624	3.1	–	Yes	Constitutional Assembly
1945	46,344,177 total / *24,412,379 adult*	7,459,849	16.1	*30.6*	408.6	6,200,805	13.4	*25.4*	Yes	President & Constitutional Assembly
1950	51,973,727 total / *27,551,075 adult*	11,455,149	22.0	*41.6*	53.6	8,254,989	15.9	*30.0*	Yes	President
1960	70,070,457 total / *36,630,649 adult*	15,543,332	22.2	*42.4*	35.7	12,586,354	18.0	*34.4*	Yes	President
1970	93,139,037 total / *48,881,962 adult*	28,966,114	31.1	*59.3*	86.4	22,435,521	24.1	*45.9*	Yes	Congress
1982	122,507,125 total / *73,809,484 adult*	58,530,653	47.8	*79.3*	102.1	48,188,956	39.3	*65.3*	Yes	Governors
1986	135,608,433 total / *80,677,779 adult*	69,309,231	51.1	*85.9*	–	65,823,591	48.5	*81.6*	Yes	Constitutional Assembly
1989	144,293,110 total / *90,690,010 adult*	82,056,226	56.9	*90.5*	40.2f	72,277,408	50.1	*79.7*	Yes	President

Table 3.1
Continued

Year	Population[a]	Electorate[b]				Voters[b]			Must Register & Vote	Election
		Total	% Total	% Adult	% Change	Total	% Total	% Adult		
1998[g]	158,232,252 total	106,053,106	67.0		29.2	83,274,223	52.6		Yes	President
	107,265,938 adult			98.9				77.6		
2002[g]	171,667,536 total	115,184,176	67.1		8.6	94,741,120	55.2		Yes	President
	115,857,116 adult			99.4				81.8		

Sources: 1821 & 1872: IBGE 1990: 30, 32 (for 1819); Souza 1979: 133. 1881–1933: IBGE 1941: 3; IBGE 1990: 33 (for 1890, 1920), 636; TSE 1934: 2–4; Neves and Machado 1999: 398; Faoro 1975: 375; Carvalho 1988: 141; Costa Porto 2002: 165, 178, 182. 1945–70: IBGE 1990: 35, 51, 636, 638. 1982–2002: PNAD 1983 (vol. 6), 1986, 1989 (vol. 13), 1998 (vol. 20), 2002; Dados Eleitorais do Brasil, www.iuperj.br/deb

a Totals refer to resident population. Adult population refers to approximate total number of residents old enough to vote according to electoral laws in force that year. During slavery, that estimate includes both free and enslaved adults because the available census data by age does not distinguish the two. Free population estimates (2,488,743 in 1821, 8,419,672 in 1872, and 9,941,471 in 1881) included all ages.

b The electorate comprises those registered to vote. Voters are those who actually cast ballots.

c See chapter 3 for a discussion of population estimates at Independence.

d The first national census in 1872 estimated 9,930,478 residents and added 181,583 people in 32 parishes that were not surveyed "in the specified period."

e Estimate of voting age population in 1886 and 1894 is based on census data for 1890, and in 1922 on census data for 1920. Estimates of number of voters for elections 1886–1930 do not include nullified and blank votes.

f This value refers to the interval 1982–1989 to be more consistent with the other intervals of percent change.

g Population estimates exclude residents of rural Rôndonia, Acre, Amazonas, Roraima, Pará, and Amapá.

that the majority of the working population made more than the annual amount stipulated, 100 mil-réis, to qualify for active citizenship when the Constitution was promulgated. Moreover, he notes that in 1876, well after the qualifying amount had been doubled in 1846 to keep pace with inflation, the lowest salary for public servants was 600 mil-réis. Thus, he (1988: 142) found that in an election held in 1876 in a rural municipality of Minas Gerais, only 24% of the voters were landowners. The rest were rural workers (46%) and artisans (13%)—most in these two categories illiterate—commercial employees (9%), public functionaries (5%), and professionals (2%).[12] The principal disqualifications among citizens during the Empire seem to have been, therefore, gender, age, and household dependence.

Based on such findings, Carvalho (2001: 30) suggests that income qualifications imposed in European countries at the time were generally more restrictive and that the Brazilian constitutional regime was therefore more "liberal." He bases this assessment on a comparison of the size of national electorates in Brazil and in European countries that did not yet have universal male suffrage. While Brazil had an electorate of around 10% of the total population in 1872, at about the same time 2% voted in Italy, 9% in Portugal, and 2.5% in Holland. In England, perhaps the most important reference for Brazilian elites in this regard, 7% had political rights around midcentury—though as a result of the electoral Reform Act of 1884 about two-thirds of adult men became eligible to vote in England and Wales. Souza (1979: 134) himself suggests that Brazil's electorate is comparatively "exaggerated." As a way of justifying his proposal for suffrage qualifications, he compares it to electorates in France (pre-1848), Belgium (pre-1848), and England (pre-1867) in his brief analysis of the 1870 data. He argues that his restrictions would produce an electorate more in line with these European ones and that its consequent "small number should [therefore] not surprise us."

I find it problematic, however, to compare these numbers from different countries directly without considering the significance of a host of other factors, such as electoral manipulation in the composition of voter lists, the designation of constituencies, the rigor of proving qualification, the number of resident foreigners, and so forth. Moreover, many European nations had either abolished voting restrictions for adult men or significantly lessened them by the third quarter of the century (see later in this chapter). Rather than simply compare numbers, therefore, I believe it more fruitful to assess the justification, methods, and especially the evolution of the restriction of political rights.

From that perspective, the qualification of political citizenship during the Brazilian Empire appears generally in line with most European standards for the first three-quarters of the nineteenth century. The rise of

industrial and commercial capitalism, the French Revolution, the prolif-
eration of movements for representative democracy, and the division of
upper classes into liberal and conservative camps produced a great variety of conflicts and strategies over the organization of suffrage throughout Europe during this period. As Bendix (1977: 93–104) observes, the
century began with the principles of estate representation generally in
force; that is, each legally constituted estate of nobles, burghers, knights,
and prelates sent its separate representatives to the center of territorial
or national authority, and often each had its separate assembly. As the
political turbulence spread throughout Europe, it produced an array of
compromises. By midcentury, only France had nationalized universal
manhood suffrage. The rest used various criteria to limit the franchise.
Each developed its own mix of qualifications, selectively combining those
of estate representation with those based on income, capacity, household
independence, residence, birthright, religion, and gender. The important
point, however, is that by the turn of the century or soon thereafter nearly
all European states had eliminated most of these qualifications, and most
had instituted universal male suffrage. Within another thirty years, many
had also awarded the electoral franchise to women.[13]

With regard to political citizenship, therefore, a broad range of nation-states experienced a transition from estate to interest representation
during the nineteenth century. The ideological ground of the latter was
the rise of liberal capitalism. Liberals argued that national affairs should
be decided only by those who had a direct interest in them, developing
on both sides of the Atlantic Abbé Sieyès' concept of active citizenship
and Benjamin Constant's notion of "real stakes." Citizens established that
they had real stakes in the nation-state through the possession of land, investment in business, and development of professional skills. Only those
with the economic independence that such interests produce could maintain their convictions without being corrupted by the political process.
Moreover, only those who had developed their intellectual capacities
would possess the sound judgment necessary to evaluate public policies
and political candidates. Hence, the argument went, the franchise should
be restricted to those who could demonstrate the basis for economic and
intellectual independence. The most commonly accepted proof of these
criteria was precisely the qualifications used to limit the vote: wealth (annual
income, capital assets, property value), education (literacy, diplomas, appointment to public office), household autonomy, gender (male), and age
(majority).

On the one hand, liberals advocated the use of these qualifications to
deny the lower classes political rights because they doubted their capacity
to make rational judgments and feared that electoral corruption would
result if the economically dependent became enfranchised. On the other,

conservatives tended to oppose such restrictions for inverse reasons: they favored extending suffrage to the lower classes because they expected to control the vote of their employees, especially those on rural estates. Hence, we might conclude that the liberal position dominated most of the century but that the conservative one prevailed by the end. By then, however, both liberal and conservative elites had to find new ways to control the onrush of mass democracy with universal suffrage, because both were threatened by the political effects of the century's unrelenting urbanization: a new laboring class of urban wage earners who gained income, skills, and organization outside the patriarchal domain of the employer had emerged.

The Brazilian evolution of political citizenship kept step with this European development for most of the century, reversing directions only at the end. Before independence, Brazilians used an estate-inspired principle, adapted to the woolly conditions of the New World, that gave local political rights to those considered *homens bons*. The rules for Brazil's first national election in 1821 to send representatives to the Lisbon Assemblies were the most generous ("liberal" is decidedly the wrong word). Based on the revolutionary French and Spanish constitutions, they enabled nearly universal manhood suffrage and imposed no income qualifications. But they lasted only a year. The electoral instructions for the constitutional assembly in 1822 that replaced them were the most restrictive because they eliminated "all wage laborers." Finally, the rules for political citizenship promulgated with the 1824 Constitution and in effect until 1881 were a compromise. They were more restrictive than the first and less than the second and generally congruent with the limitations imposed by their European counterparts. There was one significant difference: the Brazilian system did not use literacy to limit the franchise. In this regard, political citizenship in Brazil was in fact less "liberal" in being more permissive.[14] Moreover, the Brazilian electorate voted often. With very few suspensions either locally or nationally, elections occurred regularly between 1822 and 1930. Locally, council members were elected every two years. Nationally, Brazil has the longest continuous record of parliamentary elections in Latin America.

If Brazilians voted in sizeable numbers for the times and voted frequently, what did their political citizenship get them? What did it contribute to the overall quality of their citizenship? For most voters, the answer is very little and certainly not equality. In part, the somewhat greater size of Brazil's national electorate from that of most European countries resulted from the inclusion of illiterates who met income and other qualifications. But in part, it also resulted from massive electoral corruption that inflated voter lists and adulterated election results (see Souza 1979: 25–32). The level of electoral corruption was so high during

97

the nineteenth century that its agents became folkloric. A number of factors contributed. Eighty-five percent of the population could not read and
were not able, by that means, to confirm the veracity of elections. Ninety
percent lived in rural areas, overwhelmingly under the control of large
landowners and their private armies. Of the rest in urban areas, most of
the voters were on the government's payroll as public functionaries and
under its influence. Local electoral boards were all-powerful. They evaluated voters' qualifications and registration on the spot, decided many
issues by acclamation (i.e., shouting and shoving), calculated the votes,
and verified the results. Several attempts to reform them failed. Moreover,
the vote itself was not effectively secret until the 1930s. During much of
the nineteenth century, voters brought their ballots to the polls already
filled out and signed. Thus, the electoral board knew exactly who voted
for whom. A voter could even vote by proxy, sending someone to vote in
his place. Not only did these and other procedures make electoral fraud
easy. They were also designed to facilitate it, guaranteeing elections of
certain outcome.

Under such circumstances, the often-called elections served one main
purpose, especially in the countryside. At stake was not the development
of civic rights and duties. Rather, elections were the primary means to
secure local political dominance. For local landowners, electoral defeat
meant the loss not only of prestige but also of the control of municipal
and provincial offices, including those of police chiefs, tax collectors, local
judges, and judicial bureaucracies (Flory 1981:157–80). Hence, the real
contest of electoral politics was above all that of mobilizing the greatest
number of dependents to stack the results.

Specialists in electoral deceit emerged to meet the demand. Especially
renowned were the *cabalista* and the *fósforo*, each attending to a different moment in the electoral process. The *cabalista* was responsible
for registering as many partisans of his boss as possible on voter lists.
Electoral laws did not specify what kind of proof the electoral boards
would accept for qualification. As a result, it became the *cabalista*'s job
to furnish proof, generally in the form of someone paid to testify before
the board that an aspiring voter met the necessary requirements. The
cabalista also had to guarantee the vote of the voters registered. To that
end, he acted like a cattle herder on election day, keeping his voters cor-
ralled and supplied with food, drink, and prepared ballots until the polls
opened. *Cabalistas* also worked with hired henchmen, known then as
now by the Quimbundo term *capanga*, to intimidate an opponent's voters into remaining at home, an application of force that often turned
elections into violent confrontations.

The other remarkable election-time figure was the *fósforo*, literally,
"the match." Before depositing his ballot, a voter had to prove his identity

before the electoral board. Again, legislation did not define how, as qualified voters did not receive identification documents before election day. When it was known that a registered voter would not appear at the polls for whatever reason—illness, death, relocation, or intimidation—a *fósforo* would be hired to assume that person's identity. In what became something of a recognized theatrical tradition, the *fósforo* would play the part, often studied and rehearsed, before the electoral board. As Souza (1979: 29) observed in 1872, "A good *fósforo* voted three, four, five, and more times in various [nearby] parishes. ... It was very common that when a qualified citizen did not respond to the [roll] call, not less than two *fósforos* would present themselves as substitutes, it being up to each to offer better proof of his identity, each to have a better argument and louder voice to sustain his pretension." Apparently, the best "entertainment" occurred when, contrary to the *cabalista*'s expectation, the qualified voter appeared and the *fósforo(s)* had to compete with him for his own identity. If the *fósforo* won under such circumstances, he "acquired the right to double his pay" (29)![15]

Observers at the end of the Empire registered two additional complaints about electoral corruption that have long-term significance for the development of citizenship. Lower-class voters became adept at treating their vote like a commodity, offering it to the highest bidder, selling it several times over to competing *cabalistas*. That the poor sell their votes is undeniable and has often been used by those who would deny them the franchise. They claim that it is proof that the poor lack the capacity to vote intelligently and are therefore easily corrupted—a persistent refrain of the "real-stakes" argument which I heard regularly throughout the 1980s. However, the commodification of suffrage among the lower classes may just as well suggest that they are not electorally incompetent. Instead, it may represent a realistic appraisal on their part of what benefits can actually be had from political citizenship in an electoral system that was largely corrupt.

At the other extreme from the expensive and often violent strategy of maintaining droves of voters in the patriarch's camp, many elections were won *a bico de pena*, "at pen point," in absolute tranquility and accordance with the law (Souza 1979: 33). Such elections were completely falsified, either by adulterating the books of the electoral board, falsifying the returns, or both. With the stroke of a pen, electoral boards regularly performed miracles, reviving the dead, making the absent present, listing slaves as qualified citizens, substituting the contents of ballot boxes, and changing the vote counts. In duly stamped, sealed, and notarized books, they presented perfectly run elections as a set of legal documents. Indeed, to the eternal consternation of researchers, those elections that appear in the historical record as best documented, most complete, most law-abiding, and least violent are likely to be most falsified. As we shall investigate further in the next chapter with regard to property rights, from the beginnings of national citizenship in Brazil, the law and its written word have been prime instruments of subterfuge.[16]

A Long Step Backward into Oligarchy

By the late 1870s, the corruption of the electoral system had become so thorough that both liberal and conservative legislators clamored for radical reform. For the landowning class and their representatives, elections had become prohibitively expensive. The frequency of elections required year-round "standing armies" of voters, and the increasing competition between Liberal and Conservative Parties elevated both the numbers needed to win and the expenses. For liberals in the European mold, the electoral system insulted their concept of real stakes in national citizenship. During parliamentary debate, Rui Barbosa argued that Brazil needed electoral reform to exclude "the henchman, the ruffian, the manioc cake and the penny [used to maintain voter claques], the flycatcher, the certified dead, the phantom, the beggar, the *fósforo*, the illiterate, the slave, all these products of the extensive social misery, to open space to patriotism, enlightenment, independence, fortune, and experience" (cited in Costa Porto 2002: 100). By the end of the decade, Parliament had a bill to achieve such exclusions. Some of its proposals, especially the one to bar illiterates, generated criticism. For example, the deputy José Bonifácio de Andrada, the Younger, argued in 1879 that "We do not have the struggle of the worker, but we have the crisis of [slave] labor, the transition of the great estate [economy], the disorganization of commercial affairs, and all this when the project [of electoral reform] says to the masses: pay taxes, but you will not vote!" (cited in Neves and Machado 1999: 397). Some critics also suggested that mere legislation would not eliminate electoral fraud and violence. Nevertheless, the bill passed overwhelmingly in 1881.

Law 3029, known as the Saraiva Law, instituted direct elections, collapsed the categories "voter" and "elector" into one, made voting optional, and—in a compromise designed to win passage—left the annual income restriction at 200 mil-réis, the same as it had been for voters (in Jobim and Costa Porto 1996: 213–35). The law achieved the objective of limiting political participation to "truly" qualified voters with two additional measures. First, it required literacy (both reading and writing), beginning in 1882. Second, although the income requirement itself was not high, the law required numerous documents to prove income that were difficult to obtain.[17] Exempted from having to provide such proof

Table 3.2
Illiteracy Rates in Total, Rural, and Urban Populations, Brazil, 1872–1999

Year	Illiteracy Rates (%)		
	Total Population	Rural Population	Urban Population
1872	84.3	–	–
1890	85.2	–	–
1900	65.3	–	–
1920	64.9	–	–
1940	56.1	–	–
1950	50.6	66.9	26.6
1960	39.7	55.6	22.5
1970	33.8	53.3	20.0
1980	25.5	46.3	16.8
1991	20.1	40.5	14.2
1999	13.3	29.0	9.7

Sources: IBGE 2001; IBGE: 1950–2000.

Note: For the census years 1900–1999, the estimates of literacy include people fifteen years of age and older. In the years 1872 and 1890, the census considered all ages in surveying literacy, without distinguishing age groups. For 1999, estimates exclude the rural zones of Rondônia, Acre, Amazonas, Roraima, Pará, and Amapá. The census did not distinguish urban and rural literacy before 1950.

were all those with a legally recognized diploma from an institution of secondary or higher education, as well as those whose income was a function of high public office (ministers of state, deputies, judges, high-level administrators, and so forth). The capacity qualification of literacy eliminated 85% of the population (table 3.2). Having to prove the requisite income with a set of precisely specified documents eliminated nearly all the rest: although most adult men earned 200 mil-réis annually, very few could prove it as required. Indeed, then as now, many wanted to avoid documenting how much they earned. Thus, the new law pitted voting, now optional, against income reporting, now required to vote. Not surprisingly, the measure privileged those exempt from reporting and those whose wealth rendered the difficult bureaucracy docile.

The effects of the Saraiva Law were immediate (table 3.1). In the first election after its passage (1881), with income requirements in place, the electorate declined from 10% of the total population to 1%. The number of those with political rights dropped 86%. Even if we allow that the elimination of the category "voter" might have generated confusion in 1881 about the eligibility of previous voters, the impact of the law on subsequent elections is unequivocal. As the available data between 1881 and 1930 is more consistent for actual voters than for those registered,

I use the former. In the 1886 elections, the first after the literacy requirement went into effect and for which a census in 1890 provides an estimate of the adult population, the number of voters declined to just 2% of
adults and less than 1% of the total. That is to say, out of approximately
5.7 million adults, only 117,000 voted.

Thus, at century's end, most Brazilian citizens were stripped of whatever
political rights they had. Regional oligarchies now ruled unencumbered
by messy elections, and their alliances controlled national politics. They
had effectively used political citizenship to consolidate their domination
and insulate their rule from the contagion of European mass democracy.
Moreover, as some critics suspected, legislative reform did little to curb
electoral fraud. Throughout the First Republic (1889–1930), it remained
as rampant as ever, though it became less a matter of herding false noses
and more one of managing false papers.

There can be no doubt that with regard to the world development of
citizenship, Brazil had taken an enormous step backward at the end of
the nineteenth century and the beginning of its Republic. Moreover, for
the next hundred years, from 1881 to 1985, each generation of political elites reconfirmed this step backward: they continued to differentiate
political citizenship by reiterating in federal constitutions and electoral
laws the principal means of disenfranchisement first decreed in the Saraiva
Law, namely, the exclusion of illiterates. The founding Republican Constitution of 1891 dropped the income qualification but kept the other
restrictions, barring illiterates, women, indigents, soldiers, minors, and
members of religious orders. It also kept elections direct and voter registration optional. It eliminated the income restriction because it was not
necessary for the purpose of mass exclusion. The literacy requirement
was sufficient, so much so that it was maintained throughout the twentieth century in each of the five subsequent constitutions until the one of
1988. As table 3.2 indicates, fully 50% of Brazilians were still illiterate
in 1950 and 25% in 1980, just five years before the literacy qualification
was finally abandoned by means of an amendment to the 1969 Constitution. In fact, Brazil was the last republic in Latin America to allow
illiterates to vote.[18]

Thus, for much of the twentieth century the capacity exclusion remained
a fail-safe means of differentiating and limiting political citizenship. Even
though some illiterates always managed to register ex officio, this strategy
of exclusion remained extremely effective as long as illiteracy remained
high. Hence, mass exclusion through mass illiteracy also reflects the failure
of public education as a means to build an informed citizenry. It even
suggests a motive for neglecting this fundamental means for achieving
greater equality among citizens, one already accepted by ruling elites in
Europe and North America. In fact, despite some preliminary republican

advocacy for public education to this end, the intentions of the Republican Constitution could not have been clearer. Although the Imperial Constitution allowed illiterates to vote and gave all citizens the right to a free primary education—the first right realized, the second not—the Republican charter eliminated both. In keeping with the economic liberalism espoused by many framers, it absolved the state of any responsibility for educating citizens to become voters.

Table 3.1 summarizes the effects of differentiated political citizenship on the distribution of the right to vote for the last two centuries in Brazil, from 1821 to 2002. The persistence of mass exclusion from 1881 to 1982 could not be more evident. The number of Brazilian citizens with political rights stayed at rock bottom, under 5%, for sixty-four years following the Saraiva Law. By the last election of the First Republic in 1930, the electorate had not expanded significantly beyond that of the first in 1894. Regardless of political regime—under monarchy, democracy, and dictatorship—the few ruled.[19]

The Revolution of 1930—in which a civilian-military revolt deposed the president—ended the "Pax Oligarchica" and initiated a period of accelerated change. An important electoral reform in 1932 extended the vote to women, reintroduced compulsory registration (in some cases, made automatic), created an electoral justice system to oversee elections with its own regional and federal tribunals, reduced the voting age to eighteen, and further guaranteed a secret ballot. Despite these innovations, however, the electorate actually declined to just 3.7% of the total population in the 1933 elections for a constitutional assembly. A climate of revolution and repression prevailed. For the next twelve years, there were no elections, as Vargas's coup in 1937 curtailed political rights and installed a civilian dictatorship supported by the military until 1945.

With redemocratization that year, the electorate expanded dramatically, by over 400%. This expansion of political citizenship was the result both of pent-up demand for participation on the part of citizens and of more effective voter registration on the part of government. Nevertheless, in the presidential elections in 1945, the electorate included less than one-third of Brazilian adults. Moreover, only one-quarter of them went to the polls. That is to say, after fifteen years of social, political, and labor turmoil, of revolution, coups, dictatorship, and redemocratization, despite women's suffrage, the return of obligatory voting, reduction of the voting age, and the automatic registration of public employees and union members, the Brazilian electorate was barely greater proportionally for adults than it had been for most of the Empire. During the 1950s, the growth of political citizenship again stagnated, due to a law in 1955 that instituted a rigorous process of reregistration. As a result, in the last presidential election (1960) before the military coup of 1964, the electorate was proportionally the same size as it had been ten years before. Sixty percent of adults were still denied political rights.

Urbanization and the Equalization of Rights

The principal reason for the restriction of political citizenship during the period of electoral democracy from 1945 to 1964 was the same as in previous decades: a model of citizenship that emphasized differences, in this case by using a capacity qualification to exclude illiterates. The basis may have been illiteracy, but the deeper cause was a conception of citizenship that needed to use a significant difference—any one would do—to distribute political rights differentially among citizens. Gender had also served this discriminatory purpose until the women's suffrage movement countered it. However, with half of Brazilians illiterate in 1950, the capacity exclusion was just as effective.

Much of this illiteracy was concentrated in the countryside (tables 3.2 and 3.3). At midcentury, nearly two-thirds of Brazil's population lived in rural isolation and poverty. Of these, two-thirds were illiterate. In addition, they were excluded from the benefits of labor legislation developed for urban workers in the 1930s and 1940s. Hence, rural workers toiled under profoundly exploitative conditions. In consequence, they began to

Table 3.3

Urban Population, Brazil, 1872–2000

Year	Urban Population	% of Total	Annual Growth Rate (%)
1872	1,103,501	10.9	–
1890	1,784,657	12.5	2.73
1900	3,014,331	17.4	5.38
1920	7,120,157	23.2	4.39
1940	12,880,182	31.3	–
1950	18,782,891	36.1	3.84
1960	31,303,034	44.7	5.24
1970	52,084,984	55.9	5.22
1980	80,436,409	67.6	4.44
1991	110,990,990	75.6	2.97
2000	137,775,550	81.2	2.43

Sources: 1872–1920: Lopes 1972: 14; 1940–2000: IBGE 2001.

Note: Before 1940, the national census did not distinguish between urban and rural populations. For the years 1872–1920, the table indicates the number of people residing in cities of 50,000 inhabitants or more.

abandon the countryside for the city in unprecedented numbers during the next decade. If the literacy qualification for political rights had become less effective by the 1960s, it was because of this mass urban migration. Indeed, the highest urbanization rates of the century occurred in this decade and the next (table 3.3). During these twenty years, Brazil changed from a rural nation to an urban one, as enormous numbers of Brazilians settled in and built up the urban peripheries. Eventually, the vast majority became home owners, salaried workers, and mass consumers. In this new urban world, illiteracy was a distinct disadvantage and therefore diminished significantly as people taught themselves to be functionally literate. Over the next thirty years, these new and literate urban residents became new and insurgent urban citizens.

In the middle of this process, however, unsettled by the emergence of a mass urban citizenry that, for the Right, seemed to be fodder for populist and unionist manipulation, the military overthrew the elected government in 1964 and restricted political citizenship by force. However, the generals did not abolish it. Reflecting ambiguities within the military regime itself, one of the peculiarities of this dictatorship was that it maintained direct elections for some offices. Even though the national congress was closed on several occasions, many congressmen were forcibly retired without political rights, freedom of speech and press was curtailed, and political association was repressed, proportional elections were not suspended. As a result, Brazilians continued to elect federal deputies, state deputies, and city council representatives. However, all elections based on majority representation—namely, those for governor, mayor, senator, and president—were suspended or restricted. Direct popular elections for these offices were not reinstated until 1982, 1985, 1986, and 1989, respectively. For the elections it allowed, the military regime created procedures that made victory for permitted "opposition" candidates less likely. Among the more effective inventions were the "subticket" (winner determined by party with the highest sum of votes among all its candidates for a particular office) and the "linked vote" (obligatory voting for candidates of the same party for all offices).

Perhaps even stranger than holding elections under dictatorship, the electorate expanded significantly with each election. Though the electoral deck was stacked, Brazilians continued to vote in record numbers. It is a paradox of Brazilian citizenship that one of its most important political expansions occurred under military rule: At its beginning, approximately 42% of adults had political citizenship. By 1970, during the darkest days of dictatorship, a majority of adult Brazilians finally gained political rights. By the end of the regime, political citizenship had for the first time in Brazilian history become practically universal, incorporating 86% of adults into the electorate. Elections in 1933, 1945, and 1986 for

105

constitutional assemblies illustrate this expansion unambiguously: in the first, the electorate represented only 3.7% of the total population; in the second, 16.1%; and, in the third, 51.1%. Between 1960 and 1986, 53 million citizens gained political citizenship—more than the entire population of Brazil in 1950.[20]

Let me hasten to emphasize two points. First, the military regime had no intention of turning Brazil's masses into a modern political citizenry that participates independently in competitive political and electoral decisions. It is worth remembering that one of the arguments that the military and their supporters used to justify the suspension of direct majority elections after the 1964 coup was that "the people" (meaning the mass of poor people) did not know how to vote intelligently and should therefore be governed by those who did. The military regime controlled popular civic participation by political repression and electoral manipulation, not by encouraging democratic citizenship.

Second, although the vast majority of the urban poor became enfranchised during the dictatorship, they widely condemned the restraints imposed on their suffrage. As many residents of São Paulo's peripheries have told me, they resented not being able to vote "for the offices that really mattered"—in their view, president, governor, and mayor. They felt infantilized and degraded. Nevertheless, they believed they had earned the right to vote, and they wanted to demonstrate their competence. For them, qualifying to vote marked their personal achievements publicly, their autoeducation as much as their autoconstruction. It distinguished them from those who remained illiterate, differentiating their citizenship from that of less-accomplished citizens. Therefore, although indignant, although cynical about politicians, they registered to vote during the dictatorship in record numbers.[21] However, they also protested the electoral restraints by nullifying their ballot in record numbers. They voted and then invalidated their ballot in one way or another. For example, they wrote messages across it ("down with dictatorship" was common), left it blank, or checked more than one candidate. In 1945, the number of annulled and blank ballots in congressional elections was 3% of the total cast; in 1970, 30%; and in 1978, 21% (IBGE 1990: 642).

By the end of the military regime, the mass desire to vote and to vote for what mattered had become overwhelming. In the first direct election for president after dictatorship, in 1989, voter participation broke world records: 91% of adults (now defined as sixteen and older) were registered, 80% voted, and only 6.4% of ballots cast were nullified or blank. Political citizenship had become egalitarian.[22]

In the six decades after 1930, several forces combined to produce this profound transformation of Brazilian citizenship. It cannot be denied that the return to compulsory voting and the military regime's stringent efforts

106

to enforce it contributed to the expansion of the electorate.[23] But as the military's project of governance never included the creation of a democratically organized mass political citizenship, the decisive sources of this change must be sought in the intersection of three other transformations in Brazilian society that occurred during these decades: women's suffrage, democratization, and urbanization, the last being the most significant. The first allowed the incorporation of a small but growing number of women who were literate into the political process. It also initiated a more general, if still incomplete, emancipation of women as independent citizens. Today, women are the majority of voters and not only the majority of Brazilians.

The second, electoral democracy, followed two long periods of dictatorship. Although different, repression under each created strong demands for electoral participation as a fundamental right. Indeed, throughout 1983 and 1984, millions of Brazilians took to city streets to demand direct presidential elections, in the largest mobilization of citizens in Brazil's history. The campaign for *diretas já* (direct elections now) ultimately failed in its objective, as the military maintained an indirect election in 1985 for the first civilian president in twenty-five years. Nevertheless, this unprecedented national mobilization for democracy significantly influenced the direct election of representatives to the Constitutional Assembly in the next year. Moreover, the movement's organization remained energized throughout the Assembly by channeling demands for new citizenship rights to the representatives. This conduit evolved into an organized campaign of popular proposals for the new constitution itself. It was so impressive in its mobilization of popular forces for change and so successful in shaping constitutional principles that the new charter of 1988 became known as the Citizen Constitution.[24]

Nevertheless, the most significant factor in the expansion and equalization of political citizenship was the accelerated urbanization of Brazil from 1950 to 1980. Brazil's transformation from a rural to an urban nation during these decades not only consolidated and amplified the force of women's suffrage and electoral democratization. It also changed the terms of citizenship's formulation and, consequently, the nature of its conflicts. On the one hand, rapid urbanization led to the increasing isolation and backwardness of the rural sector. For example, in 1950, when half of all Brazilians were illiterate, the rural rate of illiteracy was two and a half times greater than the urban. In 1980, when 25% of Brazilians were still denied suffrage because of illiteracy, the rural rate had grown to almost three times that of the urban (table 3.2). Although this rural isolation contributed to the persistence of local oligarchic rule (*coronelismo*) in the countryside, it also led to its increasing insignificance in broader state and national politics.

On the other hand, in the cities where most Brazilians now lived, the urban electorate developed an independent and oppositional political citizenship. Urbanization resulted in unprecedented access to primary education, mass media, market consumption, and above all property ownership, precisely for those poor Brazilians who had always been excluded from these fundamental means of achieving citizen standing. Such access not only reduced illiteracy significantly, thereby rendering the capacity qualification increasingly irrelevant. It also generated a new and explicit kind of argument for participation among these new urban citizens: they began to reason that, although poor, they had in fact established "real stakes" in the nation-state as city builders, taxpayers, and modern consumers. As I show later, on that unprecedented basis, they demanded new kinds and qualities of political participation.

In the two neighborhoods of São Paulo's periphery where I have worked intensively, three developments during the last twenty years demonstrated the force of these demands. First, residents founded local cells of the Workers Party (PT). In the one I studied most closely, eighty-seven neighbors in Jardim das Camélias joined the party and organized a "nucleus" in 1980. At their own expense, they maintained a meeting hall in the neighborhood—a remarkable fact considering their poverty—in which they regularly discussed questions of interest, mobilized residents around community problems (primarily of land rights and urban services), and organized electoral campaigns for PT candidates. During the next two decades, many of these founders remained the most active and articulate members of the neighborhood's various grassroots organizations and, moreover, in cross-community social movements and political initiatives. What drew them passionately to the PT nucleus was the value the party gave to their experience and knowledge of urban problems as the basis for articulating projects of political action. They rallied to the PT as a means of contributing to the future of their city and nation on the basis of their stakes in the residential neighborhood. As one founder later explained to me, "in those years [1980–1986], our ideas were valued. The PT leadership used our experiences in the neighborhood to formulate its programs and actions." In this participation from the bottom up, they rewrote the history of their exclusion, disrespect, and manipulation as national citizens through their assertion of an urban citizenship.

The second event was the mayoral election of 1988, the first democratic contest for city hall after the end of military rule. Ninety percent of Brazilian adults had political rights, and the peripheries were well organized to assert electoral power. The results rocked the political establishment: the peripheries elected their candidate, Luiza Erundina of the PT, as mayor of the city—a candidate of and from the peripheries, a radically left-wing, female, nonelite, nonintellectual, northeast immigrant. The residents of my neighborhoods were ecstatic. I spent election day in one of them observing the *bocas de urna*, the activities of party campaigners who try to win votes for specific candidates as voters approach the polling stations. On the eve of the election, the Superior Electoral Tribunal had banned *cabos eleitorais*, as the vote getters are called, from campaigning within 100 meters of the stations. Beyond that, however, each party had dispatched its troops. At the two polling stations I attended in São Miguel Paulista, the three main parties paid each vote getter the following sums: the PSD (candidate Maluf) paid about US $12 for the day, the PMDB (candidate Leiva) $10, and the PSDB (candidate Serra) less than $5. If we consider that the minimum monthly wage was around $54, these payments were significant for a day's work. Each party *cabo* also a received a t-shirt, hat, and lunch. The PT had far fewer troops in the field that day because it paid nothing, gave no t-shirts, and offered no lunch. Yet every *cabo eleitoral* I spoke with who was working for another candidate told me that they had or would vote for the PT candidate, Luiza Erundina. As one said with a distinct glee, "I accept everything from everyone—food, t-shirts, bricks for my house, money. I accept everything, say I'll vote for the candidate who gives me something, and then I vote how I see fit."[25] Try as they might with election payola, the modern-day *cabalistas* were unable to corral the votes of these citizens. Unlike their rural ancestors, the urban poor had not sold their suffrage. Rather, they had forced the candidates to compete for it and to pay for that privilege. They had sold the appearance of support but cast their votes as they deemed best.

The third event was the election of Lula as president of Brazil in 2002. As I have already described the elation of São Paulo's working classes, I want to convey here the clear geographic and economic divisions of Lula's victory (map 3.1). In the municipality of São Paulo, he obtained 39% of the vote in the first round, compared to 28% for his principal rival, José Serra of the PSDB. Lula won in nearly all the peripheral districts. These are the poorest and most populous of the city, containing 74% of the electorate who voted in the first round. Serra won in all the more central districts, which have the highest income but far fewer voters (only 26%). This distribution is but one of many examples of the spatial division of the city into center and peripheries, a pattern of segregation analyzed in chapter 5. The difference between this example and almost all the others, however, is that the people of the peripheries turned the disadvantages of their residential condition into victory precisely by exercising their rights of political citizenship.[26]

We shall see later that these new urban citizens did not think that their rights had been bestowed on them by a beneficent state because of their moral worth as "good" workers (rather than bums or criminals), because they were clients of this or that cacique, or because they met some

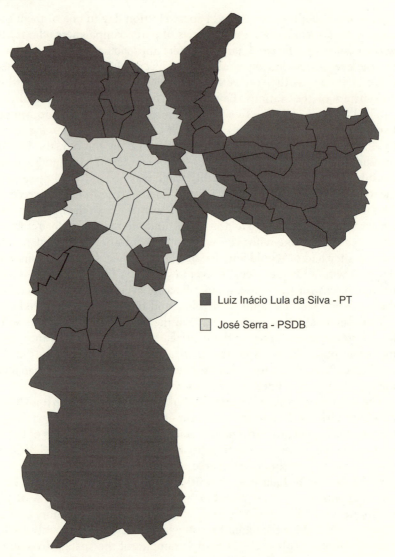

MAP 3.1. Outcome of first round of voting in 2002 presidential elections by electoral districts in São Paulo. *Source:* SEADE 2004c.

state-regulated requisite. Nor did they primarily argue for rights on the basis of their needs as human beings or even their absolute worth as citizens. More generally and consistently, they used a real-stakes argument that they refashioned. Paradoxically, they made the very argument that had excluded them the basis of an insurgent movement for rights among the urban poor, turning it against the exclusionary formulation of citizenship that, as this chapter has shown, ruled for more than one hundred years. Now literate; better informed; and property-owning, taxpaying, commodity-consuming citizens, they had gained, in their own view, the right to a fair share of resources. They had won the right to be treated with full-citizen dignity. They had earned their right to political rights.

Before examining this new formulation of rights, I must first establish, in the next chapter, the extent to which the old formulation denied most Brazilians another fundamental aspect of citizenship: I must show that under every kind of political system Brazil has known, it reduced their civil standing and alienated them from law by limiting their access to landed property. Only then can we appreciate the full impact of the development of the urban peripheries on citizenship.

Chapter 4
Restricting Access to Landed Property

Independence and republican government in many nations signal the development of movements for the equalization of rights. Yet the onset of Brazil's republic marked the beginning of even greater disparities among citizens. As a result, most Brazilians have received unequal distributions of citizenship for centuries under colonial, imperial, and republican regimes. This extraordinary persistence of mass inequality characterizes all aspects of citizenship, not only the political ones, and affects society as much as state. Brazilians have captured the vastness of this inequality succinctly in an aphorism: "Brazil is a land without people and a people without land." This chapter demonstrates that each half of the adage describes an essential element in the entrenchment of Brazil's differentiated citizenship. Yet it also shows that they indicate the terms of citizenship's transformation.

If the aphorism still accurately characterizes rural Brazil, however, its second half no longer applies to urban Brazil. With their construction of the urban peripheries, Brazilians not only massively moved to cities. A majority of the urban poor also gained access to land as first-time property owners. We shall see that their tenure generally results from a complex process of legitimation, in which illegal occupation is both the only means of access to land for most citizens and, paradoxically, an illegality that initiates the legalization of property claims. Even if, as a result, their ownership is typically insecure and often contested, it nevertheless generates fundamental changes in their citizenship.

This unprecedented access of the urban poor to landed property is of such importance for citizenship that I distribute its analysis across several chapters. In this one, I show that the exclusion of most Brazilian citizens from property resulted directly from the interaction of centuries-old policies and practices of land use, labor, and law. My point is that this exclusion from property had a number of fatal consequences for Brazilian citizenship. It certainly limited political rights, as we have seen. More important, restricted access to property had the effect of forcing most Brazilians to reside illegally, making illegality if not the norm then the predominant condition of settlement. For most citizens, the effect was overwhelming: their status as illegal residents subverted their civil citizenship. It did so in two ways. First, by placing them on the other side of the law, the condition of having to live illegally alienated citizens from law generally, diminishing their access to its rights and justice, undermining it as an institution of and for citizenship, and rendering it "for enemies." Second, their exclusion from legal property in land also denied them the civil standing that legitimate property ownership is conventionally understood to create. By that, I refer to the relation between property and personality, as political philosophy has called it, in which property ownership is the means to establish such fundamental qualifications for citizenship as independence, respect, and responsibility.

Hence, residential illegality has had paradoxical, even contrary, effects on the evolution of Brazilian citizenship. When Brazil was predominantly rural and most citizens lacked both political organization and education, residential illegality crippled the development of civil citizenship. However, with mass urbanization and the opportunities of concentration it energizes, the illegal conditions of residence politicized autoconstructors, becoming the core issues of grassroots mobilizations and providing a resilient foothold for the insurgence of both political and civil citizenship. In this chapter, I am concerned with the earlier and ruinous developments. I establish a set of correlations among access to land, labor, law, and citizenship, and analyze a related set of problems concerning the consolidation of state sovereignty, illegality as the norm of settlement, private landed property as a marketable commodity, and the emergence of a particular cast of citizens as the agents of land conflict. In the next chapter, I focus on the formation of São Paulo's contemporary periphery, where a reiteration of these same correlations leads to a very different outcome.

Property, Personality, and Civil Standing

I begin with the relation between property and civil standing to suggest that the denial of the former subverts the later, at least under the

113

circumstances I describe in Brazil. The idea that property is significant for citizenship is not, of course, my invention. Nor is it my imposition on Brazilian experience. Much of the foundational writing on modern society and state, both within and against liberalism, derives citizenship's essential ethical and personal attributes, as well as its rights and obligations, from the right to property. This discussion generally does not limit property to land but considers rights themselves as kinds of property. Moreover, both for those who trace their justification of property back to Locke's *Second Treatise* and for those whose understanding of property descends from Hegel's *Philosophy of Right*, the quintessential property right is similar, that of being the proprietor of one's own person and capacities—owning oneself. In Locke's formulation, "every Man has a *Property* in his own *Person*. This no Body has any Right to but himself. The *Labour* of his Body, and the *Work* of his Hands, we may say, are properly his."[1] From this natural property in life and labor, Locke derives a natural right to appropriate land and things, for whatever a person transforms by his labor becomes his property. As each person has this natural right of property equally, the property right is the basis of an individual's equal natural rights in relation to every other member of society.

Hegel's theory of property is developmental rather than directly constitutive and was especially influential among Brazilian jurists in the nineteenth century. While for Locke self-property is a given of nature, for Hegel it is something an individual must achieve, a subjective act of appropriation, an extension of an individual's will over nature. His discussion therefore emphasizes property as an external possession, especially of land. In Hegel's justification, property also secures the very possibility of developing a person's full potentials. Individuals go forth from themselves into the external world of nature and society by claiming things as property. Through property, they objectify their will in the world, building themselves up from within to without, achieving both the self-conscious apprehension of themselves as autonomous, free, and creative agents and the recognition by others of their struggles and dreams.[2] Hence, for Hegel, property ensures both personal and social development. It is, moreover, the basis of his anticontractarian argument that mutual recognition, and not individual consent, is the foundation of the social order. On the one hand, what distinguishes a person from others—personality—derives from property. On the other, it is only insofar as an individual's personality (or free will) is embodied in things that it becomes capable of being recognized as such by others. In this way, property owners recognize each other as persons struggling through the same processes of self-realization. They respect the other's property rights because they want the same respect in return. As a result of such mutual recognition and respect, they regard each other as equals. Thus, in Hegel's account, a person's sense of both universal equality and intersubjective distinction develops through property.[3]

Important differences notwithstanding, both the Lockean and the Hegelian lineages of property right agree on the direct relation between what could be called inner property (self) and outer property (land/things) and between property (in both senses) and citizenship. Both contend that it is the property right, above all other rights, that insures an individual's freedom. By the latter, they mean freedom from dependence on the will of others. Property is, therefore, the embodiment and externalization of an individual's free will. Thus, an individual is free insofar as he is the proprietor of his own person, a relation embodied and expressed in the ownership of land and things. As freedom is in this way a function of property, a government that is responsible for the freedom of its citizens must guarantee property as one of its principal obligations. Both philosophical traditions also consider that the appropriation of property is essential for the development of respect for persons and that such respect is foundational for citizenship. For both, as well, property owners are more likely to think responsibly about the consequences of their actions because they naturally want to leave their property to their descendents and do not want irresponsible behavior to compromise its perpetuation. Thereby, property ownership generates responsible citizens with "real stakes" in the future of the nation.

In sum, both lineages of property right claim a close connection between property and the fundamental qualifications of citizenship: freedom (economic and intellectual independence), capacity (agency, mastery, responsibility), dignity, respect, and self-possession. For Locke, individuals without property in land on which to expend their labor lose that full ownership of their own person that is the basis of their equality. As a result, their citizenship becomes differentiated from those with landed property and their rights unequal. Locke considered such propertyless and differentiated citizens unfit to participate in political decisions.[4] As ruled but not ruling, moreover, they are less free. For Hegel, individuals without property lose the possibility of fully developing their own person which is also the basis of their standing in the social world. As a result, the propertyless are not only lesser persons but also diminished citizens.

I return to these connections between property, person, and citizenship in subsequent chapters when I analyze the values of land and home ownership for residents of the urban peripheries. We shall see that autoconstruction is a measure of both their self-development as persons and their social drama as citizens. It grounds their sense that their achievements in both entitle them to full citizenship rights.[5]

For now, I want to establish the relevance of such considerations of property to the formation of Brazilian citizenship. I can convey it concisely by citing two passages by eminent Brazilians of the latter part of the nineteenth century, one from the jurist Clóvis Beviláqua (1859–1944) and the other from the abolitionist, lawyer, and politician Joaquim Nabuco (1849–1910). Beviláqua authored the civil code that was legislated in 1916 and remained in effect until 2003. On the origins and justification of property, he writes: "With the cultivation of land, the sentiment of individual property became accentuated, because productive work—creating, regularly, utilities corresponding to the effort employed—stabilized man, and, tying him strongly to the generous soil, gave him a special personality. And, with the establishment of the State, such individual rights acquired more clarity and security" (1956: 97). In this passage, Beviláqua combines both the Lockean tradition of property right (appropriation through transformative labor) and the Hegelian (personality development through subjective appropriation and its objectification). With both lineages of property right in tow, he argues for its decisive importance in organizing relations of land, labor, personality, right, and state.[6]

The implied negation of property is, therefore, no less decisive in this Brazilian formulation, namely, the devastating consequences for both person and society of not having property and of organized attempts to restrict access to it. That these consequences were clear to Brazilians is evident in Nabuco's 1884 election to parliament, in which they were at the core of his campaign. "[Land] ownership," he argued, "not only has rights but also duties. If elected, I will not separate these two questions: that of the emancipation of the slaves and that of the democratization of the soil. The one is the complement of the other."

Land, Labor, and Law

As Beviláqua and Nabuco indicate, questions of land have been inseparable from those of labor in the development of Brazilian society and the consolidation of its nation-state. In broad terms, the Brazilian state has promoted four regimes of labor from colonial to present times. Each regime is associated with a distinct mode of labor supply and with specific policies and conflicts of land acquisition. Portugal's goal of extracting maximum profits from colonial investments led it to develop an economic strategy of large-scale agricultural and mining operations powered by slave labor. The importation of free labor would have contradicted this goal because free workers would require either wages or land to produce for themselves. Either case would have compromised the profit structure of Portugal's mercantile objectives. In the early part of the colonial period, the Portuguese Crown relied on a regime of Indian slave labor, supplied through an indigenous slave traffic. From the beginning of the seventeenth to the end of the nineteenth centuries, it invested overwhelmingly in African slave labor and the international slave trade. When it became evident in the 1840s that this trade would eventually end, the government began to consider the substitution of free foreign wageworkers for slaves and to promote international immigration, particularly of European workers, for that purpose. This promotion lasted until the end of the 1920s. From the 1930s to the present, the state has focused on developing a force of national rather than foreign wage labor, available to industry and commerce through internal migration.

Each regime of labor required specific policies of land use and access, both to sustain its particular productive base (e.g., agriculture, mining, ranching, and manufacturing) and to anchor and discipline its labor force. Thus, throughout Brazilian history, land and labor supply have conditioned each other and are, in that sense, interdependent. The appropriation of land depends on the organization of labor, just as different kinds of labor require different kinds of land use. Hence, although the abundance of land in Brazil is certainly a geofact, its availability—as well as organization as property—is an artifact of a particular economic enterprise and its legal foundation. These deployments of land and labor presented Brazil's newly independent state with an extraordinary problem. To consolidate its sovereignty, it had to bring them under its authority. A standard means of doing so for nation-states is to issue and regulate land titles based on a certified demarcation of which lands are held publicly and which privately. Without such certification, the consolidation of national territory remains fundamentally incomplete, as it defines the very national territory over which states extend and exercise their sovereignty. This extension consolidates a national legal order, through which states manage the supply of land and labor. Moreover, the emission of secure land titles enables states to guarantee property rights. Without that assurance, they can neither fully constitute a class of property owners nor settle land disputes among them. Thus, for foundational reasons of state, land regulation was imperative for Brazil's central government at independence. Yet it was also impossible: after almost three hundred years of application, colonial land policy had generated overwhelming confusion, opacity, conflict, and illegality in the territorial occupation of Brazil. This dilemma of national land regulation—of its necessity and impossibility—had dire consequences for the development of state, rule of law, and formulation of citizenship which reverberate in kind to this day. Therefore, to understand these effects, we must examine the legacy of chaos in land tenure that postcolonial Brazil inherited.

117

THE TANGLE OF COLONIAL LAND TENURE

One founding premise of Portuguese colonialism was that the royal emissary's act of discovery or conquest incorporated land into the king's personal patrimony. This incorporation constituted the legal foundation for the empire's policy of ruling the colonies by creating landed elites. It established the king's right and duty to redistribute conquered land to his subjects for the conjoined purposes of economic exploitation and Christianization. The Crown had assumed the latter project when the pope ordained King João III as Grand Master of the Order of Christ in 1522, making him responsible for propagating the faith among peoples discovered in the course of Europe's maritime explorations. Hence, the Portuguese Crown claimed original title to the entire territory of Brazil by virtue of Cabral's landfall in 1500, on the basis of which it distributed land for commercial and religious enterprise.[7]

To regulate this distribution, the Portuguese employed a medieval system of royal land grants called *sesmarias*. In the late fourteenth century, the Crown devised various legal mechanisms to force the cultivation of uninhabited, unproductive, or abandoned lands. It consolidated these measures as the Law of Sesmarias and incorporated them into the legislative codes that governed Portugal and its colonies. As the central initiative was to link land occupation to productive agricultural use, the imperial codes authorized the expropriation of unproductive property for reassignment as noninheritable grants in exchange for a rent of one-sixth of the annual production. Such lands remained Crown patrimony, as only their usufruct was distributed. The law limited the size of grants to the capacity of applicants to cultivate them and specified the duration of usufruct rights. After this period, uncultivated *sesmarias* reverted to the Crown and became reassignable as *terras devolutas* (devolved lands). These restrictions of size, time, and productive use were destined to cause great conflict in Brazil.

Transferred to the Americas in 1548 with the Rules of Government that established juro-political organization in the colony, this policy became the Crown's only legal means to fix people on the land to carry out its twin projects of commercial cultivation and religious instruction. Both were based on sedentary agriculture as the Christian alternative to the nomadic "habits of heathens." Therefore, the Crown authorized its New World agents to distribute *sesmarias* only to those who possessed the considerable resources necessary to develop them for these purposes. This necessity transformed the policy. To attract such colonizers, especially to set up slave-based sugar plantations, the Crown offered generous incentives, removing inheritance restrictions and annual payments (except for God's tithe) from the grants. Moreover, even though the requirement of cultivation still applied, its meaning changed. In colonial Brazil, land it-self had little value, not only because of its abundance but especially be-cause its availability for profitable exploitation depended on the complex capital arrangements of supplying slaves. The plantation production of sugar and later coffee was predatory in nature: it exhausted land and slaves quickly and therefore required the continuous incorporation of new supplies of both. As a result, the Crown often used *sesmaria* grants to guarantee future investments in export production rather than to se-cure the actual occupation of land. Hence, land could be legitimately held for future use without being cultivated or occupied—a perversion of the original objectives of the *sesmaria* law.

On the basis of these changes, the Crown's agents used royal grants to carve up Brazil into enormous latifundia. Common concessions were of ten, twenty, and even one hundred square leagues (168, 336, and 1,680 square miles, respectively), though I have found examples of three and four times the last. Concessions were so large, according to a contempo-rary observer, that in many one could "lose Italy" (cited in Lima 1988: 58). This distribution consecrated their grantees as an aristocratic, slave-holding, commercially oriented ruling class. By independence from Por-tugal, the institution of *sesmarias* had produced the perversity I noted earlier: after three centuries of colonization, Brazil was a land without people and a people without land. According to Gonçalves Chaves's as-sessment published that year, little territory was still undistributed that was not "subject to invasions by Indians." As a result, "there are many poor families, wandering from place to place, at the mercy of the favor and caprice of the landowners and always lacking the means to obtain a bit of land on which to make a permanent establishment" (cited in Faoro 1975: 407). Moreover, if these families managed to establish a land stake, they did so illegally and, as squatters, lived in constant fear of eviction. Hence, for the free but poor, repeating cycles of land invasion and ex-pulsion characterized their settlement of Brazil and created a enduring condition of disprivilege, illegality, and violence.

The *sesmaria* system had several other lasting legal consequences. The first concerned the role of government in legitimating private property as a holding cut out from the public domain. This role evolved as the notion of *sesmaria* ownership changed. Initially part of royal patrimony, *sesmarias* were granted to applicants as administrative concessions of usufruct rights with conditional tenure. As land could not be bought or sold, there was no real estate market. The historian of land law Ruy Cirne Lima (1988: 41–43) argues that the Crown's ownership of *sesmarias* began to be considered in a different light after it imposed a annual tax (*foro*) in 1695 on the basis of ordinary property law. After that, *sesma-rias* were gradually thought of less as administrative restrictions on the appropriation of land by private individuals or public entities and more as alienations of property cut out of the royal domain, over which grantees had common property rights as symbolized by their obligation to pay property taxes. This conceptual transformation was not completed until the Imperial Constitution of 1824 guaranteed private property and the Land Law of 1850 consolidated its market foundations by establishing that thereafter public lands could only be acquired through purchase.

The second consequence of the *sesmaria* system was legal confusion, and it became a strategy of domination on both sides of the Atlantic. Throughout the colonial period, the Portuguese Crown adopted a formal, bureaucratic, and legalistic approach to the problem of land. It attempted to direct the occupation of Brazil by means of legislation transferred from the metropolis to the colony, and it saw the confusion of land tenure there as a problem of disobedience. The more chaotic the tenure conditions became, the more the Crown issued remedial legislation. Its principal objective was not to resist the abuses of land accumulation but rather to recover legal control. To that end, the Crown produced a steady stream of corrective laws, decrees, regulations, orders, and instructions during the eighteenth century. Individually, each measure may have been reasonably clear and precise. Taken together, however, they produced little more than confusion, as one act annulled, obscured, or conditioned another in contradictory fashion.[8]

Moreover, the Crown awarded many land grants with indefinite boundaries, producing endless litigation and violence over contested rights. Royal authorities often superimposed and duplicated *sesmarias* because they had only the vaguest notion of which lands were legitimately occupied. Hence, grants usually contained no exact information about location or size.[9] As a result, different people often claimed the "same" properties, each of whom might have some stake in the truth and some rights recognized. Congressional debates concerning land legislation in 1843 show that legislators suspected that the Crown deliberately granted vague *sesmarias* not out of ignorance of uncharted territories or for lack of surveying skills but to keep planters "busy plotting against each other rather than against the Crown" (Dean 1971: 607). Be that as it may, the fundamental problem was that because so many land grants were originally vague if not irregular, and because land use often followed a different logic in practice than the legislated one, each new law created new conditions of illegality. In effect, each regulation rendered yet more land holdings illegal and generated new layers of confusion and conflict.[10] Thus, far from creating transparency, the documental regime of rule and surveillance the state employed, with its technologies of regulation and clarification, produced illegality, opacity, and tangled communication.

120

For their part, the Brazilians developed legal confusion into a strategy of rule with greater brilliance. On the one hand, the grantees (*sesmeiros*) rarely complied with the requirements of their grants to demarcate, survey, register, and confirm their concessions. In fact, they had little interest in regularizing their holdings because the kind of extensive agriculture and herding they practiced demanded a continuous replacement of exhausted lands. Their objective was normally to use slave labor to appropriate land as needed without reporting it. On the other hand, having taken the best lands, the rural elites worked in the eighteenth century not only to augment their individual shares but also to dominate the system of land distribution by preventing others' access to it. Certainly, their means were violent. More effectively, however, they dominated distribution by generating such a confused heap of legislation about *sesmarias* that only those already in power could manipulate it. Their strategy was not to deny the law—as often assumed in assertions that Brazil was and is a lawless land—but rather to create an excess of it, zealously applying the Germanic-Roman legal fundament that "the law has no gaps."[11]

These landed elites sent their sons to the University of Coimbra in Portugal to study law, and they returned to constitute the upper echelons of the legal and political professions in both pre– and post–independent Brazil.[12] As judges, legislators, politicians, administrators, and heads of state, these elites ran the legislatures, packed local governments and courts, enacted laws to further their interests, manipulated inheritance regulations, obtained additional grants surreptitiously through distant family members and arranged marriages, and squatted on unclaimed and disputed lands. In sum, they learned how to complicate the legal system for their advantage. Lima (1988: 46) concludes that after a century of attaching legal restrictions and administrative procedures to land grants, these elites succeeded in creating "an invincible tangle of incongruent texts, contradictory regulations, and defective bureaucratic mechanisms, all united under a constraining pile of doubts and stumbling blocks."

To complicate matters further, squatting on Crown lands had been common practice since the beginning of colonization for settlers who lacked the resources to apply for *sesmarias* but who had the wherewithal to survive in the wilderness on subsistence cultivation. Given the immensity of Brazil and the large tracts of uncultivated and disputed territory within the plantation areas, squatting was an ever-available alternative, tolerated, if noticed, unless someone obtained a grant to the squatters' land. Such holdings, called *posses*, thus made it possible for those who could not participate in the commercial economy to survive as free settlers and served as the trump, so to speak, of poorer immigrants—the frontiersmen, sharecroppers, small farmers, and freed slaves—against the regime of latifundistas.[13] The confusion of land tenure and the predatory nature

121

of agriculture regularly pitted *sesmeiros* against *posseiros* in often violent confrontation. Yet, over time, it also united the two against the Crown's increasingly obsessive legal measures to (re)gain control of Brazil's territorial occupation.

During the colonial period, squatting had an ambiguous jural status. *Posses* were illegal because they violated the stipulation that land could only be acquired through the concession of a royal land grant. However, they were customarily recognized as legitimate if they were actively cultivated for a long time with ongoing and evident production. Thus, productive squatters had certain customary rights.[14] These derive from the idea, already found in medieval Portugal's Law of Sesmarias, that property has a social function and property owners an obligation to produce some social benefit, be it food or colonization. Such justification explains the government's concern to give legal title to those who occupied land, especially public land, productively but illegally, even if it jeopardized the rights of those who held it legally but unproductively. However, ambiguities about the meaning of productive and unproductive possession, the nature of acquisition, and property itself persist to this day in various legal and cultural forms as endemic sources of land conflict. The colonial courts generally ruled that squatters' rights over cultivated lands could be legalized if their claims were registered and taxes and fees paid within a specified period of time. This decision essentially converted a *posse* into a *sesmaria* or *aforamento* (lease). For many squatters, however, these expenses were prohibitive. In consequence, a favorable ruling often had the perverse effect of forcing them off the land or at least into unambiguous illegality. Therefore, humbler squatters rarely sought to legalize their holdings.

However, the landed elites could generally afford the conversion, and this possibility encouraged them to squat on public land as an effective strategy to augment their estates. Moreover, they could take advantage of the ambiguous meaning assigned to active cultivation by seizing large tracts of land for legalization later. Finally, when the new imperial government extinguished the institution of *sesmarias* in 1822, *posse* remained the only method recognized in law (however contradictorily) to claim land. As a result, in anticipation of a new mechanism to legalize holdings after its abolition, elite squatters claimed *posses* of staggering size, even greater than that of royal *sesmarias*, usually marking their cultivation with nothing more than a trail or corral, if that. In the backlands, squatters claimed as much as they could imagine; in the more settled regions, as much as they could hope to get away with.[15] In both areas, squatter latifundistas launched violent campaigns against other *posseiros*, large and small, to force them off the land. Thereby, these elite squatters consecrated a fundamental and perduring strategy of land acquisition in Brazil: as usurpation, if maintained, usually produced legalization, they confirmed land seizure as a dependable way to obtain legal property. Those who broke the law consistently, in other words, gained rights reliably.

During the regime of *sesmarias*, Brazilian upper classes thus developed the skills to use law, government, and bureaucracy to create "an invincible tangle" of land regulations (Lima 1988: 46). This imbroglio paralyzed the Crown's adjudication of land conflict, effectively permitting local authorities to legitimate illegal practices in their interest. In this manner, legal complication was not only a strategy of metropolitan rule. It also became a weapon against the impositions of that rule and a reliable means to pilfer its patrimony. Therefore, when the Council of Appeals in Rio de Janeiro abolished the policy of *sesmarias* and suspended the leasing of Crown lands two months before independence in 1822, it was only formally extinguishing what had already been thoroughly subverted and usurped.

NATIONAL LAND REFORM, SLAVERY, AND IMMIGRANT FREE LABOR

In addition to this expediency, two great transformations during the nineteenth century forced ruling-class Brazilians to reconsider the colonial structure of property: the advent of independent nationhood and the end of slavery. Each initiated debates on land and labor and generated related legal measures that had profound consequences for the organization of citizenship. Brazilians were well aware, moreover, that American elites also confronted the effects of independence and abolition on the same issues. In both countries, these events triggered similar concerns with regard to the regularization, commodification, and distribution of land in relation to the supply of free labor and national development. These concerns focused on the exact demarcation of public and private holdings, emission of corresponding land titles, creation of national land registries, formulation of a legal regime of private property, relation between federal and state jurisdictions, and distribution of public land to citizens, immigrants, and investors. The land measures were especially important to the consolidation of national sovereignty. Only the certified discrimination of public from private lands could secure the titles of private holdings. It was thus indispensable both for the constitution of a class of property owners and for the state's ability to resolve land disputes among them. Security of title also enabled the state to distribute public lands with confidence in the legality of its operations, a condition crucial to its ability to establish policies for immigration and the development of national resources. If these issues were in many ways similar for both Americans and Brazilians, however, a fundamentally different rationality engaged them and ordered their outcome.

123

I suggested earlier that the leaders of Brazilian independence who gathered around Prince Pedro had interests in economic liberalism but not in liberal democracy. They broke with Portugal primarily to institute free trade to benefit the local planter class, which wanted to maintain the existing social structure and its regime of slavery. Because of their antipathy to "dirty Democracy" (as José Bonifácio called it), these Brazilian elites did not develop—either with independence at the beginning of the nineteenth century or with the foundation of the Republic at the end—what is often described in European and North American political history as a republican ethos of citizenship.[16] By that, I refer to the antiaristocratic ideal that promoted the value of earned independence to replace inherited status as the measure of the "good citizen." This ideal derided unearned advantage and promoted hard work, self-direction, and self-improvement as the ethical basis of national membership (at least within certain ascriptive boundaries of race and gender).

In the United States, it was associated with land policies that advocated the creation of a mass citizenry of small-property owners. These policies sponsored the generous distribution of public lands—through public auctions, low prices, and free homesteads—for two basic purposes: as a means to draw settlers to the interior and thereby stimulate national economic development, and as a means to foster independence and equal opportunity among citizens. These twin purposes structured the American conception of the role of land in the development of the nation's democracy. In Brazil, where this democratic ethos did not generally take root, Brazilian leaders rejected such national land policy and its aims, though they were precisely aware of their effects in the United States.[17] Although they intensely debated projects of land distribution and regulation throughout the nineteenth century as a means to advance economic development, a different sociopolitical argument about land, labor, and citizenship reigned.

Brazilians forcefully engaged in these debates in 1821 on the eve of independence, as they organized provincial delegations to represent their interests at the Lisbon Assemblies. As noted earlier, the selection of these representatives occasioned Brazil's first general elections. During this process, José Bonifácio prepared a set of "instructions" for deputies representing the Province of São Paulo at the Assemblies. One chapter proposed a radical reform of the *sesmaria* system. It argued that the confusion and illicit use of this system of land tenure hindered "a united and progressive settlement," restricted agriculture, isolated villages, and caused people to live "as wild animals in the middle of the jungle, with supreme damage to the administration of the justice and civilization of the nation" (Bonifácio 2002: 130).

The instructions call for the return of all uncultivated *sesmarias* and *posses* to the national patrimony for redistribution. The reform becomes radical in proposing to end the free distribution of land to the wealthy. Instead, it recommends that all lands considered "devolved" and "empty" be sold in moderately sized, relatively inexpensive, and precisely surveyed lots never to exceed approximately 8.4 square miles (a considerable reduction of the common practice). It also proposes that the state use "the proceeds of these sales . . . to favor the colonization of poor Europeans, Indians, mulattoes, and freed Negroes, to whom would be given small parcels of land as *sesmarias* to cultivate and settle" (Bonifácio 2002: 131). Hence, Bonifácio's reform advocates turning land into a commodity, using its sale to subsidize colonization, and making it available to the masses as small holdings. It is a recipe for developing Brazil's economy and society by creating a mass of property-owning independent farmers.[18]

Preoccupied with other matters, however, the Lisbon Assemblies ignored Brazilian land reform. As a result, Brazil embarked upon independence with the problem in suspension: the *sesmarias* had been abolished, but no legal substitute for alienating public lands was established. Moreover, for an entire generation, until the Land Law of 1850, none could be agreed upon. Although in theory a new system of land regulation and alienation would benefit property owners, their practice of a predatory, mobile, and slave-driven agriculture opposed it. This limbo of law during the first half of the nineteenth century encumbered land occupation with yet another layer of chaos. It made illegal seizure (*posse*) the only way to obtain land and automatically turned all further acquisitions into acts of encroachment. Consequently, as the 1821 proposition faded, access to land and landholding became even more chaotic, violent, and, therefore, restricted to the powerful.

For the first decades of independence, land reform brooded at the edge of state affairs. As long as rural oligarchs could maintain the colonial system of production, based on slave labor and free appropriation of Crown land, they might debate reform but they could avoid enacting it. By midcentury, however, as each base eroded, they had no choice. Forced by Britain, the Brazilian Crown ratified a series of laws between 1826 and 1832 prohibiting the international traffic and importation of slaves. Yet these measures remained on the books without implementation, enacted "for the English to see" as Brazilians put it, coining an expression still popular today to characterize any similar ruse of appearances. In 1845, however, Britain responded by enacting the Aberdeen Bill, which authorized its forces to seize any ship transporting slaves, even within Brazilian seas and rivers, and to try captured traffickers as pirates in Admiralty courts. Outraged at this attack on their national sovereignty, Brazilians actually intensified the commerce of slaves, smuggling upwards of fifty thousand a year into the country between 1845 and 1850 (Costa 1985: 129–32).

Nevertheless, ruse and uproar aside, even supporters of slavery began to realize that the slave trade was doomed. When the Brazilian Parliament effectively terminated it in 1850 by enforcing severe measures against smugglers, it also signaled the beginning of the end of the economic regime of labor the traffic maintained: as the slave population did not reproduce itself naturally without the trade, there would be no slaves to work the plantations within one or at most two generations. When the more dynamic sectors of the plantation economy (mainly in coffee) understood that the inevitable end of the slave trade would result in labor shortages, their interest in land reform became urgent.

Nor could the new imperial government turn a blind eye indefinitely to the illegal encroachment of Crown land. Fundamentally, *posse* subverted the state's authority. Without a legal means to establish title, it could not guarantee property rights, let alone adjudicate land disputes. Without demarcation, the state could not even identify its own patrimony with sufficient confidence to maintain its rights over public lands or alienate them legitimately. Moreover, *posse* pitched the landowning class into conflict and encouraged violence as the means to settle land disputes.

As the land and labor foundations of the colonial system of production thus deteriorated, debates about a course of action focused on two prospects: that of replacing slave labor with the free labor of foreign immigrants and that of financing immigration through the sale of public lands. However, such sale required comprehensive land reform to determine which lands were public (either "devolved" or "empty") and thus available for sale. The strategy of foreign immigration further split into two generally competing objectives: to import immigrants as laborers for the plantations or as independent freeholders to colonize Brazil. Those advocating the latter, such as Heinrich Handelmann (1982) and A. C. Tavares Bastos (1939a), compared the perceived success of American colonization with the failure of Brazilian. They blamed the lost economic development that resulted on insecure land tenure and misguided land policies. As a means to diffuse small-scale property holding, they pointed to American land policies that instituted national surveys and registries, accurate demarcations, public auctions, and homesteading. It is crucial to follow these debates and their outcome because the access to property they established applied not only to new immigrants but also to Brazilian citizens, to the free and freed poor who constituted most of Brazil's citizenry. This application profoundly conditioned Brazilian citizenship for nothing less than the next century.

As debate over land reform revived in the 1840s, most parties agreed on the necessity of transforming Crown property into a market commodity that could be sold publicly to finance immigration. The question was immigration to what end. Well represented in government, established

126

agrarian interests dominated once again: the argument to use immigrants to replace slaves on the plantations and thereby solve the problem of their labor supply overwhelmed the one to use them to stimulate colonization by independent smallholding.[19] In fact, the latter was denounced as a certain means to produce competitors rather than laborers. The dominant position had various projects in circulation, all unified around the objective of forcing free immigrants into wage labor on the plantations. Common to them was the proposal to tie new labor to the estates in such ways that neither a market in free labor nor a market in land accessible to workers would be created. Without either market, free immigrants would have no choice but to work on the plantations. Especially for those whose passage had been subsidized, that outcome would ensure the substitution of a type of indentured servitude for slavery.[20]

For these projects, the planter class found both practical and ideological inspiration in the work of the English theorist of colonization, Edward Gibbon Wakefield (1796–1862). Wakefield developed his theories in response to failed efforts by British capitalists to retain workers on the immigrant settlements they financed in Australia. Imported at considerable expense, these workers were soon able to abandon their employers to become independent producers on free or cheap tracts of land and thereupon to compete with those who had subsidized their immigration. This process resulted in labor shortages and therefore high wages. In turn, the latter enabled new immigrant workers to become independent landowners even more quickly. In *A Letter from Sidney*, Wakefield (1829) proposed to stem this hemorrhage of labor and profit by terminating free grants of land and by setting a "sufficient price" on unoccupied lands to render them inaccessible to recent immigrants. Set sufficiently high, immigrants would have to work for wages for some time before purchasing land to work for themselves. Their wage work would produce profits to fund the employment of more workers. When they had earned enough money to become independent landowners, proceeds from the land sales would subsidize further immigration, which would replenish the labor supply, lower wages, and thus create what Wakefield called a "self-supporting system" of colonization.[21]

Wakefield's theories were not only of immediate strategic interest to Brazilian planters. They also appealed because they offered an explicit criticism of economic and social development in the United States and a workable alternative to avoid repeating it. Wakefield advanced his self-supporting system as a means to perpetuate an aristocracy of social and economic differences ("gradations") under conditions of colonization. He (1829: 148–49) considered Americans a "rotten" people, who had "degenerated from their [English] ancestors" because (among other things) they "delight in a forced equality, not equality before the law only, but

127

equality against nature and truth; an equality which, to keep the balance always even, rewards the mean rather than the great, and gives more honour to the vile than to the noble." Above all, he blamed the loss of English aristocratic organization in the United States on the availability of cheap land in the service of such equality. "In new American settlements," Wakefield (1833) wrote in a comparative study of England and America, "a passion for owning land prevents the existence of a class of labourers for hire" (1: 17). Access to land encouraged workers to become both independent and republican and burdened the great estates with higher costs for either free or slave labor. Thus, Wakefield's theories encouraged Brazil's rural oligarchs to believe that by forcing free immigrants into low wage or indentured labor, it would be possible to develop their plantation economy to compete with the United States while maintaining their plantation society.

The Brazilian Council of State developed this inspiration into a legislative initiative of comprehensive land and labor reform in 1842.[22] The expanded bill that emerged from the Chamber of Deputies a year later became a significant attempt by members of the Conservative Party linked to the Crown and to the more dynamic sectors of the plantation economy to consolidate and modernize the powers of central government.[23] As a means of state building, the bill had three objectives: to create the conditions in which free European labor would replace slave labor on the plantations; to finance this substitution by funds generated through land sale and title regularization, the cost of which would be distributed among all landowners; and to bring order to the reigning chaos of land tenure by discriminating public from private holdings and developing a legal regime of property under the authority of the central government. These measures of land reform aimed to assert central control over key aspects of local politics and to prevent further encroachments of public lands.

To achieve these objectives, the bill subjected all existing land grants to review and taxation. Its specifications implemented a version of Wakefield's self-supporting system of labor. It stipulated that henceforth Crown land could be alienated only through sale and only in lots of 4.2 square miles or more. These provisions would keep land prices high and therefore inaccessible to smallholders. It reinforced this strategy by creating an annual property tax on all private holdings.[24] The funds generated through these measures of land regularization and sale would be used to finance the immigration of free laborers. To tie them to the plantation economy as wageworkers, the bill prohibited subsidized immigrants to purchase, lease, rent, or otherwise obtain the use of land for three years, unless they fully repaid the expenses of their immigration. These same conditions also prevented them from establishing any commercial enterprise, including peddling.

Thus, the 1842 bill adopted Wakefield's theories by ending free access to land, increasing its cost significantly through sales, taxes, fees, and minimum lot sizes, and directing the funds generated to immigration. However, the Brazilian version went beyond his proposal to use a rigged market mechanism to supply and retain workers. Brazilian planters added restrictive measures to prevent them from becoming independent, in effect by gutting the development of a market in either free labor or land. Moreover, whereas in Wakefield's scheme private capitalists financed the immigration of workers, in Brazil's the state assumed the costs by collecting targeted revenues from all landholders. The importation of free labor to substitute for slaves would be a state project, not a market one.

Many deputies, especially among the Liberal Party, found the bill's measures of land reform outrageous. They complained bitterly that to limit the size of *posses* constituted an attack on property itself and betrayed generations of squatter latifundistas, that the land taxes and fees amounted to extortion, that the survey required for validation was both too corruptible and expensive to be feasible, that the bill inflated land values artificially, and that the need to acquire it at such high prices would bankrupt planters. To get the bill passed, the government retreated. It either modified or withdrew some of the offending provisions. But on the matter of inflating the value of land, the government held firm. The bill's principal sponsor, Rodrigues Torres, justified this outcome as deliberate, because it was the means to deny immigrants access to landed property: "We want to keep free workers, who come to us from other parts of the world, from being able to arrive in Brazil and, instead of working for the landowners for some time at least . . . find crown land immediately" (cited in Dean 1971: 614).

Although the bill finally passed the Chamber of Deputies, the Conservative government fell a few months later to Liberals, who tabled it in the Senate. There it languished for nearly seven years, until the return of the Conservatives in late 1849. During the interim, however, relevant conditions at home and abroad had changed. In Brazil, the end of the slave trade under British pounding had become inescapable.[25] That realization made the need for new labor even more urgent. Correspondingly, as investment in the traffic of slaves became insecure, Brazilian capital sought new markets. Real estate was one. But violence discouraged investment, and land conflict had become epidemic with the prolonged absence of both legal alternatives to squatting and legalized surveys to secure property rights. Internationally, Brazilians learned that the application of Wakefield's theories in Australia had failed. Instead, they increasingly perceived that the United States had achieved economic success by using cheap land to attract European immigrants to become smallholding producers and the sale of public lands to finance immigration. Moreover, many

Brazilian abolitionists viewed the American combination of slave and free-immigrant labor as evidence that the two could be successfully mixed in Brazil as a means to engineer a gradual termination of slavery.[26]

As a result of these changing perceptions, progressives in Brazil like Tavares Bastos and Heinrich Handelmann (the German-born author of an important history of Brazil published there in 1860) began to argue that development for new nations now depended on competing for the best European immigrants. Creating conditions for "spontaneous immigration," as they called it, meant vying with the United States, as well as Australia and Argentina. But they realized that Brazil would not succeed in this international competition if all it had to offer immigrants was toil alongside slaves on plantations or insecure property. For example, Handelmann (1982: 344–49) reports that although a number of German colonies had been founded in the south of Brazil on land donated by the Crown, they existed under constant threat of losing their lands to *posseiros* who claimed to be legitimate holders. To this fate, they were abandoned by the central government, which had neither the resources nor the power to compete with local elites.[27] As a result, European immigration to Brazil by small freeholders was a comparative failure: it averaged a mere five hundred a year before 1850. Handelmann records that in 1855 there existed in all Brazil only about eighty colonies of immigrant agriculturalists, totaling approximately forty thousand people—about the number immigrating to the United States, he observes pointedly, every few months.

Thus, when the new Conservative government revived the 1842 bill in 1850, its original objectives of labor substitution, subsidized immigration, and land regulation compelled even greater attention. However, the linking of land and labor reform now included new arguments for smallholding, competitive immigration, gradual abolition, and land markets that changed the legislative initiative. The government continued to emphasize the need to attract European immigrants to solve labor shortages on the estates. But it also justified reviving the reform in terms that would enable immigrants, as independent producers, to make the vast lands of Brazil productive and thereby competitive with the United States.[28] To these larger ends, the government of the Marquis of Monte Alegre embarked on an ambitious project of state building and national economic development. In 1850, it pushed through parliament a law effectively ending the slave trade (Euzébio de Queiroz Law), adopted Brazil's first commercial code, founded several national banks (including a reestablished Bank of Brazil and the Rural and Mortgage Bank), and inaugurated both telegraph communication and railroad construction. In the same year, it also passed Brazil's first comprehensive land law, uniting, after so many decades of debate, land reform and immigration initiative.

THE LAND LAW OF 1850

In matters of land reform, Law 601 of September 1850 reiterated the principal points of the original bill. It prohibited the acquisition of Crown land (*terra devoluta*) by means other than sale, recognized earlier *sesmarias* and *posses* but terminated them as means for future claims, established a new legal regime of public and private property, and transformed land into a market commodity. It deemed all other means of acquiring *terra devoluta* a crime punishable by fines and imprisonment, similar to encroachments on private lands. All *sesmarias* and *posses* had to be validated and legitimated, but only land in productive use qualified. As defined in the law, this included cultivation and habitual residence. Unproductive holdings "devolved" to the Crown. In addition to productive use, validation required measurement, registration, and payment of fees, with specified deadlines and penalties. Upon completion of these requirements, the state would issue a title of property ownership, without which land could not be legally sold or mortgaged.[29] Additionally, the law authorized the central government to undertake a national survey of public lands, which would discriminate private properties in the process, and to establish a national registry of landholdings to which all property owners had to conform. It empowered the government to auction these public lands, once surveyed, in gridded lots of about a half-square-mile each.[30]

To stimulate immigration, the land law offered immigrants several incentives and imposed none of the restrictions of the original bill on their purchasing land or engaging in commerce. Rather, immigrants who bought land and resided on it would be rewarded with naturalization after two years. Moreover, they were exempted from serving in the military, although not from the municipally based National Guard. The law directed the Treasury to use funds generated from land sales and regularization to finance the national land survey and to bring a certain number of free immigrants to Brazil annually. It also determined that these state-subsidized immigrants had to work as employees for prespecified periods of time and at jobs the government had prearranged, either in agriculture, public or private works managed by a public administration, or in the creation of independent immigrant settlements (*colônias*).

The Land Law of 1850 entered Brazilian history as a somewhat tepid accommodation of competing interests for land and labor reform. It was modest in many aspects and daring in just a few. Nevertheless, the law and its supporting legislation created a framework of concepts, strategies, and stipulations, as well as contradictions and consequences, that structured the organization of and access to landed property directly for the next forty years and indirectly for another century. The law struck a compromise between those intent on supplying the plantations with the new labor of immigrants by denying them access to land and those intent on promoting the settlement of independent producers. It abandoned the most controversial aspects of Wakefield's system by eliminating earlier restrictions on landownership. Instead, it encouraged smallholding in various measures and sponsored the American idea that the state should make public land available to settlers at public auction in previously surveyed and subdivided lots. Thus, it significantly reduced the size and expense of lots surveyed for sale, offered a few other incentives to settlers who purchased, and created a mechanism (however underfunded) to subsidize immigration.

However, the land law did not "completely abandon" Wakefield, as some suggest (e.g., Dean 1971: 618). Rather, at the same time that it seemed to encourage independent smallholding, it also retained the fundamental Wakefieldian principle that immigrants should not have easy access to land. First, it maintained the crucial obstacle that the state must sell and not grant public land. Thus, it affirmed Wakefield's system of financing the importation of free labor through land sales and bureaucratic fees. Second, in extinguishing the institution of *posse* as a legitimate means to property and criminalizing its practice thereafter, the law eliminated the customary if not the only way the poor obtained land. When we realize that the law established these obstacles for Brazilian citizens as well as for new immigrants (and future citizens), its scope as a means to restrict access to property becomes more apparent.

These limitations were already clear to Deputy Tavares Bastos (1939a) when he published his critical study in 1867 of the effects of land policy on immigration. He used comparative data from the United States, Australia, and Argentina to show that Brazil was not competitive in attracting immigrants for a variety of reasons: immense and unproductive *sesmarias* and *posses* monopolized the best lands; slavery gave Brazil a repellent image abroad; the absence of a national land survey rendered land tenure insecure; and there were too few financial incentives for immigrants. Yet the most significant liability in his opinion was that the state's system of selling land, instituted by the 1850 Land Law, failed to open Brazil's immense territory to citizen and immigrant alike for productive use and the generation of wealth. Achieving these results required a regime of "modern democracy" and not simply the auction of public lands.[31]

Tavares Bastos indicated three problems. First, land measurement was five times more expensive in Brazil than in the United States. Second, although the price of Brazilian public land was less, that it had a price at all discouraged immigration because most land had little market value.[32] As a result, "all refuse to buy lots [in Brazil's interior] because the price, even though the legal minimum, is greater than that of private lands in the area ... the monetary value [of which] is insignificant" (1939a: 83). Third, the United States, Australia, and Canada had dropped their prices for public lands since 1850. The United States adopted a graduated scale in 1854 and then legislated a massive giveaway with the Homestead Act in 1862. This law gave American citizens and foreign immigrants the right to a homestead on surveyed public lands, not exceeding 160 acres, at practically no cost.[33]

Brazil had nothing remotely similar. Regulations of the Land Law in 1854 and 1858 merely allowed installment purchases, which, however, increased the minimum price of land by 100% to 150%. Furthermore, a decree in 1867 raised the price of land in immigrant colonies far above that of the maximum in the United States and added another 20% if bought through installments. Although the Brazilian price included a provisional house, survey, and cleared land, Tavares Bastos (1939a: 86) points out that these benefits were irrelevant because the initial cost was prohibitive for most immigrants. Thus, Brazil raised the price of national lands just as its international competitors reduced theirs to attract immigrants to populate their interior regions.

Tavares Bastos reached two conclusions. First, Brazil's attempt to finance the European immigration of either laborers or freeholders with funds from land sales had failed. Second, the land law actually impeded access to land and its productive development for both immigrant and citizen. The combination was pernicious. In the absence of effective land regulation and favorable terms of acquisition, little public land was sold. Without sales, little revenue was generated either to sponsor immigration or to advance land regulation, the lack of which further hindered sales. Contrasts with the United States were stark.[34] As a result, Tavares Bastos recommended that in most of Brazil, the state cede surveyed lots of public land free of charge to immigrants—though he did not, apparently, include Brazil's own citizens in this recommendation.

While the 1850 law remained in force until 1891, there is no doubt that it failed miserably in all but one of its objectives to regulate landholding, finance immigration through land sales, supply immigrants to work on the plantations, open Brazil's territory to productive use, institute a secure legal regime of property, prevent seizure of public lands, and increase state authority. However, one intent achieved remarkable effectiveness, the consequences of which resound to this day: on a national scale, the law impeded the access of poor immigrants and citizens to small-scale property. It is the case, therefore, that the law's implementation simultaneously failed and succeeded. As a failed instrument of state rule, it generated contradiction and confusion that, we shall shortly see, many used for stratagem and profit and many others suffered as violence, but that in either case eroded state rule and its objectives of land reform. As effective legislation, it has been a source of extraordinary inequality and injustice in Brazilian society.

In response to its perceived failures, the state issued two regulations, eight decrees, and more than a hundred notices (*avisos*). The government also sponsored two reform bills in the 1880s aimed at overhauling the law in one way or another, though neither proposed free concessions of plots and one increased land prices. But the many rulings had little effect and the reform measures were never brought to a vote. Instead, the law eventually became a dead letter with the end of the Empire. In 1891, as part of its general plan of decentralization, the Republic's constitution transferred all uncultivated public lands (*terras devolutas*) to the new state governments. That transfer amounted to more than 80% of the nation's territory! After that, Brazil had no national land policy until the 1960s. However, as the problem of land reform remained unresolved, the convoluted terms of the 1850 law and related legislation were reiterated in state governments, where local elites retained even more control. Thus, at both the state and, by default, national levels, the 1850 framework of contradictory objectives in land law continued to structure conflict about property.[35]

With regard to labor, the issue of immigration gradually became dissociated from land reform. For a variety of reasons—from changes in technology that decreased the urgency for new labor on coffee plantations to the refusal of landowners to bear the costs of immigration as a solution to their labor problems—land reform lost appeal as a means to achieve the substitution of immigrants for slaves. As abolition appeared certain and land reform dead, European immigration began to be funded in the 1870s directly from the government's general budget. As such, it became subsidized by the entire population of taxpayers and not just by the much smaller subset of landowners.

Although immigration policy thus changed, the important point for my purposes is that the distribution of and access to landed property did not. Under new policies, the central state began to subsidize special companies and associations to import and settle immigrants. As a result, immigration became a profitable business, as some companies became employment recruiters for the plantations and others received free public land that they were supposed to subdivide and sell to immigrants. The latter enterprise had particular importance for the settlement (and legal chaos) of the urban peripheries of São Paulo—in precisely the neighborhoods of my own fieldwork, as the next chapters show. After the fall of the Empire, the new republican state governments took charge in financing this immigration: between 1889 and 1900, approximately four-fifths of the 750,000 immigrants who arrived in São Paulo had their transatlantic passage subsidized by the state government (Morse 1970: 19). At first, most of these subsidized immigrants became landless laborers on the coffee estates, replacing slaves as planters had hoped. However, as soon as they amassed enough money, they moved to the cities, where they rented accommodations and worked as artisans and merchants.[36] Only in southern Brazil did significant small-scale freeholding develop, as provincial governments there gave immigrants plots of land to form self-sufficient communities.

In the rest of Brazil, especially in the Southeast where almost 70% of the foreign-born lived, most immigrants joined the urban poor as renters. Thus, these immigrants abandoned agriculture altogether. They neither took up the labor of slaves for long nor became independent producers on the land. Rather, they became a new and propertyless urban poor. A census in 1920, the earliest record I can find concerning residential tenure, makes this point unambiguously: 79% of the domiciles in the city of São Paulo were rented and only 19% owned by their occupants (Bonduki 1983: 146). The effect on the countryside of this concentration of landless people in the cities is equally clear: in the same year, the census records that almost 80% of the national territory remained uninhabited and uncultivated public lands.

In sum, the 1850 Land Law succeeded, if it can be called that, only in preventing small-scale property ownership among the masses of Brazilians, among citizen and foreigner, free and freed, rural and urban. Instead, Brazilians remained overwhelmingly propertyless for the next hundred years and their country's immense interior mostly desolate even today. The demographic record substantiates this conclusion unequivocally. Although the Central West and the North together encompass over 64% of Brazil's territory, they contained just 6% of its population in 1872 and only 9% a century later. The population density of this colossal region was less than one inhabitant per square kilometer in the census of 1872 and less than four in that of 1970 (IBGE). Even a contemporary map shows that only the strip along the coast, extending four to six hundred kilometers into the interior, has dense and continuous occupation. Beyond that, Brazil appears empty (IBGE 2000). Moreover, although sparsely populated, the great expanses of Brazilian land still remain concentrated in the hands of a few: 1.7% of the population owns nearly 50% of the arable land.

Frei Vicente do Salvador (1931: 19) created a famous image of this Brazil when he wrote that Brazilians have "clung to the coast like crabs for over four centuries." But rather than suppose that this clinging is voluntary, the evidence indicates that as Brazil's competitor nations populated their interiors during the nineteenth century, the Land Law of 1850 anchored most Brazilians on the coast as a source of cheap landless labor. In this

135

result, access to landed property paralleled access to political citizenship: both became and remained far more restrictive in Brazil by the end of the nineteenth century.

Land Law and Market Become Accomplices of Fraud

While we already know that the 1850 Land Law's overarching objective of land reform failed, it is important to analyze the terms of its failure for two reasons. First, many remain in force today. Second, they directly conditioned the development of the urban peripheries, and thus their insurgent citizenships, because much of these hinterlands was *terra devoluta* until the late 1960s. Hence, when the urban migrants settled there, they confronted the consequences of failed land reform. The reform measures had five principal components, each of which failed and in failing were perversely productive: to establish that future access to public lands depended solely on purchase; to submit existing holdings to validation; to transform those deemed legitimate into private property through a bureaucratic process that included demarcation, registration, and taxes, and to "devolve" those deemed illegitimate; to designate the remaining devolved holdings and unoccupied lands as national public land; and to establish a new legal regime of private property ownership based on free markets. Thus, the land reform proposed to determine the legal norms by which Brazil's vast national territory would be settled and to bring order to existing occupation by means of a new national regime of real property.

It created the latter by transforming land into a market commodity. Before the 1850 Land Law, property was a public patrimony transferred to private use by concession for specific purposes, primarily cultivation. Legitimate property ownership thus required productive use of the land. Failure to meet this condition of consignment resulted in forfeiture of ownership and return of land to public patrimony. The Land Law terminated this type of property with regard to private possession. Instead, it created a regime in which property became a private patrimony alienated by contract between individuals. Thus the law represents a transition between two concepts of property, each based on a different regime of ownership: tenurial versus allodial. In the first, the essential meaning of property resides in the use to which its holder puts his rights; in the second, its meaning resides in the value the possession of those rights gives to the holder.[37]

Planter elites were motivated to commodify land because, with the end of the slave trade, they needed to find new forms of capital investment. They also wanted to use land instead of slaves to guarantee loans. Both required not only the creation of a legitimate real estate market to generate and maintain land values. The effective commodification of land also depended on the security of its title. Without it, the rights of ownership, especially those of possession and alienation, were vulnerable to legal challenge. That insecurity threatened the value of land as an asset and all aspects of its market negotiation. The only way to guarantee the validity of one title was to regulate all titles by identifying each legitimate property through legal survey and documenting the results with a unique deed of national registration.

But such land regulation proved impossible. In 1878, the Minister of Agriculture admitted that the national land survey was an "abandoned task."[38] Not only did landholders large and small resist actually legalizing their land. Especially among planters and entrepreneurs, they also sought to cloak their land claims in the appearance of legality because, above all, they profited from the chaos of land tenure. Several factors resulted in this unstable and perverse relation between the illegal and the legal—a kind of negative synergy between effective illegalization and false legalization. Landholders resisted because the law established financial disincentives: they had to bear the expenses of demarcation and registration and then pay taxes on the legalized property. More important, payment did not guarantee security. Everyone knew that the central state was incapable of enforcing property rights and that most landholders benefited from this incapacity. Enforcement depended on local police and militia, which were controlled by the larger landowners. Moreover, legalization froze the fluid incorporation of new lands on which their agricultural production generally depended. Hence, they wanted neither property rights enforced nor public lands discriminated from private because the opposite conditions better served their interests: they appropriated *terras devolutas* wherever they could and unscrupulously evicted weaker settlers wherever they encountered them in agriculturally productive areas, especially from *posses*.[39] Furthermore, with the creation of the real estate market, land speculators tried to claim and sell as much land as they could, often several times over. To do that, they expelled occupants, even those who had paid. Thus, smaller-scale *posseiros* were especially vulnerable to eviction and felt unprotected by the very law they were asked to oblige. As long as land seemed limitless, therefore, most landholders had good reason to oppose regularization.

The central government thus found itself depending on the very local forces least committed to regularization. Observers (e.g., Silva 1996: 175–76; Carvalho 1981) agree that this situation resulted from a deep conflict within the imperial state between centralizing and decentralizing forces. Although the former used the land laws of 1850 and 1854 to consolidate imperial authority over key issues of state (land reform and immigration), they had to decentralize implementation to gain passage. As a result, the laws conceded control of demarcation to the president of each province and the local authorities he appointed. Moreover, each *sesmeiro* or *posseiro* had to initiate regularization by asking these officials to measure his land at his own expense. Some jurists even argued that productive landholders could do so at their discretion. Only after the private properties in an area had been thus surveyed could the government identify the residual lands as *terras devolutas* and offer them for sale and colonization. As Silva (1996: 178) rightly concludes, this sequence short-circuited implementation, for both land reform and immigration depended on private initiative that was not forthcoming.

However, landholders also wanted the appearance of legality. As the new legislation created many new kinds and layers of illegalities that might eventually result in forfeiture, it was always better to have a foothold in the legal: better to sustain possession, defend a claim, sell on the market, extend a deadline, use as collateral, leave to heirs, confuse opponents, and so forth. To create such footholds, landholders engaged the law at its weakest points, complied only with its least significant aspects, exploited every ambiguity of definition, and practiced both gross and subtle fraud. I have already stressed that deception, subterfuge, stratagem, and complication shaped Brazil's settlement from the beginning. The 1850 Land Law refocused these attributes and gave them their contemporary significance. It not only provided strategists with an unprecedented regulatory technology to manipulate, but also seeded the real estate market it created with a new cast of manipulators. In addition to established landholders, a novel sort of land pirate emerged to exploit the law and the market. This was the outright swindler, called a *grileiro*, who pretended to have legitimate title to the land he sold through a vast repertoire of deceptions. The land scam itself is a *grilagem* and the land thus held or sold a *grilo*.[40] In fact, existing landholders also practiced *grilagem*, as *grileiros* usually established some sort of physical possession to market the land, thereby becoming *posseiros*, and more established *posseiros* regularly sold their possessions illegally. In such manner, the term *grilagem* became synonymous with illegal land practices of whatever stripe, and the *grileiro*—produced in response to the 1850 Land Law in assorted hues—became a permanent feature of the Brazilian landscape.

As the real estate market gave new purpose and synthesis to many old practices of deception, the 1850 Law initiated an era of unprecedented land fraud. During the second half of the nineteenth century, land grabbers refined the technique of manipulating law that became forevermore the trademark of *grilagem*: they gave claims to encroached lands a cloak of legality by involving them in what appear to be legitimate transactions. The two-fold objective of this strategy is to build a dossier of documents attesting to what would be a legal transaction in each case if it were grounded in legitimate property rights and, thereby, to involve as many people as possible in the apparent recognition of the usurper's claim. There are as many versions of this stratagem as there are regulations about land. To immerse the property in a web of legitimate transactions, a *grileiro/* landholder might pay taxes on his *posse*, sell a piece of it, donate part to a religious organization, have it surveyed, use it as collateral for a loan, bequeath it, or give it as dowry. His inheritors and business partners would continue to accumulate such transactions, making sure to pay at least some of the required fees and taxes. Most important, they would dutifully record them in the ledger of the local parish, which served in many places as the first registry.

All the accumulated paper of these transactions—the receipts, wills, permits, surveys, bonds, ledger pages, and so on—was proof that the state and the church had sanctioned them. The stratagems of *grilagem* require, therefore, considerable legal knowledge and use it to dissimulate usurpation and fraud within a web of legitimate claims. Although he aims to exploit this web for immediate financial gain, the *grileiro* generally has a more profound objective: to encumber such legitimate claims with too many social relations with the passage of time to dismantle, so that legalization of the illegal by executive decree, legislative act, or judicial decision becomes inevitable. In this kind of complication, fraud finds an accomplice in law.

Three legal ambiguities have been fundamental to the *grileiro*'s stock-in-trade since this period. Describing them here will save effort in the next chapters, where it becomes clear how important they remain in structuring land and citizenship conflict in the urban peripheries of São Paulo. First is the apparent contradiction in law between illegal and adverse possession; second, the definition of *terra devoluta*; and third, the matter of registration. A main objective of the 1850 Land Law was to prohibit the acquisition of public land by any means other than purchase. Hence, it made *posse* illegal. In so doing, it turned new *posseiros* into malefactors. This interdiction not only negated a method of occupying land without title that had been legally recognized as customary practice. It also seemed to contradict the ancient and perfectly valid legal right to acquire property by "prescription," called *prescrição aquisitiva* or *usucapião* in Portuguese and best translated by the common-law concept of adverse possession. If planters thought it both impossible and unwise to prohibit *posse*, many jurists resisted the Empire's assertion that public lands could not be acquired by *usucapião*.

This principle refers to the method of acquiring absolute title to land, as against all others including the owner of record, through its continuous possession for a statutory period of time. Depending on the situation, this

139

uninterrupted period is typically twenty-five or thirty years, but may be much less. The key is that possession must be not only continuous, definite, and exclusive, but also, as lawyers say, notorious (visible, undisguised, and open, to the point of being generally recognized) and hostile (actual occupation without the permission of anyone claiming paramount title, coupled with the occupier's claim of ownership).[41] In Brazilian law (as in American), *usucapião* is considered a fundamental guarantee of property rights because, in the last analysis, it supercedes all other claims of ownership, ending doubts and conflicts about tenure. Indeed, in many common circumstances of settlement, where proof of ownership may have been lost, nonexistent, or erroneously recorded, it is the only means to do so.

The ambiguity that led to much confusion and fraud is whether or not public lands, *terras devolutas*, could be acquired by *usucapião*. From 1850 on, many leading jurists have debated this question, including Teixeira de Freitas, Messias Junqueira, Azevedo Marques, and Cirne Lima. Still unresolved, the current law and constitution continue to refine the issue. Many jurists have argued through the years that as a category of things, *terras devolutas* were indeed susceptible to acquisition by prescription but that the Land Law made the essential component of this process, possession, illegal. To confuse matters more, its Article 8 appeared to allow *posseiros* with "effective cultivation" and "habitual residence" to retain possession of their land (i.e., *terras devolutas*), but with no rights of ownership. In these directives, the law was open to doubt in apparently contradicting adverse possession as a basic guarantee of property rights. Subsequent legislation on the matter, up to the present, seems to contribute little more than confusion of intention to the extraordinary confusion of fact in land tenure.[42]

In part, these doubts depended on another, namely, the meaning of *terra devoluta*, itself open to various interpretations. Since colonization, devolved lands referred to those holdings returned to Crown patrimony for violating their terms of concession. It was also common, though perhaps not technically legal, to use the expression to mean empty or unoccupied lands.[43] The 1850 Land Law ratified both senses. Moreover, it used the term to designate the national public lands it created as a residual category left over after the discrimination of private property. Jurists debated the extent to which each sense applied. Did the law's overall purpose to encourage the productive use of land mean that these criteria applied universally, to all types of tenure with claims of ownership? Did they apply to the new regime of private property, which was no longer based on concession?

In evaluating property claims, these questions were especially thorny, as the state never succeeded in knowing definitively which lands were public and which private. Moreover, it seemed patent that owners with titles issued after 1850 could leave their property uncultivated without penalty, as it was now their private commodity. The same liberty presumably applied to those with claims to property instituted after 1850 but not yet resolved. Thus, it seemed plausible that the original legal sense of "devolved" should apply only to lands occupied before the new regime of private property went into effect in 1850. These possibilities opened innumerable opportunities for manipulation. For example, those who created a *posse* with cultivation after 1850 could register their holding with an earlier date in the local parish registry and then use the fact of cultivation to legitimate their claim. However, all holdings without legal title, even if productively used, were liable to become empty public lands by residual definition and were thereby vulnerable to the schemes of clever *grileiros*. In effect, the layering of ambiguities in the meaning and use of these terms became a windfall for swindlers.

Competing forms of registration also constituted a font of confusion over title. Before 1850, the state considered legal two modes of private transaction involving land, neither of which conferred title because that could be granted only by direct concession from the Crown. First, private land transactions were legalized by drafting their terms as a document written into the official records of any governmental bureaucracy, institution, or office—most commonly at treasury offices. Such a written act (*termo lavrado*) constituted a legally binding contract. Second, the state also recognized, though more nebulously, that certain customary rights applied to declarations written into parish records. *Posseiros* in particular used this local registry to document their holdings.

After the 1850 Land Law and its 1854 Regulation, these modes changed. The state claimed exclusive rights over empty and devolved lands, which, once discriminated and categorized as such, became part of its public domain. As public goods, they could only be alienated by an act of public administrative law, not private civil law, that generated a title registered with the newly created General Land Office. Private transactions of land—now including sale—continued to be contractually binding if recorded at any state office, under the rules of civil law. However, the regulatory law clearly stated (Art. 94) that declarations of landholding written into parish records did not confer rights of ownership. Complications arose because this very same law required all *posseiros* to register the extent of their holdings at their local parish and ordered these records combined into an official and national Parish Registry. The objective of this registry was informational: to provide the state with an initial survey of private holdings in an area. However, the parish priest was obliged to record declarations as *posseiros* (or anyone) wished and had no means of confirmation. It is not difficult to imagine the fiction that got written into the national Parish Registry.

Finally, ten years later, the 1864 Mortgage Law nullified the legal validity of land sales written into the public record at government offices. Instead, it declared valid only those terms of property conveyance transacted via the public written registration of titles issued by the state. In other words, the state limited the bona fide conveyance of property (by sale or other manner), and hence proof of ownership, to a specific type of registration (a "public transcription of title"), made at a specific government office (today, the Public Registry of Land) and according to specific bureaucratic rules.[44]

Each of these changes created its own anthology of deceptions. One still common is for a swindler to sell land to which he has no title by exhibiting documents that assert his ownership in terms of a previous transaction—perhaps originating in a parish registry—and that were legally registered in some public record (except the Land Registry). Finding a buyer, he draws up a contract and registers it at a Registry of Titles and Documents, a type of notary at which anyone can register anything. With the resulting stamped and notarized document, the *grileiro* has institutionalized a contract for payment. This contract may even have some validity between signatories. But it does not transfer ownership of property. Unknowing buyers therefore reside on the land illegally. From the perspective of the real owner—or of another *grileiro* who can make his claim stick—they are squatters and subject to eviction. Such a contract does, however, transfer financial opportunity to a buyer who understands the land game, for he has purchased an accumulation of legalized documents with which to perpetuate the same scam.

Illegality, Inequality, and Instability as Norms

Nineteenth-century land reform did create a new national regime of property to order existing and future settlement. But in the absence of land regulation and title security, it developed by confusion and treachery. One result was the perpetuation of extraordinary inequalities of property and wealth, coupled with lost economic growth. Another was the perpetuation of illegality as the norm of residence for most Brazilians and violent conflict over it. With regard to economic consequences, the strategy of selling land at a high price backfired completely. As the value of land at any price was insecure, few financial institutions or instruments developed to transform it into working capital. For example, banks were generally unwilling to accept land as collateral, for as long as land was plentiful and relatively worthless, borrowing and defaulting on a loan made more sense than repayment. As banks did not want to own land by way of foreclosure, they offered few mortgages, except at exorbitant rates. For the same reasons, they were reluctant to offer farmers credit on the basis of land guarantees, even though the Mortgage Law made it a principal objective. As a result, the land market and the laws structuring it deterred the extension of credit, and Brazil forfeited an entire economy of loan-driven development based on land.

Furthermore, the possession of land, even if occupied and productively used, was not in itself a useful basis on which to build personal wealth. As most families could not borrow against their land—or their houses for that matter—they found that neither were productive assets, even though they often required the most massive investments of their lives. Rather, their time, labor, and money became locked into possessions of little fungible value. While large-scale planters had other assets, those who held small properties were unable to capitalize on their investments as a means to build an equity-based wealth. Consequently, insecure property rights meant that even productive settlers remained asset poor and had their ability to develop through investment stunted. This problem of frozen assets took its modern form after 1850 and remains absolutely contemporary, especially affecting the autoconstructed urban periphery where the extraordinary investments of residents in their homes stagnate. For most of Brazil's population, the same logic that required upfront payment for land prevented the development of loans with accessible interest rates. Both conditions crippled their economic advancement and eliminated them from the legitimate real estate market.

Above all, the failed land reform created permanent instability in the countryside. Its legal complications established illegality as the rule of settlement, facilitated land fraud, and fostered violence. We shall see in the following chapters that this confusion became even greater when the states assumed control of *terras devolutas* during the Republic, as it directly structured the experience of the urbanizing poor in city hinterlands. Contradicting the 1850 Land Law, state legislation consistently favored the legalization of illegal occupations (i.e., *posses*) by sponsoring amnesties for illicit activity and extending deadlines for regularization. Whatever favored legalizing the illegal fueled the ambitions of the new land pirates, the *grileiros*, to compete with established latifundistas in what became a land grab of unprecedented scale and violence throughout Brazil. The *grileiros* appropriated land for speculation; latifundistas for estate building and speculation; and poor migrants for subsistence. The problem of each, however, was the same: to hold land long enough to reap the benefits of their objectives, namely, sale, legalization, or, more rarely, actual cultivation. Although at different scales, their strategy was therefore identical: to seize land and defend it against eviction.

With unguarded areas subject to seizure, all sides hired gunmen—known then as now as *capangas* and *jagunços*—to defend their stakes

143

and seize others. Local *coroneis* were the kingpins in this violence. Their control of resident militia and police, judges, surveyors, scribes, clerks, tax collectors, and other officials charged with maintaining land records made them central to the private appropriation of public lands. In the absence of effective state and federal authority—and sometimes in collusion with it—their private armies roamed the countryside, warring over land. Against these forces, the tenure of the small *posseiro* could only be temporary. The modest farmers, backlanders, ex-slaves, poor immigrants, and Indians who actually settled and cultivated *posses* suffered the most from this violence. Although they had only illegal access to land, through possession and not property, they were settlers who fulfilled the original legislative objective of productive land use. Nevertheless, the more powerful branded them squatters and pushed them off their lands. Indians especially were exterminated. Completing a vicious cycle, the landless were recruited as *capangas*. In the absence of any legal means to establish title, killings became routine as conflicting land claims multiplied unchecked.

The irony of this period of instability, especially violent from the Republic's inception through the 1930s, is that those small-scale holdings that managed to develop did not generally stem from state policy for settling immigrants on public lands. Rather, they resulted from the activities of *grileiros*, who claimed possession of large tracts and subdivided them into small plots for illegal sale. This was especially so in the interior of the state of São Paulo. In fact, many conservative and nationalist Paulistas promoted the extermination of Indians and the illegal appropriation of land as the twin means to burst the state's territory open to modern development. Like the robber barons of the American West, the land swindler-entrepreneurs thus had an ambivalent identity: they were necessary criminals, pirate patriots. Without them, the legions of poor migrants, whom these promoters lionized as fierce invader-civilizers, would never have access to the land. It is worth citing a passage from the eminent conservative Oliveira Vianna (1933: 113–15) to grasp the tenor of this promotion of illegality as the means of development.

This formidable assault on the forest has two original path-breakers: the Indian-killer [*bugreiro*] and the land-swindler [*grileiro*].[45] . . . In this work of civilizing conquest of the land, the Indian-killer triumphs over the material obstacle, which is the nomadic Indian, unfruitful populator of the fruitful forest. There is, however, another obstacle, a juridical obstacle, which is the right to property. Today, to the contrary of past times, there are no lands without owners: either they belong to private individuals, as survivals of the immense early land grants [*sesmarias*], or they are "devolved lands" and belong, in this case, to the state. These lands, when they do not belong to the state, remain unexplored and virgin but "appropriated" by retarded latifundistas, very full of the grandeur of their estates—"old long-beards who hold thousands of hectares to take from them one plate of beans and a few pigs" [citing his compatriot Monteiro Lobato]. It is the "*grileiro*" who manages to resolve this difficulty. It is he who is going to give to the progressive colonizer, full of ambition and means, the right to exploit this unfruitful treasure. To do this, he creates, by chicanery and by falsity, the indispensable title of property.[46]

In these emblematic texts of Oliveira Vianna and Monteiro Lobato, the laws of progress are clear: murder generates civilization and modernity; illegality produces legality and rights. The combination of genocide and usurpation creates property, wealth, and nation. This vision of national progress promotes a cast of characters and a set of processes that had been assembled during centuries of land and labor conflict. Paradoxically, these are also forces that will generate the urban peripheries and their insurgent citizenships during the next fifty years.

Chapter 5
Segregating the City

Urban peripheries developed in Brazil as the place of and for the laboring poor. After the 1930s, these hinterlands became practically the only areas in which both established workers and new migrants could secure a residential foothold in Brazil's industrializing urban economies. They did so by building a shack in a peripheral subdivision that was typically illegal and lacked most infrastructural services. As urban migration mushroomed in subsequent decades, so did this autoconstruction of distant hinterlands, far beyond the supervision of government and employers. At the same time, a new national state sought to modernize the organization of this urbanizing economy and society. Its objective was to articulate a new public sphere of citizenship in which to channel and regulate the new urban labor force. This chapter demonstrates that between 1930 and 1980, the development of the urban peripheries and the institutionalization of social rights based on urban labor consolidated a centrifugal pattern of segregation in Brazilian cities and modernized the already differentiated citizenship of Brazilians. Thus, spatial segregation and citizenship differentiation were concurrent processes in a project of national modernization. Having established these conditions, I show in the next part of the book that the inequalities and illegalities they created came back to bite: they motivated the insurgence of a new sphere of urban citizenship.

In analyzing these processes, I focus on the city of São Paulo, which I take as both pioneering and paradigmatic for urban Brazil. After considering the significance of the category "periphery," I examine the eviction of the working classes from São Paulo's center. This eviction established an enduring pattern of peripheral segregation and urbanization. I then discuss the autoconstruction of the peripheries and, finally, the formulation of a restrictive social citizenship for urban workers. Though not exclusively, I study these processes through the lens of the two neighborhoods in which I have done fieldwork since 1987. They are always inevitably in my mind when I think about the peripheries. One is Jardim das Camélias, a neighborhood of about fifteen thousand residents in the district of Vila Jacuí (formerly São Miguel Paulista) in the far northeastern periphery of the city. The other is Lar Nacional, a neighborhood of about three thousand residents in Sapopemba, a district also in the East Zone but on its southeastern edge (figures 1.2–1.7 and map 5.1).[1] Both neighborhoods began to develop intensively in the late 1960s. Although distinct in ways that will become apparent, both are typical of newer and poorer areas of the urban peripheries in which migrants or the children of migrants construct their own houses and typically hold low-wage jobs in the industrial and service sectors. No doubt, my analysis reflects the idiosyncrasies of these neighborhoods and their inhabitants. Nevertheless, I believe that their experiences of social inequality and residential illegality are common enough to indicate the whole of urban segregation and its counterpolitics.

Center and Periphery

The use of the word "periphery" in São Paulo to refer to lands at the margins of the city probably dates from the 1940s. But only in the 1960s did it become the popular way of designating the settlements of people beyond the city's perimeter of urbanized services and infrastructure. Only when the hinterlands were filling up with millions of poor residents did "periphery" replace the older terms "suburb" and "rural."[2] Then, moreover, a number of discourses arose that homogenized the vast heterogeneity of conditions in hinterland settlements into a singular politicized concept of "periphery." In this changing vocabulary, the notion of periphery does not refer to an excluded outer space of capitalism in which the underclasses supposedly exist. Rather, it refers to relations of mutual dependence—to social productions of space—in which component parts define each other through apparatuses of domination and response. Each comprises political, legal, social, and infrastructural elements whose interrelations change and whose discursive use sometimes homogenizes. Consequently, as both places and concepts, the key terms "periphery," "city," and "urban" shift in location and significance through time and juro-political contexts, which, in any case, are almost always lost in translation.

1.	Água Rasa	49.	Liberdade
2.	Alto de Pinheiros	50.	Limão
3.	Anhanguera	51.	Mandaqui
4.	Aricanduva	52.	Marsilac
5.	Artur Alvim	53.	Moema
6.	Barra Funda	54.	Moóca
7.	Bela Vista	55.	Morumbi
8.	Belém	56.	Parelheiros
9.	Bom Retiro	57.	Pari
10.	Brás	58.	Parque do Carmo
11.	Brasilândia	59.	Pedreira
12.	Butantã	60.	Penha
13.	Cachoeirinha	61.	Perdizes
14.	Cambuci	62.	Perus
15.	Campo Belo	63.	Pinheiros
16.	Campo Grande	64.	Pirituba
17.	Campo Limpo	65.	Ponte Rasa
18.	Cangaíba	66.	Raposo Tavares
19.	Capão Redondo	67.	República
20.	Carrão	68.	Rio Pequeno
21.	Casa Verde	69.	Sacomã
22.	Cidade Ademar	70.	Santa Cecília
23.	Cidade Dutra	71.	Santana
24.	Cidade Lider	72.	Santo Amaro
25.	Cidade Tiradentes	73.	São Domingos
26.	Consolação	74.	São Lucas
27.	Cursino	75.	São Mateus
28.	Ermelino Matarazzo	76.	São Miguel
29.	Freguesia do Ó	77.	São Rafael
30.	Grajaú	78.	Sapopemba
31.	Guaianazes	79.	Saúde
32.	Iguatemi	80.	Sé
33.	Ipiranga	81.	Socorro
34.	Itaim Bibi	82.	Tatuapé
34.	Itaim Paulista	83.	Tremembé
36.	Itaquera	84.	Tucuruvi
37.	Jabaquara	85.	Vila Andrade
38.	Jaçanã	86.	Vila Curuçá
39.	Jaguara	87.	Vila Formosa
40.	Jaguaré	88.	Vila Guilherme
41.	Jaraguá	89.	Vila Jacuí
42.	Jardim Ângela	90.	Vila Leopoldina
43.	Jardim Helena	91.	Vila Maria
44.	Jardim Paulista	92.	Vila Mariana
45.	Jardim São Luís	93.	Vila Matilde
46.	José Bonifácio	94.	Vila Medeiros
47.	Lajeado	95.	Vila Prudente
48.	Lapa	96.	Vila Sônia

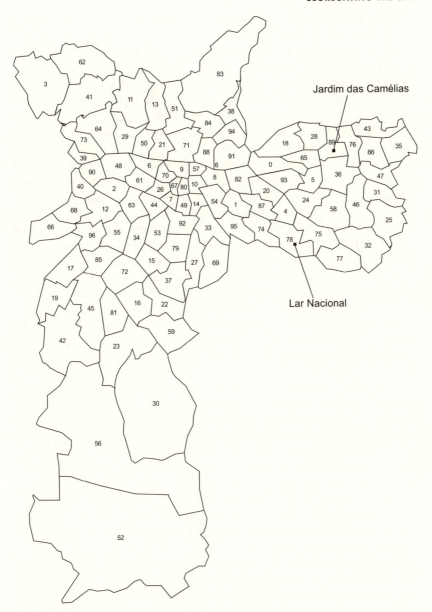

MAP 5.1. Districts of the municipality of São Paulo, 2000.

Thus cities have a different political meaning in Brazil than in the United States. In Brazil, they are defined by bureaucratic position in the administration of government, regardless of their size. Within the hierarchy of this administrative-political organization, the smallest unit of autonomy is the municipality. It is ruled by its own "organic laws" and governed by a mayor and council. The location of this municipal government, its headquarters, has the legal status of "city" (*cidade*). Therefore, in this juro-political sense, a city is the seat of municipal government, and every city is legally defined as the capital of a municipality. What determines this status is administrative power, not population size or density as in the United States. Thus, there are many cities in Brazil with less than two thousand residents and a few with less than two hundred. To facilitate rule, each municipality is divided into administrative units called districts, each having a seat with the status *vila*. Unlike in the United States, where a city and the county in which it is located have different incorporations and often administrations, a Brazilian city is not incorporated separately from its municipality. Rather, a city is the command center of its surrounding region, an idea of extensive social organization embodied in central offices. It is the concentration of power (governmental, judicial, educational, ecclesiastical, cultural, commercial, and so on) that rules the municipality, headquartered in institutions typically set around a central square. Strictly speaking, that square would be the most precise spatial referent of "city".

Colloquially, the spatial notion of "city" also typically designates the area of a municipality that is "urbanized," in the sense of having infrastructure identified with city life.[3] Yet the core definition of city remains juro-political, as each municipality defines by law what it designates as urban and rural. Thus "the urban" refers legally to the area of a municipal seat, a district seat, or to what is sometimes termed an isolated urban area, in each case according to criteria that are political and that therefore vary among municipalities. In fact, though rare, a municipal seat in a remote region could be urban politically but unurbanized infrastructurally. The inverse is unlikely, because urbanization generally results from political power and in reclassification as urban.[4]

My point is that as the designations "city", "urban", and "rural" are politically defined, they are subject to political manipulation and consequence. The legal definitions of São Paulo's hinterlands as overwhelmingly rural until the mid-1960s and of its roads as private, for example, had enormous significance for their development as periphery. These definitions meant that developers could forgo the requirements of urban legislation in subdividing the land. The result was perverse. As these subdivisions grew and were incorporated into the urban area of the municipality by new legislation, they became instantly illegal according to the very statutes that had been ignored. Moreover, as rural subdivisions were not entitled to the same municipal resources as urban, pioneering residents had to struggle politically to obtain urban services and infrastructure. Although technically based in the legislation of urban incorporation, the popular concept of periphery that emerged referred to these politicized residential conditions of poverty, administrative inequality, illegality, mobilization, and urbanization. It became the common reference term precisely as more people experienced these conditions.

If one can say that every Brazilian municipality has its city (politically powerful and replete with the urban resources available) and its hinterland (dependent, rural, and generally unurbanized), the emergence of the peripheries as a political force transformed this historical difference in São Paulo and many other cities. As millions of house-building and productively employed residents settled hinterlands, they asserted political power and urbanized their neighborhoods. Doing so, they transformed hinterland into city in fact and law. What began as the one turned into the other, as hinterlands became organized, urbanized, and urban (compare figures 1.1–1.7). Map 5.2 illustrates the extraordinary rate of São Paulo's urbanization and map 5.3 and table 5.1 its equally extraordinary population growth. By the end of the 1920s, the urbanized area of its metropolitan region—entirely within the municipality of São Paulo—had reached approximately 180 km². Over the next thirty-five years, it tripled. By the end of the 1990s, it had increased by another two-thirds to approximately 900 km² (Sempla 1995: 30). This peripheral expansion of people and city followed the push of new settlers into ever more distant areas of the hinterlands in search of affordable land. In general, those districts with the lowest population density—that is, those at the expanding perimeter of development—have the highest population growth. As the area of the peripheries is not constant, it is difficult to estimate their total population. Nevertheless, considering the number of residents in districts that qualify unambiguously in each decennial census since 1950, I estimate that the peripheries have consistently contained more than half of São Paulo's population. My rough estimate suggests that this share peaked in the 1960s, when as much as two-thirds of the municipal population lived in the peripheries. By 1970, settlers had crossed the eastern, northern, and western municipal boundaries, bringing urbanization to the surrounding municipalities of the metropolitan region as well. Similar processes of peripheralization have transformed every other major Brazilian city.[5]

As the leading edge of this expansion eroded the hinterland, the term "periphery" came to refer not only to the way the poor constructed the city through their house building and urbanization. The periphery also became and remains the place of and for the poor in São Paulo. Map 5.4 makes clear in one glance the persistence of this segregation based on

151

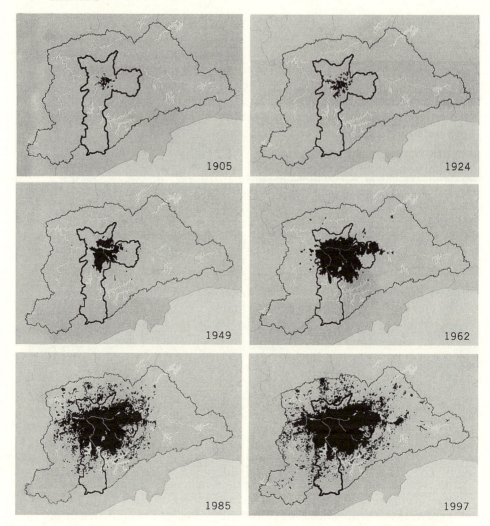

MAP 5.2. Expansion of urbanized area, metropolitan region of São Paulo, 1905–1997. Heavy line delineates the municipality of São Paulo; lighter line, the metropolitan region. *Source:* Meyer, Grostein, and Biderman 2004: 43.

the peripheralization of poverty, despite the remarkable improvements evident in figures 1.2–1.5. In 2000, only twelve districts out of São Paulo's ninety-six had an average monthly income for heads of households greater than twenty minimum salaries (MS)—the amount considered minimally necessary for one person to afford comfortable middle-class living. These districts contained merely 8% of the city's population and

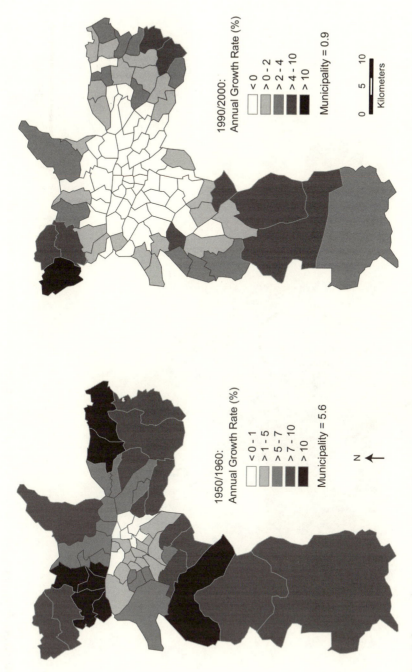

Map 5.3. Population growth rate by district, municipality of São Paulo, 1950/1960 and 1990/2000. *Source:* Caldeira 1984: 31; IBGE 1960; IBGE 2000.

1990/2000:
Annual Growth Rate (%)

< 0
> 0 - 2
> 2 - 4
> 4 - 10
> 10

Municipality = 0.9

0   5   10
Kilometers

1950/1960:
Annual Growth Rate (%)

< 0 - 1
> 1 - 5
> 5 - 7
> 7 - 10
> 10

N

Municipality = 5.6

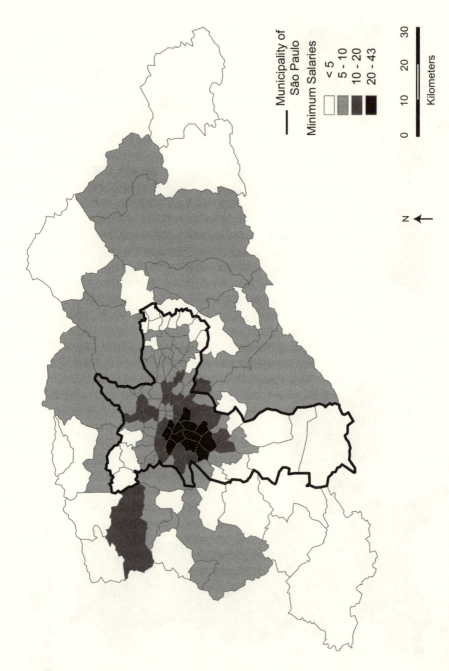

MAP 5.4. Average income of household heads in minimum salaries, metropolitan region of São Paulo, 2000. *Source:* IBGE 2000.

Municipality of
São Paulo

Minimum Salaries

< 5
5 - 10
10 - 20
20 - 43

N

0   10   20   30

Kilometers

Table 5.1

Population Growth: Municipality and Metropolitan Region of São Paulo, 1872–2000

Year	Municipality	Annual Growth Rate (%)	Metropolitan Region	Annual Growth Rate (%)
1872	31,385	–	–	–
1890	64,934	4.1	–	–
1900	239,820	14.0	–	–
1920	579,033	4.5	–	–
1940	1,326,261	4.2	1,568,045	–
1950	2,198,096	5.2	2,662,786	5.4
1960	3,781,446	5.6	4,739,406	5.9
1970	5,924,615	4.6	8,139,730	5.6
1980	8,493,226	3.7	12,588,725	4.5
1991	9,646,185	1.2	15,444,941	1.9
2000	10,434,252	0.9	17,878,703	1.6

Source: IBGE 1950–2000; SEADE 2000.

are all either central or concentrated just southwest of the center.[6] By contrast, sixty districts had an average head-of-household income of less than ten MS. They held 73% of the city's population. Only two of these districts are located in the historic center; the rest are outlying. Of these, the twenty districts that averaged less than five MS, the poorest in São Paulo, are exactly those that make up the most distant periphery, along its eastern, northern, and southern limits. They contained 30% of São Paulo's residents.[7]

Unlike the suburbanization of American cities, which created poor centers and wealthy suburbs, the peripheralization of Brazilian cities put the poor in the peripheries and left the rich in the center. This residential segregation got established in São Paulo in the 1940s and 1950s, with the growth of the first ring of periphery neighborhoods, such as Vila Maria, Vila Guilherme, and Vila Prudente (maps 5.1 and 5.3). These neighborhoods arose just beyond the old downtown (primarily Sé and Santa Ifigênia) and the first industrial areas (Barra Funda, Bom Retiro, Belém, Moóca, and Pari). As we shall see, this periphery became the only possible place to live for new migrants arriving in São Paulo after the working classes got expelled from their homes in the more central areas. After this pattern of peripheral settlement for the poor became established, the first ring filled up, its conditions improved, and it became unaffordable for the next wave of migrants. These new settlers were forced to make more distant peripheries their home. This pattern of centrifugal settlement

155

continued at a blistering pace for four decades. During the period of greatest territorial expansion, from 1960 to 1980, the inequalities between center and periphery reached their maximums. Yet it was precisely the improvements of each successive ring of nearer periphery that forced people to settle farther out. Hence, the periphery is always shifting, its location triangulated among the variables of poverty, illegality, rapid but precarious settlement, and urbanization. It is a place for the poor that, although initially destitute, improves with autoconstruction and political mobilization.

Given these changing circumstances, the periphery evokes a complex notion of inequality among the city's residents. For inhabitants of the peripheries, it denotes the development of residential neighborhoods beyond the modern city center where they live far from places of employment. In their collective memory, it refers to the unending concatenation of poor neighborhoods where some form of illegal and precarious residence is typical, including unregulated subdivisions, clandestine dwellings, and squatting. However, as with most matters of domination, the periphery also denotes struggle and, for many residents, unprecedented individual and collective achievements. This significance focuses precisely on issues of residence that condemned the peripheries: house building, home ownership, property conflict, urban services, child care, education, environmental hazards, and so forth—issues historically marginal to the traditional political arenas of men, work, unions, the state, and political parties, but ones that have in fact been more effective in mobilizing working-class Brazilians to fight for citizenship rights and to develop new cultural identities and sensibilities of self.

Thus the periphery signifies for residents a drama of extraordinary change, whose themes of inequality and struggle, segregation and inclusion, poverty and improvement, denigration and assertion are at the same time and in the most everyday ways both intensely personal and political: a drama in which the experiences of shacks, dirt roads, raw sewage, flooding, eviction, violence, faulty urban services, packed buses, and interminable commutes to work are read through the future of house building, neighborhood improvements, community organization, and modern consumption that constitutes the dream of someday having a house-and-a-destiny-of-one's-own. Residents read everyday change in their neighborhoods—each new setting of tile, appliance, sofa, and second storey, each new health clinic, school, paved road, and sewage line—as installments in this narrative of the transformation of subaltern life.

These installments routinely get homogenized by discourses that make "periphery" stand for collective agents. The Catholic Church has used them to mean "the poor and the excluded," the PT "the people," and contemporary rappers "the brothers." For the upper classes of the center, periphery often means "criminal and destitute," the unraveling of Brazilian society. Residents of the peripheries may see each new course of brick in these terms as well. Yet such elements also refer them to the heterogeneity and specificity of their histories, in which their own periphery is a space tangled in both the bitterness of expulsion, segregation, and illegality and the heroism of mastery and redefinition.

Evicting Workers and Managing Society

During the first part of the twentieth century, various forces conspired to push the poor out of the modern center of São Paulo (figure 1.1) and to make its periphery the only place possible for most of them to reside. Which processes of segregation generated this formation? If it is true that the complexities of city life and the rules organizing its space always differentiate and separate residents, then the processes and patterns of this segregation may change but they rarely disappear. Rather, they become redefined, superimposed, and layered in new spatial arrangements and adjusted to new social circumstances. In this sense, we can describe the expansion of São Paulo from a small state capital of thirty thousand inhabitants in 1872 to the world's fifth largest conurbation with 17.8 million residents in 2000, just over a century later, in terms of two comprehensive patterns of segregation. The first produced a condensed and heterogeneous form of urban growth that dominated São Paulo's expansion from the late nineteenth century until the 1940s. The second pattern produced the center-periphery paradigm of growth that dispersed the poor into the hinterlands. I analyze the first not only to demonstrate that the rich expelled the poor from the center with an elaborate justification of social management. I also show that this expulsion generated the paradigm of peripheral urbanization because it essentially closed the center to succeeding migrations. I analyze the second to establish the inequality of conditions that became the basis of a new urban citizenship.[8]

São Paulo's feverish growth began in the 1890s with the onset of industrialization and the influx of foreign immigrants. Until then, it had been a relatively small and tranquil state capital—smaller than Rio de Janeiro, Salvador, Recife, and Belem—organized around the economy of coffee, which dominated the state through the 1930s. For reasons discussed in the last chapter, foreign immigrants inundated the city as industrialization began to offer alternatives to agricultural labor. This tide crested in 1893, when the foreign-born constituted 55% of São Paulo's population, and raised the annual growth rate for the 1890s to an extraordinary 14.0% a year (table 5.1). After that, changing immigration laws, world depression,

157

and world war reduced this foreign majority to a still considerable 36% minority by 1920 (Fausto 1984: 10). The city's annual growth rate also declined, reaching 4.2% by 1940. Though this rate is still high, it reflects a fundamental change: migration to São Paulo became overwhelmingly national, as state government ceased subsidizing foreign immigration at the end of the 1920s and severe drought in the Northeast of Brazil during these and later years provided the city's expanding industrial economy with a new and steady source of cheap labor, namely, the "flagellated" Nordestinos driven to take the long journey south to find work.[9]

This turn-of-the-century expansion transformed São Paulo into a chaotic urban space. Factories, railroads, and industrial services appeared almost overnight in many areas of the city, especially along the Tietê and Tamanduatéi Rivers just beyond the central residential and commercial neighborhoods. These industrial areas were thoroughly mixed with new housing, commerce, and other services needed to accommodate the hordes of immigrant foreign workers. Rather than expand its urban perimeter to keep pace with this growth, however, the industrializing city condensed, as these heterogeneous functions were piled upon one another with little separation, planning, or regulation. Consequently, the city's density increased, from 83 inhabitants per hectare in 1881 to 110 three decades later (F. Villaça, cited in Bonduki 1983: 149). In the process, São Paulo became a typical industrial city of its time: a concentrated confusion of functions, classes, nationalities, races, and spaces.

Although upper and lower classes lived in relative proximity, three general attributes of residence segregated them: location, tenure, and type. Elites lived on higher ground, away from the flooding rivers and their disease-bearing mosquitos, in neighborhoods along Avenida Paulista (like Jardim Paulista and Jardim América) and in those developing to the west (like Pacaembú and Higienópolis, literally "hygiene city"). The working classes resided where they worked, in lower-lying neighborhoods along the rivers Tietê and Tamanduatéi and the railroad tracks that linked the city's first industrial zones in Barra Funda, Belém, Bom Retiro, Brás, Moóca, and Pari. Home ownership constituted an even greater class division. In 1920, the date of the earliest systematic records of housing tenure in the city, only about 20% of Paulistanos owned their homes; the rest rented (Bonduki 1983: 146). The rich and a small middle class lived in their own single-family homes, some very grand indeed, while almost all workers rented rooms in tenements called *cortiços*. A few skilled workers were able to rent single-family row homes, generally called *vilas operárias* and built by factory owners as a means to attract and tether the best workers. Typically, the families of these privileged workers, including children, labored in the same factory, and the threat of eviction for the "indiscipline" of any one member was an effective strategy to discipline all.

In 1926, a boy from a family of immigrants left the following description of his tenement home, recording the typical layout of poverty in the city's *cortiços*.

> Real human hornet nests, spread out over the whole of lower Moóca, Brás, Pari, Belémzinho. . . . Each door led to an immense corridor which had ten, twenty rooms in a row, where families piled up in filthy tenements. The size of our room was three by four meters and in it, six people—my parents, my two young sisters, my grandmother, and I—slept, ate, talked . . . did everything, except relieve ourselves. The latrine was right at the end of the corridor, shared by the eight other families who lived there. Near it, at the end of the corridor, was the kitchen where my mother cooked with three other women. Each had a coal stove in a three by three meter area. Five women shared the kitchen next to it in the same way. So this was a fortress for nine families: one room each, one latrine, and two collective kitchens. (cited in Paoli nd: 136)[10]

As had happened in European cities during the throes of early industrialization, São Paulo's chaos and degradation became the target of those who advocated the "scientific management" of society. The city's progressive elites—planners, economists, engineers, architects, public health specialists, sociologists, criminologists, psychologists, demographers, public administrators, and industrialists—came together to promote the so-called rational organization of production, labor, and the city itself. Their investigation of one produced research on the other. For example, they tackled the polemical question of whether the government should establish a national minimum wage as a means to increase productivity. To determine what expenses such a wage had to cover, they investigated the actual living conditions of the working classes. To promote their concept of scientific social management, they founded institutes and task forces, sponsored research, publications, and conferences, and formulated legislative initiatives and public policy. Their most important organizations in these efforts were IDORT (the Institute for the Rational Organization of Labor), founded in 1931 under the leadership of entrepreneur Roberto Simonsen, and the Institute of Engineering.[11] Active throughout the 1930s and 1940s, both institutes identified working-class housing as the key issue at the intersection of their principal concerns: to expand industrial production by creating a mass consumer market, discipline the "dangerous classes" to produce more qualified and "adjusted" workers, and reshape São Paulo to become the setting of a healthy modern society.

In their view, existing housing was the problem and new housing the means to these ends.

The villain in almost every diagnosis was the tenement-infested working-class neighborhood. Its subhuman living conditions produced crime, disease, and immorality; generated unhappy, undisciplined, and unproductive workers who were susceptible, for those reasons, to the propaganda of class struggle and communism; and limited consumption far below levels necessary for industrial expansion.[12] The solution proposed was unanimous: eliminate the *cortiço* and disperse its population into owner-occupied, single-family, detached houses. The titles of articles published by IDORT's Task Force on Economic Housing indicated the scope of this solution: "Economic Housing and Social Hygiene," "Housing as a Factor in Delinquency," "Housing and Morality," "Housing and Conjugal Harmony," "Hearth and Home: Education of the Resident," in addition to articles on building technology, house design, urban planning, and transportation.[13]

To achieve its bio-moral agenda for labor, IDORT proposed a seven-room house as the ideal *casa própria* (house of one's own) for the modern Brazilian working-class family: three bedrooms, a living room, a kitchen, a bathroom, and a veranda. Proponents argued that this design embodied a separation and rationalization of functions and sexes that would "preserve the good morals of the family" and become "a true sanctuary where the character of the nation is forged" (Andrade Sobrinho 1942: 13). This house—labeled "hygienic, educative, economic, popular, consumer-based, owner-occupied, single-family, and detached"—would discipline bodies, mold character, domesticate workers, and anchor a reliable supply of reliable labor. If the *cortiços* in the center produced social marginality, the *casa própria* in the peripheries would produce social normality.

Simonsen's inaugural address to the Task Force conference underscored the importance of home ownership in this project of social management. IDORT social scientists had demonstrated in their studies of domestic economy that after expenditures for rent and food, the working poor had practically nothing left. Simonsen (IDORT 1942: 13–28) stressed that a shift from rent to ownership, properly financed, would reduce household expenses, make them predictable, and increase disposable income. The result would raise the standard of living of the poor. That change would sustain a "rich internal market necessary to expand industrial production," as well as a new residential order of hygiene and morality. The key to such progress was to develop a mass consumer market focused on house building and household commodities, that is, on the construction, equipping, and decoration of the *casa própria* for workers.[14] As Simonsen turned the meeting over to the specialists, he declared that although private initiative could make a contribution, the problem of mass housing would escape solution without decisive state intervention.

For their part, the planning experts proposed, unapologetically, to refigure São Paulo according to a new pattern of segregation: the working classes would have to go to the hinterlands, while the wealthier classes would remain in a remodeled center. A transportation specialist, for example, takes this pattern as natural: the middle and upper classes have "an intense social life [that] is incompatible with living far from the centers of urban life because the problem of transportation makes coming to the center two, three, or more times a day impossible" (IDORT 1942: 85). Since the poor will have to go to the "suburbs" and since there is no transportation there, he recommends revitalizing the suburban rail lines and clustering worker housing around their stations. Free of the poor, the center can be redeveloped with condominium apartment buildings for the middle class. Presumably, the rich will remain in their mansions.

The urban planners are no less explicit. They recommend the "haus-mannization" of central São Paulo; that is, as Haussmann did in Paris in the 1850s and 1860s, they propose, as one wrote, "drastic laws ... to permit the public powers to expropriate entire blocks," demolish the warrens of crooked streets and tenement housing, redimension and rebuild new blocks, and sell their individual lots "for the real price increased by the costs of the areas that were incorporated into public streets" (IDORT 1942: 146–47). Obviously, the poor have vanished from these plans. For working-class neighborhoods then at the edge of the center, like Brás, this planner advises reducing their populations between one-half and two-thirds to achieve a "healthy population density." Where are these reduced people to go? He proposes doubling the size of the municipality from about 200 to 400 square kilometers to accommodate the dispersion of the laboring classes.

In fact, these urban planners expounded the principles of the master plan for São Paulo that the municipal government had already developed, the so-called Plan of the Avenues. Indeed, some of them were government officials who had participated in the plan's creation and were now responsible for its implementation. Although work on the plan had begun a decade earlier under the direction of Francisco Prestes Maia, the government made it policy and began its implementation only after Prestes Maia became mayor in 1938.[15] The plan was the most ambitious intervention of government ever undertaken to shape São Paulo. It proposed to transform the model of growth from condensed to dispersed by radiating a set of large avenues from the center to the hinterlands of the city. This radiation required the wholesale demolition and redevelopment of downtown. The result gave a new scale to the center, with new government buildings, squares, parks, monuments, and commerce all laid out in baroquely

161

radiating symmetries. As in Paris seventy years earlier, the avenues were driven through working-class neighborhoods and their residents driven out. The dislocated had no possibility of returning, as real estate speculation raised rents in the remodeled center beyond their reach. At the same time, the plan made a strategic commitment not to invest in the trolley system of public transportation. The administration viewed this system as confining city growth with expensive and outdated installations that expanded too slowly to permit it to dislocate workers to the outskirts where they would now live and to bring them back daily to the center where they continued to work. Instead, the plan inaugurated a bus system whose vehicles could range freely along the new avenues and then negotiate the dirt roads that would carry workers far into the hinterlands when the asphalt ended.

Thus, changing public transportation was crucial to the periphery's development. Until the 1930s, the outward expansion of São Paulo remained slow, as it followed the development of suburban rail lines. After the 1930s, however, it expanded rapidly on the rubber wheels of the bus system. Real estate speculation in the hinterlands had existed since the turn of the century, when speculators began to market parcels of land. As it lacked accessible transportation, however, the land remained mostly unsold and unoccupied, except for small subdivisions close to occasional rail stations. That isolation ended with the switch to buses and the opening of avenues radiating from downtown. Often in league with land developers, private bus companies appeared. Generally without municipal authorization, they built dirt roads where the avenues ended to carry their buses into the peripheries, making the development of remote new housing tracts feasible. Camargo et al. (1978: 28) estimate that twenty-six thousand such dirt roads had been constructed by the mid-1960s. By then, these private bus companies had completely displaced the trolleys, the public bus company, and the suburban rail lines in transporting commuters.[16]

The federal government also intervened in the creation of the periphery, with decisive but perverse consequences. After Getúlio Vargas came to power in 1930, it completely restructured the organization of labor. Vargas's populist rule embraced the urban working classes as the basis of its political legitimacy and focused on urban industry as the core of its economic policy. The dire conditions of urban housing therefore became a central concern to the regime, as it managed relations between labor and capital through an extensive series of interventions in labor law and social welfare. The new Ministry of Labor, Industry, and Commerce advocated home ownership for the working classes in much the same terms as IDORT, namely, as a means of instilling moral values, ensuring social stability, improving hygiene, increasing production and consumption, and so forth. Moreover, for the first time, the federal government assumed responsibility for housing Brazil's workers. Thus, when it formulated housing policy based on single-family ownership, initiated programs to build subsidized worker housing, and passed laws to protect renters, the urban masses aclaimed Vargas their champion.

To those ends, the federal government took a number of steps. In 1937, it created a set of social-welfare and pension institutes that were charged with constructing and financing affordable houses for workers. In 1946, it reinforced this policy by funding the Popular Housing Foundation. It also resuscitated state-run credit institutions (first established in 1831) to provide mortgages at rates accessible to the working classes. These initiatives marked the beginning of the direct production and financing of low-income housing by government institutions that continues to this day. However, for various and mostly ignoble reasons, these institutions failed their charge. Most of their publicly financed mortgages went to buildings for the middle and upper classes, and the few houses built for lower-income earners were distributed clientelistically.[17] Moreover, although planners estimated that the city would need about half a million new housing units between 1945 and 1960, the welfare institutes only constructed 25,428 and the Foundation only 2,959 during this period in the entire state of São Paulo.[18]

These failures had decisive consequences for the development of the periphery. The absence of publicly financed affordable housing generated both the need for autoconstruction and its impoverished residential conditions, by forcing workers to build their own houses out of the poorest materials. Furthermore, the absence of state investment and accompanying regulation left development entirely dependent on the operations of the private real estate market.

Finally, in 1942, at the height of unprecedented inflation, urban demolition, real estate speculation, rent increases, and housing shortages, the federal government issued the Renter's Law. It froze all rents at their December 1941 levels, instituted a system of rent control, and established regulations to govern the terms of renting, which had previously been privately negotiated between tenant and landlord. As fully 75% of the city's inhabitants rented, according to the census of 1940, this legislation had tremendous significance. Although it was supposed to last only two years, the government reissued it by decree in 1944, 1945, and 1946, and it remained in effect for residential properties, with slight increases for inflation, until 1964. The effects of the law were, however, thoroughly perverse. The long-term consequence was to discourage investments in new rental units, precisely when much of that stock was being lost to the demolition of urban "renewal." The immediate consequence was to encourage mass evictions: landlords tried to expell old tenants to get new ones who would pay more or sold occupied buildings to recover their capital, now devalued by the rent freeze and inflation. We will not be surprised to learn that even though the Renter's Law emphasized tenant rights, had sanctions against illegal evictions, and created special courts to adjudicate them, tens of thousands of evictions were successfully concluded. In 1945 and 1946 alone, Bonduki (1994: 106) estimates that as much as 4% of the entire population of the city of São Paulo was evicted from their homes, perhaps 75,000 people. By end of the decade, he surmises that between 10% and 15% of inhabitants suffered eviction.[19]

In response, workers organized to resist. Indeed, they had been protesting their living conditions for decades. They wanted home ownership. Even more, they wanted to remain in the center, which was close to work and reasonably equipped with services, rather than be forced into empty hinterlands. In the first two decades of the century, the trade union movement had become strong under anarchist leadership, and its many strikes emphasized housing. Primarily, the unions promoted the formation of renters' leagues and the actions of rent strikes as the means to achieve rent stability. In the 1940s, the Communist Party of Brazil organized much of the renters' resistence to eviction. It prioritized public pressure on executive and elected institutions, organizing many strikes and demonstrations. These mobilizations had little effect, however. Year after year, chief executives, including the democratically elected President Dutra in 1946, renewed the Renter's Law by decree. No elected body ever passed legislation to suspend or dampen the evictions. Instead, the poor had to face expulsion by confronting either the police or the courts, against which forces they had little chance of prevailing.[20]

As the crisis in rental housing became critical, interests converged on autoconstruction in the hinterlands. Employers ceased calculating rent into wage considerations, promoted the ideal of home ownership, and assumed that workers would find their place in the wilds of the municipality. The state did the same in its propaganda for subsidized housing.[21] No one considered that the working poor might return in significant numbers to reside in the remodeled center, except perhaps workers themselves. Instead, new kinds of investors in tract real estate and bus transportation arose to open the outskirts for house construction. Many of these speculators were, in fact, the very same employers, government officials, and proxies who had engineered the city's redevelopment. Moreover, at this moment of converging interests, the nineteenth-century *grileiro* was reborn in urban form to subdivide and develop the peripheries.

For their part, the displaced working poor had two immediate but only one long-term option. They could either try to remain in the more central areas, moving into the new favelas (squatter settlements) that arose downtown or hanging onto rooms in *cortiços*. In either case, they would remain close to work but live both in misery and in constant fear of being evicted. Indeed, most of these favelas and *cortiços* were soon demolished. Or they could move to the distant hinterlands, without reliable transportation, electricity, water, hospitals, or indeed any service. In fact, both options amounted to a sudden decline in their standard of living. At least in the hinterlands, where most went, they could build for themselves on a lot of their own.

Autoconstructing the Peripheries

The expulsion of most low-income residents from São Paulo's historic central districts was completed by the end of the 1940s. Evictions, demolitions, and higher rents also reduced their numbers significantly in the first industrial neighborhoods, those east of downtown along the rail lines, particularly Brás and Moóca.[22] Therefore, when the great migrations to São Paulo began in the 1950s, bringing millions of people from the Northeast and other regions over the next thirty years, the city's new working poor had no choice but to live in the peripheries. For example, the population of Vila Prudente in the near-eastern periphery increased precipitously from 29,511 in 1940 to 90,408 in 1950 and to 197,945 in 1960 (Langenbuch 1971: 250–51). Dispersed into the peripheries, the city's population dropped in density from a high of 110 inhabitants per hectare in 1914 to 25 in 1960 (Rolnik, Kowarik, and Somekh n.d.: 35). However, the central districts remained the primary place of work. Consequently, each new wave of migration had to commute to work from increasing distances because all confronted the same repeating process of peripheralization: migrants were forced to reside in the outskirts where they had to build their own houses, but to find an accessible plot of land, they had to go ever farther out. Thus, the population of São Miguel Paulista–Ermelino Matarazzo at the far-eastern edge of the municipality increased from 7,634 in 1940 to 137,908 in 1960. On each successive fringe of the fringe, where the only infrastructure they found was the dirt roads speculators opened to sell the land, these Brazilian migrants became pioneers of modern city building.

Between 1940 and 1960, these forces of expulsion, exclusion, attraction, and dispersal consolidated a pattern of peripheral urbanization in São Paulo. As a result, millions of workers populated the peripheries, putting up single-family shacks of concrete block or wood at astonishing rates and spending decades transforming them into finished homes and urbanizing their neighborhoods. Similar historical, social, and spatial

165

conditions generated such urban peripheries throughout Brazil. During its core development in São Paulo, from the 1940s to the 1980s, a set of interrelated processes sustained this center-periphery paradigm of urban growth: it developed by low-density dispersion from a higher-density and concentrated center; the autoconstruction of detached houses, without state or bank financing, was the primary means of settling the peripheries, while financed high-rise construction by licensed firms characterized growth in the center; the development of the peripheries occurred overwhelmingly through private market operations, with little state regulation or application of public policy; home and land ownership was the norm for residents in both center and periphery; and the lower classes were segregated in the peripheries from the upper classes in the center not only by great distances but also by every standard indicator of well-being except home ownership.

Autoconstruction is the key attribute of this pattern, for it renews the others in its realization and links them in driving peripheral expansion. Nevertheless, it yields paradoxical results, in that it both perpetuates and transforms urban segregation. Thus, settling the periphery to build a house of one's own is itself a spatial paradox: each instance of autoconstruction reproduces the periphery, pushing its leading edge farther into the hinterland; but in so doing, it brings the center and its promise of a different future that much closer to the individual house builder. Furthermore, as each autoconstructing family develops, the entire neighborhood evolves. Thus, the newest and most outlying neighborhoods have the most precarious dwellings in which reside the poorest and youngest families.[23] As these families grow in size and accomplishment, they transform their houses and urbanize their neighborhoods, and those improvements in turn displace the fringe of the periphery and its attributes of poverty to new areas of the hinterland.

As the sum of all instances of autoconstruction, the development of São Paulo's peripheries is thus a story of constant displacement and transformation. Their growth followed the expanding transportation routes of trains, buses, and cars, which brought families to outlying areas where they could afford to build and provided access to the places of employment in the center. This centrifugal pattern continued even as the peripheries gained their own jobs because employment was centrally located in each area and developed from near to far. Most of the pioneers I worked with on the history of their neighborhoods had a similar trajectory. Their first place of residence after migrating from the Northeast or from the interior of São Paulo or Minas Gerais was a rented room in a *cortiço* in one of the more central industrial neighborhoods, such as Barra Funda, Brás, and Moóca. But demolitions, escalating rent, and associated instabilities invariably drove them into the peripheries, to another rented room or perhaps a rented shack, if possible close to a train or bus stop. Depending on family fortunes, they moved in this manner regularly ever farther out along the transportation lines until finally they were able to buy a plot of land and build a house. As one pioneer in Jardim das Camélias put it, "each move was desperate, each a loss, until we got our own home [*casa própria*]."

This passage between center and periphery remains a daily commute for many workers. It averages three to four hours round-trip and generally requires several transfers between overcrowded buses and trains.[24] Thus observed, the changing cityscape presents the various forms of São Paulo's growth. In the old central industrial neighborhoods, what is left of tenements still crowd around the hems of the factories, which themselves sprawl over alleys and courtyards in such a manner that it is often difficult to distinguish between living and workplace. Almost all available space is constructed, built to each lot line, and all surfaces shaped by the forces of Paulista capitalism—even the sky is tinted an industrial hue. In this solid mass of concrete and asphalt, out of which the spaces of streets seem carved, the natural world is decidely out of place. Most of the transportation lines out of the center run alongside rivers or streams decades dead and mostly paved over. They are lined by a mix of buildings characteristic of working-class commuter avenues everywhere: bars, shops, single-room manufactories, small apartment buildings, a chaos of signs and billboards, flights of stairs between facades leading to a cluster of rooms around an outhouse or to a vest-pocket favela tucked into a hillside.

On the way to Jardim das Camélias, this commercialized thoroughfare is unremittingly drab, its buildings unpainted concrete grey. What little green one finds is of the garbage-heap variety, tough hybrids that breed on the debris of industrial society. At a certain point, the avenue climbs a hill and a break in the construction suddenly brings a bird's-eye view of the landscape into focus: From horizon to horizon, the periphery appears as one continuous building site, a hivelike enterprise in a million stages of autoconstruction. Although an apartment structure occasionally materializes, it is mostly a one-and two-storey landscape of houses and shops. After about an hour of travel by bus, building along the avenue begins to thin. Large vacant spaces appear off to both sides in the distance, accented by spots of tightly clustered settlements that are neighborhoods in the making. In another thirty minutes, the avenue ends at an open area. For years, an amusement park set itself up at this terminus, the whirling colored lights of its ferris wheel signaling both the end of the line and the arrival of an electrified modernity.

All along this route through the periphery, a turn into the neighborhoods reveals an incongruous mix of living conditions. Off the main streets, especially in the farther periphery, everything looks unfinished. The asphalt

167

often ends abruptly at dirt roads that are gullied by rain and ditches. The houses are provisional shacks of block or wood, their mostly unpainted walls either concrete grey or the weathered tones of recycled lumber. Piles of construction material occupy front yards, stocked when possible and awaiting deployment under plastic tarps. A lone pole, an outpost of electricity, sprouts dozens of improvised connections. In comparison with these houses, however, those along the main streets, especially in the closer periphery, may seem like mansions. The incipient shacks give way to crisply mortared and stuccoed houses, many richly styled and brightly painted two-storey homes in blue, green, pink, and ochre. They feature studied citations of colonial, chalet, and modernist styles, expensively appointed with wood moldings, tile, decorative wrought iron, smoked glass, and high spiked fences of silver and gold that enclose multiple-car garages. Serving them are neighborhood stores that sell tile, granite, and marble, some offering an assortment of stone angels and fauna.

Is this the impoverished periphery? In relation to the elite center, yes. Individual fortunes of inhabitants in the peripheries vary greatly, and their houses speak of that variation more eloquently than any other sign (figures 1.6–1.7). Residents read this house architecture as indications not only of economic success but also of life cycles and personalities. In this sense, the neighborhoods constitute a stage on which houses perform by giving evidence of the social drama of each resident. As a rule, nearer, older, and more-established neighborhoods feature the most diverse houses, while newer and precarious ones, those at the far edge, are uniformly shanties. In this way, house architecture in the peripheries renders legible the social and market forces that broadly organize Brazilian society as well as the idiosyncratic individual narratives that energize them.[25] In this relation between property, citizen, and person, the periphery is a cacaphony of individual expressions within a grand narrative of segregation and insurgence.

This pell-mell development results from the interaction of two sets of initiatives: those of developers, who divide, sell, and speculate, and those of settlers, who purchase or seize land. Aside from claims by federal and state governments, there has not been a great concentration of property ownership in São Paulo's periphery since the 1930s. Rather, there are many who claim to own land and many more developers. As a result, development occurs overwhelmingly through the subdivision of small parcels, often containing around two hundred lots. Some have twice that amount, but many fewer. I emphasize claims because, as we have seen, landownership is characterized more by uncertainty than definitive proof. Hence, the presumed landowner may very well be a *grileiro*. In the next chapter, I fully analyze this likelihood and its consequences in the case of

Jardim das Camélias. I defer this analysis because of the importance and complexity of the slippery relation between the legal and the illegal in the settlement of the peripheries. Here, my concern is to describe the heterogeneity of land occupation and the range of property conditions.

Three situations dominate private land development in the periphery. In many cases, the "landowner" is also the developer. This situation occurs typically when people inherit small parcels of land, in which case development is a family project, and when construction or real estate companies purchase such parcels. In other cases, "landowners" enter into partnership with developers, the former putting up the land and the latter subdividing and selling it. In still other cases, a realtor enters the deal, each partner having distinct roles. Such realtors may be employees of development companies but may also be autonomous, selling lots for several enterprises on commission.

These land entrepreneurs use several modes of speculation that create a chaotic and fragmented settlement. Most employ what I would call a "hold-back scheme" of speculation in subdividing a parcel of land. They offer the worst lots for sale first, at low prices, and hold back the best, usually those on level ground and closest to transportation. They often open the subdivision illegally without any infrastructure and wait for some of the worst lots to be occupied. After dwellings appear, they (or their minions or the residents themselves) petition local public authorities to install desperately needed infrastructure to serve the existing houses. Although installation of services generally takes years to complete, even the arrival of the first (such as potable water or electricity) greatly increases the value of the land. At that point, the developers begin to put the better lots on the market and may try to expell the earlier residents. This process of speculation works well because the demand for cheap lots always outpaces the supply.

Occasionally, either by conspiracy or accident, one finds a type of "leapfrog" speculation. Instead of expanding their subdivisions contiguously, developers leave an undeveloped parcel sandwiched between an existing and a new subdivision. When infrastructure eventually arrives to the latter, it passes from the old through the unbuilt land, increasingly its value immensely. This kind of speculation requires considerable coordination between allied developers or the concentration of numerous parcels in the hands of a single developer. Neither condition is likely. Rather, it is more common to find another mode of speculation, that of the "lone operator," in which several "owners" appear in an area undergoing subdivision. Each claims to own a few lots and sells them independently, trying to benefit from the development of neighboring lots. Most of these sales are fraudulent. Also common is the illegal scheme of duplicate sales, in which a developer superimposes a new plan of subdivision over an older and sells the same land several times in different configurations of lots, or in which several developers superimpose different plans. This mode of speculation is particularly vicious, as it depends on the expulsion of previous residents and the erasure of their purchases.

In Jardim das Camélias, I found all these modes of speculation, except the "leap-frog." The others coexist, creating multiple layers of chaotic and illegal land development in the same neighborhood. Land speculation is rampant in the peripheries because the demand for accessible land is so great that any sort of development in one parcel or even one lot provokes a significant increase in the value of unbuilt land around it. As a result, land speculation remains inventive and profitable.

In combination with developer initiatives, those of settlers also produce a heterogeneity of property conditions as they try to secure a *casa própria*. Their initial access to land establishes a fundamental distinction between two kinds of settlement: those based on land purchase and those on land seizure. The former are the most common and called *loteamento* (subdivision); the latter are labeled either "favela" or, if organized by groups such as the Landless Movement, *ocupação* or *invasão* (land occupation or invasion). The organized land seizures tend to be different by design from the classic favela, in that they are laid out according to regulation lot lines and built of concrete block. Subdivisions are further distinguished as legal or illegal. To qualify as legal, a subdivision must be in full compliance with regulations. The law classifies those that are not into three kinds of illegal subdivisions—the fraudulent, irregular, and clandestine—distinctions I examine in the next chapter. Thus, depending on resident initiatives of purchase or seizure and developer compliance with regulations, two classes of six property conditions result in the settlement of the periphery: subdivisions deemed legal, fraudulent, irregular, and clandestine, and seizures called favelas and *ocupações*. Frequently, all are present in the same neighborhood.

Such is the case in Jardim das Camélias. As settlement intensified in the area after 1967, most residents purchased lots in subdivisions. However, these were divided and sold by several developers, some several times over, with the result that while a few lots were legal, most were either fraudulent, irregular, or clandestine, and all types were found near each other. When Caldeira (1984: 69–70) completed a comprehensive household survey in Jardim das Camélias in 1979, she estimated the following tenancy conditions for a total population at that time of approximately 900 households and 4,650 people: 60% of the households lived on lots they had purchased, 26% rented accommodations, 12% lived in houses ceded to them (usually by relatives), and 3% occupied ceded lots. The last are typically the enforcers or hired guns (*capangas*) of the developers, who receive construction material and the use of a house lot in exchange for security services. By the time I started my fieldwork almost a decade later, one significant change in tenancy had occurred: whereas there were no land seizures in 1979, hundreds of people had squatted in two areas of Jardim das Camélias by 1988.

The Landless Movement (Movimento Sem Terra, MST) organized one seizure in 1982, in which eighty-four families (about four hundred people) occupied an area of vacant land over the course of two days. They named it Ocupação Pirandello, after a nearby school. The occupiers (or "invaders") divided the land into seventy-five regular lots of 6 x 20 meters, and all built three-room houses (bedroom, kitchen, bathroom) of concrete block. With assistance from MST-trained personnel, they followed as closely as possible the standards of the "more legal" subdivisions around them (e.g., lot size, setbacks, and construction methods).

The second land seizure exists on the other side of the local garbage dump. Its history is murky. From what I could gather, about seventy families, initially leaderless, seized the area and built a jumble of wooden shacks along one bank of a thoroughly polluted stream. According to some of these residents, they did so between 1978 and 1980—though both Caldeira and residents of the subdivisions told me that they were not there until 1981 or 1982. Nevertheless, all agree that the seizure was not an organized operation but rather the result of separate initiatives by generally unrelated families. At some point, a leader emerged who, at least according to what he related to me, founded a second part— he claims in 1979—and convinced new squatters to subdivide the land there into regular lots and to build houses only of concrete block. They separated this new part from the old by an unpaved road and incorporated an association of residents, the Associação da Favela Pedro Nunes. Despite this official name, however, everyone calls the organized rows of block houses an *ocupação*, following the typology of neat versus heap, and reserves "favela" for the earlier set of shacks. Moreover, all refer to the sum of the two parts as Vila Jóia (Jewel, also "cool" in slang). The president of the neighborhood association that represents the subdivisions in Jardim das Camélias suggested to me sardonically that the squatters chose that name because "it was cool not to pay anything for the land."

As this comment suggests, there are deep hostilities between those who purchase and those who squat in Jardim das Camélias—conflicts that underscore the importance of landed property ownership as a category of self-esteem and political consequence dividing the poor (and all Brazilians) into antagonistic fractions. The distinction between purchasing and seizing land became even more socially important as some favela housing became indistinguishable in appearance from non-favela housing. In its classic form, the favela is immediately recognizable by its jumble

171

of wooden shacks, unkept dirt paths, running raw sewage, and lack of basic services—features that contrast clearly with the gridded subdivisions, concrete block structures, and even paved streets in which most people have bought lots. However, beginning in the 1980s, urban land invasions became increasingly organized operations—especially targeting public land—sponsored by political parties, churches, and social movements (e.g., the MST). Such organized seizures are often successful not only in avoiding eviction but also, after much time and struggle, in legalizing the individual claims of participants to the land. Anticipating this legalization of usurped land rights, they routinely require their members to subdivide and build according to legal regulations. As a result, their seizures appear little different from more legal subdivisions in terms of spatial organization and building materials.

In whatever form, subdivision residents in Jardim das Camélias resent the "invasion" of their neighborhood by squatters. The latter in turn resent the resentment. In voicing their antipathy, the former have developed a set of correlations that constitutes a social mapping of the neighborhood. Its elements are frequently heard in conversation among subdivision residents who, as the vast majority of inhabitants, use it to dominate the neighborhood's moral economy. They relate five characteristics—settlement type, civil standing, tenure condition, house construction, and moral character—to produce the following typologies, in which each term in a set implies its cocharacteristics: (1) subdivision (*loteamento*), landowner (*proprietário*), home owner (*casa própria*), masonry construction (*alvenaria*), and worker (*trabalhador*); versus (2) favela, squatter (*favelado*), home owner, shack (*barraco*), and bum (*vagabundo*). "Marginal" or "criminal" may also substitute for bum. Those who use this taxonomy generally refer to the first set as describing conditions "up here" and to the second as "down there," regardless of where they are when they speak. A third typology in the neighborhood navigates between these two: (3) *ocupação*, home owner, masonry construction, and worker. Although less common, I have heard this last correlation primarily among those who sympathize with MST land struggles. As part of the militant's lexicon, it creates a distinction between people who squat because they are lazy and immoral and "good workers" who are forced to seize land because they are made desperate by the injustices of Brazilian society.

In these correlations, the very orderliness of the subdivisions and the solidity of their masonry houses indicate to residents that moral order reigns in the organization of houses and the families within. By contrast, the favela is "that heap with everything piled up, everything badly done, with no divisions or separations between people, a confusion," as one subdivision resident summarized the opinion of many. When pressed, residents admit that there exist regularly laid-out land seizures, that they have been in favela houses that are orderly and relatively well made, that there are poorly constructed houses and many shacks in the subdivisions, and that they know squatters who are "good workers and parents." Nevertheless, they hold to the generalization that the physical disorder of favelas causes a moral disorder among its residents.

I pressed residents further on these apparent contradictions by turning the question around: What makes the subdivisions orderly? Their answer was always property ownership, "to be the owner" (*ser dono*): the purchase of lots requires their exact demarcation, because it must be part of a valid contract of sale to result, eventually, in legal title. Thus, the foundational logic of this social mapping and its morality is ownership: the orderliness of a subdivision is an index of the civil standing of its residents as owners, and the disorderliness of a favela indicates the contrary.

But notice that the key distinction is landownership, for *casa própria* appears in all three typologies to indicate that residents of the periphery— even squatters—usually own rather than rent the houses in which they live. Certainly, to own the house is an essential part of the dream of home ownership. But as lot ownership almost always implies house ownership for a resident, and as the contrary is not the case, residents see landownership as the core meaning of home ownership. It distinguishes the highest civil standing of which home ownership is the general index. Moreover, as the rural poor have always built their own houses, the term autoconstruction arose to distinguish those who went to the urban peripheries to become land and house owners. It distinguishes, in other words, those who pay for a house lot on which to build their house from those who seize land to build with no intention of paying. Autoconstruction signifies, therefore, the kind of commitment to and imagination about the future that property ownership, especially that of land, engenders.

These distinctions are fundamental to the insurgence of a citizenship in the peripheries that became based on the struggles of city life and on values associated with the appropriation of city land. Not surprisingly, they are the values classically linked to property ownership in the history of citizenship: independence, responsibility, rational calculation, legitimacy, and so forth. In Jardim das Camélias, older residents articulated these values clearly in response to my questions about the importance of home ownership in the history of their migration to the urban periphery. As Sérgio said, "We moved from a *cortiço* in [a neighborhood in the center] to [a succession of peripheral neighborhoods] to escape rent, to escape the instability of always having to move when the rent went up. The little lot that you buy brings tranquillity. So we went to that bush [where they were finally able to purchase land and build a house] to have our independent corner." In terms of housing strategy, Zé reasoned that "at the time, I thought that instead of paying rent—which I always viewed as money that you never see again—I would make a down payment on a piece of land and buy construction material on installment, and that the payments I made on the land and the material were about the same as I would pay in rent. So I sacrificed in those days, but I was paying for what is today mine. If I had continued paying rent, I would not have the house where I am living today."

The values of ownership are also the focus of public affirmation, especially in discussions about the interminable land conflicts of the neighborhood. At a meeting of the neighborhood association in Jardim das Camélias, for example, Paulo criticized what he characterized as its strategy of defending residents against eviction without developing a legal case to secure ownership. Legitimate landownership was the key issue, he argued, not merely continued residence. Although preventing eviction was obviously an important achievement, he argued that the association never managed "to get what everybody really wants": legal ownership. "I do not want to live for free; I want to be the owner of my lot; I want to be the legitimate owner." Like everyone else at the meeting, Paulo had already paid for his lot but had been swindled. As a result, he was denied title and threatened with eviction. What he meant, therefore, in opposing house and land ownership was that until he had legitimate title to his lot, the world would see him as a squatter.

It is this dream of being the legitimate owner of one's "independent corner," of having the sense of family security and personal autonomy that people believe it brings, that migrants follow to the periphery and that enables them to endure its harsh conditions. It is also this dream that developers exploit ruthlessly. When they subdivide the land, they typically entice buyers with promises that "the dream of home ownership can be yours" for a low initial down payment. They erect billboards on site and distribute flyers at factories, bus stops, and stores, selling a future of family security and happiness through ownership. Lar Nacional Construtora e Administradora Ltda. was such a real estate development company when it appeared in the peripheries in the late 1960s. It developed a number of subdivisions on the east-southeast edge of the municipality, in the districts of Sapopemba and São Mateus. But by the mid-1970s, it had vanished, leaving a legacy of legal conflict from which residents have yet to recover. It gave its name to the neighborhood where I have done fieldwork since 1989, Parque Lar Nacional, also known as Novo Lar Nacional and simply Lar Nacional, meaning "National Home" or "Hearth."

Most developers in the peripheries sell empty lots on which people build homes from scratch, as in Jardim das Camélias. In Lar Nacional, however, the developer took the less common strategy of constructing embryonic house structures that buyers expanded and completed.

Beginning in 1967, it started to develop the neighborhood by laying out dirt roads, parceling blocks of land into approximately 500 lots of 125 and 250 m², and building skeletal houses of one and two bedrooms. As its development costs were higher, it aimed to sell its subdivision to a wealthier fraction of the working class. Most of the pioneers I worked with in the neighborhood were skilled industrial workers and some were self-employed salesmen when they purchased. Some had kept the original flyers that Lar Nacional distributed at their workplaces to advertise its "Plan for Home Ownership." These advertisements responded brilliantly to the desires of workers to become "legitimate owners." Although probably pitched to the top of the working class, they exemplify the process of sale and purchase that engaged all. Moreover, they illustrate the rhetoric of conversion by which the desperate necessity of moving to the periphery became a journey of pioneers, eliciting the provider in every man and woman, and by which the image of impoverished migrants became one of landowners building a prosperous future.

Thus, under a map showing the location of Lar Nacional in the periphery, one flyer announces that "this is the certain path for you to acquire your own home. Follow this path and free yourself from rent. Go to Park Lar Nacional. . . . There are 200 residences ready to inhabit. Become an owner paying installments lower than rent." A more elaborate fold-out brochure (figure 5.1) presents an idealized family with the key to their own home: "There are people who have still not resolved the problem of home ownership . . . they continue paying rent! And, as is obvious, no one likes to pay rent. A rented home represents, almost always, 25% to 60% of your salary already obligated (that is, half or more of your monthly money never comes back). This without counting the problems of readjustments (often absurd), evictions, etc., that destabilize any household budget. We have the KEY to the solution of this problem." Inside this brochure (figure 5.2), a well-dressed young couple points to their future home: "A dream that you can turn into reality. It is the old 'law' that 'unity makes strength.' You, alone, perhaps would not have the means (at least not so soon) to have your own home. It is exactly for this reason, for men like you, that we made the Lar Nacional Plan. Through it, you can realize your great dream: to buy your house, without down payment, without interest, without increases, and with a fixed delivery date. Why wait any longer? Acquire your own house this very day." The brochure concludes with images of the new daily life awaiting home owners: a car parked in front of a picket fence, a child riding a bicycle, a bus to take parents to work: "In Park Lar Nacional, your children will be able to run and play to their hearts' content . . . without danger! In Park Lar Nacional, the construction of houses follows an integrated plan, with grocery stores, schools, and transportation."

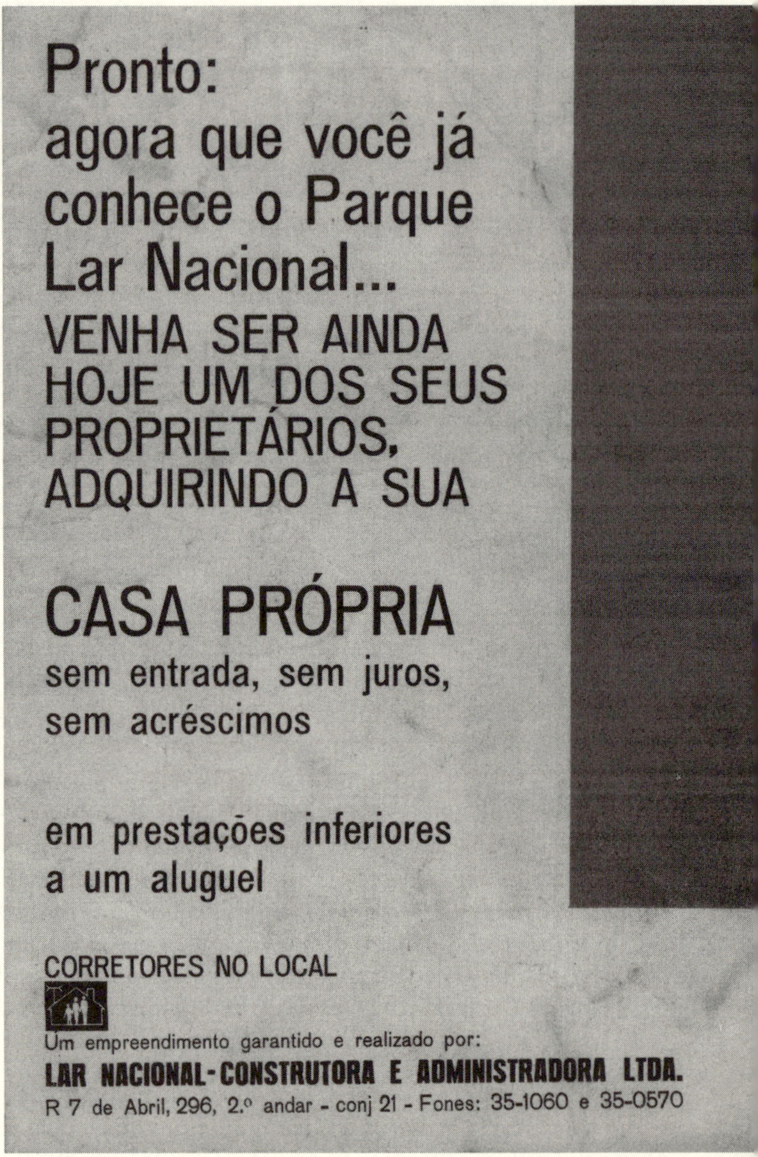

Pronto:
agora que você já
conhece o Parque
Lar Nacional...
VENHA SER AINDA
HOJE UM DOS SEUS
PROPRIETÁRIOS,
ADQUIRINDO A SUA

CASA PRÓPRIA
sem entrada, sem juros,
sem acréscimos

em prestações inferiores
a um aluguel

CORRETORES NO LOCAL

Um empreendimento garantido e realizado por:
LAR NACIONAL-CONSTRUTORA E ADMINISTRADORA LTDA.
R 7 de Abril, 296, 2.º andar - conj 21 - Fones: 35-1060 e 35-0570

FIGURE 5.1. Advertising home ownership, sales brochure, Lar Nacional, c. 19(

TEM
GENTE QUE
AINDA
NÃO
RESOLVEU
O PROBLEMA
DA CASA
PRÓPRIA...

continuam
pagando
aluguel!

E, como é óbvio, ninguém gosta de pagar aluguel.
Casa alugada representa, quase sempre, 25% a 60%
de seu salário já empenhado (ou seja, metade ou
mais da metade do seu dinheiro mensal nunca mais
volta). Isso sem contar os problemas de reajustes
(absurdos, muitas vêzes), ações de despejo, etc.,
que desequilibram qualquer orçamento doméstico.
Nós temos a CHAVE para a solução dêste problema

FIGURE 5.2. Selling the dream house, sales brochure, Lar Nacional, c. 1969.

Finally, the brochure (figure 5.3) presents a perspective drawing of the proposed neighborhood, showing it replete with community resources: "This will be Park Lar Nacional. Located in neighborhoods of great progress . . . near to ABC [three industrial municipalities], the Brazilian Detroit, is Park Lar Nacional where the house that could be yours and many others are already in the final phase of construction. Paved access roads, plenty of buses to the center of the city and other neighborhoods. All the urban comforts: water, light, schools, grocery stores, pharmacies, etc. Here will be the ideal place for your family to live." It concludes: "Become one of its owners this very day, acquiring your own home without

Um sonho que Você pode tornar realidade

É a velha "lei" de que a "união faz a fôrça". Você, sòzinho, talvez não tivesse (pelo menos tão cedo) condições para ter a sua casa própria. É justamente por isso, para homéns como Você, que fizemos o PLANO LAR NACIONAL. Através dêle, Você pode realizar o seu grande sonho: Comprar sua casa, sem entrada, sem juros, sem acréscimos e com prazo certo de entrega. Por quê esperar mais? Adquira hoje mesmo a sua casa própria.

down payment, without interest, without increases, in installments lower than rent. Real estate agents on site."

When prospective home owners reached this site, an agent presented them with the following proposal. For NCr $23,500, they could purchase a house of 43 m², consisting of a living room, bedroom, kitchen, and bath, on a lot of 125 m². This price equaled 181 minimum salaries in March 1969, the date of the information I have. No one I spoke with knew of any buyer who had paid the full amount up front. Rather, all had signed a private contract with the developer, stipulating payments over time. It required a down payment of NCr $1500, payable with a deposit of $100 at the act of signing, nine monthly installments of $150, and one install-ment of $50. After these ten months of paying off the down payment, the

179

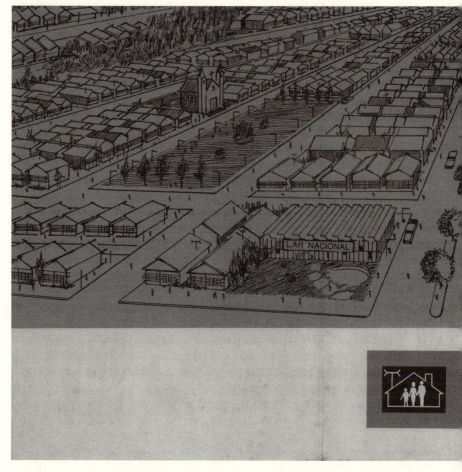

Figure 5.3. Perspective of proposed neighborhood, sales brochure, Lar Nacional, c. 1969.

buyer was obligated to make thirty monthly installments of one current minimum salary plus $50.[26] After these thirty months, the buyer would pay one minimum salary per month to liquidate the remaining balance. The contract promised that an inhabitable house, equipped with internal plumbing attached to a main water supply, wiring in each room ready for the electricity that would one day arrive, and a long list of fixtures and materials, would be delivered to the buyer "approximately 60 days after completing the down payment."

Although most subdivisions in the peripheries were sold without pre-constructed houses, their transactions were similar to the one just described. Most people bought a plot of land through a private contract based on

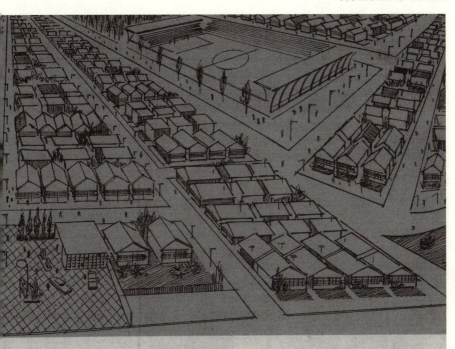

ESTE SERÁ O PARQUE LAR NACIONAL

tuado em bairros de grande progresso - entre VILA PRUDENTE e TATUAPÉ - próximo ao ABC,
Detroit brasileira, fica o PARQUE LAR NACIONAL onde a casa que poderá ser sua e muitas
utras já estão em término de construção. Vias de acesso asfaltadas, condução abundante ao centro
a cidade e a outros bairros. Todo o confôrto urbano: água, luz, escolas, armazéns, farmácias etc.
í será o lugar ideal para sua família morar.
enha qualquer dia da semana com sua família, visitar
s obras do PARQUE LAR NACIONAL e conhecer o local de sua futura casa.

installments and, having nowhere else to live, erected an inhabitable but rudimentary shack in a matter of days. In Jardim das Camélias, for example, residents who purchased in the first part of 1969 paid NCr $15,000 for a lot of 120 m², approximately 116 minimum salaries. They put 10% down and contracted for 120 monthly payments that were readjusted according to changes in the minimum salary.[27] Generally, buyers encountered several significant problems with this type of contract. One was figuring out the balance due. Although the contracts I investigated did not levy interest on the debt, they readjusted for inflation. In some, this adjustment was pegged to changes in the minimum salary, which usually occurred once a year. But in others, it could be monthly. Especially in the latter case, such changes made it difficult for residents to understand the

181

real costs of home ownership.[28] Thus, most private contracts for land sale in the peripheries obliged buyers to an ambiguous, even open-ended commitment. Some residents claimed that after years of payments, they owed more than their initial obligation. According to my interviews, however, this ambiguity deterred no one from purchasing. In any case, it often turned out to be moot, as developers commonly disappeared after a few years of making considerable profits.[29]

These contracts had another and much greater problem. It was an item that always appeared in one form or another and that usually turned out to be the most ambiguous of all. In the case of Lar Nacional, it read: "You receive . . . legal guarantee of delivery of a modern house acquired in Park Lar Nacional." In 1968, the developer sent a circular to buyers emphasizing the legality of its contracts. Under the item "title," it declared: "The absolute security of transaction is simply proved. The title of the area of Lar Nacional Construtora e Administradora Ltda. is registered with the 9th Real Estate Registry, under the number 104,585." Indeed, this registry existed, if residents chose to investigate. However, as we shall see later, such an entry is not incontrovertible proof. Moreover, Lar Nacional's insistence was unusual. In most subdivisions, the only evidence of ownership sellers presented was the sale contract itself. Lar Nacional's circular also makes evident in its "progress report" that none of the promised infrastructure had been completed: no central water supply, electricity, paving, sidewalks, gutters, or street lighting. Although the pioneers eventually installed every one of these services through their own initiatives and resources, they have never received title because they have been unable to resolve what turned out to be the compromised legality of their original purchase.

Consolidated in the late 1960s, therefore, the marching order of the day for São Paulo's working classes was to go to the periphery, "to live in the bush." Residents remember that journey as one of daily struggle, sacrifice, and not small amounts of heroism to overcome many hardships. Every pioneer seems to tell a similar story about mud as Pedro's: "When I arrived in Lar Nacional, it was bush. When it rained, all mud. Buses couldn't get through. We had to walk for hours to find a way to get to work. We carried our shoes on our shoulders, and sometimes our pants, because people would make fun of us if we showed up at work with muddy clothes." The houses were precarious, always filled with the dust and debris of construction. The neighborhoods had no markets, bakeries, or pharmacies; they only had one-room bars that sold bits of this and that and doubled for meetings and parties. For many years, there were no sewage or electrical lines, no public telephones, no educational, health, or security services. Maria, who came to Jardim das Camélias from a *cortiço* in Brás, recalls walking home for miles with groceries on her back and carrying dirty clothes in pails to a collective well. "It was an adventure, but we stuck it out," she proclaimed. In both Jardim das Camélias and Lar Nacional, residents vividly remember being caught in the cross fire of competing developers. They recall threats of eviction and beatings from *capangas*. Moacir described returning home from work to find another family occupying his house, his possessions thrown out front by a *grileiro*'s thugs.

Financial burdens also overwhelmed families. Zé from Jardim das Camélias recounts: "For the wages we got in those days, the installments were really heavy. To pay them, we sometimes had to forgo buying clothes or shoes. Sometimes we felt like eating something different at home, but we couldn't because we had to save money for the payments. We tightened our belts one notch and then another. There were times when we couldn't pay, and we fell behind. And then we had to pay interest and penalties, and interest on interest. But we caught up, because I worked vacations at the factory to make extra money. Instead of resting at home those thirty days of vacation, because the money situation was bad, I spent them working and took that extra month of money and succeeded in doing something."

In every neighborhood, the Zés and Marias of São Paulo's working poor succeeded in making their homes and building their periphery. As a result, they recall those many years of hardship with deep satisfaction as a era of self-reliance and achievement, in which the goal of a home-of-one's-own sustained them. As IDORT ideologues had hoped, but in processes of political and personal transformation not anticipated, their autoconstruction transformed them from renters and squatters into home owners in just one generation. On this result, the census data are unambiguous: table 5.2 indicates that the rate of home ownership (domiciles owned by occupants) in the municipality of São Paulo increased from 19% in 1920—when the pattern of urbanization was overwelmingly concentrated—to 41% in 1960 and to 69% in 2000. Even more remarkable, home ownership is generally higher throughout the peripheries than in the central districts and equivalent to or higher than in the wealthiest ones. In many of the poorest neighborhoods, it reaches more than 80%.[30] In 2004, I helped survey 185 houses in Lar Nacional, the lots of which constitute the principal area of disputed land titles. Of these, 87% were owner-occupied, 6% rented, 2% in commercial use, and 5% occupied in other conditions or without information.

Technically, these rates apply to ownership of the docimile but not necessarily the land. Hence, they include squatters who live in their own houses on seized land. Sorting out the data on definitive landownership is, as we have seen, a Sisyphean task and one impossible for the census. Nevertheless, we can make several approximations based on census data.

Table 5.2

Home Ownership: Domiciles by Tenure of Occupants, Municipality of São Paulo, 1920–2000

	Domiciles						
Occupied by	1920[a]	1940	1960	1970	1980	1991	2000
Owners	11,404	69,097	342,644	683,930	1,060,543	1,614,532	2,071,736
(%)	(19.1)	(25.0)	(41.0)	(53.8)	(51.4)	(63.6)	(69.4)
Renters	46,976	187,555	439,157	486,472	824,956	730,318	645,017
(%)	(78.6)	(67.7)	(52.6)	(38.2)	(40.0)	(28.8)	(21.6)
Others[b]	1,404	20,302	53,134	101,877	176,697	195,103	269,224
(%)	(2.3)	(7.3)	(6.4)	(8.0)	(8.6)	(7.7)	(9.0)

Source: For 1920 and 1940, Bonduki 1983: 146; for 1960 to 2000, IBGE 1960–2000.

[a] Data for 1920 refer to the number of buildings and not to the number of domiciles. As most owner-occupied buildings in 1920 had a single family in residence, while most occupied by renters had multi-domicile units, it is reasonable to suppose that the number of rented domiciles was significantly greater than that given in the table.

[b] The category "others" includes domiciles that are ceded rent free by an employer or private individual, those whose rent is paid by employers, and those whose rent includes nonresidential space.

First, the rates of home ownership are broad indications of landowner-ship in the peripheries for several reasons. Although the number of people living in favelas in São Paulo has steadly increased since the 1960s, and although some neighborhoods have high concentrations (above 30%), it still accounts for less than 10% of the municipal population: 1.1% in 1973, 4.4% in 1980, 7.7% in 1987, and 8.4% in 2000 (Rolnik, Kowar-ick, and Somekh n.d.: 91; SEADE 2006: 53).[31] Second, we can estimate landownership by subtracting the total number of domiciles in favelas from the total number of domiciles owned. Most of the remainder may be presumed to be occupied by those who paid for their land and thus have some ownership claim to it, since occupants would not invest in building or buying a house on someone else's land unless they were squatters, and squatters can make no such land claims. I say most because not all squat-ters own the homes they inhabit, though most do. If we assume that all do, then 10.0% of the total number of domiciles owned in the municipal-ity in 2000 were located in favelas (IBGE 2000). That number suggests a landownership rate among those who own their homes of 90%.

This estimate is borne out by a survey of lot ownership in São Paulo from the 2000 census, in which the residents of privately owned domiciles were asked to state the terms by which they occupy their lots (ownership, concession, or other). Of course, many people of all classes who say they own land cannot provide definitive proof. For the urban poor, however, what is new and of great social consequence is their widespread claim to own residential land based on purchase. In the census survey, fully 90.1%

of privately owned domiciles were occupied by those who also claimed to own the lot. In the poorest twenty-six districts of the municipality—those averaging five minimum salaries or less for heads of households—the combined average ownership rate in these terms was 87%.[32]

Thus, autoconstruction in the peripheries of São Paulo created a key distinction among the urban poor and change of status for most of them: it distinguished between those who paid for land to build a house and those who did not and therefore resided under other conditions. Even if the former were swindled in their purchase and could not prove full legal ownership as a result, the majority could claim to have transformed themselves in the process of settling the peripheries from renters, squatters, and mere *posseiros* of land into landowners. They could claim to have become urban citizens through the appropriation of the very soil of the city.

Although autoconstruction thus transformed a foundational element of Brazilian citizenship and its urban segregation, it also clarified and perpetuated many other aspects of that segregation. This paradox resulted in part because the center-periphery paradigm of urbanization separated the rich from the poor by great distances, creating stark contrasts in space. As a solution to working-class housing, autoconstruction allowed elites to rid themselves of the close presence of the poor and of responsibility for their domestic well-being. It brought an out-of-sight-out-of-mind tranquillity to elites, as the poor were left to fend for themselves far away. Moreover, the productive consequences of home and land ownership—improvements in neighborhoods, political organization, legal standing, self-esteem—took time to appear and decades to mature. In the interim, most factors of well-being and life chance continued to display the brutal disparities of nearly straight-line correlations with distance from the center. With the great exception of home ownership and the consumption of durable goods related to it (like appliances), such plots indicate the dichotomous logic by which society is organized in space in Brazilian cities and the perversity with which space continues to correlate with life chances.

Thus, for the period of 1940–1980, the distribution of inequality in space remains both largely dichotomous and centrifugal, even though pockets of poverty exist in the central districts (mostly *cortiços*) and of wealth in the peripheries (a few fortified enclaves). The center is overwhelmingly wealthy, equipped with every urban service and infrastructure, legally developed, and socially white; its residents experience much lower crime, better health, greater educational and cultural opportunities, and get around in cars and taxis. In contrast, as one moves farther into the peripheries, neighborhoods become poorer, more precarious in every infrastructural service, illegally developed, and socially less white; their residents are younger; experience high crime, poor health, low education, and few cultural resources; and spend hours each day packed like cattle on buses commuting to work.

In fact, the development of central and peripheral districts retains this centrifugal distribution of inequality up to the present, even though the peripheries generally experienced significant improvements during the period of 1980–2000 as a result of autoconstruction, property struggles, and political mobilizations. We will analyze these improvements later and see that they result from the demands of residents in peripheral neighborhoods to become fully legal residents and full citizens of the city. Nevertheless, a dramatic urban inequality and its pattern of centrifugal spatial segregation persists. Map 5.5 conveyes this persistence at a glance. It presents recent snapshots of six social indicators, each striking in its centrifugal distribution. Combined with income, their sum indicates an urban condition that remains one of profound inequality.

Social Rights for Urban Labor

At the same time that many Brazilian cities began to segregate spatially through peripheral urbanization, the revolutionary government of Getúlio Vargas (1930–1934) ordered massive state intervention to reorganize the nation's urban economy and society. Its proposal for the latter was to create a new kind of national public sphere into which to channel and regulate the new urban labor force. The framework of this interpolation was citizenship: the state constituted urban workers as special citizens by bestowing social rights they had never had and celebrating a dignity of labor it had never recognized. However, it did so as the means to absorb them into its legal and administrative orders. Vargas reformulated the citizenship of workers precisely to eviscerate any alternative public sphere of autonomous working-class organization. There is probably no chapter of Brazilian history more analyzed than the development of the corporatist and populist state under Vargas between 1930 and 1945. But as his regimes created a state-sponsored social citizenship that has lasted in part through the contemporary period, understanding it is indispensable. Moreover, I argue that Vargas's innovations did not constitute a new model of citizenship, as often supposed, but rather a modernization that perpetuated the nineteenth-century paradigm of differentiated citizenship by adapting it to the new conditions of an emerging urban industrial society. In what follows, I focus on this adaptation. However, I reserve a discussion of workers' interpretation of its social citizenship until chapter 7, where I consider the changing public sphere of rights the urban peripheries produced.[33]

Between 1889 and 1930, the laissez-faire orthodoxy of Brazil's first Republic had allowed industrializing urban capital and labor to expand their organization in an unregulated manner and to engage each other in increasingly chaotic and violent confrontation. After the union law of 1907 permitted the free organization of labor, worker associations and organized protests of all types increased dramatically. In São Paulo, there were twelve factory strikes between 1888 and 1900, eighty-one between 1901 and 1914, and 109 between 1917 and 1920. That European immigrants mobilized most of these associations and actions is not surprising, as they occupied a majority of the city's industrial jobs (51% in 1920) and had far greater union experience than national workers (Fausto 1986).[34] Moreover, many of them were affiliated with anarchist and communist groups which constituted an alternative public sphere of debate about the development of Brazil's economy and society. Through the 1920s, the state's response to the increasingly aggressive activities of this urban labor force was both to neglect the underlying causes of strife and to repress its manifestations. Backed by laws targeting union militants as subversives, it cracked heads and deported foreign workers.

Simultaneously, however, modernizing sectors of the political elite began to reconceive the state as the interlocutor of capital and labor. They imagined it as a third force that had the power to manage the interests of the other two and thereby control the development of both, by defining their conflict and imposing negotiations in terms of the state's own administrative apparatus. By the Vargas Revolution of 1930, this new state was in the making. Through the imposition of some thirty labor laws within two years, the regime proposed to make the demands of the labor movements for social rights and justice its responsibility. In exchange for bestowing rights on workers, it demanded that they relinquish all work-related organizational autonomy. To neutralize independence, the regime pledged to regulate factory life and to mediate worker and employer demands. Its aim was to absorb the interests of both sides and negate their powers of conflict.[35]

The first social law, decreed in 1930, aimed to create the national body of workers on whom to bestow the new labor rights of citizenship. The so-called Law of Two-Thirds (Decree 19,482) nationalized the labor force by requiring companies to guarantee that two-thirds of their employees were Brazilian-born and restricting the immigration of third-class passengers. By thus proposing to protect Brazilians from foreign competition during a time of world depression, the state claimed to fight unemployment among citizens. But the law also gave it control over the industrial labor market and powers to remove the foreign-born leadership of the labor movement. As a result, the state succeeded in supervising the substitution of national wageworkers for foreign, at a time

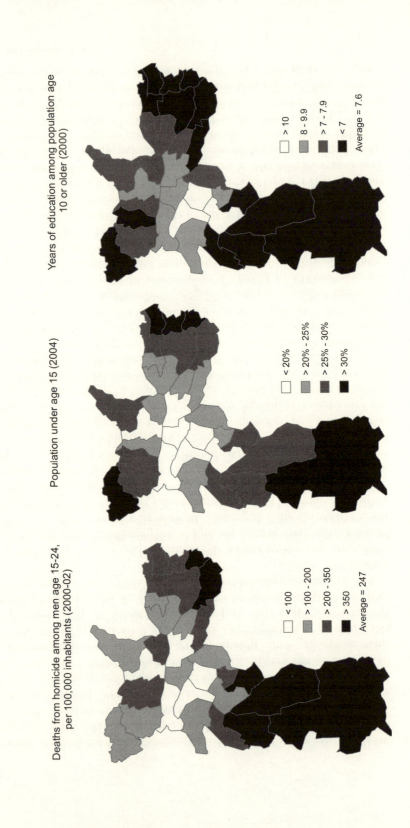

Deaths from homicide among men age 15-24, per 100,000 inhabitants (2000-02)

< 100
> 100 - 200
> 200 - 350
> 350

Average = 247

Population under age 15 (2004)

< 20%
> 20% - 25%
> 25% - 30%
> 30%

Years of education among population age 10 or older (2000)

> 10
8 - 9.9
> 7 - 7.9
< 7

Average = 7.6

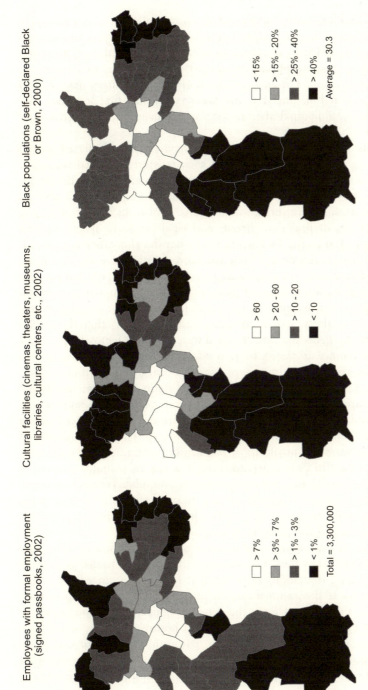

Employees with formal employment (signed passbooks, 2002)

☐ > 7%
◻ > 3% - 7%
▨ > 1% - 3%
■ < 1%

Total = 3,300,000

Cultural facilities (cinemas, theaters, museums, libraries, cultural centers, etc., 2002)

☐ > 60
◻ > 20 - 60
▨ > 10 - 20
■ < 10

Black populations (self-declared Black or Brown, 2000)

☐ < 15%
◻ > 15% - 20%
▨ > 25% - 40%
■ > 40%

Average = 30.3

Map 5.5. Six distributions of urban inequality by subprefecture, municipality of São Paulo, 2000–2002. *Source:* SEADE 2004 *a,b,c.*

when internal migration supplanted immigration as the means to supply new urban labor. Equally important, the revolutionary government used the Law of Two-Thirds to create a new meaning of national citizenship for Brazilian workers by making them the beneficiaries of its right-to-work qualifications. For citizens who had previously been denied most rights of national membership, this law created their first collective and, in most cases, individual identification with citizenship as a distribution of rights.

With its promulgation, however, the new state perpetuated an old principle of citizenship: it promoted a citizenship of special treatment based on the differentiated distribution of entitlements among Brazilians. The Law of Two-Thirds not only distinguished the employment rights of Brazilian citizens from foreign noncitizens. It also distinguished among different types of Brazilian citizens and legal residents. It gave special treatment to those citizens born in Brazil but discriminated against citizens born elsewhere who had been naturalized. After a few months, moreover, amendments to the law created a precedent that remained basic to the new state's entire project of social rights: they exempted agricultural enterprises, so that Brazilian citizens who labored at nonagricultural jobs (i.e., urban workers) had legal rights and protections that those who labored in the fields did not. If this differentiation of Brazilian citizens seemed to require no justification, it was because its principle passed as a taken-for-granted assumption of Brazilian citizenship. Rather, in addition to making workers the beneficiaries of rights, what was new in the law in relation to the labor policies of the First Republic and Empire was its legal discriminations against foreigners and its moral deprecation of them to define Brazilian national membership. This new xenophobia elicited a government justification. In a newspaper interview, the Minister of Labor, Lindolfo Collor, defended the new law by claiming that many immigrants came to Brazil because it was "an unpoliced country, in many respects a paradise for vagabonds" and accusing them of "increasing the difficulties of life in the urban centers and infecting the Brazilian worker with subversive ideas" (cited in Paoli n.d.: 166).

The Law of Two-Thirds initiated the government's strategy to create a new national labor force not only by granting rights to urban workers and controlling the employment market. It also announced the state's plan to promote the national worker to the center stage of national development. For the first time, the state recognized the laboring classes as central agents of Brazilian history and bestowed dignity upon their labor, indeed upon labor itself. For a nation in which labor had never been a source of dignity but only of its opposite, in which elites abhorred manual work, and in which those who performed it were low-life, if not slaves, this promotion was momentous.

It had two primary components, one in spectacle and the other in law. Like other populists in Latin America and Europe, Vargas pioneered the use of spectacle and culture to form a modern national mass of citizens enthralled with the personifications of power.[36] He famously addressed the nation during his rule as "workers of Brazil," forging a new public sphere for the national body out of synecdochic confusion of part for whole. This universalizing appeal made the working classes his special focus, as it rhetorically converted all citizens into workers and glorified all workers as special citizens. Moreover, it made labor the essence of working-class citizenship. Vargas was a master of this alchemy in his use of the new media of radio and cinema. Broadcasting to the nation, he scripted it into the new rituals of national identification he invented for schools, factories, and holidays. These spectacles of citizenship absorbed the humble worker into the ranks of worthy citizens. They transmogrified a figure of misery and abuse into a national role model of productivity, discipline, and loyalty. But the spectacles also made clear that in exchange for the state's promotion of their welfare and in order to receive its bestowal of social rights, workers would have to conform to this model of labor. In this stipulation, the new state effectively deflated any alternative public sphere that might compete in the formulation of Brazilian citizenship.

The regime's most effective strategy in this project was to make the state's legal definitions of labor the overwhelming focus of working-class citizenship. In addition to spectacle, it promoted the dignity of workers by recognizing their social rights in law. This recognition consisted, first, in focusing the universe of their demands for rights and justice on their labor experience and, second, in channeling those demands into the state's legal and judicial spheres. The revolutionary government of the 1930s claimed to embrace the very ideal of social justice and the legitimacy of rights that the labor movements had demanded over the decades: demands for job security, eight-hour workdays, weekly rest periods and holidays, minimum wage, job safety, pensions, and the abolition of child labor, among others. The regime accepted these demands through a series of laws that defined, regulated, and bestowed them on workers as rights.[37]

This entire construct of social rights had, however, a fundamental catch: Although the government presented it as the universal incorporation of the "workers of Brazil" into a regime of social rights and citizenship, not all workers, much less all citizens, had access to these rights. Rather, their distribution was legally restricted to the fraction of workers who had legal contracts in regulated occupations. To guarantee that the labor movement comply with its laws, the revolutionary government had initially tried to limit access to labor rights to those workers who joined unions organized according to its rules. Thus, in 1932, it decreed that only members of officially recognized unions had the right to file grievances at the labor courts it created and, in 1934, that only they had rights to guaranteed holiday benefits. Although the constitutional assembly later that year declared these laws unconstitutional and made union membership voluntary, it nevertheless excluded the nonunionized from labor's collective regulations (Santos 1979: 69). When the Constitution of 1937 eliminated that restriction, what remained as the essential qualification for labor rights was the legalized contract between employer and employee in an officially regulated occupation. With such a contract, both unionized and nonunionized workers (both of whom had to pay dues to the official union representing their profession) had rights to state-guaranteed benefits. Without it, workers relied only on their employer's beneficence.

The structure of this differentiation depended on four components. First, the union law of 1931 established that only unions organized by profession had legal standing and official recognition. Second, a series of complementary laws defined and regulated what constituted the professions in each economic category. As they exempted those in agriculture, they basically applied only to the urban labor force. Third, other laws decreed that only workers who exercised a regulated urban profession through a legal work contract had the right to join the corresponding union, register grievances at the labor boards and courts, and, most significant, access the labor benefits that the union of their profession had negotiated with the state. Fourth, the government instituted labor passbooks as the means to prove a worker's occupational classification and contractual status. Anyone who aspired to work could obtain a passbook. But only employers could make entries to establish the profession of each worker and keep track of his or her labor history (e.g., specific contract, position, wages, hiring and dismissal dates, holidays and other benefits, accidents, disputes, and so forth). As Wanderley Guilherme dos Santos (1979: 69) concludes, this professional passbook was more than legal proof of a contractual relationship between employer and worker. Its proof established both the latter's professional standing and a second contractual relation between the state and the worker that bound each to a set of labor rights in exchange for work duties properly performed and recorded. Workers' rights derived from those of the profession, and the profession only had standing to negotiate those rights by virtue of the state's regulation.

The passbook thus became "a certificate of civic birth" into what Santos (1979: 68) describes, in a well-known turn of phrase, as a "regulated citizenship":

Citizens are all those members of the community who are located in whichever occupations are *recognized* and *defined* in law. The extension of citizenship is made, therefore, by the regulation of new professions and/or occupations, in the first place, and mediated by the amplification of the scope of rights associated with these professions, rather than by the expansion of the values inherent in the concept of community membership. Citizenship is embedded in the profession, and the rights of the citizen are restricted to the rights of the place he occupies in the productive process, as recognized by law. All those whose occupations the law does not recognize, therefore, become pre-citizens.

In this passage, Santos identifies the structure of Vargas's extension of citizenship to the working classes and its mechanism of inequality: it excluded all workers, rural and urban, whose occupations had not been regulated by law and, I should add, who did not possess the required legal contract of work for that or other reasons.[38]

However, I wish to raise two problems with Santos's analysis. First, it is a misconception to distinguish a type of citizenship as "regulated." All are regulated. There is no such thing as an unregulated citizenship. Rather, as the distinguishing feature of Vargas's extension of social rights was its differential distribution, it is more useful to describe it as a differentiated rather than uniform or egalitarian type of citizenship. Identifying it as difference-specific has a significant advantage: it indicates that far from creating a new model, Vargas perpetuated the historic paradigm of Brazil's inclusively inegalitarian citizenship by giving it modern form, by adapting its differentiations to the new conditions of modern urban industrial society. Vargas breathed new life into it through a number of innovations: he added the component of socioeconomic rights, made their focus the labor of the working classes, and developed a particular scheme of legalized differential distribution. Without doubt, these innovations had momentous consequences for the modernization of Brazilian society and state. However, there can no mistaking that his was an adaptation, brilliant to be sure, of the centuries-old paradigm of national citizenship in which incorporation appears universal—through the apparent universality of law—but distribution of the prerogatives attached to membership is legally restricted. As such, it also makes little sense to define, as Santos does, those included in this distribution as "citizens" and those excluded as "pre-citizens." Both groups contain national citizens. An excluded rural worker who is Brazilian and an included urban worker with a legal labor contract in a regulated occupation who is Brazilian are both member-citizens of the same polity. It is precisely the inequality of their common citizenship that is the problem.

The independent labor movement struggled persistently during the 1930s to construct viable alternatives to this restricted social citizenship, trying to sever the link between social rights, regulation by occupation, and passbook qualification. Workers were particularly distrustful of the passbook, which they had good reason to view as a means of secret government surveillance and police repression. Indeed, at the beginning of the decade, some independent unions issued their own passbooks they claimed would establish rights to benefits. They and allied organizations attempted to build an alternative sphere of participation through unofficial factory commissions, strikes, disruptions, protests, and other forms of popular mobilization. Although this resistance was significant, although its repression unpopular, the important point with regard to the development of citizenship is that these efforts failed. By refusing to recognize any alternative to its regulations, the state resolutely maintained the link between legalized profession, contract, and rights. Unable either to compete with the provision of benefits and/or to consolidate a different sphere of rights, independent unions folded. By the time Vargas's coup in 1937 established the Estado Novo, most voices for an alternative construction of urban economy and society had been silenced—at least until the decade following the fall of Vargas in 1945, after which they were smothered again by the military coup of 1964.[39]

The 1937 Constitution that crowned the Estado Novo resynthesized the many laws that had gone into its construction. Article 136 divided Brazil's population into those who worked and those who did not, making work both a social right and a social obligation that entitled workers to state protection.[40] By the same coin, it practically criminalized those who did not work for reasons other than infirmity. The regime placed the unemployed at the moral margins of society, labeling them "bums" (*vagabundo*) and excluding them categorically from the only kind of citizenship rights most Brazilians at the time might realistically exercise. Thus, it created a new construct of social marginality and exclusion.

In addition, the Vargas state divided Brazil's *laboring* population into two unequal groups of those who worked in the legally defined professions and those who worked in other kinds of jobs and situations. The former had the right to join unions, register passbooks, and receive state-guaranteed benefits; the latter had none of these rights. Thus, Vargas's system of social citizenship generated not only a new concept of marginality, aggregating the unemployed and the criminal. It also produced that of the informal labor market which comprised all those irregularly employed and underemployed, as well as those regularly employed but in unofficial occupations. It therefore differentiated Brazilian citizens into unequally graded subgroups with regard to the distribution of social rights: urban/rural, employed/unemployed, formal market/informal market, contracted/uncontracted, registered/unregistered, and unionized/not unionized. In this scheme, only a fraction of Brazilian citizens qualified for the social rights of citizenship as defined through the universe of labor.[41]

Moreover, it even divided that fraction into antagonistic parts, as each category of worker strove to defend and increase its privileges through the particular negotiations of each profession with the state. Hence, teachers got to retire five years earlier, retirees fixed one minimum salary as the lower limit of pensions, public functionaries won job tenure, and judges successfully resisted any form of external control and review. Work-based differentiations of rights also organized retirement from work. The national social security system became tied to labor laws, especially after the passage of the Consolidated Labor Laws in 1943, and excluded those not regulated by them. For example, the Organic Law of Social Security in 1960 explicitly excluded rural, domestic, and autonomous workers from its benefits. Only after 1973 were all Brazilian workers included in the social security system. However, some categories continued to suffer differentiation. Thus, domestic workers have retirement but not labor rights. Moreover, the regulation of social citizenship by labor qualification created an obviously unequal distribution of retirement benefits, as those who contributed more by professional category and those who accumulated more than one retirement by category received greater benefits.

In sum, the struggle to shape the emerging urban industrial modernity of Brazilian society was decisively won in the 1930s and 1940s by a particular formula of rule articulated through a particular project of citizenship. It channeled the urban working classes into a new state-sponsored public sphere of law, bureaucracy, and spectacle that depoliticized their demands for justice and gutted their organizational autonomy. It also severely repressed those who manifested alternatives, if only to demand compliance with the very labor laws the state supposedly guaranteed. These laws were in fact ineffectively implemented, as employers overwhelmingly ignored worker rights with impunity and secured numerous loopholes; bureaucracy complicated them to exhaustion; and judicial remedy proved unobtainable. Workers who exercised their rights generally did so at considerable risk; those who actually realized them did so with heroic perseverance.[42]

Paoli (n.d.: 309) concludes that "workers . . . were reduced to impotence and isolation in their daily work. . . . Ultimately, what the entrepreneurs had achieved by the early 1940s was the reduction of workers' conditions to the pure models of privatization and enslavement found at the turn of the century—the difference being that they could now resort to a sophisticated state apparatus which intervened in social issues through legal means, hence reducing even further the chances of a possible reaction by workers." If Paoli somewhat exaggerates the juggernaut of this apparatus, there is no doubt about the effectiveness of its combination of law and violence on three counts.

First, the Vargas state masterminded a social citizenship based on the universe of urban labor that modernized the paradigm of Brazilian national membership while adhering to its inclusive yet inegalitarian principles. It revitalized the regime of differentiated citizenship by distributing rights as special and unequal treatment to particular categories of citizens among the new urban masses. It demonstrated that these categories may be any the state differentiates, regulates, and rewards. Although the upper classes had historically overwhelmed these categories, Vargas's modernization entailed absorbing some organized sectors of the working classes into these categories of vested privilege. This differentiated citizenship sustained his corporatism. Second, the Vargas state systematically destroyed the development of a heterogeneous public sphere in which alternative sources of social citizenship might have flourished. Third, it constructed a new public by simultaneously differentiating and massifying citizens.

From the perspective of these masses, the labor laws constituted the visible horizon of rights. As such, rank-and-file struggles to achieve them in the face of employer noncompliance and state complicity resulted, ironically, in a distinct sense of collective identity and social citizenship among Brazilian workers. Thus, as Paoli and others argue, labor law and the factory regime it regulated—that is, the universe of legally regulated work—became the space in which the urban poor developed their imaginations for citizenship in the first decades after the Revolution of 1930. However, I would stress that although the arena of labor rights became an imagined source of dignity and identity for workers, it was also an imaginary marked by a deep sense of frustration, failure, division, and dependence. Similarly, the factory was a problematic space for the development of working-class citizenship. It may have been the workplace, but it was never the workers' place. Rather, it was dominated by the employer's sense that it was his private property and his exclusive sphere of authority, over which he lorded in patriarchal and seigniorial manner. In every way, workers in the factory regime were intensely supervised and repressed.

Although I return to the working-class sense of this social citizenship of labor in a later chapter, I conclude this one by using these problems to establish a contrast between the factory and the periphery as a space of citizenship. It is in contrast to the restrictions, regulations, and repressions of the labor-bound citizenship of the factory that the mostly illegal, autoconstructed, and remote peripheries emerged after the 1950s as autonomous spaces for the popular classes. The peripheries became their space, out-of-state-and-employer sight, off work. Precisely in contrast to the factory regime, the achievement of "a home of one's own" became for the urban poor an emancipation from employer domination and state regulation and, as such, a means to reevaluate both their personal and their collective place in Brazilian society. It is to this displacement and reformulation that I now turn in the next part of the book. Ultimately, these transformations became the ground for the development of new and countervalent public spheres of citizenship, categorically different from, though still entangled with, the one based on Vargas's labor rights.

A Differentiated Citizenship

Over the course of the last four chapters, I have analyzed the development of Brazilian citizenship as a combination of two considerations. One is formal membership, based on principles of incorporation into the political community, in this case, the nation-state. The other is the substantive distribution of the rights, meanings, practices, and institutions that membership entails to those considered citizens. The historical trajectory of a particular citizenship results from the interaction of the two. In Brazil, the combination produced a distinctive formulation of citizenship, one distinguished from its competitors on the world stage of nation-states through the deliberate constructions of eighteenth- and nineteenth-century Brazilians: a national citizenship that was from the start universally inclusive in membership and massively inegalitarian in distribution. Like the French and unlike the American, it rejected the formula of "nations within the nation." However, unlike both, it offered little expectation of equality in managing the social differences of members. Instead, it made extensive use of selective disqualification based on those differences to differentiate among citizens. As a result, its inclusive dimension allows for moral, symbolic, and patriotic identification with the sense of "being Brazilian," and of being equally so, among those who occupy very different places within the hierarchy of powers and privileges that the inegalitarian dimension maintains. This inclusively inegalitarian citizenship has been remarkably consistent in sustaining its principles of both incorporation and distribution, complementarity and hierarchy, since the inception of the Brazilian nation-state almost two hundred years ago. Indeed, membership became more inclusive with independence at the beginning of this time line and differentiation more severe with the foundation of the Republic at its midpoint.

To distribute rights differentially, the Brazilian formulation of citizenship requires the use of social differences that are *not* the basis of national membership, but prior to or other than it. Thus, when ruling elites sought to consolidate this conceptualization of differentiated citizenship in response to the great changes of independence and abolition, their solution was two-fold. To control political citizenship, they made suffrage direct and voluntary but restricted it to the literate. This restriction denied most Brazilians their political rights for a century, until the 1980s. To dominate civil and economic matters, they created a real estate market to legitimate the ownership of private property and finance the immigration of free labor. But they kept land prices high and wages low so that the working masses would have practically no legal access to property and independent production and be forced, as a result, to remain a source of semiservile cheap labor. Thus, political and civil citizenship developed in step: both became more restrictive as Brazil changed from an imperial nation based on slave labor to a republican nation based on wage labor during the nineteenth century.

Along the way, law became estranged as an ally of substantive justice from citizenship. Rather, it became a misrule of law: a system of stratagem and bureaucratic entanglement, deployed by state and subject alike to create invincible complication, obfuscate problems, neutralize opponents, and, above all, legalize the illegal. Brazilian law emerged from its colonial and imperial circumstances as a brilliantly constructed system of façades "for the English to see" and "for enemies." It became a scheme of alibis for the absence of effective social regulation, a form of social management from on high and remote control from afar, a compendium of particularisms that defied universal application; a misrule, in short, in which more law was the corrective for the ineffective application of previous law and meant more opportunity for entanglement and usurpation. In this context, obeying the law had low status, because to do so signified weakness. Compliance was thus a means of humiliation, directed at opponents and the poor. Conversely, manipulating, breaking, or selectively obeying the law signified power and became a habit of wealth.

Most Brazilians, however, had not the resources to use law in these ways. Overwhelmingly, they were its dupes and not its practitioners. As such, their exclusion from political rights negated their participation in making law, their exclusion from property made illegality the norm of their residence, and their incorporation into the labor market as practically servile workers denied them dignity. These exclusions from politics, property, dignity, and law alienated the vast majority of Brazilians from law as an institution that might otherwise have nourished their citizenship. Rather, they enabled the construction and perpetuation of a differentiated citizenship.

That individuals could be active citizens of a nation-state and not merely dutiful subjects of an emperor was an idea that smoldered under the debates about constitutional monarchy, abolition, immigration, political representation, and land reform throughout the nineteenth century. With the birth of the Republic, these debates had been won by elites who formulated a citizenship that systematically denied most Brazilian citizens any such role. In the 1930s, a different set of elites led by Vargas overthrew them with a project to adapt Brazil to the development of a modern urban industrial economy and society. This modernizing project realigned the differentiated formulation of citizenship to these new conditions. It introduced a new component—social citizenship—focused it on the new universe of urban industrial labor, attributed moral dignity to that universe, and endowed it with rights. However, the project did not change the central doctrine of differentiation that distributes inequality on the basis of special treatment for certain kinds of citizens. To the contrary, it perpetuated differentiated citizenship. It segregated urban space into a pattern of center and periphery by a centrifugal distribution of inequality and incorporated the new urban labor force into a public sphere of labor law without autonomy or equality.

Over the next decades, Brazilians massively moved to cities and built the urban peripheries. These migrant autoconstructors perceived the peripheries, however precarious at the beginning of their settlement, as a vital source of their experiences as modern Brazilians. As we shall see in the following chapters, these experiences fueled the irruption of an insurgent citizenship that destabilized the differentiated at the very sites that had produced differentiation – political rights, landed property, residential illegality, misrule of law, and servility. Although these conditions continue to sustain the paradigm of differentiated citizenship, they also became the conditions of its transformation. In effect, under different circumstances in the peripheries, the sites of differentiation became those of insurgence, as the urban poor gained political rights, became property owners, made law an asset, and achieved a greater sense of personal competence through their urban practices. Moreover, as residents formulated alternative projects of citizenship, they changed the development of the state and its relation with citizens. Their insurgence has thus cracked open the principles of differentiation that for centuries legitimated a particularly inegalitarian formulation of citizenship. It turned the poor residents of the peripheries into new citizens and launched an urban citizenship that transformed Brazil.

PART THREE

INSURGENCIES

Chapter 6
Legalizing the Illegal

What does that saying mean:
"For friends, everything; for enemies, the law"?

For enemies, the law. Yes, I remember very well, when I came to
São Paulo—that was some thirty-five years ago—in the Northeast, in Bahia where I lived, there were the big planters and
ranchers. The first thing they did with their children was to send
them to the capital cities to study law, to study. But mostly it was
law, because in Bahia, for example, I know people like [name
of well-known political boss] who all the wealth they have today,
lots of them there, came from getting estates [*fazendas*] even
through *usucapião* [adverse possession] itself, that they got by
using *usucapião*, by using law. And the poor little guy on his plot
of land? That's when they didn't send somebody—the hired gun
[*jagunço*]—to make the guy disappear. And disappear he did.
Yes, the law. They used it to get rich and to screw others.
—*Zé, neighborhood leader in Jardim das Camélias*

The urban peripheries of São Paulo developed, like most of Brazil, according to the norm of law Zé articulates: as an arena of land conflict in
which distinctions between legal and illegal occupation are temporary
and their relations dangerously unstable. In this context, the law regularly
produces irresolvable procedural and substantive complexity; this jural-
bureaucratic irresolution dependably initiates extrajudicial solutions; and
these political impositions inevitably legalize usurpations of one sort or
another. As such, land law promotes conflict, not resolution, because it sets
the terms through which encroachments are reliably legalized. It is thus
an instrument of calculated disorder by means of which illegal practices
produce law and extralegal solutions are smuggled into the judicial process. In this paradoxical situation, law itself is a means of manipulation,
complication, stratagem, and violence by which all parties—public and

private, dominant and dominated—further their interests. Of the many consequences of this misrule of law, one renders it much more than an opportunistic perversion: for the subaltern in the peripheries, legalizing the illegal is the means by which they become urban citizens through the appropriation of the very soil of the city itself.

This chapter investigates a case of land fraud in the settlement of Jardim das Camélias as a means to analyze these processes of il/legalization. My objectives are, first, to provide an ethnographic account of an extraordinary land conflict; second, to show how this conflict epitomizes the struggle of residents for inclusion in the legal city and mobilizes them to create grassroots organizations that give form and substance to a new citizenship; and third, to consider the relation between law and society it reveals. The case shows that the land in this peripheral neighborhood has been in dispute for nothing less than four hundred years. This demonstration establishes that the urban peripheries owe their formation to a contemporary reiteration of the age-old relations of land, labor, and law that we have already uncovered, namely, land policies designed to anchor and discipline a certain kind of labor force and illegalities that precipitate settlement and the legalization of property claims. However, the investigation also reveals that although today's land frauds repeat these old patterns, they do so with an unexpected difference. Instead of subverting citizenship as in an earlier era, residential illegality generates an insurgence of political and civil rights among the urban poor, who learn to use law to legitimate their land claims and who thereby compete in legal arenas from which they have been excluded. Thus, my argument is that for the working classes of the autoconstructed peripheries, illegal residence initiates the opportunity not only for legitimate property ownership through the eventual legalization of claims, but also for a new kind of participation in law and a new participatory citizenship that demands full inclusion.

These extraordinary changes derive from two contrasting conditions. On the one hand, although everyday law remains a burden to engage, the urban poor have learned, largely through struggles about residential property, how to use its complications to legal and extralegal advantage. In this sense, they perpetuate the misrule of law, but for their own benefit. I focus this chapter on that result. On the other hand, their political and legal mobilizations helped generate a new constitution and related measures that specifically address their residential experiences in the peripheries. These innovations create new opportunities to distribute resources more equitably and to foster the exercise of democratic citizenship. I focus the next chapter on that outcome.

I unearth the history of this land case for strategic reasons. As land disputes oppose interpretations about the origin of rights, they are explicitly struggles over the meaning of history. At their legal heart is a title search, a search for origins that justify or debunk claims. Thus, I soon discovered that no one could make much sense of the dispute in question without following it back in time. Litigants, lawyers, judges, residents, and swindlers themselves study its genealogies to base their present-day arguments on the authority of history, which in this case begins in 1580. They operate under an assumption basic to property rights in many societies that historical precedent confers legitimacy. It need not. An alternative argues that present necessity overrides precedent, a position for instance that activists of the Catholic Church and the Landless Movement have taken in Brazilian land disputes. As we shall see, however, disputants usually adopt a historicizing strategy: they use law to give their claims believable historical origins. Most turn out to be, nevertheless, highly ambiguous and many deliberately false.

If the search for origins aims to discover precedents that justify one set of claims to subvert another, my research into origins also has its corrosive intent. I establish their legal fiction to debunk not only the appeal to history in such cases but also what remains a central tenet in Brazilian legal education and scholarship about the idea of law and its explanation by function, namely, that the social basis of law as an institution is its role in maintaining social cohesion. In this view, law serves order essentially by resolving conflict, enforcing conformity to norms, and establishing clarity in relations, usually on the basis of notions of what is right, just, and good; and its inability to do so is the result of factors extraneous to its nature, such as incompetence, corruption, and politics. Thus, in a discussion of Brazilian law, Shirley (1987: 89) attributes its dysfunctions to a "gap between the formal and the applied law." Legal education generally attributes the incapacities of legal institutions to the gap that Shirley elevates to an analytic concept. Law students learn that formal law is based on the scientific logic of transcendent and liberal legal values, all too often corrupted by real-world interests.

Such views of law are functionalist because they claim that once law has processed conflict, both law and the conflict it channels further cohesion. This functionalism also characterizes classic legal anthropology. Hence, Schapera (1955: xxv) justifies why he excludes the "many subterfuges employed to circumvent the law" from his handbook of Tswana law by claiming that the natives themselves might resent "the inclusion of what are, after all, abuses of the law and not part of the law itself."[1] Of course, anthropologists of diverse theoretical persuasions have described such so-called extrinsic features of legal systems. But in an astute observation that remains valid today, Nader (1965: 21) writes: "[F]or the most part the inclusion of such extralegal functions in the anthropological literature has been anecdotal. [They] are not meant to illustrate *the law*; rather they are examples of what should be included in any truly *ethnographic* study of the law."[2]

205

Influenced by Marx, Foucault, and critical legal studies, subsequent anthropology rejects this essentialist and functionalist view of law. Its studies focus instead on law as a system of power, the multiple interests that mobilize it, its incoherency in practice, and its rationality as a kind of discourse. They abundantly confirm Foucault's (1977: 280) observation that "the existence of a legal prohibition creates around it a field of illegal practices," as well as Marx's critique of the injustices of law.[3] In the case at hand, I wish to emphasize not only that law produces illegality and injustice but also that illegality and injustice produce law. Moreover, although law predictably generates chaos, it often does so for strategic purposes which have, however, little to do with justice. The rule of law is as much about such productions as about the objectives of fairness, clarity, and resolution. Certainly, law needs to promote such ideals or its rule forfeits the possibility of justice. However, understanding that multiple agendas inform both its application and construction prevents the assumption that the rule of law is just (or democratic) without investigating the ways a particular rule of law engages a regime of citizenship.

The case of land conflict I analyze presents a historically specific rule of law that arms conflict and in that way makes it productive. So engaged, neither law nor conflict affords an opportunity to resolve problems in the wider net of social relations, as functionalism supposes. Rather, operationalized through conflict, Brazilian land law regularly and predictably perpetuates domination, legitimates usurpation, accentuates inequality, and furthers instability. These processes overwhelm any ideals of justice the Brazilian legal system harbors and turn it into a misrule.

Are we thus compelled to reconceive law if litigation is primarily a means to perpetuate and obscure rather than resolve disputes? My argument stresses intention and norm because land law in Brazil produces so much confusion in its own terms that one suspects not incompetence or corruption alone but rather the force of a set of intentions concerning its construction and application different from those aimed at justice and fair resolution. In what follows, therefore, I am especially concerned with the theoretical and sociological consequences of banishing the disruptive from the explanatory model. I do not doubt that utopian principles may exist in law or indeed that they are desirable. What I doubt is that the law's dystopias are external to its construction.

The Illegal Periphery

The settlement of the urban peripheries perpetuates the grand historical agency of Brazilian land occupation: illegality makes it possible. The very illegality of house lots in the peripheries makes land accessible to those

206

who cannot afford the higher sale or rental prices of legal residence. As significant, this residential illegality eventually prompts a confrontation with legal authorities in which residents generally succeed, after long and arduous struggle, in legalizing their precarious land claims. Illegal residence is, therefore, a common and ultimately reliable way for the urban working classes to gain access to land and housing and to turn their possession into property. Thus, the urban peripheries of São Paulo and other Brazilian cities typically develop through two law-related processes: one of illegal occupation that opens them to settlement and a concomitant one of legalizing the illegal. The first sustains a center-periphery pattern of segregation because the development of the center is overwhelmingly legal and the periphery illegal in one form or another. The second erodes that pattern, though very slowly. It is worth repeating that this unstable but productive relation between illegal and legal first crystallized at the beginning of colonization as a strategy of planter elites, who perfected it as a means to pilfer royal patrimony and who reaped incalculably greater gains. But after four centuries of use, and especially in recent decades, this strategy has become ubiquitous. Thus, in both the wealthiest and the poorest of Brazilian families, we find legal landholdings that are at base legalized usurpations.[4]

Whether people purchase or seize land in the periphery, most seem to understand this central paradox of land occupation. I am not suggesting that residents justify seizure as a step to legalization. Although some squatters and their organizations have understood that legalizing the illegal is a good bet in the long term and have learned to manipulate this lesson of history as precisely as wealthy squatters have always done, most residents of the peripheries are not squatters. Rather, they pay for house lots thinking that their payments will buy them the dignity and respect of property ownership, are swindled, cannot get title, and suffer greatly as a result. Indeed, my interviews show that even those who can articulate the bet of legalization are morally indignant at the thought of being considered a squatter. They reject categorically any suggestion that they deliberately sought an illegal land transaction. Moreover, they argue that in addition to the moral disadvantages of land seizure as a deliberate first step to property ownership, there are economic ones: legalizing land claims takes too long to sustain their goal of leaving a legacy of property to their children. As Paulo asserted in the meeting of the neighborhood association, residents "do not want to live for free." It is a matter of deep pride and self-worth that they have paid for their land. Having done so is the basis of their demands for full property rights.

Objectively, however, the fact remains that the working classes typically gain access to land only because it is illegally occupied, developed, and sold. Although the distinction of who paid for their house lot and who did not—of *autoconstrutor* and *favelado*—is crystal clear for residents, the legal status of land occupation is far more complicated. The problem is that whether people purchase or seize a house lot, both options almost always lead to some form of illegal or irregular residence. Those who squat on seized land have no legal rights to it, though the law tends to recognize that they own their constructions and allows their relocation if residents are evicted. Those who purchase lots, and thereby have some legal claims to own them, usually find that their deeds are jeopardized by the illegal ways in which developers sell land—from outright fraud to failure to provide the basic urban services required by law. Victims of faulty sales, they are accused of squatting by those who claim to own the land and then threatened with eviction.

The legal status of property initially depends on how it is zoned. In 1915, Municipal Law 1874 first divided São Paulo into four zones: central, urban, suburban, and rural. Subsequent legislation set requirements for development in each. This initial categorization contributed significantly to the illegal development of the hinterlands because it created a perduring dichotomy between a central zone defined by an urban perimeter and the rest. Most building and planning regulations applied only to the central area. When the poor began to move to the peripheries after the 1940s, the land there was not considered urban, and its development was therefore largely unregulated. Thus, municipal zoning created a dichotomy between development in the central zone, which was urban, regulated, and legal, and growth in the peripheries, which was not.

For example, legislation specified that for a street to be legal within the urban perimeter it had to have certain minimum dimensions and infrastructure. To facilitate the development of car and bus travel into the hinterlands, however, a law in 1923 bypassed these requirements by permitting the creation of "private streets" in the suburban and rural zones to which the urban codes would not apply. Developers used this possibility to open new land for profitable sale by putting in such private streets on the edge of the advancing urban perimeter. As the peripheries became occupied, this urban perimeter expanded progressively through new legislation and amnesties that rezoned the land. As it did, it incorporated many private streets that failed to meet the requirements of urban zoning and were therefore illegal according to its regulations. Thus, as we have seen before, new legislation created new layers of illegality. Each one required executive (i.e., political) favors to create exceptions, special treatment, and amnesties. But such actions did not generally retrofit the subdivision with urban infrastructure. Rather, they left residents in precarious legal and material circumstances that made obtaining a deed unlikely.[5]

Once land is absorbed into the urban perimeter, its legal status depends on how it is subdivided, alienated, and acquired, which means essentially either by sale or seizure. By law, parcels of urban land can only be developed when they are subdivided into lots. Federal and municipal codes regulate urban land subdivisions (especially Federal Law 6,799/1979), establishing physical requirements that include minimum lot size, hookups for services, and open spaces for traffic circulation and community facilities, as well as bureaucratic regulations that stipulate the procedures for registering the subdivision and alienating the land. These are in turn founded on the bureaucratic mode of land acquisition established in the Brazilian Civil Code (Código Civil 1990: Art. 530), through which property is acquired "by the transcription of the title of transfer in the Real Estate Registry." All transactions relating to property must be so registered to obtain the relevant legal rights. These transcriptions are regulated by the Law of Public Registries (6,015/1973), which sets out the formalities constituting the privately owned, labyrinthine, and venal cartulary system of public registries in Brazil, called *cartórios*.[6] Their immense bureaucratic power is given in the Civil Code (Art. 533), which states that transactions of real estate do not transfer ownership or related rights except from the date on which they are transcribed into the legalized books of the registry; that is, "those who don't register don't own," as the saying goes. Full ownership of urban land, therefore, requires a legally registered deed, called an *escritura*, to a lot in a legally registered subdivision. Anything less jeopardizes ownership.

As defined in the regulatory codes, people buy lots in four types of subdivisions, usually existing side by side in the same neighborhood: the legal, irregular, clandestine, and fraudulent. The rarest of the four, a legal subdivision, meets all physical and bureaucratic requirements. An irregular subdivision (*loteamento irregular*) is—or better, appears to be— legitimately owned and registered by its developer but violates in some way the requirements for parceling the land. A clandestine subdivision (*loteamento clandestino*) is not registered in the real estate registry though the land itself may be legitimately owned by its developer. A fraudulent subdivision (*loteamento grilado*) is sold by a swindler, a *grileiro*, who pretends to have legitimate title to the land through a vast repertoire of deceptions. Although an illegal subdivision often combines features of several types, it is classified according to its most severe infraction. Thus, while the three illegal types violate the planning codes, the *loteamento grilado* faces additional problems because it is developed, and even registered, on the basis of fraudulent documents.

It is exceedingly difficult to know how much of São Paulo is illegally occupied and constructed. Although the typologies may be clear, historical research into land titles too often demonstrates that the evidence used to claim legal ownership is contestable and unreliable. As the available estimates do not undertake case-by-case historical investigation (an impossibility), we must therefore consider them skeptically. One of the more suggestive estimates for residential construction calculates the difference between the number of dwellings counted by the national census and the number recorded in the TPCL, the municipality's official register of urban constructions. While the census counts all residential units, the TPCL only registers those that are supposedly legal. Thus, as Caldeira (2000: 235) demonstrates for the 1991 census, the discrepancy between the two measures suggests the extent of illegal construction. Caldeira found that in central districts, where the wealthy live predominantly in apartment buildings, the difference between the two was less than 5%. In two of the richest districts, Cerqueira César and Jardim América, for example, it was 1.2% and 1.9% respectively. These figures indicate that construction in the center of the city is overwhelmingly legal. The contrast between this legal center and the peripheries could hardly be greater. Caldeira (236–37) calculated that in the poorest periphery of 1991—an aggregate of twenty-eight districts—the discrepancy between legal and illegal residential construction was 164%. That is, there were 1.6 unregistered and presumably illegal residential units for every legally registered one. In Guaianazes, the district that also had the highest population growth in the city between 1980 and 1991, the difference was 433%, or more than 4 to 1!

Estimates of the amount of *land* occupied without secure title are even more uncertain, as the historical complexity is far greater. The Municipal Planning Department calculated in 1981 that São Paulo had 3,567 illegal subdivisions, comprising over 1.2 million house lots and corresponding to approximately 21% of the municipality's total area. In 1990, the same office under a different administration estimated that the percentage of illegal land occupation was 9% of the total area (Rolnik, Kowarick, and Somekh n.d.: 94–95). The latest calculation by the department responsible for the regularization of settlement in São Paulo proposes that in 2003, there were approximately three thousand illegal subdivisions, containing three million residents and occupying 20% of the municipality's land (Resolo 2003: 25). Now, it is unlikely that in just one decade so many cases of illegality could have been resolved so as to halve the area occupied illegally. It is equally unlikely that the number would double again in the next decade, especially as São Paulo's annual rate of population growth during those years declined. Perhaps it is the case that the extent of illegal settlement has remained relatively unchanged since 1981. But perhaps it is more likely that while the authorities may know of three thousand illegal subdivisions in contemporary São Paulo, many more may not yet have come to their attention and many others would have to be reclassified as illegal if their titles were thoroughly investigated. Thus, while some officials claim that "it is possible to affirm that between

210

60% and 70% of the residents of the municipality [of São Paulo] find themselves today in a situation that contradicts the models of the appropriation and organization of space contained in the current legal norms" (Rolnik, Kowarick, and Somekh n.d.: 90), and others claim that the number is closer to 30% (Resolo 2003: 25), I can only attest with absolute conviction that it is high.

Illegal residence is not only statistically uncertain. It is also a lived experience of complex ambiguity, even though many of its consequences are brutally precise. When people purchase a lot in an illegal subdivision, they cannot obtain a legally registered deed until they correct the infraction. However, it may take them decades even to discover a problem because they can only apply for an *escritura* after completing all payments for the property, a bureaucratic formality sustaining many a swindler. Brazilian law does not have the instruments of escrow or title insurance. Rather, it regulates a real estate transaction not paid for in full by a promissory contract that establishes the terms of payment and binds the seller to transfer title after their completion. When and if residents finally perceive their legal predicament, they usually learn that their investment is imperiled, their claims hopelessly entangled in bureaucratic misadventure, and their families threatened with eviction. In 1979, Caldeira (1984: 70) found that among those households that had purchased land in Jardim das Camélias, 57% had completed payments, although only 16% declared that they had definitive title to their lots. However, even such declarations cannot be taken at face value because many residents simply refuse to admit that their property, purchased with such sacrifice, is not secure. People have told me many times that "there may be some problems around here, but everything is in order with my lot" and have shown me documents to prove it.

The difficulty is that developers of all sorts, especially *grileiros*, typically provide buyers with reams of bona fide records of transactions—for example, sales receipts, tax documents, land surveys, and protocols for preliminary registration—based on frauds or irregularities not yet uncovered. Residents may even obtain quitclaim deeds on the basis of these records that are ultimately defective and that might be challenged by other supposed owners. Such compromised deeds or promissory contracts are not entirely worthless because they can be used to establish the good faith of the fraud victim, a juridical status crucial to the struggles of the poor in land disputes. Nevertheless, they do not establish clear title and deprive buyers of its sense of ownership.

Such subterfuge exemplifies what continues to be the fundamental strategy of land swindlers of all stripes, now adapted to the circumstances of mass urbanization: the use of complication as a means to deceive. Drawing inspiration from the intricate formalities of the urban land legislation

211

itself and its bureaucracy of signatures, seals, stamps, and notarized copies, they model their deceptions on the very laws they violate. They try every legal and bureaucratic façade possible to give their operations a cloak of legality, sometimes so expertly woven that lawyers and judges are fooled, let alone humbler folk who are apt to be intimidated by official-looking documents. The result is that it is usually exceedingly difficult to determine the legal status of land purchased in the peripheries, or the distribution of property conditions within a neighborhood, without an exhaustive title search of each and every lot. *Grileiros* rely on this very difficulty, knowing not only that people are gullible and that interviewing about property is unreliable, but also that standard title searches are not likely to reveal frauds because, for example, legally registered documents in one registry may be based on false or irregular documents from another.

The following case illustrates this stratagem. Squatters have long occupied a 72-acre area along one bank of São Paulo's Tietê River in the northeastern periphery of the city. In 1987, y sold the land to z, who registered the sale at the 7th Notary Office of São Paulo. This *cartório* based its transcription of the conveyance on the property's registration that same month at São Paulo's 17th Real Estate Registry. That registration states that the land belonged to a couple born in the 1860s, married in 1890 in Santos, and living in 1986 in Guarulhos near São Paulo, who sold the land in that year by power of attorney to y. The problem is that in 1986 the couple had been dead for many decades, according to death certificates registered at São Paulo's 19th Civil Registry. Digging considerably deeper, we find the original fraud: the 17th Registry based its registration on a deed transcribed in 1986 in the registry of a small town in the southern state of Paraná, which attests that a certain x presented himself as having the couple's power of attorney to sell the land to y—a lawyer, by the way. I predict that the courts will take many decades to conclude that z and the estate of the couple were defrauded by x and y, who made off with a lot of money, provided that z (who may have represented other buyers) was not a partner in the fraud or that the claims of the old couple do not turn out to be illegitimate, neither of which is a remote possibility. In either case, I wager that given the legal complication of any of these possibilities, the squatters will end up with the land—if they can mobilize to demand that the government legalize their usurpation because of "social interest" as permitted by the new federal constitution.

Even if the intrepid researcher survives the paper chase in such cases, it is often difficult to determine who owns what beneath the layers of complication. Hence, as in the next example, these disputes are frequently impossible to settle in court. Rather, they circulate forever through the bureaucratic system, awaiting more conclusive but nonexistent evidence on the merits of competing claims. Needless to say, irresolution best serves the interests of swindlers, as these cases are usually solved through extra-judicial and politically onerous maneuvers, such as accords and periodic amnesties, in which executive or legislative institutions of government intervene to declare the judicial system checkmated and abrogate one set of property claims in favor of another. Inevitably, such interventions legalize usurpation and thereby insinuate illegal and extralegal practices into the law. They are, moreover, modern-day versions of old practices that have inspired countless illegal land operations. Thus, as a delegate to São Paulo's 1935 state constitutional assembly reminded his colleagues during debate on an amendment to give legitimate title to those who claimed land without it if they had paid state property taxes, there is a perverse and well-known correlation between making and breaking law. "The land policy of São Paulo," he complained, "has always been to try to avoid future land frauds [*grilos*] by legalizing past land frauds" (São Paulo Assemblea Constituinte 1935: 228), thus pointing out that distinctions between legal and illegal in this area of vast social consequence were conceptually slim, noncategorical, and temporary. Perhaps because it merely restated the norm, however, his observation had no effect on congressional deliberation.

A Case of Land Fraud in Jardim das Camélias

To understand the vitality of this land policy and its importance in the formation of the periphery, I shall analyze an example of land fraud in Jardim das Camélias. The case involves 207 families who purchased lots between 1969 and 1972 but who were unable to get legal title to them because they were sold fraudulently. It is one instance of the kind of *grila-gem* and consequent legal chaos tormenting millions of residents in São Paulo's peripheries. I first outline the chronology of the land dispute since the residents became ensnared and then analyze the various ownership claims whose contradictions have made it judicially insoluble and whose complications stretch back to the sixteenth century.

In 1969, a man named Rafael Garzouzi, or "the Turk" or "the Lebanese," as residents call him, appeared in the sparsely settled Jardim das Camé-lias. Through his real estate company, Adis Administração de Bens S.A., he opened a few dirt roads, set up an on-site office, fenced in eleven 6 x 20 meter lots, and began to sell them. To buyers, he exhibited a plan to develop the entire neighborhood and deeds to the area that had been registered at the appropriate *cartório*. He offered a promissory contract that bound purchasers to monthly installments for periods of two to ten years and that pledged Adis to furnish receipts and a quittance after final

213

payment. With these in hand, the buyer could then register his purchase and transfer ownership. Among the many things that Adis did not tell its customers, however, was that although notarized as a document, its subdivision plan had not been approved by the planning authorities—nor could it be. It not only violated planning codes but, more seriously, disfigured a plan already approved in 1924 for the very same area in the name of José Miguel Ackel.

In early 1970, the estate of Nadime Miguel Ackel, José Miguel's brother, sued Adis to repossess the eleven lots it claimed to own. Adis brought countersuit claiming that it had held legitimate ownership rights since 1958, and its predecessors since 1890, to an enormous tract of land that included the lots. Adis sought damages, charging that the Ackel estate had in fact usurped these rights in developing the 1924 subdivision plan and in selling approximately seventy lots since then. Adis expertly manipulated the judicial bureaucracy so that charge and countercharge circulated through the legal system for several years without any effect. It used the time, however, to subdivide the rest of the neighborhood and sell another 233 lots, part of which it renamed Vila Tyrol. It also sold two large areas to business associates, who resubdivided them for sale as Jardim Ocidental and Jardim Eliane. The area now had four different names and subdivision plans with differing lot locations, irregular roads, and substandard lot sizes—all of which facilitated the sale of the same lot more than once. The 1924 plan was thus thoroughly disfigured by multiple layers of contradictory developments and an ever-expanding number of third parties who had ownership claims. Moreover, in response to Ackel's challenge, Adis and associates launched a campaign of intimidation: they installed *capangas* who demolished constructions, tore down fences, refenced according to different lot sizes and locations, and otherwise denied access to those who had not bought from their bosses.[7]

Residents responded in various ways. Many contracted lawyers who appeared in the neighborhood to offer their services and who disappeared as soon as they received advances on their fees. Some were duped by door-to-door document peddlers claiming to represent the real estate companies or even city hall. Others ignored the situation, believing their lots were legal. Finally, suspecting illegalities on all sides, about eighty people organized a Neighborhood Friends Association in 1972 to defend their interests collectively. They sought advice from a group of lawyers affiliated with the University of São Paulo, the Catholic Church, and leftist political parties, and known for their work with other grassroots organizations. This relationship turned out to be enduring, as one of these lawyers, Antônio Benedito Margarido, has remained dedicated to the case ever since.

Once the dispute was juridically engaged, the state of São Paulo intervened in 1972, claiming that in fact it owned the land and ordered the eleven lots sequestered. The Ackel estate opened a new suit in 1973 against both Adis and the state to repossess all 207 lots it claimed, to which Adis responded with a countersuit and the state with an order to sequester the entire subdivision in 1975. This writ ordered residents to make all remaining payments to a court-monitored account in a state savings bank, pending resolution of the ownership dispute. To this day, however, the dispute remains pending. This judicial irresolution meant that residents had to complete payments without receiving proof of ownership, that they could not sell their lots legally, and that neither the subdivision nor any of its constructions could be regularized. Nevertheless, I have not heard of any resident who stopped payment. Indeed, all the ones I know personally completed theirs into the court-monitored account, though I am told that some continued to pay Adis instead.[8]

The state's action meant that Adis received few installments. As the writ of sequester did not explicitly prevent it, Adis responded by serving residents with eviction notices to intimidate them into making lump-sum payments. During this period, however, the neighborhood association and its attorney learned how to use the legal system to prevent eviction. The lawyer demonstrated, on a case-by-case basis, that residents were making regular deposits into the court-sanctioned bank account, and the court voided the eviction proceedings. The more cases Margarido won, the more residents deposited their payments in the bank. Eventually, this strategy complicated Adis's activities in Jardim das Camélias to the point of inactivation. As one resident told me, however, "this [legal strategy] resolved the problem of not being evicted, but not the problem of [individual] title or regularization of the neighborhood." Moreover, regardless of whom residents paid, their money vanished. Adis absconded with whatever it could, eventually disappearing from the neighborhood, and the bank account seems to have vanished as well into a sinkhole of government bureaucracy. Perhaps when, if ever, the legal dispute is resolved, the bank deposits will reappear as a boon to survivors.

Until Margarido, no other lawyer representing residents had been able to beat the *grileiros*. At most, they had been able to arrange out-of-court settlements in which their panicked clients paid to cancel eviction proceedings; at worst, their clients were evicted. Eviction had happened, for example, in 1988 to a group of residents from fifty-nine houses in Ocupação Pirandello, when another *grileiro* brought eviction proceedings against them. They had not followed the association's legal strategy and were suspicious of its president and lawyer because they were openly "negotiating" with Adis. Instead, this group was represented by an attorney from the Workers' Party (PT), who was affiliated with the Landless Movement (MST). He told me that he refused on principle either to negotiate with "criminals"—referring to the *grileiros*—or to manipulate

215

legal "technicalities" on his clients' behalf because such technicalities had always sustained bourgeois rule and humiliated the poor. He was, he claimed, a *político* not a *técnico*. In any case, as far as I could tell from questioning him, he did not know much about the technical tactics of land law. Not surprisingly, his clients lost in court. They were evicted on a rainy day in a tense confrontation with a cavalry unit of the military police. With the horsemen preparing to move against them, they agreed to leave and were permitted to remove their possessions. Many sat on the sidewalk weeping, amidst their wet and ruined belongings, while their attorney gave an interview to Globo Television about injustice.

By contrast, the association's lawyer, Margarido, convinced members to contain their fears until their day in court. Then, at each hearing, he challenged Adis to prove ownership definitively, which he demonstrated it could not do in any instance. He argued, furthermore, that the residents had not defaulted on their contracts or invaded the lots but were buyers in good faith who were making full payments as requested by the court, pending resolution of the dispute. As a result of this legal strategy, he forced Adis to request postponements or to withdraw lawsuits altogether. In the end, after spending a considerable sum of money in legal fees, Adis lost or abandoned every case.

I witnessed the development of this new legal approach among residents during the eviction proceedings against Ocupação Pirandello. Families from sixteen of its seventy-five lots agreed to be represented by Margarido and to follow the legal orientation of the association. The others refused and remained with the lawyer from the PT/MST. At a meeting in one home, Margarido presented the association's strategy to these sixteen families. The association president then re-presented the plan "in simpler words," as consisting in "making a contract with the *grileiro* and by that ceasing to be an invader and, yes, [becoming instead] a buyer; then, you start paying him and then you stop paying him, depositing instead at court [*em juízo*] until he proves that he is the rightful owner of the sub-division, which he cannot do. This is the strategy of the association with its attorney." As predicted, these sixteen families were not evicted, while the others were.

A few years earlier, moreover, the association had denounced Adis's disfigurement of the 1924 subdivision plan to the department of records at city hall, which ordered the company to pay for a new survey and plan regularization. As the association expected, the new plan was regularized but could not be registered in Adis's name. This failure publicly compromised Adis's ownership argument. Furthermore, regularization dismembered each lot from the larger area claimed by Ackel and Adis. It identified each with exact measurements and location for tax purposes and assigned an individual tax number—an important recognition of the residents' rights and duties as owners, not squatters, to pay property taxes. As a result of these combined legal strategies, the association learned how both to disarm its enemies through legal engagements and to build a dossier of official documents to support its claims. By the end of the 1980s, its members did not yet have title to their lots, but they were no longer in danger of being evicted.

This mastery of the rules of the land game was a pioneering achievement for lower-class protagonists in a land dispute. It counters the norm that even when represented by counsel the poor lose head-on encounters with land barons and speculators. The association owed its success in this case to the abilities of its president, José Nogueira Souza, and its lawyer to achieve a new understanding of law and its bureaucracy as a strategic resource to exploit on behalf of the poor. With this approach, they overcame the essentialist views that have long characterized the poor's deferential, alienated, and subordinate relation to law. These views accept the bureaucratic and upper-class exploitations of the legal system as external corruptions of what they consider in itself an embodiment of principles of justice to venerate, of established procedures to endure fatefully, of complex knowledge and moral axioms best left to educated others, or even—in revolutionary and millenarian movements—of political ideologies to reject out of hand.[9] Though not a final victory, the association's success thus far constitutes a new relation to law on the part of its traditional victim, one that we may identify as strategic opportunism because it considers law to be a resource governed by circumstance as well as by fixed principles. Effectively, this innovation redistributes to the lower classes a legal strategy first perfected by Brazil's colonial elites.

The federal government's intervention completed the legal imbroglio of the dispute in Jardim das Camélias. It too claimed to own the land as federal patrimony and refused to recognize the validity of any transaction or judicial proceeding concerning the area from which it had been excluded, thus effectively negating most of its legal history for the last few hundred years. Federal intervention obstructed and confused every judicial action already undertaken to clarify ownership: it stopped demarcations and lawsuits in process and prevented both the city and the state from expropriating, legalizing, or in any way regularizing the disputed lands. In 1975, the case went to the Supreme Court as the only tribunal empowered to judge a conflict between federal and state governments. To proceed, however, it first had to evaluate each claim, discriminating the various private from public property interests in the area. As a result, the case languished in the high court for lack of evidence, resources, and probably nerve to decide which among the multitude of ownership claims had most merit.

As the years passed, the major parties to the conflict opted for extrajudicial strategies. In 1983, Adis and the estate of Nadime Miguel Ackel signed an accord to extinguish their suits against each other—though it had no effect on those also involving the state. Ackel conceded the 207 lots in dispute to Adis, which in turn conceded an equivalent number to Ackel in other areas of Jardim das Camélias. Neighborhood leaders considered the agreement nothing more than a pact among thieves to establish a united front against the increasing activity of squatters in the area. Nevertheless, a year later, the Neighborhood Friends Association signed an accord with both. It accepted the terms of their 1983 agreement if, in exchange, they suspended eviction proceedings, promised not to litigate against members of the association in the future, agreed that those who had completed payments in the court-monitored account had fulfilled their contracts, and accepted a number of other points securing tranquility for residents. Why should each party have acccepted this extrajudicial, so-called "friendly" solution to the dispute? Adis and Ackel wanted to have as much recognition of their ownership claims as possible, and the residents wanted to determine a clear owner to whom they could make payments in exchange for receiving legal title. They were willing to pay; indeed their morality required payment to distinguish them from squatters. The question was to whom?

At this time, the residents also mobilized politically to reach beyond the neighborhood. The association gathered signatures to petition the state governor, Franco Montoro, for an audience. It argued that as the first governor elected democratically after military rule, he was obliged to meet the residents and address their concerns. It delivered the petition to the governor through the mediation of a state deputy, Marco Aurélio Ribeiro, who was well known in the East Zone for his work on local issues and who also employed Margarido, the association lawyer, on his staff. José Nogueira, the asssociation president, remembers "filling up three or four buses with residents" and meeting Franco Montero at "the governor's palace," which they "occupied with humble people." At the meeting, however, no resident spoke. Rather, their case was presented by the lawyer and the deputy, who pressed the governor to accept the friendly solution the local parties had signed as a means to resolve the land conflict in Jardim das Camélias. This agreement required both the state and the federal governments to renounce their ownership interests. Although the governor denied that request, he instructed the attorney general to form a commission to analyze the problem of such land disputes in the entire eastern periphery of the city. The residents were jubilant that their mobilization had produced an effect at the highest levels of government.

The commission of state prosecutors met regularly over the next few years, with occasional participation of neighborhood leaders. In 1986, it concluded, in the words of the attorney general, that "the already chaotic legal situation of the area, abandoned for so many years to the greed of '*grileiros*,' has become practically insoluble given its procedural complexity, characterized by the simple fact that an enormous number of original defendants and their successors allege that they have legal evidence to support their claims." Given the impossibility of a judicial solution, the commission proposed resolution "by politico-administrative actions" based on a presidential decree abjuring the federal government's interests in favor of the state of São Paulo. In turn, the state would renounce in favor of friendly accords, such as the one in Jardim das Camélias, where possible; or, if not, it would expropriate disputed land and award it to residents.[10]

Although two state governors have signed agreements to form a joint state and federal commission to work out the details of this proposal, no further action at either level of government was taken. When asked why, residents grumble about lack of political will and about corruption but do not seem too surprised after twenty years of confusion. The neighborhood association continues to seek "friendly accords" between new *grileiros* and new residents in the area and to develop other strategies that we consider in the following chapters. Meanwhile, all around São Paulo, and indeed all around Brazil, the fraudulent transaction of land continues unabated under the cover of procedural complexity, which is to say, under the cover of law.

Histories of Dubious Origins

The Brazilian legal system features an ad hoc mode of irresolution in which people of all sorts, some intentionally criminal but most not, seek advantages through the deliberate use of the tactics and powers of law to influence an easily manipulated bureaucracy. As a construction of law, however, the system is too inoperative, contradictory, and confusing in its own terms to attribute these characteristics to corruption, incompetence, or individual manipulation alone—even though legal education does just that, typically presenting law as a science in which ambiguity, opacity, indecision, instability, and the like appear only as corruptions.[11] Rather, the law's predictable and reliable dysfunction in cases like the ones I consider indicates a more systemic mode of irresolution. It suggests that the legal system skillfully embodies intentions to perpetuate judicial irresolution through legal complication. For that very reason, the law facilitates stratagem and fraud. As we have seen, it is not only the malpractice or devious practice of law that generates this complication. Using the law legally also creates "practically insoluble procedural complexity," as the state attorney general admitted, and generally does so in important conflicts. In this way, using the law legally legalizes usurpation.

219

Although legal irresolution certainly promotes corruption, I suggest therefore that it has a more profound consequence in Brazilian society: it is also a means of rule that systematically produces irresolution for a society in which irresolution is a means of rule. Of course, there are other kinds of rule in Brazil, and judicial resolution is not unknown. Moreover, legal ambiguity need not entail administrative uncertainty. However, the more significant the dispute, especially involving land, the less likely it will find such settlement. The ruling classes use law to avoid for as long as possible court decisions in which they have to submit to the uncertainties of justice. Instead, they launch legal maneuvers to keep conflicts open and bureaucratically tied up until they can secure an extrajudicial and political solution. Going to court for a judgment between such elites may be an act of desperation because it means that they have exhausted their networks of power and favor to find such solutions. However, going to court against those who cannot manipulate the judicial process is an opportunity to demonstrate their domination.

That the residents of Jardim das Camélias and their lawyer have learned to orchestrate this process to avoid decisions and to develop extrajudicial solutions means nothing less than that they are redefining the legal arena. They are not changing the rules of the game but using them to challenge the exclusivity of its strategic players. Thus, people invoke the law's complications not only for fraudulent purposes but also to bring conflict into the legal arena as a way to keep it unresolved but contained, thus controlling it until the political will is found for solution. In perpetuating conflict, therefore, juro-bureaucratic irresolution may be politically functional but not in any functionalist sense.[12]

To demonstrate the contemporary force of irresolution and usurpation in the law, I shall unravel the tangled sets of ownership claims to land in Jardim das Camélias. Their history takes us again to the colonial foundations of Brazil and reveals the remarkable degree to which both territorial occupation and land law developed out of the need to legalize usurped rights—initially to further the fortunes of Brazilian colonists against those of Portuguese rule and, after independence, to consolidate them. As we follow the litigants' own arguments back in time, we find that the so-called *grileiro* in this case is not the only party to use law to construct historical origins and that it will be difficult indeed to determine which origins are less dubious.[13]

FEDERAL OWNERSHIP CLAIMS: *SESMARIAS* AND INDIANS

The federal government claims that it owns the lands of Jardim das Camélias because they fall within the boundaries of the ancient Indian settlement of São Miguel and Guarulhos, established by royal land grant in 1580 and officially extinguished in 1850. I found two arguments to support this claim. One reasons that the Land Law of 1850 and subsequent legislation incorporated indigenous villages created by *sesmarias* into the national patrimony. All federal constitutions except the first have reaffirmed this incorporation. The first—the Republican Constitution of 1891—placed indigenous lands under the patrimony of individual states, a decision reversed in the 1934 Constitution. The federal government's second argument accepts that by the first constitution the states had acquired rights in 1891 to former Indian settlements declared abandoned and vacant (*terra devoluta*) but claims that the lands in question were never in this category. Rather, it argues that the national government retained ownership because it has leased these lands to non-Indians since the seventeenth century on the basis of numerous executive and legislative interventions.

Several counterarguments have been advanced against these claims. Some assert that the states acquired real rights to Indian lands in 1891 that cannot be repealed by subsequent constitutions. Others maintain that the federal government has ownership interests but not rights because it never discriminated the residual indigenous lands from private holdings as required. Nevertheless, the important point is that all of these positions have juridically plausible aspects, which even the Supreme Court seems incapable of sorting out. This impasse derives directly from the legacy of legal chaos that postcolonial Brazil inherited from the Portuguese system of royal land grants, one of which was the Indian settlement of São Miguel and Guarulhos. As we have already dug deeply into this "invincible tangle" in chapter 4 to unearth the ground rules for usurpation it established, it remains to specify the case of São Miguel.

Established by Guaianase natives around 1560, the village was soon transformed by Jesuit missionaries into the model Indian settlement proposed in the Rules of Government. In 1580, the Jesuits obtained a *sesmaria* for it of about 100 square miles, making it an official reserve of Christianized Indians.[14] The Jesuits intended not only to separate the converted and the lands necessary to teach them the ways of civilization through agriculture. They also hoped to gain the Crown's legal sponsorship so that the grant would protect the Indians from enslavement and their lands from seizure by neighboring colonists in the expanding *vila* of São Paulo. Nonetheless, the Indians lost both their freedom and their lands. Not surprisingly, these deprivations occurred under the cover of law, and they offer a lesson in how legal complication and ambiguity serve illegal practices and how these practices in turn produced more law.

The enslavement of these Christianized Indians was a legal travesty. The local government first arrogated control over their secular affairs and

221

then created legal ambiguities and procedural complications concerning collective work responsibilities that permitted their de facto bondage.[15] Motivated by the usual complex of gold, greed, and expansion, it also usurped Indian lands through the legalization of illegal acts. First came outright land seizures. Then, at the beginning of the sixteenth century, the local government legally awarded to colonists *sesmarias* that illegally included Indian land. Such "irregularities," as officials described them, went unresolved for half a century until 1660, when the regional council managed to authorize itself to distribute lands within the reserve to colonists "as long as the Indians were not thereby disadvantaged" (cited in Bomtempi 1970: 64). This contradiction notwithstanding, it now legally regularized the irregular grants and issued new ones. In 1679, an appellate judge came to São Paulo to "correct," as the procedure was called, disjunctions between the law-in-books and the law-in-practice. Considering the land problem, he simply rewrote the former to fit the latter by recognizing officially what the council had already usurped, namely, its authority over the Indian settlement and the right to distribute its lands without restrictions. He further ordered the council to oblige all squatters in the reserve to pay an annual tax, thereby regularizing their seizures by converting them into leaseholds and transforming their status from mere invaders of public land to legally recognized leaseholders. These leases, called *aforamentos*, established usufructary rights to land that were both alienable and inheritable. As they were far easier to arrange than royal grants and as they initiated a private market in land rights, they enabled the council to dispose quickly and legally of the remaining Indian lands— all supposedly inviolable by the still-valid title of *sesmaria*.

From time to time, the Crown took note of these apparent contradictions. But it always deferred resolution in favor of temporary measures that indirectly recognized the validity of the leases, such as its declaration in 1703 that only its representative had authority to collect the rents. When the Crown finally voided the council's rule over the reserve in 1733 and ordered the land returned to the aborigines, the council rejoined that for over a century it had accumulated legal support for its land policies from numerous regional, colonial, and royal administrations. Like any smart *grileiro*, it brought out its dossier of collected documents (*sesmaria* titles, tax records, land surveys, leases, and so forth) to prove its point and succeeded in tying up the litigation in procedural complications until 1745. At that point, the Crown dropped its case, having determined that the appropriation of indigenous lands was irrevocable because there were few Indians left to retrieve them.

Thus, the genealogy of the federal government's claim to own enormous areas of the contemporary peripheries of São Paulo has an ancient history indeed, based on the incorporation of Indian settlements into the national patrimony. A probe of that history clearly demonstrates, however, that when it uses that claim to block the struggles of residents in Jardim das Camélias from gaining legal title to their house lots, it does so on the basis of centuries of usurpation through the legalization of illegal acts.

ACKEL OWNERSHIP CLAIMS: *POSSE* AND SQUATTER'S RIGHTS

The ancestry of the Ackel family's claims to Jardim das Camélias may be traced to the period of even greater confusion that began with the abolition of the *sesmarias* in 1822. For an entire generation, as we have seen, until the 1850 Land Law, no legal substitute for alienating public lands could be agreed upon. The effect was to encumber occupation with another layer of chaos: it made illegal seizure, *posse*, the only way to obtain land and automatically turned all further acquisitions into acts of encroachment. As chapter 4's analysis of the apparent contradiction at law between illegal and adverse possession (*usucapião*) established, the fundamental problem is that all of Brazil's federal constitutions and civil codes have created conditions under which *posseiros* may acquire legitimate property rights to the *posses* they continuously occupy and productively use. This possibility of turning possession into property has long been a primary source of Brazil's endemic land violence and usurpation, as well as a primary motivation for *grileiros* to develop their repertoire of deceptions. The usurpation of lands within the Indian settlement of São Miguel and Guarulhos is a case in point.

Sometime between 1822 and 1850, the parents of Gabriela Fernandes established a large *posse* within the Indian settlement. When Gabriela married Felisbino Santana, they gave her a parcel of 600 acres as her dowry. By the time she died in 1886, this land had been registered at the local parish and legalized under the terms of the 1850 Land Law. Her four children thus inherited it in equal shares. In 1924, one sold his parcel of 150 acres to José Miguel Ackel and a partner. Within the year, the former bought out the latter, developed a plan to subdivide the land into about one thousand lots, registered the approved subdivision as Jardim das Camélias, and put the lots up for sale. The enterprise failed. No doubt, it drew few buyers because at that time São Miguel Paulista was a distant and disconnected suburb of São Paulo, without its own places of employment or convenient transportation to others. Only in the late 1930s did this situation begin to change with the installation of bus and train service and a few small factories. During this incipient period of growth, José Miguel sold 207 of his lots to his brother Nadime Miguel, a sale transcribed at the 7th Real Estate Registry of São Paulo in 1935.

223

Thus, Ackel property in Jardim das Camélias originates in the sale of encroached indigenous lands and the legitimation of squatter claims. Its history shows that despite its titles and registrations, the Ackel claim does not differ from those of the other litigants because it reveals a strategy of law they all share in their origins: the use of some mix of custom, fraud, and legal complication to turn the mere possession of land—by seizure, lease, proclamation, or even purchase—into property. If the Ackel history highlights the importance of custom in this strategy, the last claim we consider exposes fraud.

THE OWNERSHIP CLAIMS OF ADIS AND THE STATE OF SÃO PAULO

The origins of Adis's claim in Jardim das Camélias also account for that of the state of São Paulo. They are at the center of one of the most notoriously complex land cases in Brazilian history, which is indeed quite a distinction. Because its complexity seems endless, I cannot declare that I understand it fully or that the following outline is free from distortion or error. It is clear, however, that there is no undistorted version, as distortion structures the use of law in the case. Its legal manipulations were designed to create multiple and plausible, yet discordant and flawed accounts in relation to which the notion of legal truth dissipates and the possibility of resolution appears only in the impositions of conjunctural politics. Like the other litigants, Adis's principal argument is a genealogical one: it justifies its claim by presenting a supposedly legitimate pedigree. It traces this line to 1890 through seven generations of property rights, each certified by registered documents that in turn refer to earlier ones as giving legitimate origin to its claim. Once we examine this property tree, however, it becomes evident that Adis and its predecessors have been creating illicit but never entirely false origins all along the way.[16]

We have already seen that when the imperial government promulgated the Land Law of 1850, it intended not only to establish legal means to regulate land titles and to prevent further seizure of public territory. It also intended to use land policy to bring European immigrants to Brazil, initially as free laborers to replace slaves on the plantations and later as free settlers on their own land. To that end, in 1890, the provisional republican government awarded 50,000 hectares (about 200 square miles) of supposedly devolved land to the engineer Ricardo Medina, in equal parcels on each side of the Tietê River east of São Paulo. The south parcel of this enormous concession included São Miguel Paulista and indeed all of what is today the East Zone of the city. Medina's contract depended upon several conditions. He had to found an agricultural colony of five hundred families in each parcel; construct a center for each colony with a

224

pharmacy, hospital, school, and factories to process agricultural produce; survey the area at his expense to discriminate unclaimed lands from those previously acquired by others and to which he had no rights; pay a fixed price for the former, which he could resell to the immigrants; and complete the land survey and purchase within one year and the settlement and construction of the first colony within two years. Failure to meet any of these conditions voided the contract. In that case, however, the grantee would retain rights to half the lands acquired under its terms but forfeit the other half to the grantor. Six months after receiving the contract, Medina transferred his concession, with all its conditions, to the Banco Evolucionista, which he had founded—one of the many precarious development banks the new land policies spawned. However, the bank failed to colonize the areas by the deadline and lost the contract. It did manage to survey the south parcel and offer payment for it but did not differentiate claimed from unclaimed lands within it. On this basis, the republican government gave the bank title to 25,000 hectares in 1892. Although this act established the bank's proprietary rights, it subjected them to all the conditions of the original concession.[17]

A year later, the Banco Evolucionista mortgaged this conditional title to another bank, the Banco de Crédito Real do Brasil, which foreclosed when it failed in 1900. Although the new titleholder also went bankrupt, in 1909, its president, Eugênio Honold, bought the title at auction during the bank's liquidation. In turn, he sold it in 1917 to the real estate company, Predial. In the meantime, however, other creditors of the Banco Evolucionista sued to gain their shares of its assets. The state of São Paulo had also intervened, claiming that it and not the defunct bank owned the vacant lands in question by virtue of the 1891 Constitution. The case went to the Supreme Court, but its decision in 1928 seemed to complicate rather than settle the dispute: the Court affirmed the validity of the Banco Evolucionista's recisionary rights to one-half of the lands it had acquired under the original concession of 1890. However, it calculated this area to be 12,500 and not 25,000 hectares, because the grantee had only measured, discriminated, paid for, and thereby acquired rights to the latter amount. It also ruled that the state of São Paulo had acquired rights to the other half on the basis of the same contract. The Court named the state and not the federal union as reversioner, arguing that by the time the bank had defaulted on the contract, the Constitution's provisions had awarded unclaimed lands to the states. Thus, the Supreme Court recognized that the bank and the state each had rights to 12,500 ideal hectares which were subject to the same, original requirement to distinguish claimed from unclaimed holdings.[18]

This ruling had two principal effects. First, it gave legal origin to the ownership interests of the state of São Paulo in places like Jardim das

Camélias throughout the eastern periphery of the city. Second, the Court's recognition of the bank's title, though reduced by half in ideal terms, permitted its successors to continue to use the title in banking and business transactions. As the lands were never discriminated and as there were many successors, the title became involved, always ambiguously and sometimes fraudulently, in innumerable transactions. Thus, when Predial sold it in 1958 to Nagib Jafet, a former president of Adis, one clause of the contract stated that the seller "is not responsible for any divestment of rights." In the same spirit, Jafet sold it to Garzouzi in 1966, who transferred it to Adis when he became its sole shareholder in 1968.

For one hundred years, therefore, a multitude of banks, real estate companies, and third parties have been using this title to complete countless property transactions—some involving the title itself and many more actual pieces of land, but all fundamentally compromised by its conditional nature. The dealers of this fetishlike item have depended on two things to perpetuate its transaction: its accumulated complications and fraud. The title's complexities keep it potent by preventing the courts from settling any one dispute without resolving all. As this task is practically impossible, the courts never declare the title's powers exhausted. Hence, opportunities multiply for *grilagem*. It is significant in this regard that the Supreme Court's 1928 decision lamented the existence of "rulings by local Paulista courts and federal courts that recognize the dominion of the Banco Evolucionista as full and definitive over the lands in question," because these rulings were defective, "some contaminated with manifest incompetence" (cited in Pereira 1932: 113). In other words, the High Court admitted that even when land disputes reach the courts, judicial decisions concerning ownership can be suspect. It would seem that the only solution to this particular legal mess is to regularize, by extrajudicial intervention, every hectare within the title's scope so that it loses force because it has no object, that is, unclaimed or ambiguously held land. The commission of state prosecutors convened to examine the problem in 1986 reached precisely this conclusion, recommending nothing less than a presidential decree to resolve the land disputes in Jardim das Camélias.

In investigating the perpetuation of the Banco Evolucionista's title, I have found sixteen different types of fraud. Some are blatant, such as falsifying documents, tampering with boundary markers, corrupting officials, and destroying registry records. Others are subtle, long-term stratagems that use the law to establish precedents in the swindler's favor. For example, a *grileiro* uses doctored documents pertaining to a piece of land as a way of opening a lawsuit to regain possession against an accomplice who plays the part of illegal occupier. The latter defends himself badly and is evicted, establishing court actions and precedents that the *grileiro* invokes later to support his claim of ownership. Perhaps the most remarkable fraud occurred at the very beginning. In foreclosing the Banco Evolucionista's mortgage, the Banco de Crédito Real claimed to have acquired real estate described in an out-of-court "letter of adjudication." The problem is that the mortgage could only refer to conditional rights to ideal hectares and not to full rights over specific lands—a detail that condemns both federal and state ownership claims as well in my view. However, the so-called letter included a survey that defined an area of 21,600 hectares.

This magical transformation of ideal into real and conditional into full is an example of a type of mortgage scam popular among well-connected swindlers. In one way or another, a *grileiro* obtains documents giving him rights to vaguely or ideally defined lands. He mortgages these lands to a partner as collateral for a loan on which he deliberately defaults. As foreclosure requires an inventory of assets, the partner hires a surveyor to produce a description of the mortgaged property, which is nevertheless often impossible to verify for subtle technical omissions. This survey becomes part of a private letter of agreement or auction that liquidates the debt, and the settlement is then legally executed. As the documents are now part of a judicial proceeding, the *grileiros* have relatively little difficulty obtaining a registered deed to lands which may not even exist but which they have defined within a net of perfectly legal operations. In the documents of Adis and its predecessors, such alchemic mortgages, letters of agreement, and surveys appear over and over as the origins of their claims.

The Misrule of Law

After four hundred years of settlement, one thing is certain: no one has unambiguous title to land in Jardim das Camélias—or indeed to enormous areas of Brazil. As a result, and in spite of many claims to the contrary, there is simply no clear owner from whom residents can receive an incontestable deed to any of the 207 lots whose disputed history I have traced. Each litigant in the conflict has used law to create a version of this history that gives a plausible origin for their claims. These origins are inventions of law, literally legal fictions. The central government first created a legally inviolable sanctuary for the Indians of São Miguel and then, in various incarnations of colonial, imperial, and federal rule, legalized its usurpation. It seems undeniable that while the federal government may have acquired ownership interests in the area as a result, these are not full rights because it never discriminated the residual indigenous lands from other kinds of holdings. Thus, it has no publicly registered title for the lands it supposedly acquired and, in one of those satisfying twists of history, it cannot prove ownership in terms of its own Law of Public

Registries. On this matter of proof, the law seems clear, as Pereira (1932: 121) argues, citing the famous opinion of Azevedo Marques: "The Union, the States, and the municipalities, when they acquire or alienate [land], are subordinated to common law. There is no law that excuses them. So much is this the case that any time they acquire [land], they require a deed."

The situation of the state of São Paulo and the Banco Evolucionista is similar: their interests remain tied to the unfulfilled conditions of Medina's 1890 contract, and they too lack registration. Although the claims of the Ackel family and Adis are backed by titles and registrations, these are ill-gotten. The former derive from the sale of encroached Indian lands and the legalization of squatters' holdings. Ironically, Adis's claims have more official recognition in tax records, public registries, and court rulings, but only because they are the more skillfully and ambitiously fraudulent. Which claim, therefore, has most legal merit?

A definitive answer seems impossible, not only because of the importance of illegality in each claim but also because of the unstable relation between the legal and the illegal. Indeed, the historical study has shown both that usurpation is a prime mover of Brazilian territorial occupation and that land law itself developed in great measure out of strategies to legalize encroachments through extrajudicial maneuvers. During the colonial period, land law became an arena for contesting Portuguese rule by complicating it to the point of inactivation. It was thus a means of achieving autonomy for the colony. However, this mode of resistance was also one of local hegemony: legal complication sustained land conflict to the extralegal advantage of the planter elites, who could make the illegal legal. Then as now, land seizures helped poor settlers gain access to land and were recognized as legitimate on the basis of customary rights if productively occupied. Although this mix of custom and law aided the humble, it also and to a far greater extent permitted swindlers (many from elite society) to dissimulate fraud within a web of legitimate transactions. Thus, illegal appropriation became a basic means of land acquisition and illegality a common condition of social organization at all levels of Brazilian society. Out of this universal necessity to turn illegal and usufructuary possession into real property developed the fine art of legal complication.

For centuries, therefore, the law's orchestrated irresolutions have promoted land seizures by creating confidence in their eventual legalization. In this time-hallowed process, illegal practices produce law, extralegal solutions are incorporated into the judicial process, and law is confirmed as a channel of strategic disorder. In such circumstances, law has little to do with notions of neutral or fair regulation. Rather, it ensures a different norm: the maintenance of privilege among those who possess extralegal powers to manage politics, bureaucracy, and the historical record itself. In this sense, legal irresolution is an effective, though perverse, means of rule.

As we have seen repeatedly, this misrule of law has tremendous force in Brazilian history. Paradoxically, it made legalizing the illegal and encumbering the legal basic functions of law itself. There is no doubt that these attributes characterize the practice of law in Brazil. I refer here primarily, though not exclusively, to civil and administrative law rather than criminal. But I would apply them more generally to the construction of Brazilian law as a system of regulatory legislation for normalizing behavior. This legal system is so torturous that "getting things done" according to the letter of the law becomes a bureaucratic hardship. I have given ample evidence that such encumbrance is a function of the design and not a failure or corruption of the legal system and its bureaucracy. On the one hand, it is a resource deployed to paralyze conflict until an extrajudicial solution can be found, to pad usurpation with enough layers of complication to keep it profitable for usurpers until its utility is spent or it becomes a fait accompli, to humiliate adversaries with less power to manipulate the system by forcing them to submit to the law, and to subjugate citizens. When they desire such objectives, Brazilians apply the letter of the law—"for enemies, the law [lei]," as the maxim instructs; and to keep this resource potent, they produce an extraordinary amount of law and litigation.[19]

On the other hand, precisely because using law generates complication and delay, everyone knows that it is far more efficient to do something extralegally or illegally and bet on legalizing it later, than to try to meet all the legal and bureaucratic requisites at the outset. In this cultural context, people voluntarily obey the law only when convenient. Otherwise, common sense brands those who follow the letter of the law "for friends" as naive, foolish, or powerless.[20] As a result of these values and practices, maneuvering around the letter of the law became accepted as a normal way of doing business to get both exceptional and quotidian transactions accomplished. Such maneuvers are often romanticized as *jeitinhos*, a knack for getting things done by bending, stretching, shortcutting, and circumventing the bureaucratic requisites of legal procedure. While little transgressions pass barely noticed because they keep the transactions of daily life moving, bigger ones await the legalization that results from using patronage and political power to secure executive amnesty or exculpating legislation. Moreover, each seal, stamp, and signature in this legal culture of encumbrance and transgression, each requirement for yet another layer of legal bureaucracy, creates a new opportunity not only for distrust but also for deceit and usurpation—instituting, in turn, another instance of the misrule of law, with a new cycle of legalizing the illegal.

229

These components of the misrule of law—normative illegality, bureaucratic entanglement, legal stratagem, law for enemies, extrajudicial solution, and the dependable legalization of illegal practices—have been instrumental in transforming São Paulo's rural hinterlands into urban peripheries. They enabled speculators to convert desolate regions into an El Dorado of profit, precisely because the illegal conditions of the subdivisions they opened rendered the land accessible to poor Brazilians, made the dream of home ownership they sold attainable, and kept the land markets they created productively volatile. However, this misrule of law generated an unexpected outcome. Home ownership disciplined the working classes, as the ideologues of industrialization had supposed. But rather than produce the docile and sanitized workers they had imagined, home ownership politicized them: the same precarious legal and material conditions that made the autoconstructed periphery possible galvanized homebuilders into organizing neighborhood-based associations as the means to overcome these liabilities.

Jardim das Camélias is typical in this regard. For the lower classes, grassroots organizations fostered new kinds of participation in law, focusing on their difficult experiences of urban life in the peripheries. For most people, the core of these difficulties concerned the security of their homes and the struggle to obtain legal title to their house lots. As we shall explore in the next chapter, an array of issues about the neighborhood and the city expanded beyond this core of the home to become the substance of unprecedented demands for citizen rights. Yet it was from this core that a change of fundamental and generalized significance developed: during the last thirty years, these struggles have produced a broad expansion among the urban poor of the expectation that as citizens they not only have a right to legal rights but also that their problems can be redressed in terms of the rights and dignity of democratic citizenship rather than by other means, such as patronage, favor, or revolution.

This expansion has changed the scope of the legal system. In the course of a generation, poor Brazilians have become legal strategists with increasing frequency and efficacy. A case in point is a court hearing in 1989, at which Ezequiel, a pioneer settler in Jardim das Camélias, contested a possessory action to evict him from his house lot. I attended the hearing in full. Ezequiel was called to testify about the history of his residence in the neighborhood, and the attorney of the Residents' Association presented evidence to prove that he was not an invader but a legitimate purchaser of his lot. A mason by trade and family man, Ezequiel was a founding member of the association and regularly attended its Sunday meetings. However, I had never heard him ask questions or make comments during the collective discussions about property conflicts, and I had never conversed with him about their legal developments. After the hearing, I asked Ezequiel what had happened. I wanted to know how much he had understood, as it had transpired in about fifteen minutes almost entirely between the judge, the state prosecutor, the association attorney, and the attorney for the suing party in language that was difficult for anyone without a legal education to fathom. Moreover, no one—including Ezequiel's lawyer—had "translated" the proceedings or explained the outcome. Ezequiel looked at me with great seriousness of purpose as he responded to my question:

> Well, it seems that it was good. The law [*a lei*] is beautiful, isn't it, because it beckons the truth. It works for us. I trust Dr. Margarido [his lawyer]. It's going to turn out all right because we have rights [*direitos*] and we want what is right [*direito*].

It was clear to me that Ezequiel had not grasped much, except that the outcome was not a tragedy—probably because his support group (lawyer, president of the association, and me) was still in a good mood afterward. And when I asked his wife, she offered only a saintly smile to express agreement with her husband's statement. Yet what struck me was Ezequiel's appropriation of civil rights, that is, his conviction that he has subjective powers that derive from his having objective rights at law, that this power would triumph, and that this relation of subjective and objective right is "beautiful" not only because it "works" but also because it is morally "right."

Later, over coffee, the president of the association explained the hearing to me in considerable detail. Twenty-five years earlier, Zé Nogueira had arrived in São Paulo from the Northeast at age thirteen, with as much formal education as he would ever receive: three years of elementary school. Being smart, disciplined, and dedicated, however, he had risen in the ranks of a textile factory from child laborer to chief foreman. He had also become an expert in Jardim das Camélias's land conflicts. He kept track of every document and development and had assembled an extensive archive of historical records. In fact, he had become so knowledgeable that he was now the paid assistant of the association's attorney, responsible for researching the physical and legal situation of house lots in cases of property conflict in his and several other neighborhoods. Zé explained that the judge had questioned Ezequiel to establish his long-time residence and good-faith status as buyer of the house lot; that his attorney had requested a court-appointed investigator to survey the lot and research all ownership claims to it (i.e., those of Ezequiel, the federal government, the state of São Paulo, Adis, and another "developer" in the area) with the objective of establishing definitive title; that the costs of the expert be paid by the state rather than his client; and that the judge had agreed to these requests as standard procedure in such cases, without making any determination of the merits of this particular one. As a result, Zé concluded with satisfaction that the judge had sent the case "into space" where it would stay for a very long time because the investigator would not be able to establish definitive title and because the inevitable appeals by both the state and the union of that finding would send it to "Brasília"—that is, to the outer space of the Supreme Court in the capital, "where it would be lost in the piles and piles of cases gathering dust in the corridors of justice."

The new strategic appropriations of law that Ezequiel and Zé express in this case both undermine and perpetuate the classic misrule of law. Clearly, residents of the peripheries have learned to use the law's complications to tie up land conflict to their advantage. Through their associations and leaders, many of these new legal players have already succeeded in beating the developer-swindler and the government at their own game, using law to avoid being its victim. Yet, in learning to generate legal irresolution, they perpetuate the game's premise that irresolution enables those with superior power to transform the illegal into the legal through extrajudicial means, a power they have so far lacked. Thus they have avoided eviction but have not legalized their possession.

Eventually, one could imagine that the legal system might change under the weight of similar engagements: vastly increased participation of this kind could render extrajudicial solution to legal conflict too cumbersome or radical for anyone's benefit, and the particular misrule of law that it supports would end. Yet this outcome seems only possible with the type of complete paralysis that the current system manages to avoid by permitting people to use irresolution and illegality to garner benefits of various sorts. However, another change in the relationship of the poor to law—expressed in Ezequiel's hybrid sense of his citizen rights and dignity and his mix of moral and textual understandings of right—has also taken root in the urban peripheries. This transformation is generating a different rule of law, to which we now turn.

In 1972, an official from the São Paulo courts went to Jardim das Camélias to notify residents that a writ of possession had been issued against them, ordering their eviction. It was the first indication residents had that their deed contracts were fraudulent and their tenure in jeopardy. A crowd gathered in the streets as the news spread. When it met the official delivering his orders from house to house, the men assaulted him. They knocked him down, scattered his papers, and chased him out of the neighborhood. He returned with the police, who arrested several of the assailants. Residents marched to the police station to demand their release. Several more were arrested. Over the next few weeks, neighbors formed an association to fight the eviction and hired one of the lawyers who suddenly appear in Jardim das Camélias offering legal services. Soon afterward, however, the lawyer was gunned down, murdered as he left a neighborhood house. As one resident told me, "at that time, it was a war, between us and the *grileiros*. The law didn't exist. The only law was might; it was violence. We didn't know anything about rights. All we knew was to beat up the court official."

Thirty-one years later, another official came to Lar Nacional to rescind a resident's title to his house lot because of a discrepancy in measurements. The courts had recently issued this title as an original deed of ownership by virtue of adverse possession (*usucapião*). Organized by their neighborhood association, residents had spent more than ten years petitioning the courts for such validation. This was the first case to return from the inner recesses of the justice system, favorably judged and executed. The courts had ordered the new title issued in the resident's name, with its own site plan and tax number. Now, an official from the Municipal Treasury Department wanted it cancelled because the measurements recorded on the title did not match those on file with the Department of Engineering. The residents knew why: the area's developers had superimposed so many subdivision plans over the years in their efforts to usurp land and swindle buyers that none corresponded to what had actually been built. As requested by the association's attorney, however, the courts had appointed an official appraiser in each case of adverse possession to create an accurate site plan that would supercede all other plans by defining the actual conditions of occupation as original for any title eventually issued.

Aguiar, an executive director of the Society of Friends of the Neighborhood or SAB, has followed such cases through the Byzantium of the justice system for over a decade and all legal cases of land conflict in the area for over three. As a result, he told me, "we of the Society were prepared, expecting that this [kind of contestation] would happen sooner or later." Hence, the association had issued standing orders to all residents: "Never enter into any polemic or fight with any official who appears at your door; send him to the Society to talk." When the Treasury official claimed that "the resident's house was wrong, we knew that it wasn't because we had the [new] title, ratified by the judge; and the judge only ratified it based on the official appraiser, who is the eye of the law." Armed with that knowledge, Aguiar confronted the Treasury official by law talking him. He defied him to produce a better document than the court-ratified title and site plan, one which would, he argued, have to overturn the judge's ruling. Moreover, he challenged the official "to look for the law," by which he meant to find out exactly what the law stipulated in this case, what the courts had ruled, and to what effect. Then, he meticulously explained to the official what he would find if he went to all that trouble. He elucidated the purpose and consequences of adverse possession, and he exhibited documents from the society's archive to show that the earlier plans had been cancelled by court order and superceded by the new title. In this manner, he rebutted the official's claim that the measurements were off because the resident had encroached on someone else's lot. After about an hour of this law talk, the official left, conceding that his allegation seemed indeed to have "no merit." Neither he nor anyone else from the Treasury returned to pursue the matter.[1]

What happened to residents of the urban peripheries during these three decades that converted their violence into law talk, their reaction into proaction? Their struggles to legitimate their residential property, construct homes and neighborhoods, refute charges of squatting, and validate their standing as city builders produced not only an unprecedented involvement in law that made their leaders confident enough to confront justice officials with legal reasoning. These experiences also generated a new urban citizenship among residents based on three core processes. The first created a new and alternative public sphere of participation through which they engaged their needs in terms of rights—citizen rights that addressed their urban practices and constituted an agenda of citizenship; the second gave them new understandings of the basis of these rights and of their dignity as bearers of rights; and the third transformed the relation between state and citizen, generating new legal frameworks, participatory institutions, and policy-making practices.

This chapter analyzes these developments. It does so with emphasis on the land conflict in Lar Nacional because, more than other factors, the difficult conditions of illegal residence motivated people to pursue new articulations of citizenship. These demanded full participation in the legal city, an inclusion residents based on their appropriation of its very soil through autoconstruction. The sum of their efforts created a new source for citizenship rights: the working-class experience of suffering the city and building the city. It produced new kinds of citizens and created alternatives to clientelistic relations of dependency. I stress that the older conception of differentiated citizenship is still vital. Yet, by bringing the urban conditions of the poor under the calculus of citizen rights, the mobilizations of the peripheries initiated a new conception. Though entangled with the old, this new citizenship is nevertheless an unprecedented development of Brazilian democracy. The inclusion it claims entails the invention of a new society rather than merely a perpetuation of the old.

New Civic Participation

To follow the emergence of a new urban citizenship in the peripheries of São Paulo during the 1970s, we need to chart the existing conditions of working-class citizenship within which an alternative developed. In 1964, the military seized control of the Brazilian state. By the end of the decade, as scores of peripheral neighborhoods like Jardim das Camélias and Lar Nacional were being founded, the repression of dictatorship reached maximum intensity. Through censorship, surveillance, restriction, and violence, the military regime controlled all established institutions and expressions of citizenship. It maintained the system of differentiated citizenship within a brutalized public sphere that denied citizens independent participation in either political or civil organizations and eliminated organized forms of opposition that it did not authorize. In short, the military subjugated every space of citizenship that it could identify and invade.

235

With regard to political citizenship, it is the case that both the size of the electorate and the number of voters increased significantly throughout Brazil during the years of military rule. As chapter 3 demonstrated, this increase ensued in large measure from the intense urbanization during the period of 1950 to 1980 and the consequent reduction of illiteracy among urban populations. As a result, increasing numbers of urban residents qualified for political rights and were required to vote. In São Paulo, where these twin processes were among the most accelerated, 34% of the municipal population voted in the 1970 legislative elections as compared with 24% nationally.[2] Moreover, residents in the poorest districts of the city (Area VIII) increased their share of the vote 83% between the elections of 1970 and 1978, from 9% to 16% of the total votes cast, while those in the wealthiest neighborhoods (Area I) saw their share decline by 20%, from 11% to 9%.

However, obligatory voting does not signify that the city's population participated actively in the electoral system or had their interests represented through it. First, the majority still remained without political citizenship. Second, those with rights could not vote for any executive offices and only for two parties, one supporting the military regime (ARENA) and one officially opposed (MDB). That restriction made independence in political debate and choice practically impossible. Moreover, these parties limited their popular political activity mostly to election times and tried to draw voters to them in typically clientelistic ways that promised benefits in exchange for votes.[3] Among Paulistanos with political rights, most reacted to this rigged political citizenship by refusing to legitimate it: although required to vote, they protested by invalidating their ballots. In the 1970 elections, the number of ballots left blank or annulled by municipal voters reached almost 34% for Senate candidates and 40% for House. Moreover, as Lamounier (1980: 72–73) observes, the percentage of invalidated ballots increased progressively from Area I to Area VIII, that is, from the wealthiest central districts to the poorest peripheral ones. Although residents in all areas protested by invalidating their ballots, those in the poorest periphery did so in greatest numbers. Thus, it is evident that although more had gained political rights than ever before by the beginning of the 1970s, the vast majority of working-class Paulistanos found neither meaningful participation nor effective representation in the established sphere of political citizenship.

The working poor were also overwhelmingly denied access to civil and social citizenship during the years they pioneered the urban peripheries. Their status as mostly illegal residents, impoverished, unschooled, and without title to their house lots, alienated them from law, undermined their access to its rights, and subverted the development of their civil citizenship at the traditional sites of its realization in law, property, and education. Important civil institutions—such as the Order of Attorneys of Brazil (OAB), the Brazilian Association of the Press, various human rights groups, committees for amnesty, and the student movement—continued to exist either underground or under strict surveillance. Many pressed the military regime to uphold principles of liberty and justice. But working-class participation in these groups was minimal. The exceptions were two types of neighborhood-based organizations, the Christian Base Communities (CEBs) of the Catholic Church and the Societies of Friends of the Neighborhood (SABs).

The latter have had three phases of development. Their origin may be traced to an organization founded by Paulistano liberal professionals and business elites in 1934, the Society of Friends of the City.[4] Like other associations of elites inaugurated during this period (e.g., IDORT, discussed earlier), this organization was concerned with the direction and management of São Paulo's rapid industrial growth. During the next two decades, it inspired the creation of similar organizations in neighborhoods of the expanding peripheries. However, these were dedicated much less to long-term urban planning and social engineering than to demanding urgent improvements in local services from municipal authorities, typically through the patronage of political leaders and parties. Overwhelmingly they became clientelistic organizations.

Such neighborhood improvement associations expanded considerably throughout São Paulo's peripheries during the 1950s, under the tutelage of Jânio Quadros, populist deputy (1950), mayor (1953), governor (1954), and president (1960). Quadros was immensely successful in mobilizing popular support by denouncing the miserable conditions of life in the peripheries. He energized the working-class neighborhoods by forming hundreds of election committees that delivered massive victories. To consolidate this electoral base, Quadros and his associates transformed many of these committees into SABs. In this second phase of development, the SABs functioned explicitly as an exchange of votes for benefits financed by public funds, providing an organized but entirely clientelistic articulation between the poor peripheries and the apparatus of government. By 1970, there were eight hundred of these client-based SABs registered in the metropolitan region of São Paulo, 88% of them founded since 1955. When the military seized power, it imposed a uniform model of organization on the SABs and substituted its party patronage. This substitution perpetuated SAB clientelism, but under authoritarian conditions of decision making and representation that alienated many residents from existing SABs and discouraged their foundation in new neighborhoods. The third phase of SAB development began in these new subdivisions of the expanding periphery of the 1970s. It marks a basic change in their nature, which I describe in the next section.

In terms of social citizenship, the state continued to offer urban workers the illusion of mass participation through labor rights while restricting actual access to the few who exercised officially recognized professions with signed work books and union membership. One study (Camargo et al. 1976: 105) estimated that in 1970 only 5% of the population of the peripheries, where most of the working class resided, participated in trade unions. The military authorities and their delegates controlled both unions and factories by enforcing compliance with the organizational framework it imposed (essentially a version of the 1943 Consolidated Labor Laws) and by applying constant supervision and varying degrees of coercion. Unions were excluded from the process of deciding wage adjustments, lost the right to strike, and suffered frequent government intervention to remove elected leaders. Even under these harsh conditions, opposition groups within factories and trade unions continued to exist and to protest. However, as these working-class organizations lost basic liberties, autonomy, and effectiveness in winning demands, they also lost the active participation of workers. They became hollow as spaces of citizenship.

The effect of state repression on political, civil, and social aspects of citizenship was thus to drain popular interest from the militarized public sphere, fracture civic organizations, obstruct the centralization of conflict and mobilization, and contaminate public relations with fear and suspicion. Consequently, it tended to isolate people within their homes, families, and neighborhoods, confining them to local relations. This evisceration of the established public domains of citizenship created, however, a paradoxical possibility, that of developing a sphere of independence precisely in these interior and—from the perspective of central authority—remote spaces. Indeed, the only institution interested in this possibility was the Catholic Church, which renewed its evangelical mission by ministering to the poor in these spaces. It was thus in contrast to the alienations of the ballot box, clientelistic SAB, union hall, and factory that domestic life in the neighborhoods sprouting in the distant peripheries became the focus of working-class commitment. There, organized around the social life of residence, beyond immediate state, party, and employer sanction, new spaces of civic participation and collective evaluation emerged.

The development of SABs in Lar Nacional and Jardim das Camélias illustrates this emergence. It exemplifies what was new about the so-called new social movements and organizations of the peripheries in the construction of an urban citizenship. In many ways, however, the SABs of these neighborhoods developed differently. Their differences indicate that no single path led to the construction of a new kind of civic participation. Rather, several coalesced to produce a broad-based insurgence of new citizenship.[5]

Both SABs were founded in 1972 when residents in each neighborhood discovered that they were threatened with eviction. However, the SAB in Jardim das Camélias developed according to the clientelistic model sponsored by several already well-established SABs in the district of São Miguel Paulista. Its first president was a member of the ARENA Party, who courted city politicians, supported the military, organized the SAB by the government standard, established a hierarchical command structure, and ruled without much consultation of members. The SAB had a single focus, the land conflict, and its principal activity was defending residents against eviction.

By 1980, however, new kinds of associative and "revindicatory" activities had proliferated in Jardim das Camélias.[6] Almost all initially developed outside the organization of the SAB. A prominent resident of the neighborhood, who has been president of the SAB, described the accomplishments of these activities to me. Each resulted from a mobilization of residents:

> Thirty years ago, when we founded the Society of Friends of the Camélias, in June 1972, there wasn't pavement on the streets; there wasn't a public school or a day-care center. Today, we have two public elementary schools, we have a municipal preschool, we have a state health clinic, we have a municipal nursery, and we have a center for child development, also run by the state. Where there was once a huge and unhealthy garbage dump, we got it filled in. Today it is a park, with its own name, Spring Park. We hope, through one more struggle we are going to make, to get recreational facilities for it. In addition, we have a Catholic church that we built here in the neighborhood, that did not exist. Today we have the majority of streets completely paved with asphalt, all well made, sewage lines and piped water in all the streets, public [street] lights, and electricity in all the houses. All this, when I came to live here in 1970 did not exist. From that point on, we began to struggle to obtain this development.

These mobilizations for neighborhood improvements were organized by the Christian Base Community (CEB) of the local Catholic church, founded some five years after the SAB, the local chapter of the Workers' Party (PT), and a group of women residents.[7] Most members of the last two were active participants of the CEB but not of the SAB. The key point is that the SAB only began to participate in these movements after the CEB subverted the SAB's clientelistic and authoritarian model of organization by getting its own members elected as president and directors in 1981. These officers implemented the CEB's model of collective deliberation, direct rather than clientelistic action, and avoidance of party endorsements. At that point, the reconstituted SAB collaborated with the CEB in organizing neighborhood mobilizations of all sorts. It succeeded in involving many residents in the broad campaign of revindicatory movements described above, even while the land conflict persisted as its core struggle. As the first president of the renovated SAB recalls: "[These improvements] were the fruit of struggles of the residents, of the SAB, of the Catholic Church. We always saw the movements together with the CEB as movements of the SAB. We were all together in all the struggles that existed in the neighborhood." This CEB-inspired SAB remained the articulator of neighborhood organizations and struggles even after the women's group had disappeared and the CEB itself ceased to be a mobilizing force by the mid-1980s.

Although these groups did unite, differences within them developed in the 1980s over the justification of demands. Especially pronounced in the SAB, it was a foundational difference between needs-based and rights-based arguments—one that became evident to me in interviews, documents, and group meetings in Jardim das Camélias and other neighborhoods. The CEB and those it inspired justified the demands of social movements on the basis of needs. Following Liberation Theology, they argued that the social needs of the poor trumped other justifications for claiming resources, including those of legal rights and precedents.[8] During the 1980s, this needs-based justification lost traction in both SABs and CEBs. It may have provided moral support to residents for initial actions, but it became apparent that its rejection at court and by public utilities was costly. It worked with politicians, but only by establishing old-style clientelistic relations that paid off irregularly, unreliably, inadequately, and, if at all, only around elections. Moreover, as residents learned more about their land conflicts, it became obvious that such relations would never gain them title. They would never produce the universally recognized respect and rights of *proprietários* but keep them dependent on the favors of others as mere *posseiros*.

A crucial change occurred in the urban social movements and organizations when residents began to understand their social needs as rights of citizenship and to generate rights-based arguments to justify their demands. Many influences contributed to this change, to making it possible for residents to consider that their needs would be best served not only by claiming existing rights but also by inventing new ones that emerged from their specific political and legal struggles over actual practices—indeed, by seeing new rights as the objective of these struggles. My interest is less to investigate the history of this development, however, than the salience of rights in these struggles and the nature of their conceptualization and argumentation.[9]

Rights-based arguments appealed to residents of the peripheries not only because they provided a strategy with which to fight the massive inequalities and disabilities of city life they suffered. Discourses of armed revolution do that as well. They also appealed because they offered a strategy of countering (not furthering) illegality and marginalization through the demonstration of competence ("know your rights") and negating humiliation through the dignity of participating in the public sphere as bearers of rights. In part, rights arguments do so precisely because their medium, law, has an accepted aura of social legitimacy and power. Moreover, even though historically law is a means to humiliate the poor, the labor laws of Vargas had given the urban working classes a sense of the dignity of rights, however restricted their realization.

Yet more important, the rights arguments of the urban social movements transcended a specific reference to law to signify a change of subjectivity. That is, their articulation was like a performative that changes the status of performers, in this case from subjects historically denied rights, whom the state and its elites did not recognize as national citizens who intrinsically bear rights, to citizens who do so regardless of other attributes. In other words, the rights arguments constituted their proponents as bearers of the right to rights and as worthy of that distinction as any other class of citizen. In this performance, they produced a transformation in the understanding of Brazilian citizenship itself of great social consequence, from a distribution of privilege to particular categories of citizens to a distribution of the right to rights for all citizens. The rights-to-the-city arguments of the urban social movements embodied the struggles of residents for this recognition of being citizens who bear the right to rights. This change in citizen subjectivity was neither linear nor without contradiction. It continues to be entangled with justifications of need, clientelistic relations, and special treatment rationalities. Yet the mobilizations of the urban peripheries articulated, in several modalities, a participatory right-to-rights citizenship. The rest of this chapter investigates these articulations.

THE MOBILIZATION OF LAR NACIONAL

The residents of Lar Nacional founded their SAB in 1972 after justice officials arrived to execute a writ of possession to an enormous tract of land that included their neighborhood. Residents were shocked. How could their subdivision be part of a lawsuit between two parties they had never heard of who claimed to be rightful owners of their land? How could they be subject to a lawsuit about which they knew nothing and which did not even name the real estate company Lar Nacional Ltda. from which they had purchased their lots in good faith? How could they be evicted if they were not informed parties to the possessory action? Nevertheless, the justice officials notified residents that the courts had awarded recovery to one of the litigants of land that included their lots and that this decision entailed the eviction of any unauthorized occupant.[10] However, the officials were themselves surprised, as they noted in their report, to find a neighborhood of inhabited houses called Lar Nacional, because the court writ made no mention of "houses and improvements existing on the land under execution of judgment." Hence, the officials decided "not to proceed with the evacuation of these houses [but] to await instructions."[11]

In the interim, the victor in the lawsuit, Humberto Reis Costa, told residents that he would not evict them if they repurchased their lots from him. Residents were outraged at this proposal and refused. But he also installed a patrol of off-duty military policemen to add weight to his offer. It barred people from moving into houses they had bought from Lar Nacional Ltda. but not yet occupied, and it threatened any opposition with violence. According to residents I interviewed, Reis Costa simulated several evictions to terrorize them further, hiring off-duty and corrupt justice officials to evict residents with whom he had made prior deals. Violence erupted in one eviction as residents defended the family of a man who, unbeknownst to them, had "gone over to the other side." After that incident, leaders of the resistance were regularly harassed and occasionally beaten by the patrol. Most residents continued to pay their installments to Lar Nacional Ltda. for fear that it had the power to evict them if they did not honor their contracts. Nevertheless, the company soon abandoned its outpost in the neighborhood, forcing residents to go to another office to make payments. Then, about eighteen months later, Lar Nacional Ltda. vanished without a trace, disappearing with the original records of the residents' purchases.[12]

Soon after the initial confrontations with Reis Costa, residents organized a SAB. It was their first organization. Unlike Jardim das Camélias, however, they were encouraged to do so by a CEB in a nearby subdivision with which they were not affiliated. As no church had yet been built in the area, this CEB was organized by a nun from another neighborhood and met in an improvised shack. On its own initiative, it advised residents to form a SAB and hire a lawyer, and it helped them do both. Initially, the new SAB held meetings with the CEB, and many of its members—including most elected directors—joined the latter. But as the SAB's membership grew to include almost all the 210 families of Lar Nacional, it rented a neighborhood house and then, after a few years, bought it. Members contributed monthly dues to support the SAB's activities and pay for its headquarters, motivated by both self- and collective interest. "We contributed because it was something for us," one member told me, "and I was always participating [at the SAB] because I wanted to know about my house. I had never had a house, and this was my only opportunity."[13]

242

Thus, from the SAB's inception, it and the CEB shared members, leaders, interests, and actions. The CEB held its meetings and masses in the SAB's new headquarters, while SAB members helped pay for the construction of the CEB's church through monthly contributions. When the SAB mobilized residents for a demand action, the CEB did the same. This mutual reinforcement lasted about a decade, until a rift occurred in the early 1980s. According SAB members, the CEB became envious of its successes and began to schedule events at the same time to "divide us and steal away our people." Their members disassociated, ending the close relationship. As in Jardim das Camélias, three factors contributed to the rupture, though I could establish no overwhelming cause. First, rights-based justifications became predominant in the logic of SAB protests, displacing the needs-based arguments of the CEB and its moral authority. Second, as democracy became a national demand and the dictatorship increased political liberties, people's interest in the safe haven of the Church diminished. Finally, the CEB withdrew into more explicitly religious concerns, while the SAB continued its neighborhood actions.[14]

Of the SAB's mobilizations, those involving the land conflict remained its priority. During the 1970s, they were practically its exclusive focus, as Reis Costa used his 1972 appellate court victory to terrorize residents with numerous suits of repossession and eviction (see note 10). Legally, no eviction could be executed until the Supreme Court judged the case. Nevertheless, Reis Costa would petition local courts for the repossession of several lots, publicize the action, and use it to bully occupants into paying him for the land. Almost all refused, insisting that they had already paid Lar Nacional Ltda. and turning instead to the SAB for legal defense. The SAB had hired and fired a number of attorneys, claiming that it was deceived by each, before consulting the 11th of August Academic Center of the University of São Paulo in 1976. This association of law students was becoming known in the peripheries through affiliations with CEBs and human rights groups for effective legal work on behalf of residents. The center assigned law student Antônio Benedito Margarido to the case, as well as to the conflict in Jardim das Camélias. He has continued as the principal attorney of both SABs ever since. Margarido eventually won every legal confrontation with Reis Costa, deploying the same innovative legal strategy that he used against *grileiros* in Jardim das Camélias discussed in the last chapter. He either persuaded the courts to dismiss a suit on formal grounds or forced Reis Costa to withdraw because he could not prove the merits of his ownership claim. Although this strategy did not win title for residents, it prevented eviction.[15]

As important, it also created an exceptional involvement of SAB members with the workings of law. Some became Margarido's research assistants and, in effect, gained both a legal education and an idiom for engaging civic and political institutions. For years, they conducted extensive archival investigations at municipal departments, courts, and *cartórios* into land titles, regional maps, subdivision plans, surveyors' records, and so forth, in an effort to discredit Reis Costa's claim, unravel the tangled history of titles in the area, and substantiate their own claims as good-faith buyers. They also built at the SAB their own archive of relevant documents. To gain access to these institutions, they directly lobbied both political leaders (governor, mayor, deputies, and councilmen) and bureaucrats. They presented their dilemma, demanded that officials recognize its urgency, and argued their right to investigate. On many occasions they met with city attorneys to communicate the results of their research and contest errors of record. They also brought officials to Lar Nacional to attend meetings of the SAB, hear directly from members, and see the situation firsthand. Their legal work was one of learning, informing, and arguing. One the most active researchers and leaders, Arlete Silvestre, told me how she learned about the courts:

> To tell the truth, I couldn't even tell one court from another; I didn't know what their names meant, like the 5th or the 6th. I didn't know anything about them. I was a housewife with a baby. I had only finished elementary school. But I learned with Sr. Francisco, that man of color who was a member of the Society [SAB] and a Director at the time. He worked at the Central Forum of Courts serving coffee. He was very intelligent and knew a lot. He taught me what this name meant and that one and where to go to file this kind of paper or talk to this person. I didn't know anything, but I kept learning things after I joined the Society. And one day Dr. Margarido asked me and Sr. Francisco and Sr. Aguiar to speak at the Law School. I had never even entered a university! And so we did. We spoke to the students about the land business and everything, exactly what happened here, how it was and how it wasn't.

In 1982, an important change occurred in SAB leadership: in the biennial election, a team of three women won the top offices, lead by Silvestre as president. These women transformed the SAB from an association that focused almost exclusively on the land crisis to one that organized educational, recreational, and revindicatory activities. Under their leadership, the SAB became the neighborhood center of social life. It instituted classes to develop the capacities of individual members and sponsored events that brought organized recreation to people whose schedules varied little between work and house building. It also expanded considerably the range of demand actions for neighborhood improvement. For adult education, the women developed courses in literacy, typing, and sewing. They gained state resources for the first and invested in the equipment for the last two. For fun and as a means of raising money for SAB projects, they sponsored bingos, dances, holiday parties, and an annual beer fest. For youth, they organized a sports club and dances. They also created a preschool where working mothers could leave their children for half the day, which included morning milk, lunch, and eventually a vaccination program.

Gaining resources for this preschool was the women's first citywide revindicatory campaign. Their initial move aimed at the top: they petitioned the governor of the state, Franco Montoro. They got to see him at the Governor's Palace on the ruse of presenting him with a Christmas card from the neighborhood association. When, after much insistence, he finally received them, Silvestre presented herself "as a housewife fighting for her home and the needs of neighborhood children and talked his ears off about their rights as honest citizens." They left with a letter from him asking the regional administrator to provide resources for the preschool, including roofing material to cover the backyard of the SAB. Their next target was the mayor, Mário Covas, whom Silvestre described as "kind of blunt and difficult to reach through his staff." Instead, they adopted a "guerrilla strategy" when they had an urgent matter: they would follow him to public events, "plant" themselves in his path, and demand a meeting. They often succeeded. Through Covas, they gained access to the staff and records of many municipal departments and, through that, to resources for the neighborhood, research data, and new arguments for the land struggle. In this manner of direct confrontation, the SAB mobilized residents—especially women—to accost public officials at city institutions to demand neighborhood improvements. Its campaigns included those for potable piped water, sewage lines, street paving, public lighting, better bus service, and a health clinic. Remarkably, it achieved each of these objectives. The sole exception has been its failure to solve the land conflict and gain definitive title for residents to their house lots.

The SAB's typical strategy for a mobilization is to draft an official letter of demand (duly signed, stamped, and registered), attach a petition with neighborhood signatures, and organize a caravan of residents to deliver the demand petition directly to the highest relevant authority.[16] Delivery usually involves occupying someone's office and refusing to leave until heard. For a meeting with the mayor, the SAB deploys a caravan of buses; for one with a department head of Water and Sewage, a carload or two. The development of mobilization strategies that I have witnessed always requires decisions to be deliberated first among the directors and then presented to the assembly of residents for approval by vote. When I asked Arlete Silvestre how the SAB justified its demands for urban services, she replied with a rights argument: "We would say 'Look, it is our right to have clean water to drink, to have lighting in the streets at night.' Because I think that as a citizen, I have the right. Don't they say that I have the right to make claims [*reivindicar*] as a citizen? Once you pay taxes, pay everything correctly, I think that you have the right to ask." Furthermore, residents always insisted that they were willing to pay individually for services, if necessary, "to take responsibility for what we demanded, as long as it wasn't too expensive and could be paid in installments," as one leader explained. In fact, residents had to pay out of pocket for the street asphalt, individual water and sewage hook-ups, lunches for the medical staff at the health clinic (to keep them visiting the remote location), and tips that workers from each service provider demanded. In return for such payments, the SAB insisted on its right to inspect the public works, hold the providers accountable, and call in the press to publicize any perceived negligence, which it occasionally did. Thus, in articulating and justifying its demands, the SAB emphasized the rights of residents as unconditional citizens, taxpayer citizens, and consumer citizens—a mixed foundation for rights I consider in a moment.

Women dominated the SAB's leadership throughout the 1980s. When the most prominent retired, mainly for health reasons, and men reoccupied the top offices, most of the activities the women had pioneered ended. Silvestre observed that "as the men worked, they would arrive at night and just didn't have the energy to participate in SAB activities." Once again, the unresolved land conflict became its nearly exclusive concern. Participation in SAB meetings and events also declined during the 1990s. Although some children of the pioneers became regular members and a few assumed leadership roles, many among the first generation of residents complain about the younger generation's lack of interest. In this sense of decline, Lar Nacional's SAB contrasts with Jardim das Camélias's, which continued to develop new activities, recruit members and leaders (though older ones disengaged), and launch mobilizations around diverse issues.

Nevertheless, the demobilization that Lar Nacional pioneers lament may be less significant than they imagine. First, at the many regular meetings of the SAB on the second Sunday of each month that I have attended during the last decade, attendance has been stable, usually between fifty and seventy people. Second, as older residents admit, "before there was nothing, so we had to run all the time; now, there is little if any necessity" because nearly all the objectives of SAB mobilizations have been achieved. The great exception is definitive land tenure, which remains the primary focus of Sunday meetings. In addition, as we shall see later, when the land conflict exploded with renewed potency in the first decade of the twenty-first century and mass eviction became imminent, the neighborhood once again rallied decisively.

It is generally the case that residents throughout the peripheries have experienced many such de- and remobilizations in their neighborhoods during the last four decades. Therefore, rather than insist that the urban social movements have declined because they regularly demobilize, it makes more sense to understand their realm of political participation as a noncontinuous mobilization that is institutionalized: residentially based organizations forged a sphere of local citizenship that involves citizens directly in the management of their collective affairs and that mobilizes them when necessary. Thus the capacity to remobilize indicates the strength of these civic associations.

REINVENTING THE PUBLIC SPHERE

This public sphere of participation is new and insurgent for several reasons. It developed largely outside of the established domains of citizenship available to the working classes, in contradistinction to the restricted universe of Vargasian social citizenship and to the repressive public sphere of military dictatorship. In effect, the very urban conditions of segregation and inequality in the peripheries made this development possible: remoteness enabled a certain off-work and out-of-sight freedom to invent new modes of association, at the same time that illegality motivated residents to demand inclusion in the property, infrastructure, and services of the legal city. These demands were not funneled through the established institutions of political parties, unions, and SABs. Instead, the working classes of the peripheries invested in new and reinvented forms of organization—CEBs, new SABs, and other neighborhood groups and mobilizations—in which the criterion of membership is residence and the core agenda the articulation of claims to resources.

As I have argued, these claims were not generally made on the basis of clientelism, cronyism, and flunky-ism—not bargained for with political operatives as an explicit exchange of benefits for support. Rather, a new sphere of associations emerged in the peripheries in which residents claimed resources as a matter of rights to the city without a necessary quid pro quo of support. These right-to-rights arguments structured a civic sphere categorically different from that based on special-treatment labor rights in Vargas's formulation or on the clientelism of patronage politics. That the latter continues to exist in Brazil (as in the United States) does not mean that Brazilian citizenship has not changed or that this change has not transformed how clientelism operates. Both are indisputable. However, that certainty does not lead us to expect that clientelism and particularism have or will disappear. To distinguish between incidents of citizenship and clientelism, it is necessary to analyze the *basis* of people's

247

claims for benefits on the one hand and their provision on the other. The key is not whether people accept a load of bricks from an aspiring candidate (who would not?) or vote for those candidates who deliver them (a rational choice of interest). Nor does it seem useful to multiply analytic categories of clientelism as a means to gage whether interests are more or less "emptied of their political content," as if interests (not to mention government provisions of resources) could ever be apolitical.[17]

Rather, the key is whether alternatives exist to direct and coerced exchanges of resources for political support. The sphere of civic participation that the residential organizations created established this alternative. It did not wholly replace other forms of state/society exchange. But it posited an expanding alternative. Objectively, it required politicians to compete for support that was not guaranteed even if they delivered goods. Subjectively, it allowed members to perceive that their needs might be met not by having to give something up (their vote, freedom of choice, dignity) but by claiming something unprecedented for the lower classes: participation in the new civic associations of the neighborhoods enabled residents to demand recognition from the state of their worth, in rights, as citizens who had achieved stakeholds in the city as city builders, property owners, taxpayers, and consumers. This claim does entail a kind of quid pro quo. But its basis in participation and rights is entirely different from that of client-patron favor. Let us examine the foundation of each in the making of this public sphere.

The new civic chorus of residents, often led most articulately by women, formulated new strategies of mobilization. They developed projects of mutual assistance and self-help to improve conditions of life that the state failed to govern. In that sense, their revindicatory, associative, and educational activities confronted the state with its absence and negligence as a provider of essential services for the well-being of citizens. In this confrontation, a much more autonomous society of associations and citizens emerged. It fundamentally challenged the conception of Brazilian society that the modernizing-developmentalist state of Vargas and subsequent rulers had sponsored. That one assumed Brazil's masses to be silent and mostly ignorant citizens who were incapable of making competent decisions on their own and who needed to be brought into modernity by an enlightened elite and their plans for development. In the insurgent formulation, the residents of the periphery imagine that their interests derive from their own experience, not from state plans, that they are informed and competent to make decisions about them, and that their own organizations articulate them. They consider this organized experience the basis for an exercise of citizenship through which they participate in and hold accountable the institutions of society, government, and law that produce the conditions of urban life.

248

This new form of citizen participation, management, and mobilization entailed a different process of decision making as well. Pioneered in CEB and PT organizations and developed in the neighborhood SABs and mobilizations, this process of deliberation is direct, bottom-up, and consultative; it eschews disagreement, emphasizes consensus, and assumes conscientious individuals. It is grounded in a demand to equalize rights that dominates local CEB, SAB, and PT activities. This equalization establishes both a recognition and an imposition of equality that is uncomfortable with individual differences and strives to level them as the means to create a sense of local community and solidarity (Durham 1984; Caldeira 1988). This demand for equal rights not only grounds specific demands for access to resources and institutions on behalf of members, but also aims to produce a universal equality, dignity, and access. In this manner, the insurgent public sphere of citizenship entails a particular project of social justice and fosters a specific democratic imagination, one focused on equalization and not differentiation. I emphasize that this new participatory citizenship has not replaced the old formulation in which citizenship is a means for distributing inequalities and differences. Rather, the two now coexist and confront each other in the same social space of the city.

Finally, in addition to pioneering new vertical relations between state and citizen, the neighborhood associations forged new kinds of horizontal confederations of citizens throughout the city and beyond. These translocal organizations considerably fortified the development of an autonomous civic sphere of citizenship. Generally, they grew from conjunctural problems into thematic issues. That is, specific problems that rallied neighborhoods began to mobilize confederations of local organizations, as residents of the periphery realized that most confronted similar concerns. Consequently, they established interneighborhood contacts with residents who had become competent in a particular problem and with associations willing to pool research and tactics. These alliances developed primarily around three kinds of issues: urban conditions, cost of living, and human rights. By the mid-1970s, local organizations concerned with housing, tenure conflicts, infrastructure, services, and management had confederated into several citywide movements, some of which became national as well, including the Housing Movement, the National Housing Forum, and the Movement of São Paulo Favelas.[18]

Protests against increases in the cost of living and the inadequacy of the minimum wage grew from neighborhood to city, state, and national organization by 1980, gathering millions of signatures for various initiatives along the way. The First National Encounter of the Cost of Living Movement in 1979 gathered more than two hundred representatives of city and state confederations. This movement pioneered new strategies of mobilization in what was called a new pedagogy of citizenship. It sponsored street theater, youth groups, door-to-door petitioning, factory commissions, and musical productions, in addition to forums for discussion and debate. These new methods of civic participation contributed significantly to the development of a new understanding among the urban poor that fundamental socioeconomic needs could be rethought in terms of the universal human rights of citizens.

Indeed, the language of human rights became a general idiom of citizenship during this period. Human rights abuses by the military police had united neighborhood and religious organizations in a broad campaign to divulge information about rights, denounce their violation, create archives of relevant data and publications, promote courses in human rights awareness, and provide legal services. Centers for the defense of human rights sprang up in the peripheries and promoted citywide conferences to "defend the rights of the people" and "mobilize citizens to exercise their rights." Although their first priority was police violence, these organizations developed a broad understanding of human rights as both the individual and collective fulfillment of basic social, civil, economic, and cultural needs. They promoted human rights, in short, as the core of citizenship itself.

With the hindsight of history, we can see that these new horizontal linkages among organized citizens prepared them to participate massively and unprecedentedly in the framing of the 1988 Constitution. This mobilization turned the insurgent citizens of the urban peripheries into key protagonists in a national struggle over the nature of the new charter for Brazilian society. They fought not only to make the constitution formally democratic. Their more significant campaign transformed the role of "the people" in its elaboration: they insisted on participating directly in drafting the constitution. Their objective was to insure that it embody their experiences—their conflicts, needs, rights, and perspectives as the modern urban working classes of Brazil—as a basic source of substantive rights and social justice. Along with their compatriots in the countryside, their battle was, in essence, for the democratic imagination of the Constitutional Assembly (Assembléia Constituinte, 1986–1988) elected by direct popular vote.[19]

The articulation of this vox populi had four fundamental aspects, elaborated across Brazil by thousands of citizen groups of the most diverse types and levels of association. In many cases, it resulted from the convergence of citizen movements and nongovernmental organizations providing legal assistance, staffed by "alternative lawyers" who fashioned the specific social problems the movements presented into legal initiatives. In this process, the movements became educated in the strategic construction of law. The first aspect was to educate the population about the constitutional process and powers through public debates (seminars, committees, forums, and plenary sessions) and publications. The second focused on the election of candidates to the Assembly who were committed to the inclusion of an agenda of popular initiatives in its deliberations. The third developed this agenda in two ways that fundamentally transformed the internal workings of the Assembly and its constitutional project. Mobilized citizen organizations generated so-called amendment proposals as the principal instrument of popular participation in drafting the constitution. To substantiate each initiative, they launched a petition drive to secure as many signatures as possible. In addition, once the Assembly convened, they battled over its internal rules to insure that these popular amendment proposals would be duly considered. Finally, popular citizen organizations monitored the Assembly's progress and lobbied for the passage of sponsored amendments.

The most remarkable thing about this mass insurgence of citizenship was its success in shaping the constitution. The decisive moment came when the Assembly passed Article 24 of its internal regimen allowing "the presentation of proposals to amend the Project of the Constitution, as long as subscribed by 30,000 or more Brazilian electors [those with voting rights], in a list organized by a minimum of 3 associative entities, legally constituted, which are responsible for the validity of the signatures." During the convention, citizen organizations submitted a total of 122 popular amendments that qualified in these terms. Combinations of 288 different plenary organizations sponsored these initiatives, representing thousands of groups throughout Brazil that had debated, articulated, and validated each proposal-petition. Of these plenary organizations, approximately 14% were employer associations, indicating that all sectors of Brazilian society took advantage of the new means of participation that the popular mobilizations achieved. The 122 proposals were backed by more than 12 million signatures. Some had more than 700,000 each. These signatures represented approximately 12% of the electorate, an enormous portion considering the extensive formal requirements for documenting each signature and the entirely unsubsidized expenses involved.[20]

Citizen groups sponsoring amendments packed the galleries of congress for the entire two years of the convention, developing into a formidable lobby. Although few of their amendments passed as such, they saw the substance of many of their proposals incorporated into the articles of the Assembly's initial draft of the constitution and ratified in its final version. Many of these initiatives concern new means of guaranteeing the participation of organized society in the management of government and citizen affairs. For example, Article 29 instructs municipalities to adopt charters that incorporate "the cooperation of representative associations in municipal planning" and "popular initiatives for legislative projects of interest . . . to at least 5% of the [municipal] electorate." As a result, many municipalities passed charters that require citizens to participate in developing annual budgets, mandate public debates for urban plans, and create advisory citizen councils on matters of socioeconomic well-being. They are, without doubt, innovations in participatory democracy. Other popular amendments that developed into constitutional principle and statutory laws address the conditions of the urban poor, including those of land tenure, health, and children's rights. These are innovations in social justice.[21]

I discuss some of these initiatives in planning and property in the next chapter, as both are central to developments of urban citizenship. Here, I emphasize that the sphere of insurgent civic participation that began in the impoverished autoconstructed neighborhoods of the peripheries, in illegality and inequality, generated a national transformation of citizenship. The current of change went from local to national. Not only did local practices of poor urban citizens become sources of constitutional law. They also led to the creation of a national charter that both assumes and requires that the masses of Brazil, "silent and backward" just forty years prior, have become an organized participatory citizenry. Moreover, this reorganization of society happened outside the boxes that the national government of military dictators had imposed. Thus, when the dictatorship "decompressed" at the end of the 1970s, it was not in fact their controlled "opening" that allowed society to reorganize democratically—though historians and political scientists often adopted these terms from the regime's own description of its "liberalization."[22] Rather, the dictatorship was forced to recognize what had already occurred. When it opened the pressure valves to decompress, it found that society had already escaped into new practices of local citizenship that quickly materialized into new forms of national participation.

This participatory citizenship so strongly marked the development of a democratic imagination among residents of the peripheries that almost ten years after the Assembléia Constituinte, I still noticed a striking lexical phenomenon in my interviews. One woman from Lar Nacional told me: "It's beautiful to read, look, I have this right. If you take the *Constituinte* to read—I have read various parts—you look at it and say: Wow, can this be a fairy tale? Is it true? If I don't use it, I won't know if what is written really works. . . . But I myself already have the knowledge to say, look, that person there achieved something by using law such-and-such." I first thought that this use of *Constituinte* was an idiosyncratic error in syntax. But after transcribing many interviews from both neighborhoods, I realized that this switching of terms is consistent: When residents talk about the *Constituição*, they frequently use the word *Constituinte* instead. That is, they often refer to the text of the national charter by the agency of making it. This iteration of agency—their agency—has come to define for me the spirit of insurgent citizenship.

New Foundations of Rights

Why do you think you have rights?

Well, one part is just what we were saying. I am an honest person, thank God. I don't steal from anyone. I am a worker. I fulfill my obligations at home, with my family. I pay my taxes. But today I think the following: I have rights because the *Constituinte* [i.e., Constitution] gives me these rights. But I have to run after my rights. I have to look for them. Because if I don't, they won't fall from the sky. Only rain falls from the sky. You can live here fifty years. You can have your things. But if you don't run after your rights, how are you going to make them happen? (Resident of Jardim das Camélias since 1970, SAB member, retired textile worker)

The public spheres of citizenship that emerged in Brazilian peripheries forced the state to respond to their new urban conditions by recognizing new kinds and sources of citizen rights. These rights concerned issues of both substance and scope that the state's existing laws and institutions had generally neglected. In that sense, they developed on the margins of the established assumptions of governance: they addressed the new collective and personal spaces of daily life among the poor in the urban peripheries; they concerned women and children as well as men; they established duties to provide state services. Without doubt, the greatest historical innovation of these rights is that they initiate a reconceptualization: their advocates began to conceive of them as entitlements of general citizenship rather than of specifically differentiated categories of citizens, such as registered worker. In these ways, the emergence of new participatory publics in neighborhoods like Jardim das Camélias and Lar Nacional not only expanded substantive citizenship to new social bases. It also created new understandings and practices of rights.

Yet, as the statement above suggests, this foundation of rights remains a mix of new and old formulations. When I asked residents in the neighborhoods why they think they have rights and on what basis, they consistently invoke an amalgam of three conceptions. They speak about rights as privileges of specific moral and social categories (e.g., "I am an honest worker"), as deriving from their stakes in the city ("I pay my taxes"), and as written in the Constitution ("the *Constituinte* gives me rights"). In other words, they present a hybrid of special-treatment rights, contributor rights, and text-based rights. Moreover, this typology has a temporal organization, as indicated in the strategies residents deploy in their housing and land conflicts. The first type appears as practically the exclusive foundation of rights in historical recollections of the periods before the settlement of the peripheries (1930–1940) and during its first phase (1940–1970). The second appears along with the first in discussions of rights that refer to the mobilizations of the neighborhoods until the new Constitution, from the end of the 1960s to 1988. The third appears after the Constitutional Assembly and remains mixed with the other two in discussion. This is not to say that people never referred to earlier constitutions and laws. But when a few occasionally did, it was to complain that, with the exception of labor rights, these charters did not apply to them.

In these three formulations, people use the same concept to describe the realization of rights. They speak of "looking for your rights" (*procurar os seus direitos*) or "running after them." However, doing so generally means something different in each case, with a different outcome. The conceptualization of rights as the privilege of certain kinds of citizens has grounded, in various incarnations, the system of differentiated citizenship. As long as it prevails, citizenship remains overwhelmingly a means for distributing and legitimating inequality. In the post-Constitution periphery, however, this conception confronts an insurgent one of generalized text-based rights. The latter proposes that citizens have an unconditional worth in rights, not dependent on their personal social or moral statuses. It therefore creates conditions for the realization of a more equalitarian citizenship. The concept of stakeholder or contributor rights ambiguously propagates both systems of citizenship. It does so because, although widespread, it excludes some residents. But as it emphasizes the self-determination and accomplishment of contributor-citizens, both individually and collectively, it tends to promote a citizenship of universal "autoconstruction" and therefore has a kind of egalitarian agency absent from the differentiated paradigm. In the contemporary peripheries, all three conceptualizations of rights remain vital and mixed in the development of citizenship.

RIGHTS AS PRIVILEGE

For most people in the peripheries today, their sense of rights as special treatment ultimately refers to the kind of labor and welfare rights initially established in Vargas's social legislation. However, only those few residents who actually held registered jobs in the legalized professions— or, more often, whose parents did—and who as a result participated fully in the labor unions talk about the Vargas system of citizenship as a distribution of rights for workers. For the rest, their sense of citizenship in the pre– and early–periphery period amounts to one of national identification experienced through public symbols and events (Portuguese, soccer, the flag, *carnaval*, Vargas himself, and so forth), but means little as a recognition and distribution of rights. They certainly discuss specific benefits, such as minimum wage, retirement, and holidays, but they do not generally use the category "rights" to articulate them. Rather, this citizenship of special treatment has a different salience: they describe it as a distribution of inequality and injustice. An older resident in Lar Nacional makes this point with reference to his parents (more or less for the period 1930–1970):

> A citizen was a guy, in the time of my parents, loaded with money. It's true. The citizen was the chic, the rich, the owner of a business. . . . The worker was not a citizen, no. That didn't exist. The worker was a peon [*peão*]. Peon, peon, peon, his whole life. My father came to São Paulo a simple sharecropper and died a simple construction worker. But he met all his obligations, all his duties. And when he went somewhere and needed some right, no one treated him as a citizen. They made him into a marginal, as if he were trash. I saw that and I experienced that too. The injustice made me furious.

The paradigm of citizenship this man describes produces the paradox he denounces: Brazilians can consider some Brazilians as "citizens" who have rights and other Brazilians as "marginals" who lack rights—a distinction that only makes sense from within the system of differentiated citizenship that treats some Brazilians as if they were not citizens because, for reasons that have nothing to do with their national membership, they are denied rights.

In her study of Jardim das Camélias in the late 1970s, Teresa Caldeira (1984: 224–35) noticed that the relatively few residents who used the category "right" did so in three modalities. Today, everyone talks about rights. Yet the three modes that Caldeira analyzed persist, albeit with additional meanings. The word "right" appears in both the singular and the plural. In the singular, it denotes a specific right (*direito de*), usually a political or civil right, like the right to vote or strike. In the plural, it means a condition of having rights (*ter direitos*). In Caldeira's fieldwork, the plural form always referred to Vargas's labor and welfare rights. In my fieldwork, residents still tend to refer primarily to socioeconomic rights when they speak of having rights in the plural. But the basis of these rights is no longer, or not only, the Vargas-derived system of labor laws.

In both the singular and the plural, residents then and now typically think that having rights depends on a third modality of right, namely, that of "being right" (*ser direito*) or "walking right" (*andar direito*). This mode

continues to refer to a moral condition of correctness, as Caldeira originally described. The retired worker articulates this relation in the opening statement above: having rights depends on being right and being
right is a matter of achieving certain statuses, basically those of "a good
worker, family provider, and honest person." Those who have citizen
rights deserve them because they are morally good and socially correct
in these publicly recognized terms. Similarly, those who fail to be morally right—criminals, squatters, deviants, and so forth (an expandable
category to be sure)—deserve to be denied rights. By extension, the logic
of this special-treatment citizenship also produces the a priori judgment
that those who lack rights—the poor, for example—must be assumed to
have failed morally. Both negative judgments allow Brazilians to assume
that other Brazilians lack rights in relation to themselves and therefore
that they have no duty to them if they consider them marginals in one
way or another.

Thus access to rights in this conceptualization of special treatment depends on two conditions. On the one hand, people think they have rights
because they hold statuses recognized and legalized by the state. On the
other, the state only bestows these rights on the right people. Laws establish both conditions. For example, the 1937 Constitution created a
perduring construct of social marginality and exclusion with regard to unemployment and informal work.[23] However, having or not having rights
is not only a determination of law. Rather, legal rights may be available to
all workers in theory (as Vargas's populism proposed), but they can only
be acquired and realized by those who deserve them in terms of specific
personal attributes (e.g., whether they became literate or registered in a
profession). For most of the working class, therefore, the exclusions of
differentiated citizenship often appear to result less from legal and political causes than from personal failings. This depoliticization perpetuates
the legitimacy of exclusionary citizenship rights by blaming the excluded
for not having them.

Before analyzing this contradiction further, it is important to note that
because these rights can only be acquired by the right citizens, people
who need to use them "have to chase after their rights." In the context of
special-treatment citizenship, the ubiquitous phrase "look for your rights"
means not only knowing what rights adhere to a particular status. Above
all, it means having to prove to the proper authorities that you possess
the right status and deserve its rights. Caldeira (1984: 233–34) found that
this proof had three components in the first period of the peripheries. My
fieldwork shows that the performative "look for your rights" has developed significant new meanings and practices since then. Nevertheless, the
components Caldeira identified remain fundamental to the negotiation of
citizenship whenever special treatment dominates.

First, people have to discover what rights they have. Twenty-five years ago, such knowledge was not easily obtained and typically required the help of someone in the know, generally a "good boss," union official, or older worker. Second, the petitioner must demonstrate to the authorities who provide the benefits of rights that he or she is an "honest person" with a "clean record," not a marginal of any sort. Third, to qualify, the petitioner needs to "pay for rights," as in "fulfill obligations" and "pay into the pension and welfare system." Thus I frequently heard the argument that "people have rights because they paid for them." In this context, however, payment is less of economic than moral significance. That is, paying is the primary means to establish that a petitioner is personally worthy, because only honest persons and steady workers are assumed able to pay. Hence, receipts attest that a person is not a marginal and that he or she should have the right in question.

However, this proof is not only a matter of having the right receipt, although the paperwork is essential. A fourth and mandatory component is that to be rewarded with a right, the correct status and behavior of the petitioner must be acknowledged by the provider, typically a bureaucrat, official, or employer. This personal acknowledgment is required not only because special-treatment rights always depend on the identification of subsets of statuses within the general status of citizen. More significant, it is necessary because the application of law in Brazil is rarely routine or certain. Rather, it must be made to apply through the personal intervention of someone in a position to acknowledge the good standing and just deserts of the petitioner. The need for such special pleading exacerbates the struggle of the poor to run after their rights. It always puts them on the defensive, forces them to find the right person to intercede on their behalf, renders uncertain their dignity and respect, and makes them acknowledge their inferiority. Consequently, proving one's worth to find one's rights is always frustrating and often impossible for them. It is therefore not surprising that being "treated like trash" is a reason I frequently hear to explain why people desist pursuing their rights. Moreover, in the context of differentiated citizenship, the poor often get the phrase "go find your rights" thrown in their faces as a cynical threat when they accuse others of violating or neglecting their rights. The message is clear: the search for rights will be in vain; therefore, don't bother and either accept what happened or try an extralegal resolution.

The personalization of rights means that their exercise depends on the discretion, not the duty, of someone in a position of power to recognize the personal merit of the petitioner and grant access to the right. This discretionary power converts rights into privileges, in the sense that it becomes a privilege to obtain what is by law a right. A right creates a duty when it makes someone vulnerable to a claimant's legal powers. In that sense it empowers the claimant. When these relations depend on personal intervention, discretion, and mediation, they become legally subverted. In Hohfeldian terms, the acknowledger now has the power to decide when rights apply and yet no duty to make them available. He is not liable to the claimant's legal power and has thus gained an immunity. In turn, the claimant is vulnerable to the exercise of that power, having no right to determine its course. He therefore suffers a disability that can only be overcome by personal intercession. When the latter occurs, the claimant exercises his right only as the favor of the person who grants it. In a system of citizenship rights thus based on the immunity of some and the disability of others, rights become relations of privilege between some who act with an absence of duty to others, who, in turn, have no power to enforce claims. The disprivileged lack rights and are vulnerable to the power of others. The privileged experience citizenship as a power that frees them from the claims of others, leaving them unconstrained by legal duty and exempt from legal responsibility. These relations of privilege and disprivilege epitomize the dominant formulation of Brazilian citizenship.

Thus a citizenship of special treatment creates relations of immunity and disability that entail privilege and disempowerment in the mediation of rights. The "search for rights" therefore engages the poor in a perverse exercise of citizenship that those with immunity and privilege bypass: it not only perpetuates but also legitimates the distribution of inequality because it gets individual workers to defend special treatment for themselves and disqualification for others as the means to confirm their particular worthiness and attain their hard-won recognition, respect, and recompense. In this exchange, it induces the poor to accept the legitimacy of citizenship's distribution of unequal treatment as a just means to compensate for, if not reward, preexisting inequalities. In this way, the lived experience of differentiated citizenship turns the poor into advocates of Rui Barbosa's maxim of justice.[24] It gets them to approve compensating inequalities of privilege by legalizing more privilege.

In my interviews in the neighborhoods, I asked residents to explain Barbosa's maxim to me, whether they agreed with it, and under what circumstances. The sentence confused some people, who tended to become twisted up in its play of similar words. But many understood it, as the lawyers I also asked, to mean that unequal treatment is a just way to offset preexisting inequalities, especially among the poor. However, some grasped an implication that none of the lawyers noticed: they observed that its compensatory logic also legitimates the rights of elites to special treatment. They understood that as a general social principle, it also justifies unequal treatment for the preexisting measures of elite inequality (i.e., their superiority), even though that may amount to legalizing more privilege. Thus one resident commented that "legally, the rich prisoner is treated unequally in prison. . . . [I]f a person from the periphery is jailed, see if anyone lets him have a television in there or a private cell as happened with that banker who was jailed."

Nevertheless, this resident maintains a contradictory position. After condemning this scheme of justice for perpetuating elite privilege, he uses its logic to justify special-treatment rights to compensate for inequalities among his own class. I found this contradiction among many residents and typically expressed, by both men and women, with regard to special rights for women to retire five years earlier than men:

> I think it is just. Because if you think about it, a housewife who has a job outside works double. When I arrive home from work, what do I do? I take a shower, watch television, sit on the sofa doing whatever; or I go to the bar and have a beer. What does the woman do? When she arrives from work, she makes dinner, takes care of the children, cleans the house, arranges the kitchen, washes and irons clothes. She works about double my work, if you analyze the question. Therefore, I think that she should have even more time [than five years] to retire before a man, because there still exists a lot of discrimination in the work of women.

Like nearly every man *and* woman who discussed the issue with me, this resident does not think to change the social relations of work and gender, let alone his own behavior, as the means to redress this discrimination. Rather, he wants to keep the laws discriminatory by allowing a compensatory legal privilege that rewards women for their extra work but leaves the causes of inequality untouched.

Most residents held similarly mixed or contradictory opinions with regard to various kinds of rights. They gave some version of universal constitutional equality, as in "the *Constituinte* says that all are equal; it doesn't matter if you are white, black, or Japanese. If you are in Brazil, you are equal." Yet most accepted affirmative action for blacks in education, separate courts for military police, and both special compensations and restrictions for women (e.g., paid maternity leave, early retirement, and off-limit jobs).[25] Many argued that illiterates should not have political rights because they lack independence and would not know how to vote; that children should have special rights but really problematic ones could lose them by becoming wards; and that "even though criminals are citizens, they don't deserve rights."[26] There was, moreover, general agreement that "honest people, good workers, and taxpayers have to have rights" and that "criminals, layabouts, and squatters do not." The same resident who says in one breath that "today, for me even marginals are citizens," says in another that "we consider ourselves citizens because we

259

are honest persons." When we discussed the many social inequalities that exist in Brazil, many affecting them directly, none had a problem legalizing new inequalities in the form of special-treatment rights as a means to redress existing inequalities.

These pioneers of an insurgent and participatory urban citizenship thus continue to perpetuate key elements of the regime of differentiated citizenship that discriminates against them and that they oppose in many ways. They generally accept the principle that existing social inequality justifies further unequal treatment as compensation. In doing so, they also legitimate the reproduction of more inequality and privilege throughout the social system.

CONTRIBUTOR RIGHTS

The conceptualization of rights that remains tethered to special treatment confronts, however, two new understandings of citizen rights in the peripheries. These emerged as residents developed the new participatory spheres of citizenship. Their coexistence creates a mixed and at times unstable foundation for the development of citizenship. The first to emerge refers to what I call contributor or stakeholder rights. Whereas the rights workers "paid for" under the old regime of citizenship were overwhelmingly labor rights, contributor rights constitute a different set, of new substance and ethical significance. They concern the "rights to the city" that were fundamental in mobilizing the new practices of citizenship in the peripheries—rights to public services, infrastructure, and residence that pertain to urban life as a condition of dwelling. I call them contributor rights because residents advance them as legitimate claims on the basis of their contributions to the city itself—to its construction through their building of homes and neighborhoods, to city government through their payment of taxes, and to the city's economy through their consumption. They are stakeholder rights because residents ground their legitimacy in the appropriation of the city through these means.

Contributor/stakeholder rights are, therefore, based on three identities unprecedented for most of the working class: property owner, taxpayer, and mass consumer. These identities engage an agency of self-determination entirely different from that embedded in state-supplied labor rights. Yet, as not all Brazilians share these statuses, they also ambiguously perpetuate some elements of special-treatment citizenship.

The fundamental identity organizing the bundle of contributor rights is that of property ownership. For most people, it motivates both their claims and their duties in relation to the city. For most, their identities as taxpayers and consumers also develop around the requisites of property, as they pay taxes and fees for their residential lots, buildings, and services, and as much of their consumption consists in purchases for their homes. Chapter 5 demonstrated that the rate of home ownership in the periphery is remarkably high, varying between 70% and 90% according to various measures. In Lar Nacional, it reached 87% of the 185 houses I surveyed. Thus the identity of home owner is predominant in peripheral neighborhoods. Yet, with regard to landed property, ownership excludes squatters and renters. Although they account for a small number of the residents in most neighborhoods of the periphery (about 10% on average), we have seen that the distinction between owners and others is crucial to both the moral and political economy of residence. The division between owner and squatter is especially antagonistic. I have rarely heard owners in Jardim das Camélias say that the squatters there have rights to the city. Mostly, they view them with contempt as freeloaders. Nor have I often heard squatters in Vila Joía talk about urban services as rights, though that is beginning to change as a result of new constitutional measures. Moreover, most owners emphasize their status as good-faith purchasers of land precisely because their title conflicts threaten them with the stigma of squatting. As one pioneer argued with regard to her lot,

> I am fighting for that which is my right. It's not like we invaded the land, as if we were squatters. Some people think we are squatters. But we are not. Everyone here tried to buy, and therefore my rights are supported in law.

Another pioneer remembered that during the violence of evictions in the early 1970s, she lined up with other residents to pay their installments: "But I have to pay," she declared to thugs trying to disrupt the line; "it's mine, I bought it."

Precisely because their land titles are in doubt, residents want to pay property taxes as proof of ownership. For many years, however, they were unable to do so, having only promissory deeds on which to base their property rights and their distinction from squatters. Of all the taxes residents pay, the principal one they refer to is the property tax, the IPTU (Tax on Urban Structures and Land). This tax depends on the registry of each lot in municipal records, with exact measurements, owner's name, identifying tax number, and assessed value. Due to fraudulent developer practices of superimposing the plans, titles, and sales of lots, each of these requisites has been erroneously recorded and disputed for practically every lot in my two neighborhoods. Each requires a complex bureaucratic-legal struggle to rectify. Consequently, lots were not individually or correctly dismembered from the larger land parcels for decades, and annual tax bills were grossly inaccurate and inflated. If delivered at all, residents could not pay them, a default land scammers exploited to try

261

to evict them. Moreover, in part because residents were not paying the IPTU, they were charged special fees for the installation of infrastructure and services. As a result of this knot of problems, one of the most significant legal struggles residents wage is to receive an accurate annual tax bill for their individual lot. Although I have heard some residents grumble that regularization means having to pay taxes, most display a rectified tax bill as a badge of pride that attests to legal recognition of their property rights. Even though this document does not in fact solve their title problems, it provides them with a strong foundation on which to demand public recognition of their standing as stakeholders in the city. To them, it declares that they own the city's land, build its environment, and supply funds to run its government.

This sense of having stakes in the municipality is not confined to lot owners in the peripheries. Squatters often own their homes, many of which are well furnished and equipped. Moreover, most residents pay a variety of service fees and taxes as consumers, including those for utilities, retail sales, and industrial production (the ICMS and IPI). Moreover, some pay income tax. One squatter in Vila Joía (which succeeded in obtaining most urban services by 1985) put his sense of consumer rights this way:

> During the dictatorship, people thought that they shouldn't complain about things. Today, whatever thing you buy that isn't right, you go and complain. You buy something and it's broken, you complain; the electric bill is high, you complain; the water bill is high, you complain. Everything, everything like that people complain about today. Nobody stays without complaining.

Thus, although the identity of stakeholder is without doubt strongest among owners of real property, residents very generally view home ownership, taxpaying, and consumption as evidence of their stakes in the city. This conviction not only legitimates their demands for rights to the city. It also gives residents the sense that they are citizens of the city, for many a first substantive understanding of their citizenship and its agency. "If he pays his taxes, he is a citizen and must be respected wherever he goes" is an assertion I heard routinely in various versions. The sense of being an urban citizen is, not surprisingly, directly linked to residents' demands that public officials respect them. Their reasoning is straightforward, as the former president of the SAB in Jardim das Camélias explained:

> There are still public departments where bureaucrats treat you like trash. But that's not right. If you go, for example, to city hall, you are a municitizen [*munícipe*, a citizen of the municipality], you are a tax-payer [*contribuinte*] of city hall. We, the people, are paying the public

employees. We are paying the IPTU, ICMS, IPI, and so forth with our money and that is what pays their wages. So there is nothing more correct than that they treat us well.

Thus, in the stakeholder conceptualization of rights, the "municitizen" merits respect not because he or she is a good honest worker or family provider. He does not have to prove some personal moral attribute individually to an official or have it acknowledged by the state to "find his rights." Rather, urban citizens find their rights by demanding them. They insist, as municitizens, without relying on the quid pro quo of deference and favor.

This change in attitude results from the conviction that urban citizens have earned their rights and respect by building the city and paying its bills. Just as they substitute *constituinte* for *constituição* to emphasize their new agency of citizenship, so they demand their rights on the basis of self-determination, accomplishment, and earned independence. Contributor rights thus promote a citizenship based on an entirely different agency than that of the state-sponsored labor rights of differentiated citizenship. Whereas the latter is fundamentally other-determined, the agency of urban citizenship is autoconstructed. This autoconstruction of house, self, and citizen in the periphery is both individual and collective. Its agency is individual because it refers to individual achievements. But these become intelligible and their meanings powerful especially as expressions of the great social narrative of the peripheries' settlement, as each reiterates an installment of a collective drama of segregation and insurgence. Thus, although not everyone in the peripheries can claim this autoconstructed agency equally, it engages most residents because it refers to the making of the peripheries themselves and because, owner and squatter alike, they evaluate their own lives in relation to that development.

We have to consider later the degree to which this agency continues to engage succeeding generations if the long-term inclusionary projects of home ownership, employment, and family that organized the peripheries become less available. However, it is evident that those who see themselves as makers of the peripheries achieve rights and respect because, in contrast to differentiated citizenship, they make municitizenship general (if not quite universal), egalitarian (if not quite equal), and collective (without being depersonalized). Thus, as city builders, taxpayers, and consumers, these urban citizens have inverted the real-stakes argument that nineteenth- and twentieth-century liberals used to exclude Brazil's poor from citizenship rights. Instead, they use that very argument, recasting it in somewhat different terms, to justify their rights to full citizenship.

TEXT-BASED RIGHTS

Before 1988 it was not written, it was not clear. Before, you would say: I have a right, but it was not proved in law in the constitution. . . . Before, a lot happened outside the law. You could do what you wanted. There was no one to hold you accountable [*cobrar*]. Today, things are more under the law. Today you have a book that you can get and see it. Look: it's in the *Constituinte* [the 1988 Constitution]. I have that right according to the law; I have the right to use and enjoy [*usufruir*] this benefit. The *Constituinte* speaks clearly, such-and-such a right, more for citizens themselves. The law is written. I can research the law. Look: I can use this right. (Second-generation resident of Lar Nacional)

People have to know their rights in the *Constituinte*. If you have a doubt, it's there, the law of the country, the *Constituinte*. You have to get it and read what it means. If you don't understand, look for someone who knows. . . . It is the knowledge of the *Constituinte* that gives the right for you to fight for your rights. (Pioneer resident of Jardim das Camélias)

On occasion, I have seen people at neighborhood meetings pull a concise edition of the Citizen Constitution from their back pocket or purse to make a point. More frequently, I hear them refer to what it "says in the *Constituinte*." This reference to the constitution and the legal codes deriving from it secures the second new understanding of rights to emerge in the peripheries. It is based on textual knowledge. To residents, text-based rights are evident, clear, accessible, and, above all, knowable precisely because they are written down for all to see. People access them in three ways. They read them in inexpensive paperback editions of the 1988 Constitution available at any newsstand. Some, like the woman who made the first statement above, consult them online. Many also utilize new government institutions associated with innovations in the Constitution. These aim to democratize access to and information about rights as a matter of policy and to make them work for citizens by simplifying legal bureaucracy. Hence, residents frequent Small Claims Courts, Poupa Tempo (literally, Save Time), Procon (consumer rights bureau), and various departments of public administration that are now more numerous and accessible in the peripheries. As one resident put it, these institutions constitute "a source for you to go to and get a return for your effort; today, you can get a return." It is no small historical irony that this confidence in text-based rights has turned the popular classes of São Paulo into enthusiastic positivists, not so distant from those of the "Order and Progress" positivism that some of Brazil's nineteenth-century nation builders venerated.

The keystone of this new foundation of rights is access to knowledge. If, in the past, it was almost impossible for a poor person to know her rights without the intercession of a superior, today's access to this information is practically self-evident. It is common in the contemporary peripheries to hear people speak about law in terms of researching its texts. If they have a problem, they search for the legal text that establishes their rights. For example, one resident bought a defective microwave oven. He went to the local Procon office to research his rights according to the Consumer Protection Code (1992). The staff gave him a copy of the code and also explained which aspects applied. When I asked him why he did not go directly to the store, he replied that it would deny any responsibility unless it understood that he knew his rights. When he finally made his case at the retailer, successfully, he had a copy of the Code in hand. Residents are particularly proud of their text-based knowledge when dealing with government. Another resident, exceptionally articulate in text-based law talk, explained that "when I go to these city departments, and I start to talk with them, like I'm talking to you now, they perceive immediately that I know what I'm talking about and that it's no use trying to fool me."

Access to text-based knowledge has given the urban popular classes an unprecedented confidence in their struggles to achieve citizen rights and respect. Coupled with their sense of being stakeholders, it provides an effective means to challenge the culture of deference that dominated the practices of differentiated citizenship. The following exchange between three residents of Lar Nacional illustrates this overcoming:

M: It's that in the past, a person was afraid, was embarrassed, to look for his rights. Today, no.

A: Today, he fights more.

P: Today, people are much more enlightened [*esclarecida*]. So they know that their rights exist and they no longer have that fear. . . . Today, a person has more security because of his own knowledge. He knows that there exists something that is going to protect him, and it is exactly for that reason that he is going to look for the law.

M: Today, we find an answer to what we want to know. You go, search, and find the answer. Just a short time ago, you searched and nobody was interested.

A: There was little access to information. Today there is more information. Today you can even study. For example, you are looking for something, a right. You can study to see if it really exists.

This sense of security in knowledge does not mean that residents do not tremble before the law. Many times I have gone with them to court hearings about their land conflicts. When we discuss the event afterward, they often express fear.[27] No doubt, the inquisitorial style of Brazilian courtroom procedure imposes deference. Yet the encounter seems not to produce a feeling of impotence. To the contrary, although they experience fear, residents often emerge exhilarated that they "have been called." The same man who told me he was "shaking" expressed this exhilaration when he also said "it was in there [the hearing] that I realized that I was existing in this thing [the conflict]. Because until you are called there, you think you are John Nobody, you don't exist. You only know when you are recognized, when you are called to go there."

The access to text-based law and the sense of empowerment it brings have thus fundamentally changed the meaning of "look for your rights" for working-class citizens. Today, they not only emphatically say that "a person has the right to look for his rights," echoing precisely Hannah Arendt's (1958) notion of justice. The important point, they overwhelming agree, is that "if you look today, you always find them." They are certain of this outcome because the rights they seek are accessible, demonstrable, tangible, look-and-point-at, written text. These battle-seasoned residents know that knowing rights does not insure getting justice. But as a director of the SAB in Lar Nacional observed, "without knowing the laws, one cannot know justice."

Moreover, the justice they seek is not only that of social rights and labor law. Text-based rights now refer to other kinds, including property, consumer, personal, human, and ecological rights. Among the most significant change in this regard is greater concern with civil rights, which, as we have seen, are among the most problematic aspects of Brazilian citizenship. In discussions about what looking for rights means, residents most frequently give examples from their real property and consumer conflicts. But issues of ownership and possession have also initiated a broader concern for civil rights, particularly for the general right to justice as the key civil right to rights. Less often, their illustrations include examples of interpersonal conflicts and what American law calls torts—private wrongs involving a breach of legal duty and responsibility in interpersonal conduct, such as a dispute among neighbors over a wall or between family members over abuse. Such changes suggest that residents are beginning to include more of their own social life and personal relations "under law," that they not only want the law "for enemies" but also for themselves, their family, friends, and fellow citizens.

In large part, this momentous change depends on citizens conceiving of their citizenship as a means to establish a common ground and equal measure among them. In turn, this commensurability depends on their sense that their status as citizen has an absolute, unconditional, equal worth in rights, one not based on individual market value or on any other status. In that evaluation, rights become universally egalitarian rather than differentiated. There is much to suggest that the deep involvement of the urban popular classes with the 1988 Constitution and its text-based rights is creating conditions for that kind of assessment. Even though the constitution contains many provisions for special treatment, residents overwhelmingly understand it as a charter that establishes equal rights. Although contributor rights are also egalitarian for most, as I argued earlier, they ultimately distinguish noncontributors. That ambiguity is especially apparent in discussions of rights to health services, a vital issue of popular concern. Yet in this aspect of citizenship, the popular understanding of the constitution as a charter for universal equality is also evident, as an older resident in Jardim das Camélias illustrates:

> I remember very well when the national health insurance (INPS) was part of labor rights. When you went to the hospital to get medical care, you had to take your work identity card to prove that you had paid the INPS. Without it, you weren't seen. But I think that, as it clearly states in the *Constituinte* that rights are equal, I think that independent of whether you are a contributor or not, you have to be seen. If you pay or if you don't pay, you have to be treated well. It doesn't matter if you never paid. If it says that rights are equal, they're equal.

The equalizations of text-based rights in such cases seem to combine the agencies of special-treatment and contributor rights, because residents think of them as the product of both the new democratic state and the mobilizations of citizens. The powers of both combine in the constitution to make law an asset for citizens, regardless of differences.

A new agent of Brazilian citizenship thus emerges. It is the anonymous citizen, a condition that has virtually no utility in the regime of differentiated citizenship. Among the popular classes, therefore, the new foundation of rights in the text of the constitution confronts the old regime by advancing anonymity as the condition and equality as the outcome of citizenship practices. Nevertheless, the development of citizenship in the peripheries remains contradictory: residents support anonymous citizen equality while also holding that various kinds of social inequality justify the legalization of unequal treatment. Yet, coupled with new civic participation, the new understandings of rights sustain the growth of significant measures of egalitarian citizenship. The equality of inclusion it demands is insurgent, even though it also elbows into the existing system. It is insurgent because the right to rights citizens claim is not minimal. It already assumes the totality of possible rights. Hence the recognition of these citizens as right-to-rights-bearing members creates a radical opportunity to remake Brazilian citizenship for a democratic society.

PART FOUR

DISJUNCTIONS

Chapter 8
Dangerous Spaces of Citizenship

Brazilian democracy has advanced significantly in the last two decades. Indeed, it has pioneered innovations that place it at the forefront of democratic development worldwide. Yet, precisely as democracy has taken root, new kinds of violence, injustice, corruption, and impunity have increased dramatically. This coincidence is the perverse paradox of Brazil's democratization. As a result, many Brazilians feel less secure under the political democracy they have achieved, their bodies more threatened by its everyday violence than by the repressions of dictatorship. At the same time, moreover, that a generation of insurgent citizens democratized urban space, creating unprecedented access to its resources, a climate of fear and incivility also came to permeate public encounters. These new estrangements produce an abandonment of public space, fortification of residence, criminalization of the poor, and support for police violence. These conditions debilitate democracy. They erode a public sphere undeniably broadened by novel popular participation in making law. Despite legal mobilizations that shaped the 1988 Constitution and continue to develop its participatory principles, the institutions of justice—particularly the courts and the police—have become even more discredited with democratization. Instead of its anticipated glories, Brazilians experience a democratic citizenship that seems simultaneously to erode as it expands, a democracy at times capable and at other times tragically incapable of protecting the citizen's body and producing a just society.

Researchers have now examined many of these contradictions as they twist and turn through Brazilian society, taking shape in violence, police abuse, segregation, privatization, misrule of law, racism, and illness.[1] However, accounting for their relation to the process of democratization itself remains problematic. The difficulty is to avoid dismissing them as externalities, disrespecting democratic intentions, or predetermining antidotes modeled on idealizations of particular North Atlantic democracies. Given that the extraordinary global democratization of the last thirty-five years is overwhelmingly non–North Atlantic, occurring in societies of vastly different cultures, such convergence of models seems as unconvincing theoretically as it is unlikely empirically. Even its suggestion strikes many proponents of democracy in Latin America and elsewhere as a new North Atlantic imperialism. If, as I think, neither convergence nor dismissal constitute adequate accounts, then democratic theory must be rethought in terms of the new conditions that characterize the current worldwide insurgence of democratic citizenships.

Of these conditions, it is especially the concurrence of democratic politics with systematic violence and injustice against citizens that reveals these limitations of method and theory. In many regions of the world, not only Latin America, increasing violations of *civil* citizenship in the forms of urban violence, corruption, and discredited judiciaries appear to accompany increasing political democracy. Indeed, their entanglement has become an intractable problem of emerging democracies worldwide.[2] For Brazilian democracy, it is a particularly bitter development. The victories of Lula and the PT at all levels of government in the elections of 2002 seemed a resounding triumph for democratic politics and an insurgent citizenship of social justice. But after just three years, both his administration and party are beset by corruption scandals of unprecedented magnitude. Each appears more villainous than the last; each reveals networks of politicians using corruption not merely to get rich but to govern; each extends throughout the entire political system.[3] To date, more than 20% of congress and many others at all levels of government have been implicated—112 federal deputies and senators (60% from the PT coalition) and hundreds of mayors in the ambulance scam alone. Three key ministers were forced to resign, as were the executive directors of São Paulo's PT. Yet none of these officials is on trial or in jail. Although congress opened impeachment proceedings against more than seventy-five members, it has managed to revoke the political rights of only four. Two more resigned. Others have already been acquitted by secret congressional ballot despite hard evidence, the rest bet on the same fate, and most were blithely running for reelection in 2006. President Lula declares himself absolutely ignorant of any corruption in his administration, which, one might think, would make him appear either incompetent or complicit. Nevertheless, his own reelection was secure, as he was far ahead in the polls. Indeed, he could not resist the appeal of populism when he stated defiantly that "the ballot box will absolve the PTistas accused of corruption."[4]

At the same time that the political system of Brazil's democracy appears bankrupt, and both the public and the judiciary numb to its unending and unpunished corruptions, urban violence has mutated into the terror of organized crime. First in Rio and then in São Paulo, gang cartels (*comandos*) organized massive prison rebellions, during which they denounced the hellhole conditions of state imprisonment, demanded justice, and killed their rivals. Their organizations spread to the poorest neighborhoods where they both run the drug trade and supply social services the state neglects. Beginning in May 2006, the Primeiro Comando da Capital (PCC), repeatedly paralyzed the city of São Paulo, attacking police stations, government buildings, banks, buses, and prisons. Almost two hundred police, guards, suspected gang members, and innocents have been killed, many summarily executed. These insurrections reveal gross failures of the state and its justice system to enforce the law, protect citizens, respect the rights of prisoners, and develop policies of security beyond truculence. The irony is not lost on Brazilians that both the congress and the *comandos* sustain organized crime. Both use the language of rights. Both discredit democratization.[5] To their enormous frustration, this delegitimation shows Brazilians that political democracy does not necessarily generate a rule of law that is democratic and that without democratic justice, democracy corrodes.

Thus Brazilian democratization is at a critical point. It has not been able to overcome the violence and impunity that lacerate all social groups. Simultaneously, however, these counterconfigurations have not prevented the consolidation of significant measures of democracy and democratic innovation. Above all, they have not prevented the legitimation of democratic citizenship in its extensive sense and its adoption as the language in which the most diverse sectors of society, including organized crime, frame their interests. For the time being, neither democracy nor its counters prevails in Brazil. Rooted yet rotted, they remain entangled, unexpectedly surviving each other.

In this chapter, I analyze three contradictions of civil citizenship in order to understand this entanglement. In different ways, they demonstrate a fundamental characteristic of democratization: the equalities of democratic citizenship always produce new inequalities, vulnerabilities, and destabilizations, as well as the means to contest them. Thus the equal rights of citizens to associate generate organizations of unequal capacities and powers. As citizens advance their interests, these groups are set against each other in the arena of citizenship. In this way, citizen equality becomes the foundation on which new inequality is built and challenged.[6] If that is so, it follows that citizenship's contradictions are internal and

273

not incidental or extraneous to democracy's theory. It must also be the case that significant contradiction and disjunction are inevitable in the development of all democracies, established and emergent. Hence, if we cannot consider Brazil's democratic development abnormal for being disjunctive, the problem to investigate is the specificities of its contradictions in relation to its expansions.

As three examples I consider everyday incivility, judicial injustice, and gang manifestoes. I argue that because the old formulations of differentiated citizenship persist, these examples embody a confrontation between the insurgent and the differentiated that creates inherently unstable and dangerous spaces of citizenship in contemporary Brazil. Without doubt, the insurgent citizenship disrupts established formulas of rule, conceptions of right, and hierarchies of social place and privilege. In the process, it erodes entrenched practices of domination and deference that gave the everyday its sense of order and security. However, such destabilizations produce strong reactions. Some attempt to reassert old regimes of order and others damn their persistence, now made more evident because confronted. New inequalities, injustices, and discriminations arise along with new means to combat them.

I stress that there are many causes for the increase in violence and injustice and that my objective is not to provide either a sufficient or global explanation. It is rather to show that democratization provokes kinds of social conflict, including violence, specific to the destabilizations it inevitably brings to entrenched social and spatial regimes. Democratization does not account for all destabilization and violence in contemporary Brazil, for other important processes of social change—such as urbanization and neoliberalization—also destabilize. Each of these processes brings its own kinds of disruption, and each gets entangled with the others. Nor do I suggest that Brazil has become both more democratic and more violent primarily because of a clash between entrenched elites and insurgent citizens. There are many contributing factors. My aim is not to reduce the analysis to any one factor but to consider their complex and incendiary mix.

Once charted in this way, my examples show that Brazil's hybrid spaces of democratic citizenship produce a sphere of social change in which the legal and the illegal, legitimate and criminal, just and unjust, and civil and uncivil claim the same moral ground of citizen rights by way of contradictory social practices. This conjunction of opposites is certainly perverse. Yet throughout this book I have demonstrated a deep structure of intimacy between the legal and the illegal in Brazilian society. It is not unreasonable to propose, therefore, that the current conjunction reiterates this relation in new terms, that is, in those that have become the current language of public legitimation: democratic citizenship. This condition

may eventually exhaust Brazilian democracy. But for the moment, it indicates the consolidation of a common language of democratic measure
where none existed before—a new commensurability that confronts an
older public sphere of citizenship grounded in very different values. It
shows, moreover, the limitations of democratic theory based on narrow
yet totalizing conceptions of the political and suggests the advantages of
the anthropological view that considers the lived and contingent conditions of citizenship—however messy and disjunctive—as a better means
of understanding contemporary forms of democratic development.[7]

Everyday Incivilities

I return to the performances of citizenship in everyday public encounters with which this book began. If civility is a code of behavior associated with participation in the public life of a particular paradigm of
citizenship, then incivility offends its principles and disrupts its practices.
Disrupting assumptions about paradigms of citizenship is not an abstrac-
tion. It has powerful individuating effects that get under people's skin.
Moreover, in an encounter of antagonistic citizenships, the civility of one
appears as an incivility to the other. Incivility may thus be as principled
as civility. However, while paradigms of citizenship may be contraries,
their development is rarely dichotomous. Just as different formulations of
citizenship usually get entangled, their in/civilities also become mixed.[8]

Brazil's formulation of differentiated citizenship emphasizes, we have
seen repeatedly, ideologies of universal inclusion that effectively blur—in
the sense of making less appreciable—its massively inegalitarian distributions of rights and resources. Its civility thus accentuates inclusion, accommodation, ambiguity, and heterogeneity as idioms of social relation,
expressed in a variety of nationalist ideologies (e.g., "racial democracy"),
cultural institutions (e.g., carnaval), and social conventions (e.g., play of
race classifications). As insurgent citizenship disrupts the differentiated,
these dominant formulations of inclusion wear thin and the inequalities
they cover become intolerable. Increasingly exhausted, they get replaced in
everyday relations by in-your-face incivilities and aggressive aesthetics—
rap and funk, not samba—that express new polarizations of class, race,
and rights. From this perspective, incivility appears necessary as a public
idiom of deep democratic change.

In the earlier discussion, I looked at encounters between anonymous
others in bank lines as expressing calculations about relative distributions of power and equality that relate the status of citizen to the significance of other social identities (of class, race, gender, age, and so forth).
The example I analyzed presented a confrontation between a higher-class

whiter man ("I authorize it") and a lower-class woman of color ("This is a public space and I have my rights") that engaged two citizenships and their civilities. I described the one as entrenched and the other as insurgent. The latter demanded equal rights in and to the public, transforming the various identities of those waiting into one of equivalence. That commonality negated the value of other social categories as a means for determining privilege. The entrenched tried to assert those categories as the norm of public relations. In the context of bank lines, the insurgent and its new civility triumphed—though its expression was not without contradiction ("You only rule in your kitchen and over your wife"). Nonetheless, although the habits of the entrenched regime of citizenship no doubt remain the assumed standard for many of the formerly privileged, they have lost efficacy in determining the outcome of encounters in this type of public space. No longer do either customers or banks tolerate special treatment in lines, except for reasons of pregnancy and infirmity.

The outcome of encounters is often much different at the interface of private or privatized spaces, compounding the contradictions of contemporary Brazilian citizenship. An example is car traffic. Cars provide drivers with immediate power, agency, and opportunity, assets typically exercised in Brazil under conditions of anonymity, dominated by the aesthetics of speed, and little supervised even though driving is supposed to be rule bound.[9] At the wheel of this enclosure of private space, drivers make public performances on the basis of private assumptions about public encounters. Unfortunately, these performances are exceedingly dangerous. If one is to believe the traffic safety campaigns of recent years, they result in more vehicular and pedestrian fatalities than anywhere else on the planet. In this context, calculations of agency and power lead regularly to the negation of rights and refusal of duties and, instead, to the attempted imposition of privilege that assumes impunity and often produces tragedy. The paradigm of differentiated citizenship prevails.

As common but more ambiguous are public encounters in the circulation spaces of apartment buildings, both at street entrances and in elevators. In this case, interactions are not between anonymous others but between those who know each other in a variety of employment and service relations. Middle-class apartment buildings swarm with such relations, in which the apartment principals (owners or renters) are in constant traffic with domestic laborers (cleaners, cooks, nannies, and drivers), outside service providers (installers, repairmen, construction workers, deliverers, and attendants), and building staff (janitors, doormen, security, and supers). They provide the middle classes with an experience of the diversity of Brazilian society at home, on terms that ought to be predictable and controlled for that reason. For many elites, this intense domestic urban sociality establishes the reference of interpersonal relations from which they generalize about the class and racial complexities of Brazilian society. In my experience, apartment residents tend to expect that these encounters should follow the conventions of privilege and deference characteristic of master-servant relations—always, preferably, with a pleasing but ambiguous sense of play that camouflages the hard facts of low wages and long hours.[10] Increasingly, however, those who serve expect to be treated, if not (yet) with better wages and work conditions, then at least with citizen equality in the building's public spaces. They disrupt the expectations of deference not with direct verbal confrontation but with new spatial practices. These produce both new proximities and new incivilities in social relations.

This everyday drama arises because the customary organization of domestic space, for all but the poorest families, embodies the segregations of differentiated citizenship that are now challenged. Based on the organization of the middle-class house, the Brazilian apartment is divided into three functionally independent zones: the social, intimate, and service areas. This plan reflects the division between masters, who occupy the social and intimate areas of the apartment, and servants, who work and sometimes live in the service area. This division is a norm of social life, for even modestly middle-class families employ the cheap labor of the lower classes to clean, cook, and care for children. With the exception of a multipurpose room called the *copa* attached to the kitchen, the three zones are kept separate. In fact, building codes require that corridors isolate one area from another.[11] This principle of separating functions and classes gets most articulated in planning the service zone, which has two components: a circulation system for the apartment building and a service area for each apartment. The latter consists of kitchen, laundry, work space, and bedroom(s) and a bathroom for live-in domestic(s). The organizing principle of both components is controlled separation to ensure minimal informal contact between the servant and master classes, except in the *copa*, as servants circulate through the building and perform their tasks.[12]

The need for this separation generates the convention, as far as I know unique to Brazilian architecture in the Americas, that every apartment building except the poorest must have two independent circulation systems. They begin at the street with two entrances, a social entry (sometime called "noble") and a service entry, ideally on different sides of the building. Most important, each leads to its own elevator. Corresponding to each elevator, the apartment must have separate entrances for its two classes of inhabitants: a social door off the front hall and a service door off the service corridor. In modest middle-class buildings, where the service corridor has been eliminated to save space, the social necessity of maintaining two circulation systems produces an overdetermined situation: the two elevators and two apartment doors are set side by side. Thus, mistress and maid may wait for the elevators together but should part company and ride separately. In this way, the architecture assigns each her place and reinforces social relations of privilege and deference daily.

The utilization of this double-track circulation is supposed to be asymmetrical and hierarchical, like the social order it supports. While the service class may not use the noble entrance and elevator, "nobles" can use both, according to rules of etiquette: they should take the service route when walking the dog, transporting packages, returning from exercise, or otherwise "dirty." The presence of these asymmetrical systems of circulation in every apartment building thus perpetuates a pervasive regime of social differentiation. Inequity persists palpably in Brazilian social relations not only because the privileged insist on maintaining their special treatment rights. It also persists because it continues to structure the embodied habits and spatial practices of everyday life.

In recent years, in my own middle-class apartment building in São Paulo, this organization of social place and its distinctions has become disrupted. Today, most domestic employees use the social elevator, not only when they arrive and leave but also during the day when they run errands. There is, moreover, a plaque now mounted inside the social elevator that states in bold letters the law prohibiting any discrimination in "accessing the elevators of this building." Legislation from 1996 requires its display in all social elevators. In my building, the social elevator is more crowded as a result, as masters and servants stand side by side, viewing each other obliquely in the mirrors. Some masters welcome this development. Some engage in small talk with the service class. But the hellos do not unmake the awkwardness for most of the new proximities of these different bodies in everyday space. For masters, this proximity is uneasy because it is an imposed legality. It is a proximity they cannot control or choose to experience, as elites have always done in the "acceptable" kinds of inter-class-and-race body mixings of carnival, sex, and child rearing. For servants, it is uneasy because they know exactly what they are doing: they are transgressing the dominant social codes of place and privilege by their spatial tactics and are doing so, significantly, with an underlying threat of legal sanction. As if to match them, I have noticed that some masters now engage in similar transgressions: they ride in the social elevator with their dogs—to register, no doubt, their view that the whole social system of distance and distinction has gone "to the dogs."

The new confusion is only compounded at the street. Here, the subversion of the building's code of place and privilege appears to many residents to reflect a broader disruption of social relations in the city itself. Many in the building now live in fear of the street and its elements of crime and violence. Assessments of building security a few years ago led an overwhelming majority of residents to decide in assembly that having two street entrances, one on each side of the building, made it vulnerable to assault. They voted to compromise the dual system of circulation by closing the service entry. Initially, they attempted to maintain separations by operating two doors in the security gate that was installed across the front of the building. The social entry was placed on one side of a small guardhouse, from which the doorman marshals all traffic, and has a double door system to create a "holding pen" for greater surveillance. On the other side was positioned a gate for car entry and next to that a single service door. Those domestic employees who had already abandoned the old service entry continued to use the social one. However, all other service people had to use the new service door twenty feet away.

Nevertheless, it was soon determined that the doorman could not properly screen those wanting entrance there because of that distance. Expediency dictated that he admit them first and then question them at the guardhouse. That procedure was deemed hazardous. So, the service door was closed and everyone had to use the social entrance. At that point, residents established the rule that all outside service providers had to walk from the social entry down the driveway, into the garage, and all the way to the back side of the building to pick up the original path of service circulation. Naturally, however, many just cut through the social areas of the building to get to the service elevator. Occasionally, the building administrator reopens the new service door to try to maintain some separation, only to close it again after complaints about lax security.

The result of these anxious deliberations about security, separation, equality, and hierarchy is that although residents may now have a sense of greater physical security with the service entrance closed, many feel socially assaulted. Certainly, some applaud the breakdown of spatial discrimination in the building. But if only a few argue specifically that their rights to private property have been violated, many feel generally that their status and the quality of life that depends on it have declined. They grumble about the "confusion" of people wandering around, the "decadence of appearances," the "loss of value," and even the "bad smell" in the social elevator. Yet they have always shared their residential space with service people. What has changed is that they must now do so on terms they cannot dictate, terms that establish new kinds of proximity as well as distance. Both upset assumptions of place.

I found two principal components to this elite sense of displacement. One concerns the inability to maintain a spatial order of privilege in relation to the social order emerging in the peripheries. The other concerns the erosion of the kind of everyday symbolic distinctions of status that are composed precisely to be exhibited in public and that elites are accustomed to use to confirm their sense of social place. My neighbors register both concerns with different scales of example: they fear being assaulted "by marginals from the periphery"; they are bothered by the mixing of social and service areas; they complain about the spray-paint "tagging" (*pichação*) of wall surfaces everywhere as a defacing of their neighborhoods by "delinquents from the periphery"—indeed, as an aggressive assertion of the peripheries in their faces.[13] In these examples, they focus on the imposed proximities that make them feel estranged from the outdoor public of the city and yet imprisoned in their homes by their own security measures. Other examples seem caricatures of social complaint: some are offended that their domestic employees arrive for work wearing knockoff designer handbags, fashionable blue jeans, and shirts adorned with Disney figures, all similar to those they use.[14] Their irritation that these small signs of distinction have been usurped seems petty. Yet it represents their larger realization that the lower classes now have access not only to the consumer knowledge that makes these things valuable to elites but also to the things themselves.

Most of these cases map onto the familiar signs of daily-life resentments over the commonalities of rights, knowledge, and agency that the expansions of urban democratic citizenship have produced. As tales of displacement, they express a dissonance of fact and sentiment. There is no question that the poor have forced elites to recognize them as citizens with substantial rights in shaping the future of city and nation. In 1933, a mere 3.7% of Brazilians had political citizenship. These elites ruled the development of modern Brazil absolutely. Only fifty-five years later, 57%—that is, 91% of all adults—had rights to vote in Brazil's first election for president after military dictatorship (table 3.1). For those accustomed to rule, the new facts of citizenship have changed the social world in ways unimaginable over the course of a single generation. Moreover, this transformation is not only one of the ballot box. From administration to residence, from infrastructure to consumption, Brazil's insurgent citizens have pushed themselves into urban spaces and even personal spaces elites used to dominate with complete assurance.

Predictably, many elites view these new proximities as intrusions—indeed, violations—and respond by creating new kinds of distance. From the perspective of democratization, these responses appear as new incivilities because they affront its expanding equalities and agencies. The elite development of this cycle has taken several forms of privatization and abandonment in São Paulo. Motivated by fear and suspicion, elites withdraw from the sort of everyday personal contact that made their style of rule famous for its congeniality and ambiguity. Instead, they develop an array of new social and physical barriers, which Caldeira (2000) and others (e.g., Fix 2001) analyze. On the one hand, they exhibit explicit disdain. This mindset culminates in racist criminalizations of the lower classes, which oppose human rights and support police violence. On the other, they wall themselves into residential and commercial enclosures, guarded by private security and high-tech surveillance, that create new segregations of urban space.

These strategies of withdrawal produce a destabilized urban landscape. Although the accomplishments of insurgent citizenship are visible throughout the city, so are the interiorizing and privatizing rejections of them. At the same time, for example, that neighborhoods in the peripheries exhibit many improvements in infrastructure and social resources, buildings there and everywhere bristle with the hardware of security. Even as local governments invest in new cultural facilities (e.g., museums, parks, and performance centers), middle-class families abandon neighborhood parks and squares, which deteriorate as a result, for the recreational spaces of private clubs, malls, and residences. The city thus seems simultaneously renewed and decayed. Moreover, as the city builds an efficient subway, the middle classes have also largely abandoned public transportation for private modes in which they increasingly hide from view behind dark glass and bulletproof armor. These contrasts—of public investment and routine privatization, renovation and decadence, democratic access and elitist interiorization—have become pervasive in São Paulo and explicit in ordinary urban experience.[15]

At the extreme of privatization are the new fortified residential enclaves into which some elites have sequestered themselves. In expanding areas of the metropolitan periphery, they have built walled islands of wealth that become girdled with new favela settlements. Although relatively few in number, these enclaves are of great public significance because they juxtapose "the most shocking landscapes of adjacent wealth and poverty" in the city, as Caldeira (2000: 254–55) describes them. Based on her research in several enclaves, she concludes that

> In the context of increased suspicion and fear of crime, [their] residents show no tolerance for people from different social groups. . . . Rather, they engage in increasingly sophisticated techniques of social separation and the creation of distance. Thus, the fortified enclaves. . . . constitute the core of a new way of organizing segregation, social discrimination, and economic restructuring in São Paulo. Different social classes live closer to each other in some areas [i.e., enclave and favela] but are kept apart by physical barriers and systems of identification and control. . . . [This] model of obvious separation put in place in recent decades may be seen as a reaction to the expansion of [the] very process of democratization, since it functions to stigmatize, control, and exclude those who had just forced their recognition as citizens.

281

In my study of Brasília (1989: 310–14), I conclude that although there is no simple correlation between urban form and politics, the creation of elite enclaves is not without efficacy for certain types of political regimes and social orders. Such enclosures are today both entire city centers (e.g., Brasília's prototypically modernist Plano Piloto) and the fortified enclaves (also modernist) found in most large cities. In these cityscapes, modernist design segregates city populations by eliminating the type of urban and architectural forms characteristic of the street as a freely accessible public room and by dividing urban life into discrete homogenous zones. The result is that the heterogeneous sociality of the outdoor city public all but disappears: its space is emptied and its crowd separated into an indoor public of elites, who frequent restricted interior spaces of residence, work, commerce, and recreation that require prior privileges, and an outdoor public of the working poor who, beyond work, have no place in these modernist places. This is an urban order that interiorizes some and either removes the rest or keeps them under surveillance. These displacements not only segregate space but also change the nature of the public using it: the elites of Brasília's Plano Piloto and São Paulo's walled enclaves no longer see themselves as participating in an outdoor city public of social life while the popular classes see themselves marginalized, if not criminalized.

In Brasília, these results were not intended, at least not initially. Rather, they followed from fundamental but unexamined contradictions between the architectural strategies of modernism and its political intentions (both authoritarian and egalitarian) to reinvigorate urban society. In São Paulo, these results are intended. Elites and their architects use modernist form and planning because, free from egalitarian illusion, they understand their segregating powers clearly. The Plano Piloto is exceptional because, at the scale of an entire city, it is devoid of the kind of public spaces and urban crowds that require mediations of social differences. Hence, its social separations appear overwhelmingly stark and nonnegotiable. The fortified enclaves of São Paulo are fragments of Brasília. However, they are set in a city that is vastly more complex, with unavoidable sidewalk crowds and streets crammed with every species of urban life. The Brazilian society that can be almost entirely avoided in the empty spaces of the one city cannot be unencountered in the other. Although elites try to remove themselves as much as possible in both, the multilayerings and sheer congestion of São Paulo's urban forms force most to mix. Everyday contaminations of difference occur inescapably.

As a result, the city public of São Paulo is generally tense, often uncivil, and sometimes violent. But it remains vital. The confrontations, insults, defiance, distrust, and disgust between people who have differing conceptions of privileges and rights make up the incivilities that have become

routine in Paulistano daily life. Yet this incivility, for all its unpleasant-
ness, is also public admission that the dominant orders of citizenship that
once managed the encounters of difference with propriety are breaking
down under the challenge of new terms. It is the shrill voice of the resistance of some and the insistence of many that a new type of social proximity, based on the equalizations of citizen rights, will not be undone. In
the empty spaces of Brasília, it may be possible to escape this realization.
In São Paulo, the incivilities of daily life remind residents that it is not.

This grating reminder generates another expression of antagonism to
the changes of democratic citizenship, more subtle than walls and interiorization but significant nonetheless: nostalgia. From everyday conversation to talk-show opinion, São Paulo's current problems commonly get
assessed in terms of a longing for what the city was like "before." It is not
only an old social elite who reminisce about strolling downtown, going to
theaters, and even riding the bus. Many critics of the contemporary city
conjure up an image of an older urban public in which São Paulo's different inhabitants "got along so well," in which their social, ethnic, and
racial diversities had little organized expression because they got subsumed in the common identifications of work and progress that united
all Paulistanos under the banner "São Paulo can never stop."[16] In these
nostalgic evocations, there is little violence to disrupt the pleasures of
public mixing and the industry of the street's heterogeneous society.

Such comparisons enable critics to present contemporary violence
and injustice as unprecedented. However, their nostalgia misses a crucial
point: although of new types and intensities today, violence has always
been endemic to the constitution of Brazilian society. Often advanced by
democracy's critics, nostalgic visions suggesting the contrary ignore two
conditions that made possible the "peace of the street" as a public idiom
of interaction. First, it was maintained by a discriminatory and repressive regime of citizenship that ensured that everyone knew their place
and that responded severely to threats of displacement. As I have shown
throughout this book, the perduring denials of citizen rights, alienations
of the legal system, and conditions of illegality exposed many Brazilians
regularly to repression, violence, and injustice. In fact, the regime of differentiated citizenship has always accommodated high levels of public
and private violence, impunity, judicial discredit, police abuse, corruption, scofflawism, and privatizations of justice and security (think of *coronelismo*), in addition to the structural violence of malnutrition, abysmal
health care, and all the reduced life chances of massive poverty. Indeed,
the systemic violence and repression of this citizenship have never been in
doubt—precisely as Washington Luís, governor of the state of São Paulo
and future president, confirmed on the campaign trail in 1920 with his
famous remark: "The social question is a question of the police."

283

Second, these brutal characteristics of Brazilian society have been for centuries effectively blurred by an arsenal of well-known ideologies of inclusion that Brazilian elites have used to create national projects: a nationalism of race mixing, populism based on urban labor, state-sponsored modernization, modernist and developmentalist planning, and the formulation of differentiated citizenship itself—all used, as we have seen, to produce identifications with the nation-state that are universally inclusive in membership but massively inegalitarian in the distribution of rights and resources. These ideologies of inclusion are complemented, furthermore, by cultural conventions of seduction that give personal relations of gender, racial, and economic difference a gloss of complicit accommodation, a sense of intimacy that obscures but maintains fundamental inequalities: I refer to the seductive ambiguities produced through the (untranslatable) artifices of *jetinho, malícia, malandragem, jinga, jogo de cintura,* and *mineirice,* and universalized in the institutions of *samba, carnaval,* and *capoeira*—all celebrated in Brazilian culture but beyond my purpose here to describe.[17]

My point is rather that these ideologies and conventions of inclusion have only recently become less convincing, discredited by the insurgence of democratic citizenship and its new agencies. The problem for contemporary Brazilian society is that although the inequitable distributions remain, their blurrings have lost efficacy. This exhaustion increasingly exposes the hard facts of inequality "for Brazilians to see." The undeniable exaggerations of violence, injustice, and corruption in the current period of political democracy may thus be considered in these terms: the gross inequalities continue but the political and cultural pacts that have sustained them are worn out. This flaying of a social skin transforms city and society. It produces rawness, outrage, and exaggeration. I have suggested that the deep democratic changes embodied in this process necessarily produce incivility as a public idiom of resistance and insistence. Although expected therefore, the question is what prevents this incivility from pitching into extremes, as seems to be happening today? Can there be effective restraint without a creditable justice system?

In/Justice

The police have a close collaborator in maintaining the society that Washington Luís portrays: a persistently remote, formalistic, and astonishingly inefficient judiciary. Brazil's violent police and complicit judiciary are pillars of a justice system that has firmly sustained the regime of differentiated citizenship in its propagation of inequality. This system includes the courts, the bar, the police, and the prisons. At issue with each is the right to justice that guarantees the realization of all rights. This right determines whether citizens have access to their rights in cases of dispute and whether access entails fair treatment and not only the application of statute. In other words, an effective justice system must account for the problem that what is strictly legal is not always just and vice versa. As the right to all other rights and to the sense of fairness that legitimates law itself, justice is the crucial civil right. As the institutions most associated with its exercise, the justice system constitutes the defining element of the civil sphere of democracy. Within it, the courts bear primary responsibility for securing the right to justice. That imperative shapes the entire justice system and is the crucible for the kind of law without which there is no democracy. Therefore, where citizens perceive that courts lack commitment to their right to justice, the justice system as a whole becomes discredited. Its delegitimation subverts not only civil rights but the entire project of democracy. Thus, for Brazil's democratization, the courts' engagement with this project is decisive.

The historical problem for the Brazilian judiciary is that every constitution has contained more or less adequate provisions for formal due process and fundamental civil rights to life, liberty, and property—provisions directly inspired, as we have seen, by French and American constitutions. However, in practice, the courts have consistently protected only property and only certain kinds at that, a negligence evident in the case of land dispute in Jardim das Camélias that has languished in the courts without decision for more than thirty years. It is not only that Brazilian citizens do not habitually use the courts to protect noneconomic civil rights. It is also that Brazilian courts do not invite such use because they do not have a tradition of defending them. Rather than give life and liberty rigorous judicial protection against infringements by the state, the courts tend to acquiesce to their deprivation when they consider them at all—as failed challenges to government censorship, illegal detention, coerced confessions, and police killings illustrate. What has been conspicuously missing from Brazil's judicial tradition is the sense that courts protect the rights of citizens generally and the right to justice especially.

The failings of the judiciary are legendary in this regard. As I and others have discussed them at length (e.g., 1999), I need only make a few observations to establish the key points. To use an everyday example, domestic employees can easily find lawyers to bring charges against the owners of apartment buildings who try to deny them access to the social elevator. However, everyone knows that such cases will never have a final day in court. Rather, they will circulate through the justice system endlessly, bouncing from one technical postponement to another if they make it to a judge's consideration at all. Thus, the statute posted in the social elevator may embolden the servants, but it will not fundamentally constrain

285

the masters. If the latter are willing to sustain the legal hassles and class warfare that will surely result, they will impose discrimination without fear of judicial penalty.[18] Crooks are inspired by such irresolution. When the president of São Paulo's state judiciary took office in 2005, he declared that the appellate courts alone had 550,000 cases awaiting judgment![19]

The effect of such judicial ineffectiveness is double. On one hand, Brazilians cannot expect the institutions of state to secure their rights. On the other, once their rights are violated, they are equally unlikely to expect redress through the courts. When residents in the peripheries comment on the judiciary, they describe it invariably as a remote and untrustworthy institution, protected by impenetrable bureaucratic formalities and corporate privileges. They feel that judges possess extraordinary powers but too much independence because they are only accountable to their own corporation. This combination of features produces the worst possible outcome: mostly, the judiciary is perceived as an institution "without teeth," incapable of enforcing the law and protecting rights. Yet, when it does act, it appears arbitrary and self-referential, concerned overwhelmingly with the formalities of law and not with justice.

Nonetheless, people do not neglect the legal system to further their interests. To the contrary, the insurgence of democratic citizenship has resulted in an unprecedented use of law, in ways far beyond the traditional strategy of manipulating legal formalisms to neutralize judicial resolution. However, this new use also brings unprecedented demands on the justice system. The result is that democratization has magnified its incapacities, multiplied its abuses, and amplified the problem of impunity.

Based on provisions in the Citizen Constitution, for example, many states instituted judicial ombudsmen to hear citizen complaints against the military and civil police. They were mostly placed within departments of public security; that is, within the police apparatus itself. Nevertheless, in its first three years of operation, the ombudsman in São Paulo received an astounding 30,319 complaints (and 119 compliments), from individuals, human rights organizations, and others, including charges of torture, killing, extortion, and abuse of authority. After internal review, about half the complaints were dismissed and half forwarded to the police units in question for further action. Similarly, offices of ombudsmen were installed to monitor other areas of public administration, including health, education, and prisons. To date, the state of São Paulo has 129 such Ouvidorias, the phonelines of which are perpetually flooded. Moreover, pressured by popular demands for accountability and armed with new constitutional authority, both federal and state legislatures have instituted many parliamentary investigative committees (CPIs) during the last decade, based on judicial-like public hearings with broad powers to subpoena witnesses, procure evidence, and issue warrants. Although the courts have voided some of these warrants, the CPIs have nevertheless succeeded in generating much media coverage and public support for their investigations into organized crime, including several focused on corruption within congress and the judiciary.[20]

But what, we must ask, results from all this effort to provoke judicial action and enforce citizen rights? Mostly, impunity. Evidence abounds that most civil and criminal violations remain unpunished. Consider homicide, the best-documented crime. Human Rights Watch (1991) reported that 1,681 rural workers were murdered in Brazil between 1965 and 1990. Of these cases, only 26 went to trial and 15 resulted in convictions. It is uncertain, moreover, that any of those convicted did jail time. The conclusion is nonetheless clear: hired guns murder with near impunity. So do police. The emblematic event of police violence during the 1990s was the massacre of 111 prisoners at São Paulo's Casa de Detenção in 1992. Several investigations established beyond doubt that although prisoners had rioted, the victims were summarily executed after surrendering. As a result, a civilian prosecutor presented charges against the commander of the operation and a military prosecutor did the same against 120 policemen for various crimes, including homicide. Yet, after a decade, there has been only one inconclusive trial. Most of the accused continue to work in the military police. The commander himself ran for state assembly, highlighting his role in repressing the rebellion and using 111 as his ballot number. He placed second, eventually served, and was reelected.

With regard to police ombudsmen, results are no less impressive. Of the 3,806 citizen complaints accepted in 1998 in São Paulo for further investigation, 1,942 were lodged against civil police. Of these, only 134 (6.9%) were actually investigated and 30 (1.5%) resulted in punishment, which means administrative penalties (e.g., demotion and warning) and indictments. It does not mean trial or jail—data about which are unavailable, perhaps because there are few instances. Although the CPIs have captured national attention with their courtlike drama, the outcome is much the same: they end in "pizza," as Brazilians say, that is, next to nothing—the protagonists dine together and forget the dispute. After uncovering stupendous corruption, the Judiciary CPI managed to get only one judge sent to jail. Moreover, almost a decade later, comprehensive judicial reform remains practically nil. Although CPI investigations of banking crime led the government to close several private banks in the last decade for illicit enrichment and other violations, not one bank executive ever went to trial, much less prison.[21]

The inescapable conclusion for Brazilians is that impunity reigns. The incapacities of the justice system create the firm belief that citizens cannot enforce their rights, that their legal disability encourages criminality, and that the courts cannot arbitrate social relations in ways that would impose sanctions on the offenses of the powerful and the agents of the state. Hence, citizens retain the generalized expectation of either impunity or abuse from the justice system. From the perspective of the judiciary, its failures to achieve effective justice mean not only that most Brazilians avoid it when they militate for rights, turning instead to executive and legislative institutions. They also mean that the judiciary has been slow to confront the transformations of contemporary society. Of all the branches of government, it remains the most resistant to the whirlwind of democratic change. Its failures have crippled Brazilian political democracy with an undemocratic rule of law. Should we be surprised that many citizens support police violence and private security forces as a better bet for justice?

If Brazilians widely consider the judiciary ineffective in protecting their rights and removed from their social needs, its insulation has been an institutional design. The office of judge is intended to be impregnable to outside influence: entry to office is by public examination or nomination, not popular election; the institutional career guarantees immovability, automatic promotion, and irreducible salary; life tenure comes after two years in office at the entry level and immediately for those getting superior judgeships. Furthermore, autonomy and stability in office are directly associated with principles of equilibrium and impartiality at the core of Brazilian jurisprudence. These principles hold that "the guarantee of equilibrium is inertia" (Silva 1992: 506). This idea is conveyed to every law student in the Roman maxim "there is no judge without an agent," interpreted to mean that the judiciary must not act without formal provocation. The point taught is that to be balanced, judges must be "static and inert," waiting for others to approach them with problems to solve (Calamandrei, cited in Silva 1992: 506). As judges cannot be activists of any sort, their relation to social change must be null.

However, the principle of inertia and its presumption of impartiality are not free from assumptions about the relation between law and society, though these remain mostly undeclared. One could interpret the principle to mean provoked by agents beyond the courtroom. Thus stimulated, judges could let it be known that they are interested in receiving certain kinds of cases or in considering cases at hand in light of their embedded social circumstances. It would seem, therefore, that what restrains Brazilian judges from being activists or constructionists is not a notion of agency, which, after all, may be understood in various ways. Rather, judges are roped in by a tradition of legal formalism, which Brazilian jurisprudence justifies as a "science of law" (derived from Roman, Napoleonic, and German legal thought) but which developed, I have argued, more as a means of using law to manipulate and complicate conflict in favor of extrajudicial solutions. By these means, the interpretative space of judges is shrunk, ideally, to naught: on the one hand, their scope of prov-ocation is restricted to courtroom procedure; on the other, their scope of jurisdiction is limited to applying statutes to cases at hand. This legalism has significant consequences for the judiciary's relation to society: it rec-ognizes only the state and its codifications as legitimate sources of law, rejects any form of judge-made law, and requires only the logic of statu-tory consistency to justify decisions. Thus, judges may not interpret cases by way of previous decisions or sociohistorical context.

The rejection of judicial precedent as a source of law—and thus of the doctrine of stare decisis—means that similar cases often receive differ-ent judgments. For example, courts at every level of jurisdiction can find a legislative act unconstitutional, a model of diffuse review adopted in 1891 from the U.S. Constitution. However, a court can only do so in the context of adjudicating a concrete conflict in which the act is applicable. Its ruling only affects the case at hand. As the law in question remains valid, another court might decide a similar case differently based on its own analysis. Because their decisions do not become binding precedent, judges cannot be accused of making law when they rule that an act vio-lates the constitution. Rather, they are only deciding that a statute cannot apply in a particular case or "fact situation." As in constitutional review, so with decisions in every domain of law: identical cases may and often are decided differently by different judges. From the perspective of the ju-diciary, this model of idiosyncrasy creates nearly complete independence for each judge and eliminates potential conflicts of doctrine and disputes between branches of government. However, for citizens, as I show later, it creates a judiciary whose rulings appear unpredictable and arbitrary, one in which judges have extraordinary individual powers that are practically unchecked.[22]

How has the popular mobilization of democracy affected this judi-ciary? The new constitution crystallizes three developments that challenge its consideration of justice and relation to society: the legitimation of new sources of law, innovations of constitutional principle, and a move-ment of alternative legal criticism. I focus on the first two.[23] All force the judiciary to confront contradiction and thereby contest its complacency, though the process is slow and the results uncertain. As described in the last chapter, grassroots mobilizations of citizens successfully pressured the Constitutional Assembly to accept new sources of law embedded in their own social experience. They got it to acknowledge that many exist-ing laws were intolerably out-of-date, especially in the civil (1916) and commercial (1850) codes, because they imposed norms rejected by most Brazilians and yet failed to account for contemporary social practices. By receiving the popular amendments, the assembly admitted that the social experiences of citizens—especially of lower-class Brazilians with

289

residence, property, employment, and marriage—contradicted existing legislation to such an extent that they compelled its reformulation by means of new constitutional principles and rights. With these innovations, the constitution recognized new sources of law in the social practices of citizens.

Many of these constitutional innovations create more legal problems than they solve. Critics have widely faulted the new constitution for its crippling dependence on enabling legislation, inclusion of unrealizable social rights, confusion of principle and ordinary statute, and excessive detail in its 250 articles and innumerable paragraphs. In particular, most of its innovations have little impact because they exist in principle only. They are not self-executing and require enabling legislation to take effect, legislation that congress "hesitates" to enact.[24] In 1990, the outgoing Minister of Justice estimated that the constitution required passage of 285 ordinary statutes and 41 complementary laws to implement its provisions fully (cited in Rosenn 1990: 778). Only a few have passed since then, each with difficulty.[25] Thus, the constitution's provisions for new social rights, guaranteeing most imaginable goods, languish for lack of executable statute and policy. One might conclude correctly that the assembly was able to respond to grassroots mobilizations because it knew full well that many of the socially progressive demands it incorporated into the constitution would have little effect without the unlikely passage of enabling legislation. Thus, entrenched interests in congress have been able to thwart the audacity of the constitution through calculated inaction.

For these reasons, the Citizen Constitution has often been dubbed a temporary or transitional exercise, more an appeasement of conflicting political forces than a workable charter.[26] I think this assessment misses a crucial point. Surely, it is not redaction that makes a constitution an agent of transformation. What is powerful about the Citizen Constitution is, above all, that it emerges from and engages tremendous popular demands for democracy. Without doubt, this context generates both social conflict and confusion, which, precisely because transformative, got expressed in the charter. Yet those who dismiss it seem not to understand the paradoxical power of confusion itself, especially for the judiciary, in the context of widespread mobilizations for democracy. I suggest that the new constitution is a potent agent of change exactly because, in requiring so much redefinition, it has the potential to generate significant confusion in a legal system that needs to be shaken to the core. In addition, it provides a number of new remedies and procedures and occasionally yields enabling legislation of real innovation to do just that.

With regard to the highest court, for example, the constitution (Art. 103) considerably expands the number and kind of parties who have standing to demand abstract review—that is, a review of the constitutionality of a statute or policy not requiring particular litigation in a concrete case in which it applies. Under previous constitutions, only the attorney general, representing the executive branch, had such standing. Now, almost any organized interest group can turn an issue of rights—for reasons of "commission or omission"—into a constitutional conflict at the highest judicial level.[27] A case in point is the flurry of petitions the Supreme Court has received over the last decade to review the constitutionality of economic policy and related legislation, beginning with the infamous Plano Collor I in 1990. From then on, it has been increasingly difficult for the Supreme Court to remain aloof from political controversy in questions of economic policy.[28]

But such new judicial authority is highly problematic. Consider the powers of "mandatory injunction" that the constitution (Art. 5, LXXI) gives the courts to implement rights whenever the absence of enabling legislation makes their exercise impracticable. This radical provision would seem to provide an end run around congressional inaction. In fact, however, it only permits the courts to inform a delinquent party that it must initiate corrective measures to ensure the petitioner's rights within thirty days. It provides no power to oblige legislation or to allocate funds to make judicial orders effective. Furthermore, given the amount of missing legislation, it asks judges to weigh matters of extraordinary political and economic impact. Not surprisingly, although often petitioned, the courts have been reluctant to grant these remedies. It is clear in this and many other cases that the constitution's innovations require much testing and reworking.

Nevertheless, congressional inaction and constitutional confusion have led to an unanticipated outcome: they have empowered the judiciary at the expense of congress. In effect, the ambiguities, contradictions, and new remedies of the constitution beckon litigation, mountains of it, and that possibility provides grassroots and alternative-law movements with unprecedented opportunities to force the hand of judicial complacency. Thus, congressional inaction exposed the judiciary to attack, forcing it to consider the new contradictions and redefinitions of law. Necessarily, such considerations erode the legislature's monopoly on lawmaking, not only by elevating the authority of the judiciary as the oracle of law but also by forcing it to rethink the theory, method, and scope of judicial discretion. At the same time, they politicize the courts by forcing them to expand their horizons beyond the traditional sources of law to justify deliberations. As a result, the judiciary is thrown open to society and into crisis.

Let me focus this turmoil on the problems of land and illegal residence that have been fundamental to the insurgence of new citizenship movements in the urban peripheries. One of the popular amendments that

291

they presented to the assembly generated the constitution's section on urban policy. Article 182 states that the objective of urban policies is "to organize the full development of the social functions of the city and to guarantee the well-being of its inhabitants." To realize this objective, it establishes that "urban property fulfills its social function when it meets the fundamental exigencies of the organization of the city expressed in the master plan," which it requires all cities with more than twenty thousand inhabitants to develop. Additionally, the article determines that local governments can promote the social function of urban land through expropriation, forced subdivision, and progressive taxation. Article 183 creates *usucapião urbano*—adverse possession for urban land—as a means of resolving the predicament of illegal residence that affects so many poor Brazilians. It allows the residents of small urban house lots (250 square meters or less) to obtain original ownership title if they can prove five years of continuous residence without legitimate opposition. These two articles became the basis for a series of legislated acts, regulations, and planning initiatives that have transformed urban policy in Brazil into an instrument for social justice of considerable scope and innovation.

For more than a decade, the national congress debated the enabling legislation required to define more precisely the concept of social function and the mechanisms for its implementation. Finally, in 2001, it enacted the Estatuto da Cidade (City Statute) as federal law. This legislation incorporates concepts developed by the urban citizen movements and various local administrations (especially PT). It is remarkable in the history of urban legislation, policy, and planning not only in Brazil but worldwide for at least four reasons. First, it defines the social function of the city and of urban property in terms of a set of guidelines that are substantive in nature. Second, on that basis, it frames its directives from the perspective of the poor, the majority of urban residents, and creates mechanisms to redress some of the most evident patterns of illegality, inequality, and degradation in the production of urban space. Thus, it establishes social equality as a principal objective of urban planning and turns planning into an instrument for social equalization and justice. Third, the statute requires that local master plans and policies be developed and implemented with active popular collaboration. Fourth, it is not framed as a total plan (as in the paradigm of Brasília) but instead as a series of innovative legal instruments that allow local administrations to realize and enforce social function. Unquestionably, the City Statute is the result of the insurgent citizenship movements since the 1970s. It is an important indication of the ways in which democratization has taken root in Brazilian society and of how the grassroots experiences of local administration, legal invention, and popular mobilization have made their space in law.[29]

Of these democratic innovations in urban policy, that of *usucapião urbano* (Art. 183) affects the judiciary directly. This process of transforming the physical possession of land without legal powers of ownership (*posse*) into legal possession with property rights (*propriedade*) is entirely a judicial matter of litigation between private parties (individual or collective). Public land remains ineligible. By contrast, expropriation for reasons of social function converts private land into public with indemnification. Thus, expropriation is a process driven by the executive offices of government and depends on their political will and economic circumstances. Article 183 became effective in 1990. In that year, the SABs in Jardim das Camélias and Lar Nacional began to test it as a strategy for resolving their land disputes. I received permission from the relevant court in São Paulo, that of Public Registries, to observe the adjudication of cases of urban adverse possession. For about six months, divided into two three-month periods in successive years, I regularly attended the court. I was generously allowed to examine cases, witness hearings, and accompany discussions among the judges. At the same time, I followed the cases of residents I knew in the two neighborhoods, prepared by the attorney of both SABs, Antônio Margarido. The number of residents petitioning for property rights under Article 183 gradually increased from a handful in the beginning to approximately 150 in Jardim das Camélias and 70 in Lar Nacional by 2005.

Thus I was able to evaluate the judicialization of these land disputes at both ends. I found the results disappointing. As a citizen-driven innovation of democracy, Article 183 did provide lower-class residents unprecedented opportunities to access the courts and use civil law. It also brought the social drama of illegal residence in the peripheries into the courtroom as never before. However, although forty-four residents in Jardim das Camélias and four in Lar Nacional have now received definitive titles based on *usucapião urbano*, all experienced the judicial process as capricious, complicated, unjust, and unbearably slow. For residents in Lar Nacional, it has been nothing less than terrorizing.

During the first ten years, not much happened. The cases inched this way or that, according to conditions that seemed arbitrary and absurd. The court of Public Registries has two branches in São Paulo, the First and Second Varas, of identical jurisdiction, status, and power. Each has three judges and an affiliated registry (*cartório*) which prepares the documentation for each case. Cases are distributed randomly to each judge. Nevertheless, significant differences developed between and within the two courts. The First Vara found ways to streamline, while the Second complicated. For reasons that remain opaque to me, the personnel of the former tried to simplify judicial procedures, eliminate bureaucratic excess, and minimize technical requirements. Those of the latter did not.

293

Was it a matter of circumstance, personality, or individual biography? The Second Vara required lawyers, for example, to provide a twenty-year history of the judicial record of each name associated with a petition to determine whether the plot in question had been seized. The research involved was staggering, not least because many petitioners have names in common. One judge required handwritten declarations of financial worth if a petitioner requested a waiver of court fees, including notarization of signature—difficult tasks for those who do not write well. In 1992, three of the judges left for new assignments. Two of their replacements thought that the five-year period of eligibility was not retroactive but began with the constitution in 1988. In consequence, they rejected the petitions in their charge as ineligible. The residents affected had to wait another year and start all over.

Even if their petitions survived these and other procedural infelicities and were declared bona fide and bureaucratically fit, most residents had in effect accomplished next to nothing: As required by law, the judges routinely notified the federal government of each case. The Union then intervened in the majority of them, claiming ownership on the basis, as we have seen, of reversionary rights to land located within the old Indian villages of São Paulo. If upheld, such rights invalidated the petitions. The lawyers appealed, demanding that the Union prove its ownership. The appeals went to the Supreme Court, where they remained unresolved.

Nevertheless, there were rare surprises that kept residents hopeful. In 1992, for instance, after two cases from Jardim das Camélias had received favorable judgment at the local Vara, employees of the federal judicial bureaucracy went on strike. When they finally returned to work, the statutory time for federal interventions in the cases had expired. The Union protested, but the presiding judge ignored its request. Instead, with some spiteful satisfaction, he issued two original titles in the names of the residents and ordered them registered. For a very long time, these were the only "successful" cases in the neighborhood. At another point, one judge stopped notifying federal prosecutors, adjudicating the petitions as if the federal government had no interest. He told me that he wanted "to see what happens if the Union appeals," because he doubted that it could prove ownership. When I asked another judge in the Vara about this tactic, he shrugged "I don't know; I see it differently. Each one has his own interpretation." As it turned out, some of the unnotified cases slipped under the Union's radar and others did not. In any case, not long after, the judge in question resigned his office and went into private practice.

It soon became evident that federal intervention would be an insurmountable obstacle to the realization of Article 183 for millions of poor Brazilians who lived in the peripheries of many cities on land once within Indian villages that had been extinguished long ago. In 1996, Antônio

Margarido and I submitted a report to the Minister of Justice on the absurdity of this situation in the Eastern Zone of São Paulo. We examined the legal, historical, and social aspects of the problem, argued that the judiciary could not solve it, and recommended that the Union issue an executive order withdrawing federal interest in these cases of *usucapião*. No doubt on the basis of a number of similar evaluations, the attorney general did just that in 2000. Although it only applies to lands within the ancient indigenous settlements of São Miguel and Guarulhos, Administrative Order (Súmula) Number 4 has both future and retroactive effects. Celebrations erupted in the neighborhoods in anticipation that cases favorably judged at the local level but stuck at the federal in Brasília would soon return for final sentencing and award of title.

For the residents of Jardim das Camélias, this was indeed the outcome. The cases began to return to their origins, though slowly and unpredictably. Since there were no other outstanding conflicts to resolve with regard to the house lots, the local judges granted definitive title as the cases crossed their desks. For Lar Nacional, however, few cases returned because few had gotten past the local court to be sent to Brasília on appeal. Rather, the lawsuit for repossession of land that included Lar Nacional, initially filed in 1966 and won in 1972 by Humberto Reis Costa, created an additional complication for their adjudication.[30] That is, Reis Costa claimed in each case that the 1972 decision had awarded him definitive possession and recovery rights to the lots. His protest sent the cases to São Paulo's superior state court. By 2000, only a handful had been judged there. In all cases but one, the superior court justices ruled unanimously that the real estate company Lar Nacional and therefore residents who had purchased lots from it had not, in fact, been parties to the original possessory action. Thus, Reis Costa had gained no rights to these lots. Relieved of that burden, the petitions went back to the Varas where, favorably judged, they were challenged by the federal government and sent to Brasília. When the Union stepped aside, these few were eventually returned, and by 2003 four had been awarded definitive *usucapião* title.

What no one anticipated, however, was that the celebrated Administrative Order 4 would shake loose from Brasília not only the cases of adverse possession but also all others in which the Union claimed ownership on the same basis. Hence, as the *usucapião* cases trickled back to the courts of Public Registries, the possessory action of 1966/1972 also returned to its original court of jurisdiction, the 6th Civil District Court, to resume its normal course. Because the Supreme Court did not judge the merit of any of these cases but returned them on technical grounds, that meant execution of original sentence with no consideration of the intervening thirty years. When the action finally landed on the judge's desk in 2003, she was, as her order of execution states, appalled that the winners had been waiting thirty-seven years to receive their due. She argued that this delay between judgment and execution "had caused [the heirs of Reis Costa] innumerable damages" and had discredited Brazilian justice. In determining execution, however, the judge based her orders on the decision of the one chamber of the superior state court that had, in a single case, ruled that the residents of Lar Nacional *were* parties to the possessory action and therefore subject to its judgment. On that basis, she accused the residents of willfully disregarding the courts in proposing "judicial maneuvers" of various kinds over the years (e.g., *usucapião* and other defensive actions), which only proved their "intention to perpetuate the conflict . . . indefinitely . . . to avoid the execution of the sentence . . . a situation that cannot be tolerated . . . [and that] generates enormous instability in the juridical world." Her writ of execution declared that the residents were "invaders" who had lacked "good faith" in their purchases and had no rights to the litigated lots.

With a stroke of her pen, the judge ordered the eviction of the entire neighborhood, all 210 house lots—less the four that had received title by means of *usucapião urbano*. These the judge excluded. But what, residents gasped, was different about these four lots? Nothing, other than their random selection in the judicial process of adverse possession. Yet, not only did the judge "return" all the other land to the heirs of Reis Costa. In the final twist of the screw, she awarded the houses as well. After thirty-five years of constructing Lar Nacional, residents were given six weeks to leave or be evicted by force.

Disbelief, agony, and panic engulfed the neighborhood. Attorneys for the estate of Reis Costa announced that only payment for the lots *and* the houses would prevent eviction. Residents vowed to die in their homes fighting the police. Within a week, the SAB mobilized them into an organized resistance. It pursued three strategies. Attorney Margarido initiated legal actions to stay the eviction. Those submitted to higher courts in an effort to bypass the district judge were rejected as "premature" because they had not exhausted all possibilities at the lower court; those addressed to the lower, the ruling judge either denied or ignored. After a few weeks, Margarido seemed to have reached a legal dead end. Residents widely thought that the district judge was corrupt; they had no other explanation. The SAB designated one resident to feign negotiations with the estate "to know the enemy." At their first meeting, one of its lawyers told him that she thought the residents had to pay because they were all squatters who had "lived for free all these years." The reconnaissance revealed ignorance, class hatred, and impossibly high prices.

The SAB's political strategy had two prongs. I organized a media blitz, with help from the Nucleus for Studies of Violence at the University of São Paulo. We issued press releases to radio, television, and newspapers

FIGURE 8.1. Protest in Lar Nacional (2003). Founding-, second-, and third-generation residents organize against eviction: "Brazil, does justice exist?"; "Enough injustice— Housing + Peace"; "In our youth, we bought and paid in good faith. Now seniors, retired, judged, and condemned to eviction." Photo by James Holston.

and got reporters from each on site. We also organized a mass demonstration a week before eviction, with speakers (mostly PT affiliates) from the mayor's office, city council, and state assembly. For the event, residents draped houses with black sheets of plastic and marched down the main street in protest (figure 8.1). During these six weeks, the drama received extensive media coverage, including significant editorials that presented the case as emblematic of "the problem of justice in Brazil" (*Estado de S. Paulo*, 24 August 2003, A3).

The second political strategy was to invoke Article 182 and the City Statute to convince the mayor to expropriate the land for reasons "of social interest" and then return it to the residents. After consulting with PT councilmen, state representatives, and their staff lawyers, the SAB presented its case to the city's Secretary of Housing and asked him to get the mayor to issue what is called a Decree of Social Interest (DIS) for expropriation. With only twelve days remaining until eviction on 27 August, the Secretary agreed to try and outlined a sequence of events: The city's declaration of intention to expropriate would suspend the eviction; once the city had placed a deposit on the land, jurisdiction in the case would be transferred to a different court; the city would have two years to indemnify the estate of Reis Costa, which payment would once and for all recognize him as the legitimate owner; the city would then sell the land back to the residents "at a just price" and favorable terms. Once the land had become public by expropriation, however, all pending *usucapião* cases would be extinguished. Until then, it seemed, the cases could proceed normally. When I asked residents about paying for their lots again, they all said that it wasn't right. However, they felt that expropriation would make the city the sole and definitive owner from which they could buy with security. Due to overlapping titles in the area, any purchase from Reis Costa remained risky. Moreover, the city would propose a fair price. Nevertheless, the contradiction between expropriation and adverse possession unsettled them. It was unclear whether they should continue paying for the latter or abandon it. At the next SAB meeting, attorney Margarido advised them to continue. Tempers flared about having invested so much in a dead-end strategy and then being asked to invest more. A pandemonium of disagreement irrupted. Suddenly, two men started slugging each other. Although order was eventually restored, dissension and suspicion proliferated in the coming week.

Nevertheless, the various factions worked together to organize the demonstration, which brought nearly everyone into the streets to carry signs and hear politicians deliver rousing speeches. At a climactic moment, a legal advisor to the mayor arrived and told the crowd that Mayor Marta Suplicy would issue the decree. People screamed and cried. The neighborhood was saved. What the advisor didn't say was that, for technical reasons, the decree could not be prepared until after the date of eviction. The question was whether the judge would accept the city's intention to do so. The mayor presented a formal request to the court and the estate of Reis Costa. Even though it was better business for the latter to receive payment from the city than suffer through the chaos and expense of the eviction, the estate delayed responding until the afternoon before E-Day. A few hours before midnight, the judge stayed her order.

The DIS was issued about six weeks later. What residents failed to notice in their excitement was that although entitled "Declaration of Social Interest for Expropriation," it actually proposed two courses of action: "The private properties [in Lar Nacional] are declared of social interest to be expropriated judicially or acquired through agreement" (Decree 43,937, 9 October 2003). In February, the city announced a change in course, alleging lack of funds. There would be no expropriation, only facilitation of direct negotiation between residents and the estate of Reis Costa to purchase the lots. The city would try to procure inexpensive loans from private banks though it guaranteed nothing. The residents felt betrayed.

298

The city was urging them to make the kind of accord with an alleged owner that they had resisted for thirty years. Moreover, it offered them no legal protection whatsoever. They organized a political committee to remobilize politicians to pressure the mayor into reinstating expropriation. Nothing worked. Those officials who rallied in August seemed to abandon the neighborhood. The residents became demoralized. "There are so many people in São Paulo who invaded and then succeeded in getting property rights. And we, who paid? We can't. Is that just?" The Department of Housing applied pressure on residents to settle with the estate. According to them, its representative became brutal: "It's of no interest who doesn't have the money; I don't want to hear about the little old ladies. There is no choice. Pay or go to the street. It's your problem." Residents suspected corruption. In fact, the vast majority did not have the money to pay what the estate demanded. Most would be evicted.

The SAB developed a new strategy: "Keep all doors open." It would pursue the judicial process of *usucapião urbano* and the process of negotiation, even though they contradict each other. The former has become even more absurd since the eviction order: the First Vara is denying all petitions randomly assigned to it while the Second approves all! At the same time, the SAB assured the estate that residents were ready to negotiate as soon as it furnished a definitive title to prove ownership. Although the two sides meet occasionally to discuss terms, this strategy is one of complication and delay.

For its part, the estate periodically submits a petition to reinstate the eviction. In November 2004, a new judge at the district court complied. Terror again overwhelmed the neighborhood. However, the justice official in charge of execution agreed, off record, to delay until after Christmas. By then, Margarido had demonstrated that the order mistakenly included part of Lar Nacional that was legally regularized in 1986. Recognizing his mistake, the judge withdrew the order. Mysteriously, it was not reissued. Since then, negotiations have lagged on both sides—especially after the PT lost city hall (residents in Lar Nacional voted overwhelmingly against) and all departments changed personnel in 2005. In July, Margarido heard that the court had again ordered eviction. This time, however, the judge failed not only to exclude those with final *usucapião* title but also to publish the writ in the Official Diary. Technically, it had no validity without publication. But the judge had already sent the order to the military police for execution. The neighborhood mobilized. The SAB decided to send Margarido to reason with the judge, who "recognized the errors" and rescinded the order. Nevertheless, four of the neighborhood's better-off residents verbally accepted the estate's latest offer. The terror of imminent eviction was having effect. At a SAB meeting, the four were accused of betrayal and nearly beaten. Under intense pressure, they renounced

299

their accord. Subsequently, the SAB articulated three conditions for re-purchase: the sale can only refer to the land and not the houses, to which the estate must admit that it has no rights; the estate must offer proof that it is the definitive owner; and the sale price must be fair.

As if in response, another new judge at the district court reissued the eviction order. Yet her dispatch (9 September 2005) seemed to contain a difference. After declaring "it is certain that the possessory action will be imposed," she offered a "however": "However, over the course of four decades there have been sentences favorable to innumerable people al-lowing them to maintain possession of the lots they occupy." In view of this history, she gave the estate five days to present the names of all those against whom the eviction could not be executed, so that it could be implemented against the rest. She also offered the city forty-eight hours to review the case, presumably to prod it into action.

Are these stipulations evidence that the court (or this particular judge) has developed a new sensibility to the social history of this con-flict and its relation to law? Do they suggest an attempt to apply law in ways that consider changing social conditions, making the judiciary more open to society's demands for accountability, more attuned to the histories of injustice that structure social relations, more adept at achiev-ing justice and not only imposing statute? Do they indicate that the court is making space for social as well as scientific interpretation in exercis-ing judicial discretion? Perhaps, a little. But they may also indicate an update in the repertoire of judicial terror that residents have experienced for a great many decades. At this point, I can explore neither possibility further because the estate never submitted its assessment and the order of eviction seems once again to have lapsed. For the residents of Lar Na-cional, working-class buyers in good faith who were defrauded through no fault of their own, who were repeatedly failed and abandoned by their government, who have suffered the arbitrariness of countless judi-cial maneuvers and idiosyncrasies, it is certain, however, that this terror will return.

Gang Talk and Rights Talk

The judicial terror commonly inflicted on Brazilian citizens makes the following case of the entanglement of democracy and its counters only somewhat less perplexing. I refer to the use by notorious criminal gangs of the language of democratic citizenship, rights, and justice to represent their own organizations and intentions.[31] This use offers strange proof of the generalized legitimacy of democratic discourse in Brazilian society. These criminal *comandos* originated during the early 1990s as gangs within the state prisons of Rio de Janeiro and São Paulo. They initially formed in large measure to defend the rights of prisoners in the horrifically abusive prison systems. This defense was central to their recruitment and organization of members. Today, however, they command vast operations in drug trafficking, extortion, and other criminal enterprises, both inside and outside prisons. To the chronic embarrassment of officialdom, these activities are coordinated from within the prisons via an underground network of cell phones. Ensconced as well in some of the poorest peripheral neighborhoods, they dominate a certain amount of urban territory with a rule that distributes summary execution along with diapers, milk, medication, and employment, combining terror and public works. In this combination, they are not unlike the state itself.[32]

Regularly, these criminal cartels also launch surprisingly well-coordinated attacks against entities of government they claim commit crimes against prisoners. They consider themselves at war with the security apparatus of the state. They target especially the persons and property of the justice system, assassinating police, prison staff, and judges, and sponsoring "mega-rebellions" in the prisons. In São Paulo, the PCC has also attacked public transportation, burning empty buses in campaigns of violence that have paralyzed the city repeatedly in 2006. Their violence against rival and apostate gang members is exceptionally brutal. They do not merely kill. They torture and mutilate, decapitating, disemboweling, and burning— though the PCC is also known to offer those they condemn the choice of a "suicide kit."

The *comandos* occasionally make public pronouncements, typically during a prison rebellion, city assault, or police operation. Curiously, this gang talk takes the form of rights talk. It justifies crime and terror with the rationalities of citizenship. Thus, on 24 February 2003, the Comando Vermelho (CV) issued a statement to the city of Rio imposing a shutdown of commerce in the name of justice. It ended with the following:

> So ENOUGH, we only want our rights and we are not going to give them up, so shops had better keep their doors closed until midnight on Tuesday (25-02-2003), and the one who dares to open his doors will be punished in one form or another[;] it's no use, we are not joking, those who joke are in politics with this total abuse of power and with this generalized robbery[;] the judiciary must begin to empty the prisons and act within the law before it is too late. If the laws were made to be followed, why this abuse?[33]

The gangs often justify their mass acts of public violence as the only way to gain attention for the flagrant abuse of prisoners. In August 2006, the PCC kidnapped a reporter and assistant of the TV giant Globo. It released them unharmed only after Globo broadcast a video clip in which a hooded man read a manifesto protesting the abuses of the Differentiated Disciplinary Regime (RDD) of solitary confinement:

> As a member of the PCC, I appear via the only means found by us to transmit a message to society and its rulers. The introduction of the RDD by law 10,792 in 2003 . . . coherent with the perspective of the elimination and incapacitation of [prisoners] . . . confers on the penalty of prison a clear character of cruel castigation. The RDD offends the priority of the resocialization of prisoners in force in world consciousness since the Illusionism [*sic.*; i.e., Enlightenment] and keystone of the penitentiary system, the Law of Penal Procedures. Its first article establishes . . . [that] any modality of sentence that does not apply the two legal objectives, punishment and social reintegration . . . is illegal, in contradiction of the Federal Constitution. We want a prison system with human conditions, not a defunct system, inhuman, in which we suffer innumerable humiliations and beatings . . . without medical attention, legal assistance, work, school. . . . We are not asking for anything more than what is in the law. . . . The Democratic Rule of Law has the obligation . . . to give the minimal conditions of survival to the sentenced. We want the law to be followed in its totality.[34]

What can we make of such appeals to rights, justice, and the democratic rule of law by organized crime? What do they suggest about Brazilian democracy, its trajectory, and the social transformations it induces? Should they be taken as indicating anything about such matters? Or should we view them with skepticism, as nothing more than cynical attempts to dissimulate and mock? I confess that I have no certain answers to these questions, at least none regarding the deeper views of gang members. Moreover, I can only discuss the public discourse, as sustained ethnographic research inside these gangs is practically impossible and interviews notoriously unreliable. What I can do more productively is analyze this gang talk by means of a triangulation, locating it in relation to the historic paradigm of Brazilian citizenship that democratization destabilizes and evaluating this destabilization with regard to violence. My objective in this mapping is not to give a history of these criminal cartels or to attribute their growth solely to the injustices of differentiated citizenship, though they are an important factor. Nor do I think that addressing these problems will end gang criminality and violence, though respecting prisoner rights will eliminate an important motivation for joining prison gangs.

Rather, my mapping shows that even at the perverse outer bounds of Brazilian society—in gang and police death squads—criminals and police use a similar language of insurgent democratic citizenship as a standard of evaluation to explain their murderous violence. This slippage between the legal and the illegal is a deeply paradoxical development for political democracy. But as I have shown throughout this book, the productions of the legal and the illegal have long been reciprocating processes in Brazil, a symbiosis key to the perpetuation of differentiated citizenship. Should we be surprised that they now share the legitimation of rights talk?

The paradigm of differentiated citizenship endures because its historical sites of production—misrule of law, illegality as a norm of residence, restriction of political citizenship and education, state violence, servility, and so forth—remained potent under every kind of political regime. I have also shown that this history haunts the present in two ways. It both perpetuates the past and provides opportunities for its destabilization. Thus, although the forms and functions of differentiated citizenship produced the urban peripheries, the experience of their autoconstruction activated irruptions of an insurgent citizenship at the very same sites that sustained the differentiated. This experience of the city subverted the old regime of citizenship even as it perpetuated it in new forms of spatial and social segregation, as residents gained political rights, became property owners and modern consumers, achieved rights to the city, created new spheres of participation and understandings of rights, and made law an asset.

We would hardly expect, however, this insurgent urban citizenship to be stable in its expansions. It too has holes into which it collapses. Exactly because the old formulas of differentiated citizenship persist, new incivilities and injustices arise with democratization. Hence the intertwining of the differentiated and the insurgent has contradictory effects. It erodes the coherence of taken-for-granted categories of domination that gave daily life its sense of order and security. If it did not, it would be inconsequential. But one consequence is that it provokes violent reactions that undermine the new democratic practices and institutions, some with the objective of restoring the old paradigms of order. These reactions are articulated around the historic sites of citizen differentiation, and they shape distinctively the conditions that characterize this contradictory period of Brazil's democratization, including criminal and police violence, incivility in public encounters, criminalization of the poor, indignation at impunity, massive property conflicts, new privatizations of security, and popular support for violent measures of social control. They do not generate these attributes alone, as there are other factors and types of destabilization. But insofar as this engagement of citizenships provokes democratic change, democracy brings its own kinds of violence that irrupt where it destabilizes older formulations of order and repression.

Emblematic of this unstable mix of old and new formulations of citizenship are not only the high levels of everyday violence by both criminals and police but also the combined sense of violation, impunity, and outrage

303

they generate. So much has now been written about this violence that I only need observe that violent criminality has increased continuously in Brazil since the early 1980s to the point that by the mid-1990s, the rates of homicide in most of the country's metropolitan regions ranked among the highest of the world. Moreover, the police have committed about 10% of the homicides in São Paulo's metropolitan region in the past fifteen years. They are therefore coresponsible for the high levels of violence.[35] By 2006, fully 50% of the residents of the city of São Paulo and 35% of the state had been assaulted; 80% knew a victim of criminal violence; 84% of these crimes occurred in the outdoor public spaces of the city. Among the victims, only a third reported to the police. Of the 1.2 million crimes registered with the police between January and June 2006, less than 13% resulted in a police investigation. The discredit of the police with the population is as evident as that of the courts.

The combination of democracy, violence, injustice, and impunity saturates contemporary experience with a pervasive sense not only of perversity and instability but also of outrage. For key agents of everyday violence—police and gangs—this anger is the voice of their responses to the destabilizations of the present, which to the police subvert their taken-for-granted social order and to the criminals expose the egregious failures of that same order. Both sorts of violence appear in reaction to its perceived unraveling. Police violence appears as a recourse to reestablish that order; criminal violence appears as a consequence of its being undone.

Let us look at several public proclamations by police and *comandos*, made in reaction to their perceptions of the present, to substantiate this argument. We will see that they both refer to democracy's rights and rule of law and, moreover, that both resignify them to justify violence. However, they do so in opposite ways and perhaps with opposite ends at stake.

During the transition to electoral democracy in the mid-1980s, the human rights movement that had originated in the demand for amnesty for political prisoners shifted its focus to defend the human rights of common prisoners. It vigorously denounced police abuse and exposed the degradations of Brazilian prisons, condemning, in other words, the historic regime of citizenship that was business-as-usual for the police. As many have analyzed—none more astutely than Caldeira (2000)—police reaction against the human rights campaign was swift and violent. Here is a passage from the Manifesto of the Association of Police Chiefs of São Paulo, directed to the city's population on 4 October 1985 and widely distributed among police units. The chiefs made this declaration at a crucial moment in the process of democratization. They released it at the peak of the campaign for the first direct mayoral elections since dictatorship. Moreover, it was during a period when the first directly elected state governor, Franco Montoro (1983–1987), was trying to reform the police use of lethal force. Predictably, the police chiefs attacked this initiative, savaging the project of human rights and its supporters:

> The situation today is one of total anxiety for you and total tranquility for those who kill, rob, and rape. Your family is destroyed and your patrimony, acquired with such sacrifice, is calmly being reduced. Why does this happen? You know the answer. Believing in promises, we chose the wrong governor, the wrong political party, the PMDB. How many crimes have occurred in your neighborhood and how many criminals were found responsible for them? You also know this answer. They, the bandits, are protected by the so-called human rights, something that the government considers that you, an honest and hardworking citizen, do not deserve.

In this argument, the police evoke human rights according to the historic paradigm of differentiated citizenship, in which rights and justice are privileges of certain social categories, essentially privileges of those who have the power and resources to manipulate the legal system. According to this logic, human rights for criminals are nothing more than "privileges for bandits"—as the expression popularized during this period puts it and as Caldeira (2000: 340–46) analyzes. If justice and its rights are privileges and if the majority of Brazilian citizens are denied them, it is clearly an outrage to provide them to criminals. In terms of my analysis of citizenship, therefore, the police chiefs use the differentiated order of citizenship to undermine the insurgent. Their "solution" is not to condemn that order by demanding that human rights become available to *all* Brazilians as absolute attributes of their citizenship. Rather, they use the historic order to condemn democracy and its human rights for abetting criminal violence and to justify their violent repression of civilian criminal suspects—escalating progressively during this period from just over 500 killings in 1989 to 1,470 in 1992.

This same logic is evident in the policies of the state governors, under whose command the military police operate. Thus, when the number of police killings started to rise considerably in São Paulo after 1989 as a result of these policies, the state secretary of public security declared: "The fact that this year there were more deaths caused by the military police means that they are more active. The more police in the streets, the more chances of confrontations between criminals and policemen. . . . From my point of view, what the population wants is for the police to act boldly."[36]

Both the police chiefs and the governors evoke the moral ground of citizen rights and dignity as a means, perversely, of denying it. They hold it up as something unavailable to the majority to justify its continued negation.

305

Because it is unavailable to the majority, it should be unavailable to criminals. But who are the criminals? Before they are convicted, they are suspects. As the police generally view the poor as criminally suspect, the majority are suspects and should be denied human rights as a matter of security. This logic of security evokes citizenship, therefore, to undermine democracy, to disarticulate its language of insurgent values and common measures. If we may take the countless accusations of police abuse and corruption throughout Brazil as evidence, documented since the beginning of democratization by human rights organizations and Brazilian citizens, these efforts to represent police violence as a means to wrest society from chaos and to limit police and prison reform have been largely successful.[37]

Nevertheless, the police have not remained entirely immune to democracy. Within a decade after the manifesto just cited, the Military Police of the State of São Paulo felt compelled to change its public image. Adopting new initiatives, such as community policing, it tried to counter its reputation as an institution that regularly abused citizens. It developed a new website in 2001 that framed the institutions and actions of the police in terms of democratic citizenship:

> The 1988 Constitution brought a new concept that became strong in our society: *citizenship*. People became more aware of their rights, more demanding in relation to the Institutions, and this was an invitation to those willing to serve well to revise their posture. The question was not only to expand services, but also one of attitude. . . . With the new established order, something more was necessary than just placing ourselves in the clients' position and imagining new products. . . . It was an invitation to a cultural change. . . . It was necessary to shift from a bureaucratic model . . . to a new model, the managerial, which was introduced at the Military Police of the State of São Paulo through a Program of Quality Improvement. Its goal is to get closer to the population via the improvement of the services rendered to the population.[38]

In this statement, the police announce a new model of operation and institutional identity governed by the constitutional rules of an insurgent democratic citizenship. The passage indicates the legitimacy that this citizenship has acquired. Additionally, the model presents citizens as demanding clients and public security as a product the police offer. Its organizing logic thus mixes legal and market rationalities, unified by a notion of management—a packaging that indicates that the military police have also followed the neoliberal turn of global democratization in the 1990s.

Yet if the military police has changed its discourse and even aspects of its organization, the same cannot be said about its repressive practice.

In spite of efforts to reform the police by unifying some of their operations, instituting an ombudsman, creating community policing, and requiring that officers receive training in human rights, São Paulo's police
continue to kill civilians in very high numbers throughout the state: 807
in the year 2000 and 703 in 2001. As investigations conducted by the
police ombudsman reveal, the majority of those killed had no criminal
history (Cunha 2000). That these violations continue despite good intentions to control them indicates the resilience of these limits to Brazil's democratization. It suggests, moreover, another perversity: as my interviews
with Brazilians of all social classes make clear, and as Caldeira (2000,
2002) has analyzed, police killings often correspond to the expectations
of citizens who are frustrated with the inefficacy of the justice system and
who do not believe in the likelihood of security in a society with immense
inequality. In this context, many citizens view police killing as a realization
of their right to security.

Let me return to the other indication of limit with which I began, to
the public proclamations of the prison-based gangs that combine the rationalities of crime, justice, and revolution. In spite of their barbarity,
even these criminal cartels cannot do without the language of insurgent
democratic citizenship. They talk about justice, rights, and the rule of
law in ways similar to human rights reports, portraying themselves as the
victims of entrenched social inequalities, abuses, and violence, in which
they, Brazilian citizens, are victims of their own historic system of national
citizenship. When asked in a congressional hearing (2001) if he were the
leader of the PCC, Marcola replied: "I am a person who fights for his
rights. I have read the Penal Code and the Law of Penal Procedures, and
I know that I am violated in all of my rights. . . . So, [I ask you], where
is the state? . . . In this context, what is society for me? . . . The PCC revolts against this hypocrisy." The statute of the PCC (1993)—for these
gangs have founding statutes—joins this discourse of rights to that of
revolution and crime and ends with a battle cry: "In coalition with the
Comando Vermelho—CV and PCC we will revolutionize the country inside the prisons and our armed fist will be the 'Terror of the Powerful,'
oppressors, and tyrants who use the [prisons] as instruments of society's
vengeance. . . . Liberty, Justice, and Peace!!!"[39]

The declaration of the CV to the city of Rio that I cited at the outset
uses an explicit talk of rights, citizenship, and rule of law to frame its
demands. After denouncing "the terror [that the government] practices in
poor communities," it proclaims:

> So now is the time to react firmly and with determination and to show
> this repulsive and oppressive politics that we deserve to be treated with
> respect, dignity, and equality, because if this doesn't come to pass, we

307

will no longer stop causing chaos in this city, because it is absurd that all this keeps happening and always remains unpunished.

The judiciary also continues doing whatever it wants with its power . . . because it is violating with a total abuse of power all the established and legal laws and even the Lawyers are targets of hypocrisy and abuse, and they can do nothing, so if someone has to put a stop to this violence that someone will have to be us because the people don't have how to fight for their rights, but clearly they know who is robbing and massacring them and this is what is important, because the time has passed when the bandit was from the favelas and behind prison bars, well, these days, those one finds living in a favela or behind prison bars are nothing more nothing less than humble and poor people, and, our President Luiz Inácio Lula da Silva, the country only counts on you to get us out of this mud, because does there exist a violence greater than robbing the public's money and killing the people with bad food, without a decent minimum salary, without hospitals, without work, and without food[?] Will this violence succeed in ending the violence, for violence generates violence[?] Is it possible that there exists among the prisoners of this country one who has committed a crime more heinous than killing a nation with hunger and misery[?] . . . So ENOUGH, we only want our rights. . . . If the laws were made to be followed, why this abuse?

I do not intend to romanticize these statements. They are made by criminals whose lives have spiraled into the personal insanity of an especially cruel and terrorizing violence. They are made, moreover, to justify this violence. Even though the *comandos* must be credited with introducing some protection within prisons—in particular, reducing rape—and educating prisoners about their rights, their dominion is based on other kinds of violence inside and outside jail. Furthermore, although they demand a democratic rule of law, there is nothing democratic about their own military-like organization, which "admits no disputes of power in the leadership" (Art.12). In that aspect, one might argue that they are like many other civil-society groups. Yet their draconian order also requires members in liberty to make monthly contributions on pain of "death without pardon" (Art. 7). If the *comandos* began with the anger of revolutionaries, they are today also dedicated to the big business of narcotrafficking and racketeering outside prison. They remain, in other words, violent criminal gangs.

Nevertheless, their language is striking, not only for its use of rights talk but also in its contrast with the manifesto of the police chiefs, who are also violent individuals justifying violence. The police manifesto denies democracy's legitimacy as the frame of reference for citizenship.

It undermines Brazil's new democracy by advocating violent and illegal practices. For the chiefs, the law is still, as it has always been, "for enemies." In contrast, the gangs hurl their outrage at the historical abuses of this misrule of law and frame it in terms of the new democracy and its project of social justice. Their outrage is that of the Brazilian poor against the despicable quality of Brazilian citizenship. If, in the past, the oppressed found expression in millenarian religious movements, today they have a secular voice and it speaks in rights talk.

What is remarkable about this gang talk/rights talk is that even at this perverse extreme of society, insurgent democratic citizenship has become the common language and moral discourse for justifying the illegal as well as the legal. This new commensurability refers to the city and the nation beyond it as a public sphere to which all citizens have rights to a fair share. The rights claims of the poor—including those of the gangs—about this public substance constitute their understanding of a new democratic project of citizenship. Moreover, this new rights talk of the poor suggests that the law, which has oppressed them for centuries, has become something intimate to their sense of belonging to the public, something people want for themselves, no longer "for enemies" but for citizens. We can only conclude that this change in the culture of law promises to be fundamental for the development of Brazilian democracy.

The perversity of this democracy continues to be that it has not yet realized significant social justice and egalitarian rule of law. However, Brazil has never had either under any regime. It is too late for the gang members to avoid an awful fate. But at least they tell us, even if they cannot show us, that Brazilians have made social justice and rule of law central aspirations of their democracy and that Brazil's citizens, even at the extremes, have found in that project of citizenship a common ground.

Insurgent Citizenships and Disjunctive Democracies

Democracies that cannot protect a citizen's body or produce a just city far outnumber those that do today, even though the promise of these achievements constitutes much of democracy's appeal. To understand what is at stake in this problem, some (including myself) have elaborated Bobbio's (1989: 155–56) argument that contemporary democracy develops "above all through [its] extension beyond politics to other spheres." By that, he emphasizes "the transfer of democracy from the political sphere (where the individual is regarded as a citizen) to the social sphere (where the individual is regarded as many-faceted)." Thus, in one influential essay, O'Donnell (1992: 49) writes that democratic consolidation requires "the extension of similarly democratic . . . relations into other [not just political] spheres of social life"; and, in another, he (1993: 1361) argues that "even a political definition of democracy (such as that recommended by most contemporary authors, and to which I adhere) should not neglect posing the question of the extent to which citizenship is really exercised in a given country." Although this question may not be defining for him, it is "politically relevant," both because "the ineffectiveness of the state-as-law" produces "low-intensity citizenship" and "brown areas" in new democracies, in which citizen rights are systematically violated, and because these conditions of citizenship have dire consequences for democracy.

I have only disagreed with limiting this kind of assessment "to the political theory of political democracy" (1993: 1361) and to emerging democracies. Typically produced in political science and international relations, most accounts do not acknowledge the centrality of more than political citizenship and related civil liberties for contemporary democracy. Rather, most focus on the transformation of political systems—on regime change, electoral competition, and their preconditions—and on the operations of government that are hallmarks of North Atlantic democracy. Such considerations are certainly fundamental. They establish that a majority of countries (63%) have now become democratic in the sense that they are electoral democracies and have done so at a pace in the late twentieth century never before experienced.[40] However, this kind of political focus fails to account adequately, if at all, for precisely the sort of disjunctions of citizenship that I have analyzed in Brazil and that are prevalent among most emerging democracies—namely, the coincidence of democratic politics with widespread violence and injustice against citizens. This disjunction has become just as global a condition of contemporary democratization as free elections.

These problematic developments mean that the realization of democracy for most citizens requires social and cultural changes that escape a classically narrow understanding of the political. They strongly suggest that although necessary, political democracy is not enough to secure civil and social citizenship or to produce a democratic rule of law. Without both, the realization of democratic citizenship remains disabled, and political democracy itself loses legitimacy as a mode of government. Therefore, the problem with narrow political conceptions of democracy is that they fail to analyze the very contradictions that characterize contemporary democratic developments worldwide and that undermine actually existing political democracies. Accordingly, these histories demand a revision of many standard assumptions about democratization. They demonstrate both the insufficiency of democratic politics for realizing democratic citizenship and the limitations of democratic theory based solely on politics for understanding this problem. Moreover, as the new democratization is overwhelmingly non–North Atlantic, they indicate the inadequacies of democratic theory anchored in North Atlantic history and culture for understanding democracy's global reach and practice.[41]

Rather than a specific politics or a set stage of institutions, actors, and scripts, I have emphasized two perspectives: first, that the realization of citizenship is the central and not the collateral issue of democracy; and, second, that the processes and practices that define citizenship are inherently disjunctive–not cumulative, linear, or evenly distributed among citizens but always a mix of progressive and regressive elements, unbalanced, heterogeneous, and corrosive. In this view, democracy is necessarily connected to a fuller conception of citizenship, one expanded beyond the political, and its evaluation bound to the complexities of citizenship's realization in particular historical contexts. This complexity of ethnography and history, experience and institution, and performance and script constitutes what I view as an anthropological consideration, in which access to infrastructure (like electricity and sewage lines) and the security of the body can no more be neglected in the analysis of democracy than the right to vote. Thus, I stress that the extension of democracy to the civil, socioeconomic, legal, and cultural aspects of citizenship is as central to the concept of modern democracy as its extension to the political. Does that scope make democracy unattainable? No doubt, as a totality it does. However, I have suggested abandoning the idea of democracy as a totalizing project, arguing instead that what is productive about democracy is its condition of incompletion and contradiction, its wager to be always unfinished.

At stake in considering the disjunctions of contemporary democracy is thus the very conception of the political. Since Aristotle's *Politics* established the distinction, the canon in western social theory has constituted the political as a sphere of interests that excludes the realm of household affairs. As Agamben (1998: 1–8) reminds us, Aristotle (1978: 1252b) distinguishes the domain of the political, the *polis*, as that which "exists for the sake of the good life" from the household, the *oikos*, as that which attends "to mere life." Feminist scholars (e.g., Okin 1992; Pateman 1989) have long observed that this juro-political domain is defined in opposition to the domestic-kinship domain—to residence, family, reproduction, and the personal necessities of daily living—and therefore bars the participation of those people identified with it: women, children, servants, laborers. However, the political does not exclude this domestic realm by mere omission. The *polis* acts on the *oikos* by confining it to the custody of the head of household, the paterfamilias, as its sole authority. These distinctions establish a basic set of oppositions that characterize the two domains into which social life in the classical world is divided. The political constitutes the domain of the city or city-state as an association of citizens who are free adult men, equal as members, and equally obliged by the laws they make in the course of managing the city. The domestic is the domain of household management, the affairs and members of which are ruled hierarchically by a paternal authority.

In one way or another, these oppositions of classical thought inform the dichotomous conceptualizations by which the political has been configured ever since, as public and private, political and personal, state and family, street and house, rule of law and lawlessness, juridical-institutional and biological, and so forth. There has, of course, been a chorus of criticism attacking such dichotomies, including Marx's (1967b: 227) critique of the project of political emancipation grounded on "the splitting of man into public and private," feminism's counter that "the personal is political" and its challenge to consider women as citizens who are not "like men," de Certeau's (1984) tactical readings of the practices of everyday city life, and Foucault's (1978, 1991) reconceptualization of politics as biopolitics in which questions of sovereign power increasingly revolve around managing the biological life of populations. These critiques and others mark the politicization of the *oikos* and its private, domestic, personal, everyday, laboring, sexual, and biological affairs as a decisive change in the development of modernity, transforming the classical orders of the social into the modern.

If it may be argued that classical citizenship also politicized everyday "mere life" by confining it to the realm of the household and its head, it did not do so to insure the subjection and servitude of citizens by reducing their living to a mere minimum. However mistaken, Aristotle considers his organization a "natural" means to further prosperity, education, and tranquility among residents of the *polis*. Yet what distinguishes many modern citizenships—as this book has shown for the Brazilian—is precisely this intent: they deploy a politics of legalized differences to reduce the lives of the vast majority of *their citizens* to persistent inequality and misery. That these reduced citizens retain their personal dignity, their laughter, and their music is certainly a measure of human resilience. But it is also a strategy of rule. Anyone who has ever dined with elites and then set foot in the slums of their cities and plantations understands the deep efficacy of this politicization of daily life, which reduces conditions of living to bare minimums but nevertheless allows certain vitalities. As a strategy of domination, the deployment of these differentiated citizenships as much deprives most citizens of their physical well-being as it diminishes their standing as citizens. By 1972, when residents of Jardim das Camélias beat up the court official, most Brazilians had been systematically denied political rights, disallowed education, excluded from legal property ownership, forced into segregated and often illegal conditions of residence, victimized by and estranged from law, and incorporated into the labor market as servile workers.

These conditions are a commission and not an omission of a particular kind of citizenship, one that Brazilian elites consolidated over the course of the nineteenth century in response to nationhood and the end of slavery, one that was from the start universally inclusive in membership and massively inegalitarian in distribution. Among its key features, I have shown that illegality has been indispensable to both its formulation and its exercise and thereby to the constitution of the Brazilian polity itself. Illegality is not only a pervasive condition of residential life that many citizens are made to suffer, with all the consequences that we have explored for their citizenship. It is also a political technique elites master for constituting legitimate power, in which illegal acts anticipate, reliably and predictably, legalization. Far from holding apart the legal and the illegal, just and unjust, public and private, and political and domestic, this regime of citizenship is based on managing their intersection.

Yet, under the sign of the city, the very same factors that produced this entrenched regime mobilize an insurgence of citizens. The same forces that effectively fragmented and dominated the rural poor by reducing their existence to a "mere life" incite the urban poor to demand a citizen's life. However, it is not at the factory or the union hall or the ballot box that they articulate this demand with greatest force and originality. It is rather in the realm of the *oikos*, in the zone of domestic life taking shape in the remote urban peripheries around the autoconstruction of residence. It is an insurgence that begins with the struggle for rights to have a daily life in the city worthy of a citizen's dignity. Accordingly, its demands for a new formulation of citizenship get conceived in terms of housing, property, plumbing, daycare, security, and other aspects of residential life. Its leaders are the "barely citizens" of the entrenched regime: women, manual laborers, squatters, the functionally literate, and, above all, those in families with a precarious stake in residential property, with a legal toehold to a house lot somewhere far from elite centers. These are the citizens who, in the process of building their residential spaces, not only construct a vast new city but, on that basis, also constitute it as a *polis* with a different order of citizenship.

Many cities throughout the global south today experience similar insurgent citizenship movements. Indeed, in these times of global urbanization, the basis of such new citizenships is likely to be that of the autoconstructed city, as I have investigated in São Paulo. Yet if this study demonstrates how an insurgent citizenship can irrupt on the very foundations of the entrenched, it also shows that the insurgent inevitably gets bogged down by the past it inherits as well as confronts. Their entanglement both corrodes the old regime and perverts the new. It turns the ethnographic present in which insurgent citizenships and their new democracies must take root to flourish into an unsettling yet vital terrain.

Chapter 1: Citizenship Made Strange

1. In the 1989 election, Collor, a member of the Northeast's high elite, ridiculed Lula's slogan. He argued that it demonstrated that Lula was incompetent to hold the presidency because the highest office obviously required special qualities and not ones merely equal to those of common Brazilians, who were just as obviously not qualified for the job.

2. If both anthropology and history consider practice and experience basic modalities of investigation, they turned to them to study the social lives and logics of those who did not directly produce written documents—tribal peoples, peasants, subalterns, the poor, and so forth. They often presumed them to be, moreover, less biased by theory as kinds of evidence of social life and conflict (in contrast, for example, to concepts like class and ideology). Although social historians such as E. P. Thompson, Eric Hobsbawm, and Eugene Weber looked to anthropology, they articulated an earlier theoretical justification for their reliance on "experience." For example, see Thomas (1963) and Thompson (1963). Much has since been written on the problems of essentializing experience as the evidence of history. I have found Scott's (1992) critique helpful in this regard.

3. I discuss pedestrian and car traffic as a matter of citizenship in the last chapter.

4. I draw my use of power and liability here from Hohfeld's (1978) correlative scheme of sociolegal relations. Both the civil law tradition (descendant from Roman law and dominant in Europe and Latin America) and the common (Anglo-American) recognize these relations in somewhat different ways. The former holds that objective law is the rule to which an individual must conform, and subjective right is the power of an individual that derives from the rule. The latter uses the notion of remedy, which entails empowerment, holding that where

there is a right there must be a remedy. For a useful comparison of the civil- and common-law traditions, see Merryman (1985).

5. Historical examples abound. Most well-known is the military and police destruction, often by massacre, of nearly every urban and rural socioreligious movement in the nineteenth and early twentieth centuries (e.g., Canudos and Contestado). Often as effective are legal strategies developed for the same ends. Thus, to disband labor movements, legislation permitted the swift deportation of immigrant "undesirables" (i.e., labor leaders) and made the propagation of certain ideas a crime. Similarly, when confronted with serious dispute, local and federal governments have regularly suspended constitutional rights. The iron fist of oligarchy learned to govern early in the Republic with the glove of liberal constitutionalism. I discuss some of these strategies of rule later.

6. Let me specify my use of the term "elites." All sociological terms that describe groups of people suffer from imprecision when compared to exact historical specification. However, such denotation is often so specific as to make comparison impossible except in narrowly constructed studies. Rather than proliferate denotative terms, therefore, I prefer to specify the conceptualization of the few I use. As in other immigrant nations, elite status in Brazil is much less a matter of descent and its traditions than of wealth and privilege. As such, Brazilian elites have been especially successful in prolonging their powers by absorbing successful newcomers, regardless of origins. Thus elites perpetuate the vitality of the upper classes, even as the sources of wealth change. With regard to my subject, elites established the system of differentiated citizenship to benefit themselves with rights exercised as privileges. In my analysis, elites are those, therefore, who benefit from historically privileged categories with regard to the distribution of rights. For example, ruling elites established literacy as the requirement of political citizenship in a society overwhelmingly of illiterates. Those who create and occupy such privileged categories have generally been the moneyed. However, it also makes sense by extension to speak about elites within other groups—such as elite workers—precisely to refer to those who accede to privileged categories of right. As we shall see in chapter 5, the historically dominant regime of differentiated citizenship modernized in the first part of the twentieth century exactly by absorbing small numbers of working-class Brazilians among the new urban masses into its practices and privileges. Ruling populists generalized the rhetoric of this absorption, while strictly limiting its realization.

7. Although DaMatta (1991: 181) claims that in Brazil "we find the two notions [individual and person] operating simultaneously," his analysis dichotomizes them: "It is up to sociological research to detect the context in which each notion is called for. In the case of Brazil, it seems quite clear that the individual is a modern notion superimposed on a powerful system of personal relationships." I see the two as coincident in the development of citizenship and law from the beginnings of the Brazilian nation-state. DaMatta argues that "the opposition between individual and person has never been dissolved . . . the person continues to be more important than the individual . . . [and as a result] we find it very difficult to create the voluntary associations that are the core of 'civil society.'" I argue that the legal system (as well as other systems of public and private relations) dissolves the one into the other all the time.

316

8. See my essays in Holston 1999 for the argument that contemporary cities are especially salient sites for the emergence of new forms of citizenship that unsettle national belonging. My 2001 essay also makes the case that one of the significant consequences of the globalization of democracy for city-regions is the development of new urban citizenships among marginalized citizens in emerging democracies and resident noncitizens in established ones.

9. In his classic study of 1950, Marshall (1977) understood each as consisting of specific rights and those institutions most connected with their exercise. He defined the political component of citizenship as comprised of those rights and institutions necessary to participate in the exercise of political power, either as an elector or as a member of an elected body. By civil, he meant those rights and institutions (the courts, bar, and police) necessary for liberty and justice. He understood the social to refer to rights to minimum standards of economic well-being, secured by the state, and to rights to a shared culture and history (what he called "the social heritage").

10. Although I am indebted to Marshall for pointing the way to expand the analysis of citizenship beyond political institutionalization, I do not share his historical perspective in at least five ways. First, he explains the development of British citizenship as a three-stage sequence that expands progressively and cumulatively from the civil to the political to the socioeconomic over three centuries. His history is all one of homogeneous expansion. In contrast, I view the development of citizenship and democracy as always disjunctive. They both expand and erode, progress and regress in complex ways. Second, I do not view the three-stage historical sequence that Marshall plots as the norm of development. In fact, although it may be an accurate description in some cases, such as Britain, in general it is not. Rather, the spread, timing, and substance of citizenship vary substantially with historical and national context. In most emerging democracies, including Brazil's, political and socioeconomic rights develop long before civil rights and in any case not in discrete or linear sequences. Thus, the aspect of timing is usually different from the sequence Marshall proposed for Britain and needs to be evaluated in each case. Third, Marshall always treated citizenship as national, as rooted in the unit of the nation-state. As I have argued elsewhere (Holston and Appadurai 1999), this assumption is mistaken in some cases and increasingly unconvincing in many more. Moreover, as I argue here, the city remains crucial to the emergence of new forms of citizenship. Fourth, Marshall analyzes the exercise of collective rights exclusively in terms of social classes. It is more evident today than when he wrote that groups based on difference-specific identities and cultural memberships also claim rights and that such group claims contest the liberal theory of difference-neutral citizenship. Finally, when he discusses it at all, he treats the illegal as an aberration, external to the construction and operation of law. I view it as central.

11. As has been often observed, neither the social contractarians nor the French revolutionaries they influenced intended the claim of free birth as a historical fact or truth. It was rather a theoretical claim, a necessary hypothesis and radical means to legitimate a new political order. My citation of French constitutions here and in the next chapter uses Anderson's (1908) compilation.

12. I base my translations of Brazilian legislation on the official publications of their texts.

13. See especially book 5 of the *Nicomachean Ethics*, where Aristotle (1962: 118) argues that a just distribution allocates the right share to the right person, such that "the ratio between the shares will be the same as that between the persons. If the persons are not equal, their just shares will not be equal."

14. Until 1985, every Brazilian constitution since the founding of the Republic stipulated that illiterate citizens could not register to vote and that only registered electors could vote. Article 295 of the current Code of Penal Procedure maintains the right of Brazilians who have completed a university degree of any kind to an individual (and typically better-appointed) jail cell if arrested. An expert in the Brazilian prison system I consulted thought that the date of the original statute giving this article its current form was around 1970. Although I verified later that this was not the case, the expert added that "before then, the right was customary as there was simply no need to state the obvious." When I have asked elites about it, I generally get similar justifications: people of high cultural formation should be able to choose when and where to mix with those of low (during carnival, for instance) but should not be forced to do so, especially in the confinement of prison. I have gotten a variety of explanations as to why this should be so, ranging from seigniorial privilege, to problems of contamination, to protection of the high from the inevitable retributions of the low, to frank incredulity that I should need to ask.

15. To hold democracy and liberalism apart in this discussion, I want to recognize that liberalism has at least four dimensions of historical development: (1) It appeared as a critique of the divine or naturalized basis of political society, that is, as a critique of political power as an extension of supposedly natural hierarchies between men and women or between kings and subjects. (2) Liberalism also emerged as a proposal for a particular organization of the social, embodied most broadly in the notion of self-regulation and articulated in a variety of concepts of revolutionary effect concerning the development of civil society as a sphere of social relations not regulated by the state, the public/private dichotomy, the priority of right over good, self-disciplining intersubjective relations, and so forth. This emphasis on self-regulation also informs the other two dimensions of liberalism's historical development. (3) It offers a conception of the individual as the seat of rights, of the self that an individual owns in a proprietary relation, and of natural rights that belong to the individual independently of state and that limit its powers. (4) Finally, liberalism becomes synonymous with capitalism and a theory of economics based on the priorities of a self-regulating market, governed by an "invisible hand" with no need for state intervention. The rise of modern democracy depends on and gets entangled with several of these developments, but with a different agenda of citizenship. In this sense, the imperial and republican nation-states in Brazil may be considered liberal but not democratic.

16. These differences may be cultural traits, like language and religious practices, or conceptions of what is right and good, like heterosexuality and indigenous land claims. Current examples include French Muslim citizens who demand the right to use the veil in public schools, American Fundamentalists who demand that public schools teach "intelligent design" as science, and the French-speaking majority in Quebec who require that businesses with more than fifty employees operate in French and outlaw commercial signs that do not include it. See Benhabib 2002; Galeotti 1993; Ong 2003; Taylor 1992.

17. See Hale 2002; Kymlicka 1995; Minow 1990; Postero 2007, as well as references cited in the previous note.

18. There are now a number of significant works that historicize the development of these citizenships, such as Kettner 1978; Smith 1997; Shklar 1991; Brubaker 1992; Pateman 1989. They show how concepts such as equality-as-sameness, procedural neutrality, equalization of rights, and uniform application of law developed from conflicts over the regulation of social differences and equalities.

19. Relevant to the comparative discussion of the next chapter is the observation that the equal protection clause of the U.S. Constitution does not forbid legalizing distinctions and classifications based on differences among citizens. The question Americans debate is rather in what manner distinctions may be legalized. That problem generates endless conflict. The extent to which the American concept of citizen equality allows differentiation has been so divisive that the courts have created a jurisprudence of "strict scrutiny" to determine whether the legalization of a discriminatory practice (such as affirmative action for veterans and minorities) is constitutional. This test asks, for example, whether the practice serves a socially compelling goal that cannot be achieved otherwise and whether it is sufficiently tailored to avoid generalizing discrimination. That legalizing difference remains an open yet deeply problematic question, potentially available for specific purposes but contentious enough to require continual reexamination, seems to me vital to the democratic quality of justice. For Brazilian citizenship, however, legalizing difference in the distribution of rights has been a fundamentally unproblematic norm.

Chapter 2: In/Divisible Nations

1. In both Portugal and its colonies, the Portuguese Crown outlawed the importation, possession, or reproduction of all printed materials associated with the French and American Revolutions. Nevertheless, leaders of the Brazilian independence movement of 1789 are reported to have passed these texts from hand to hand and recited them by heart. Indeed, the Crown based its trial and execution of one, Tiradentes, in part on the accusation that he had translated a French edition of the American Constitution. Another incident that remained important to Brazilian independence was the meeting and correspondence between José Joaquim da Maia, a Brazilian student at the French University of Montpellier, and Thomas Jefferson, then representative to the French government. See Luz 1977; Costa 1977: 23–26; Costa 1985:1–23 and 53–77, for more on Brazilian engagements with the Revolutions and subsequent national developments. For a discussion of the foreign literature Brazilians read during the independence period, see Burns's (1964) study of the holdings of two Brazilian libraries.

2. In one important matter, however, the central government reserved a special disability for French Jews: it refused to assume Jewish communal debts when it nationalized the deficits of all other dissolved corporations in 1793. As a result, the Jews had to revive their communal organizations as special commissions to collect taxes to liquidate their prerevolutionary debt. They continued paying into the 1860s.

3. Thus deputies from the Antilles invoked the universal equality of the *Declaration of the Rights of Man and Citizen* to argue for the removal of colonial trade restrictions. Yet they staunchly denied applying those same rights to their black slaves (Schama 1989: 498).

4. After abolition, the colonial administration tried to rule by imposing new substantive exclusions and liabilities on ex-slave citizens (Dubois 2004). But rather than sustain this contradiction of the revolutionary principle of citizen indivisibility, the state preferred to reverse history by turning these citizens back into slaves. As one adminstrator argued, trumping an uncompromising principle with a particular prejudice, "the true liberty of civilized man was not made for the nègres of the French colonies" (411). Abolition was not finally achieved until 1848.

5. See Brubaker's (1992: 89–91) excellent discussion of the presumption of attachment and its limitation of the principle of descent in the development of French citizenship.

6. This conceptualization is articulated, for example, in the revolutionary writings the Abbé (Emmanuel-Joseph) Sieyès, who wrote the initial draft of the *Declaration of the Rights of Man and Citizen*. An amalgam of Rousseauian and Lockean ideas on the social contract, these works also significantly influenced the 1791 Constitution. It is exactly this conceptual division of the nation-state into a political state of abstract citizens and a civil society of private individuals that Marx attacks in his famous essay "On the Jewish Question." He analyzes the project of Jewish emancipation during the French Revolution to reveal the limitations, if not contradictions, of political emancipation generally if grounded on the "splitting of man into public and private." Marx observes that the Revolution achieved political emancipation from religion by displacing it from the public law of the state to the private rights of civil society. Religion becomes the private affair of individuals, the sanctity of which is guaranteed by political citizenship. His criticism of this displacement is twofold. First, in his view, the private rights of civil society, the so-called rights of man, are nothing more than rights of self-interest, by nature "egoistic" and isolating. Second, as stated in Article 2 of the Declaration, the "aim" of political citizenship has become the preservation of these private rights. Hence, he concludes that "the political liberators reduce citizenship, the *political community*, to a mere *means* for preserving these so-called rights of man and that the citizen thus is proclaimed to be the servant of the egoistic man . . . and finally [that] man as bourgeois rather than man as citizen is considered to be the *proper* and *authentic* man." For Marx, this "*political* emancipation is indeed a great step forward . . . [but] not, to be sure, the final form of universal human emancipation" (1967b: 237, 227; italics in original).

7. My discussion of citizenship in the Civil Code of 1804 and the later expansion of *ius soli* is based on Brubaker 1992: 85–113.

8. The notorious examples of the debt discrimination against Jews and the unequal status of women in matters of property and inheritance were eliminated by mid century.

9. Two years later, accused of a number of crimes against the Revolution, de Gouges was guillotined for her "delirium . . . for having forgotten the virtues appropriate to her sex," as a contemporary report explained (cited in Gutwirth 1993: 23). See also Landes 1988.

10. Although passive citizens would seem to be more *sujets* than *citoyens* in Rousseau's sense, even with "passive" attached its use negates "subject" in signifying a uniform, ungraded relation to the state, especially in terms of equality before the law.

11. See Joan Scott's (1996) discussion of this surprisingly late date for women's suffrage. The ideal of equal universal suffrage continues to roil French society, though today the conflict is somewhat different: people now debate voting rights for legally resident but nonnative foreigners (e.g., guestworkers and ex-colonials).

12. Freeborn "mixed-bloods" were also generally denied membership through the "one-drop rule" that assigns persons with any "bad blood" entirely to the rejected racial category.

13. The reasoning behind the birthright principle was similar to that of *ius soli* in France, though more radical because it was not conditioned by descent: the mere fact of birth in the United States (or under its jurisdiction) was sufficient evidence and the best guarantee that a person had received an American upbringing, participated in its culture, and thereby become attached to its values, above all to republican self-government. Such socialization remains the fundamental qualification for citizenship. Hence, the principal requirement for naturalization is residence for a set number of years. However, until the passage of the Fourteenth Amendment, the application of this birthright to establish both national and local citizenships, and the extent to which the one obliged the other, was a matter of intense debate and confusion.

14. My account of debates concerning these exclusions owes much to Kettner's (1978) study—extraordinary in argument and detail—of the development of American citizenship from English origins through the Civil War.

15. The first Naturalization Act in 1790 limited admission to "free white men." Its replacement in 1802 restricted access to "free white persons" and set federal immigration guidelines that remained in force until 1952. Landmark cases in the interim often concerned extending the category of whiteness to those allegedly not white. By 1899, naturalization law included a "List of Races" that specified those considered white for purposes of admission.

16. See Cohen 1982: 78–134 for a discussion of the western removal, its legal foundations, and allotment legislation.

17. For example, federal guardians managed the education of Indians, suppressed their religious freedom, funneled them into economic activities (primarily agriculture and grazing), regulated their commerce, held their assets "in trust," and "protected them from their own appetites" (e.g., by denying them alcohol).

18. Thus, in the *Matter of Heff* (1905), the Supreme Court declared the federal laws of alcohol prohibition unconstitutional because it concluded that Indians became full citizens immediately upon accepting land allotment and not after the 25-year trust period; Congress responded quickly with the Burke Act (1906) which circumvented *Heff* by withholding citizenship from allottees until the trust period expired for Indians judged "incompetent"; and, in *U.S. v. Nice* (1916), a different Supreme Court overturned *Heff*, deciding that Indian citizenship was not incompatible with guardianship after all.

19. My discussion of this conflict derives chiefly from Kettner (1978: 287–333), Porter (1918), and Williamson (1960: 223–41).

20. Each state claimed sovereignty in matters of suffrage. As a result, the history of its qualification is complex, as states enacted and repealed restrictions of real estate, personal property, taxes, residence, education, and religion, in addition to race. Of the original thirteen colonies, all had real-or personal-property qualifications for suffrage before the Revolutionary War, forcing poor white men to struggle to achieve the franchise as a distinction of their citizenship. After independence, the development of restrictions on manhood suffrage for citizens was generally similar: first a realty qualification, then a personalty alternative, and finally a substitution of state-or county-tax payments for both kinds of property. As nearly all adult males were subject to such taxation, taxpaying suffrage was almost a universal franchise for whites. However, by 1826, four of the colonies had also abandoned taxpaying and, by the end of the Civil War, it was gone in all but three—though poll taxes were later introduced in some states. Moreover, after 1817, no new state entered the union with either a property or a taxpaying qualification. Thus, white male citizens enjoyed universal suffrage without qualification, except residency and majority, in some states by the first quarter of the nineteenth century and in all but a few by midcentury. See Porter 1918: 91–111 and Williamson 1960.

21. Porter 1918: 148. Aliens also had the right to vote in six states in 1860, though none of these allowed the same for blacks or Indians. The Pennsylvania Supreme Court ruled in 1853, for example, that even though freeborn blacks might be citizens, neither "the black population of Africa, [nor] the red aborigines of America" could yet be accepted "into political partnership" (cited in Kettner 1978: 316).

22. For example, in 1872 the important liberal deputy Francisco Belisário Soares de Souza (1979: 127) criticized a speech by a fellow congressman advocating universal suffrage for Brazilian citizens. Souza condemned it as "a speech swarming with French ideas, those that imagine the entire world immersed in darkness until the revolution and '89 and in which liberty would never shine without the emphatic declaration of the rights of man, [that] great mockery on the eve of the tremendous catastrophes that in this same country would engulf them [the French] for so many years."

23. There were two minor exceptions to this formula, both of which remain current as well. *Ius soli* citizenship was denied only in the case of children born in Brazil of a foreign father who resides there "in the service of his nation"; and *ius sanguinis* citizenship became unconditional only in the case of the children of a Brazilian father who were born in a foreign country while he was there "in the service of the Empire," even if they never established residence in Brazil (Art. 6).

24. There is some disagreement as to whether the Brazilian colonial state viewed Indians as vassals or as nations with whom "just wars" were possible (personal communication, Manuela Carneiro da Cunha). I favor the former, though I admit that amid the mountains of colonial legislation about Indians are occasional references to them as "nations." However, the comparative evidence of actual treatment is unequivocal: the U.S. federal government concluded some 389 treaties with Indian nations before converting to a policy of assimilation in the late nineteenth century; the Brazilian colonial state concluded two and its independent state none.

25. The significance of this inclusiveness for the development of a Brazilian understanding of national identity cannot be underestimated. In the United States, many white Americans exclude blacks and Indians from fundamental roles in American history. The recent introduction of Black History Month into the curriculum of public schools to redress this problem demonstrates its enormity. Brazilians need no such lessons. When asked to discuss "what makes Brazil Brazil," Brazilians of all classes generally give some version of the three-races narrative: they assert that Brazilian culture and history developed from the intersection of African, Indian, and European "races" (Asians typically get left out). In my experience, moreover, they often add a bit of self-mockery by describing the combination as a mix of the supposedly worst traits of each.

26. A few years after independence, the English naval officer Henry Lister Maw gave an accurate description of one aspect of this misrule of law in an account of his explorations in Northern Brazil: "The fact is, that in the remote parts of the province of Pará 'might makes right,' and power and interest, rather than justice, form the practical administration of the law. The emperor may send forth edicts, and the president [of the province] orders, but the isolated branco [whiteman] is himself an emperor, and much more absolute than Don Pedro at Rio [de] Janeiro. Nor is this mere figurative language. The emperor has declared all his Indian subjects *free*; the brancos still hunt and enslave them. Where then is the power? Where the absolute authority?" (1829: 434)

27. Caio Prado comments perceptively on this combination of obsession and distrust: "All these limitations of the authority of the governor are consequences of the general system of Portuguese administration: restrictions of powers, strict control, obsessive oversight of the activities of functionaries. It is a system not dictated by a superior spirit of order and method, but a reflex of the activity of generalized distrust that the central government assumes in relation to all its agents, with the poorly dissimulated presupposition of negligence, incapacity, and even dishonesty in all of them. Trust, with the concession of autonomy, counterbalanced however by an effective responsibility, is something that never penetrated into the practices of Portuguese administration" (1992: 308).

28. See Cope 1994 for an analysis of race mixing in colonial Mexico and Knight 1990 for postcolonial. For other Latin American countries, see essays in Graham 1990. Especially useful for the study of race and social policy in Brazil during the period 1870 to 1940 is Skidmore 1990 and 1993. Columbians and Venezuelans came close to Brazil's advocacy of race mixing during the nineteenth century, though not earlier. See Wade 1993 for Columbia.

29. Although approved, Bonifácio's proposals were not incorporated into the Assembly's draft constitution. After Emperor Pedro I dissolved the Assembly a few months later, the Imperial Constitution promulgated in the following year contained no mention of Indians.

30. See Skidmore 1990 and 1993. Hence, in 1889, on the eve of the Republic, the leading critic José Veríssimo wrote: "I am convinced . . . that western civilization can only be the work of the white race, and that no great civilization can be built with mixed peoples. As ethnographers assure us . . . race mixture is facilitating the prevalence of the superior element. Sooner or later it will perforce eliminate the black race here. And immigration . . . will, through

the inevitable mixtures, accelerate the selection process" (quoted in Skidmore 1990: 12).

31. Of the many ambiguous categories of whiteness in Brazil, one example is *branco da terra* (white of the land). This phrase designates people of mixed ancestry who have become, through individual success, socially and culturally white, completely assimilated to whiteness and "purified," even though phenotypical traces of other racial destinies remain evident. A famous example of such cultural redefinition of race occurred when the great novelist Machado de Assis died in 1908. In his obituary, José Veríssimo referred to him as a "*mulato.*" The abolitionist politician Joaquim Nabuco was so scandalized that he wrote the latter to protest that "for me Machado was a white man, and I believe that he became one. If there was any strange blood, it did not at all affect his perfectly Caucasian character" (quoted in Skidmore 1990: 30).

32. Gomes (2000: 40) notes the only two exceptions: the Portuguese crown found it necessary to sign peace treaties in 1691 and 1791 with two Indian tribes. Neither treaty prevented the eventual destruction of the tribes and absorption of their lands by ranchers.

33. The nineteenth-century indigenist legislation I discuss may be found in the useful compilation edited by Cunha (1992). Whether the Brazilian state (colonial or imperial) recognized that the Indians had primordial *rights* of ownership in addition to "God-given" occupation of their lands remained contested. Cunha (1992: 15) argues that the state did, both "clearly and implicitly," recognize "the anterior rights of the Indians to their lands" and cites the 1808 Carta Régia as proof. No doubt Bonifácio thought so. But I read this and related legislation as open to greater ambiguity of intention and interpretation—a view embraced by the many Brazilian jurists who have argued opposing positions, each advanced with expertise and brilliance, for several centuries. Thus I may read the 1808 Carta as expressing a different rationale. It uses a language of restoration to crown patrimony—"territory newly restored . . . newly rescued from the incursions" of Indians, which had been "given previously in *sesmarias*"—precisely because the Crown claimed legal title to the entire territory of Brazil by virtue of Cabral's "discovery" in 1500 and had distributed this territory by concession on that basis after 1532 into *capitanias* and later *sesmarias*. With the 1808 legislation, therefore, the Crown is reclaiming its land, the rights to which the wild Indians had usurped through unauthorized occupation. Why else would it use a language of restoration? Be that reading as it may, questions of Indian land rights and the status of Indian lands have been the sport of Brazilian jurists forever, as they consistently manage to wring competing positions from the dense prose of Crown law. In the end, however, the technical fineries of legal reasoning mattered less than the obvious conclusion: even if Indians had such primordial rights, they become extinguished when the Indian who bears them ceases to exist.

34. Cunha (1992: 20) cites several examples in which the federal government actually followed this provision in assigning the ownership of lands in extinct Indian villages.

35. The Law of 27 October 1831 established the authority of the Orphan Courts in these matters, applying the sixteenth-century provisions that the Ordenações Filipinas (Book 1, Title 88) defined for such courts.

36. Officio Provincial of 25 February 1858, in Cunha 1992: 253–54.

37. Chalhoub's (1990: 35–43) own point is equally important: at the risk of reproducing a "natural theory of slavery," the legal status of slaves as things must not be taken to mean that they were incapable of autonomous action, mere passive relays of their owners' values. His study of slave conflicts and court cases in nineteenth-century Rio demonstrates that slaves exercised a complexity of conflicting agencies very much their own.

38. For example, the slave miner, barber, musician, or artisan often lived away from his master and could keep a small part of his earnings to use for his own purposes.

39. One was the Law of the Free Womb, which granted freedom in 1871 to all children subsequently born to female slaves. Although it signaled that without domestic reproduction slavery would gradually vanish from Brazil, it proved ineffective and perverse. As a master could retain a slave's child in service until it reached twenty-one, the law resulted in a new kind of slavery because it did not regulate the conditions under which these "free slaves" labored and lived.

40. On manumission letters, see Chalhoub 1990, Karasch 1987, and Mattoso 1986.

Chapter 3: Limiting Political Citizenship

1. Title 67 of the Ordenações Filipinas stipulated these electoral instructions (in Jobim and Costa Porto 1996:12–13). The Brazilian constitutions and electoral legislation I discuss are found in two useful compilations: Jobim and Costa Porto 1996 and Campanhole and Campanhole 2000. Also helpful is Costa Porto's (2002) study of Brazilian elections, in which he compiles extensive passages from electoral law and procedure.

2. Copying a footnote from Laxe ([1868] 1962: 19 n. 3), Faoro (1975: 184) repeats the former's error in attributing the origin of the notebook method of qualification to the Court Order (Alvará) of 12 November 1611. In fact, as reproduced in Jobim and Costa Porto (1996), this order does not mention "notebooks." Rather, as far as I can determine, the legislative foundation for this method appears to be the Ruling of 10 May 1640, sections 2 and 3. Laxe (ibid.) further notes that according to the Provimento of 8 May 1705 "manual laborers, those exiled, Jews, and others who belonged to the class of peons were not qualified." Although I searched the Law Library of the University of São Paulo, I could not locate this provision to confirm it as a legislative basis of these exclusions.

3. See Neves and Machado (1999: 66–84) for a discussion of this constitutional movement in Portugal and its effects in Brazil, and Berbel 1999 for a fuller discussion of Brazil's participation in the Portuguese Constitutional Assemblies.

4. Election officials used a population estimate from 1808 to determine that a total of seventy-two deputies, distributed proportionally among the provinces, would represent the 2,323,286 free Brazilians. Of this total, sixty-seven deputies were actually elected (Costa Porto 2002: 23).

5. A comment about the exclusion of *criados de servir*, translated as domestic employees or servants, is relevant. There is no doubt that it deprived a large

number of citizens in imperial Brazil from political participation. In his classic study of debates about the franchise in seventeenth-century England, Macpherson (1962: 282–83) argues that the term "servant" meant all people who labored for wages in the service of another—as it did in suffrage debates throughout Europe until the late nineteenth century. Such wage earners were widely excluded from the franchise because it was thought that their economic dependence on their employer would compromise their ability to make responsible political decisions. As with most social categories, however, terms like *criado* were used with far greater ambiguity in Latin America. Moreover, in Brazil, *criado de servir* was restricted to domestic servants, most of whom did not receive wages. My point is that although the category included many citizens (in addition to slaves), who were thereby denied political rights, most wage earners would not have been so classified. In any case, during the nineteenth century on both sides of the Atlantic, specific income requirements came to replace the ambiguities of social classification in the qualification of political rights.

6. The purpose of the electoral system during the Empire was not to select a government, at least in terms of executive powers. Rather, the emperor selected the political party to form a cabinet and that party organized the elections. The presidents of the provinces had a fundamental role in their organization. They were appointed directly by the emperor, and they used all their powers to secure the success of their party, including the distribution of offices and the use of electoral fraud. Thus, elections served to guarantee parliamentary support for the cabinet and party in power. During the Empire, five different electoral systems were implemented. The purpose of each change was the same: to insure the representation of minority parties in the national assembly so that the party chosen by the emperor to form the cabinet and organize the elections would not hold all seats. Even so, of the sixteen legislatures elected during the Second Reign (1840–1889), five were unanimously held by one party and one had only a single opposition deputy (Nicolau 2002: 25–26).

7. The Imperial Constitution offered a simulacrum of religious freedom. The chapter that guarantees the civil and political rights of Brazilian citizens states, in Article 179, section 5, that "no one can be persecuted because of religion, as long as they respect that of the state [defined in Article 5 as Roman Catholic] and do not offend public morality." However, Article 5 prohibits other religions from any public expression of their place of worship, and Article 95 denies their members the political right to be elected representative. Throughout the colonial and imperial periods, the Roman Catholic Church exercised a strong direct influence over political citizenship, as specified in electoral law: voter assemblies were based on parish residence; the number of electors allotted to each parish equaled the number of "hearths" (*fogos*) found there, a list of which was posted on church doors; elections were held inside the parish church, after mass, with the parish priest seated to the right of the president of the electoral board; and so forth—practices officially ended only with the relatively anticlerical sentiments of the Saraiva Law in 1881 and the Republican Constitution in 1891.

8. Nicolau (2002: 11) suggests that electoral legislation between 1824 and 1842 limited the voting of illiterates because the ballot had to be signed. However, as cited above, specific provisions allowed illiterates to vote with the help

of an official of the electoral board, a practice in effect since the earliest elections in Brazil. Additionally, the electoral reform of 1 October 1828 reiterated that the ballot had to be "signed on the back, either by the same voter or by another at his request" (Art. 7). In an effort to curb fraud at the poles, Decree 157 of 4 May 1842 required a preestablished list of qualified voters, prohibited voting by proxy, and eliminated the signed ballot. Though its fraud prevention failed, the last measure made it easier for qualified illiterates to vote.

9. Souza published his study of the Empire's electoral system in 1872, when he was a deputy in the National Assembly. As a liberal, he argued passionately against universal suffrage as a natural right, calling it "the blind and docile instrument of all despotisms" (1979: 129). He advocated an electoral reform that imposed literacy and poll-tax qualifications as the means to identify the most capable voters. Nevertheless, his is certainly the best study of the electoral system written by a contemporary. It is, moreover, an excellent example of the intense interest that Brazilian elites maintained in European and North American developments. The study demonstrates a detailed knowledge both of political systems and events in these regions and of their leading political philosophers, and engages them as a means to analyze problems in Brazil. The study is also emblematic of the firm tradition among Brazilian writers of concentrating more on doctrinal than empirical analysis, which means that it contains precious few accounts of specific Brazilian elections and electorates. Although "electors" were also "voters," the 1870 ministerial report Souza uses distinguishes the two in its tallies. Thus, their sum gives the total number of active citizens.

10. Accurate and systematic election statistics are difficult to obtain before 1932, when an electoral justice system with both state and federal courts was created to assume responsibility for voter registration and election returns. Before 1932, that responsibility was decentralized and subject to such corruption that much electoral information has been lost, misplaced, or adulterated beyond reconstruction. Between 1937 and 1945, moreover, there were no elections. Thus, in effect, it is only after 1945 that the electoral justice system has organized reliable election data. Therefore, the election statistics of table 3.1 for the years prior to 1945 must be taken as approximations.

11. The first set includes Costa (1985: 23) and Nelson Werneck Sodré, cited in Costa Porto (2002: 115); the second, Carvalho (2001 and 1988), Costa Porto (2002), and Faoro (1975).

12. Mircea Buescu's study is one of the few that tries to disaggregate voters from the total population (cited in Costa Porto 2002: 115–16). He sampled electoral registries of the years 1870 to 1875 in various parishes of the city of Rio de Janeiro. Of the 135,896 residents he studied, only 6,743 were registered as voters; that is, 5% of the total and 6% of the free population. However, when he subtracted from the total population the number of slaves (18.7 percent), free women (30 percent), and those under twenty-five years old (27 percent), he found that those 6,743 registered voters amounted to 20.4 percent of the free adult male population.

13. Universal male suffrage appeared, for example, in Germany and in Prussia in 1849, though in the first it only became effective in 1866 and in the second it was a weighted three-class franchise. In Spain, it was first enacted in 1868, later

rescinded, and then definitively instituted in 1890. Austria universalized male suffrage in 1872 and Belgium in 1893. The English Reform Acts of 1832, 1867, and 1884 expanded suffrage for adult men progressively until it became universal in 1918. English women gained voting rights ten years later. Sweden extended the franchise for men significantly in 1866 and universalized it for both men and women in 1918. In Italy, near-universal male suffrage was enacted in 1912. In Portugal, the electoral reform law of 1918 universalized male suffrage, abolishing previous literacy restrictions. However, the prejudice against welfare remained widespread in Europe and men who received public assistance or were in bankruptcy were generally denied political citizenship.

14. The enfranchisement of illiterates had a long tradition throughout the Portuguese empire, which suffered both at home and abroad from severe shortages of manpower. Perhaps the simplest explanation for why illiterates were permitted political rights is that in the far-flung colonies many men who would qualify by achievement if not by birth as *homens bons*—the traditional basis of Portuguese estate representation—were illiterate.

15. The word *cabalista* comes from *cabalar*, to conspire, intrigue, scheme. Like its English cognate, cabal, it derives from the name of the Jewish philosophy, the cabala, that is based on esoteric interpretations of the Hebrew Scriptures. I have not found the etymology of the electoral meaning of the word *fósforo*. The dictionary *Novo Aurélio* lists "intruder, interloper" as one of the meanings of *fósforo*, attributed to vernacular speech in the state of São Paulo, though neither I nor Paulistas I asked have heard it used that way. It may also be that the meaning has a more iconic reference, in that the electoral double appears as a particular identity only for a brief moment before disappearing, like the flame of a match.

16. Perhaps the spirit of legal unaccountability and stratagem began at the very top of Brazilian politics, with imperial power. Among other things, the Imperial Constitution is notable for its creation of "the moderating power," in addition to the legislative, executive, and judicial powers. It "delegates [this fourth power] exclusively to the emperor, as the supreme chief of the nation and its first representative, to keep incessant vigil over the maintenance of the independence, equilibrium, and harmony of the other powers" (Art. 98). Further defining this moderating power, the next article contains what is probably the Constitution's most notorious phrase: "The person of the emperor is inviolable and sacred: he is not subject to any responsibility whatsoever."

17. Among the documents needed to prove annual income were, for property owners, a legally registered title with the purchase price noted and an official property assessment; for tenants, a lease contract specifying the amount of rent and at least one year's worth of receipts; for those with income from commercial or professional services, certificates of income and income taxes paid and a commercial registry attesting to capital investments.

18. In countries that had a literacy requirement, its abrogation occurred in the following order: Uruguay (1918), Colombia (1936), Venezuela (1946), Bolivia (1952), Chile (1970), Peru (1980), and Brazil (1985).

19. The Revolution of 1930 halted the national census scheduled that year, which did not resume until 1940. As a result, much demographic data for the early 1930s is not available. Although I was able to calculate the number of voters

in the presidential election of 1930, in which Júlio Prestes defeated Gétulio Vargas but never took office, the size of the electorate remains a mystery. The relevant data are not part of the archive of the Superior Electoral Tribunal, whose records date from 1932. I would like to thank the Library of the Tribunal and the Office of the President of the Republic for their assistance in this research.

20. Constitutional Amendment 25, passed in 1985, ended the disenfranchisement of illiterate citizens. It modified Article 147 of the 1967 Constitution (in its amended 1969 version) by requiring subsequent legislation to determine "the form by which the illiterate could become registered electors and exercise the right to vote." When the Citizen Constitution reestablished Brazil's democracy in 1988 after more than twenty years of military rule, it declared "suffrage universal" (Article 14). Continuing the tradition of previous Brazilian constitutions, it made both registration and voting obligatory for citizens between the ages of eighteen and seventy. However, in what may be viewed as a partial acknowledgment of the earlier disqualification, it made both voluntary for illiterates.

21. Anthropologist Teresa Caldeira (1980: 81–115; 1984: 235–46) studied voting in Jardim das Camélias, a neighborhood in the eastern periphery of São Paulo, at the start of the "opening" of the military regime in 1978. In interviews with residents, she clearly documents their sense of resentment and cynicism about politics under repression and of the diminished value of their vote. Yet she also documents that especially residents who had gained the right to vote during the period after 1945 had a strong sense of themselves as political citizens and that this sense structured their opinions of the contemporary regime. Beginning a decade later, my own interviews about that period in the same neighborhood confirmed those sentiments.

22. The problem of annulled and blank votes is more complex than I can discuss here. In the next two presidential elections, in 1994 and 1998, the number increased to 19% in both. In congressional elections, it was even higher: 41% in 1994 and 20% in 1998. However, in the 2002 presidential elections, it dropped to 10% in the first round and 6% in the second. It would seem that these last elections captured voter commitment in a way the previous two had not. Not only were they massive in scale, with all state and federal offices in dispute (except for mayor and municipal council member). They were also the first to use an electronic ballot box in all races, which may well have set a world standard for simplicity and efficiency.

23. There is considerable debate today over whether voting should remain compulsory or become optional. I am in favor of the former for a number of reasons. One may argue on theoretical grounds that in a democracy the state not only has a duty to present itself for public legitimation through elections. A democratic state also has the right to have its rule either thus legitimated or reformed, for ruling without electoral legitimacy is undemocratic. Hence, if the state has the right, the public has the duty to participate in the political process of legitimation/reformulation. The historical record is also compelling. In a country of such vast and systemic inequality as Brazil, compulsory voting under universal suffrage is one of the few rigorously instituted instances of the equalization of rights and duties among all citizens. Indeed, it was precisely when suffrage was optional, from 1881 to 1932, that the political system was most exclusive (table 3.1). Optional

voting was not the prime factor of exclusion, but it was a contributing one. More important, the equality of compulsory suffrage is actually enforced, a rarity in itself in Brazil and thus an important example for improving the democratic rule of law and curbing the impunity that plagues it: election reform in 1965 established that, in addition to fines for not registering or voting, a delinquent voter who has neither paid the fine nor been legally excused is barred from obtaining a passport or an identity card, applying for jobs or promotions in the public sector, and borrowing from public institutions. Conversely, to do any of these things, Brazilian citizens have to present a receipt that they have voted, paid the fine, or been excused.

24. Chapter 7 considers this popular participation in drafting the constitution.

25. I believe people confided in me because I was, by then, well known in the neighborhoods. Of course, they could have been telling me what they thought I wanted to hear, although I think I have developed a good ethnographic ear for a put-on. In any case, the election results strongly suggest that they did indeed vote for the PT candidate.

26. In the second round of the election, about a month later, Lula got 48% of the vote and Serra 46%. The margin of Lula's earlier victory nearly disappeared because Serra maintained his strength in the central electoral districts and won an additional nine in the north and east for a total of twenty-one. The key to victory, however, was that in the twenty districts that Lula won, all in more distant peripheries, resided the majority of voters (56%). In these peripheral districts, the average monthly income of head of household in 2000 was R $900. In Serra's districts, it was R $2,700. As the SEADE (2004c: 78) concluded after analyzing these data, "the election was decided by those who had less, the dispossessed."

Chapter 4: Restricting Access to Landed Property

1. Locke, *Second Treatise*, sec. 27. In the English tradition, Overton (*An Arrow against all Tyrants*, 1646) had established the precept of being a proprietor of one's own person somewhat earlier than Locke, deriving civil and political rights from it. See Macpherson (1962: 137–42, 197–221) for both theories of property right. Though some authors differ with aspects of Macpherson's analysis of "possessive individualism," there is little doubting the centrality of the property right in the development of modern citizenship.

2. Thus Hegel (1967) argues in the *Philosophy of Right* that it is only in possession of property that "I as free will am an object to myself . . . and thereby also for the first time am an actual will." As such, "property is . . . the means whereby I give my will an embodiment" (§45–46A). Hence, "the rationale of property is to be found not in the satisfaction of needs but in the supersession of the pure subjectivity of personality." (§41A). For Hegel, the self-possession that property produces is not a natural given. Rather, "the embodiment which my willing thereby attains [in property] involves its recognizability by others" (§51).

3. See Waldron (1988: 343–89) for a discussion of Hegel's justification of private property as a right of personality. Although Waldron thinks that the link between private property and the ethical development of the person is "rather

obscure," he argues that the Hegelians "establish a connection between respect for property and respect for persons" and also probe "important relations between the existence of private property and things like individual self-assertion, mutual recognition, the stability of the will, and the establishment of a proper sense of prudence and responsibility" (47). He distinguishes the Lockean and the Hegelian approaches to property especially with regard to the implications of propertyless-ness. In Locke, society is under no obligation to subsidize those without property in land or things. They belong "in the poor house" and lose citizen rights accordingly. By contrast, Hegel's approach is distributive: "If the argument works, it establishes, not only that private property is morally legitimate, but also that, in Hegel's words, 'everyone must have property'" (4).

4. There is some disagreement about this consequence in Locke's theory, as people always have a property right in themselves. I am persuaded by Macpherson's (1962: 231) position that although Locke emphasized the natural equality of rights, he also reasoned that the initial equality of natural rights cannot survive the differentiation of land. "Once the land is all taken up, the fundamental right not to be subject to the jurisdiction of another is so unequal as between owners and non-owners that it is different in kind, not in degree: those without property are, Locke recognizes, dependent for their very livelihood on those with property, and are unable to alter their own circumstances... To put it in another way, the man without property in things loses that full proprietorship of his own person which was the basis of his equal natural rights."

5. See also Holston 1991a for a study of autoconstruction as an aesthetics that home builders use to express both their achievements in the world and their inner intentions, a representation they characterize with such terms as "personality." I do not believe that property ownership is absolutely or uniquely necessary for developing self-possession, self-realization, mutual recognition, citizen respect, and so forth. In my view, an individual can develop such traits in other ways. Nevertheless, it is the historical and cultural case that under the remarkably broad and deep influence of liberalism, many states and societies have structured their sense both of social development and of the kind of person best qualified for citizenship in terms of the acquisition and conservation of property, especially of land and home. Some other achievement, right, or relation could have been the opportunity of such understandings, but none has been so as consistently as property. Therefore, in much of the modern world, including Brazil, property may be considered necessary in the sense that there have not been equally valued substitutes.

6. My colleague, law professor José Reinaldo Lima Lopez of the University of São Paulo, reminds me that "as a good Brazilian positivist," Beviláqua was also, along with many of his generation, indebted to the social and ethical evolutionism of Herbert Spencer.

7. Whether or not the Crown exempted Indian lands from this claim of original title is a complicated matter. As in all questions related to land, there seems to be evidence to support both sides of the argument. Cunha (1992) suggests that the Crown recognized the original seigniorial rights of Indians to their land. I am skeptical—at least when history is understood as a process rather than a series of discrete points in time—because the Crown claimed the "right of conquest"

without doubt and drove the Indians from these lands by one means or another without reprieve. As chapter 2 demonstrated, it did so until it could view them without contradiction as "empty." Moreover, the very legal definitions of land as "empty," "occupied," or "devolved" were extraordinarily complicated and contested, as I discuss in the rest of this chapter. See n. 43.

8. For example, neither land grants nor land laws were uniform in their requirements. Some grants specified time limits (themselves irregularly determined) for various purposes, and others did not; some regulations were retroactive, and others annulled the retroactivity. The most useful depiction I have found of such legal confusion is Lima (1988) for the colonial period and Silva (1996) for the mid-nineteenth century.

9. For instance, early land grants often used bow shots as their unit of measure. See Bomtempi (1970: 52) for examples.

10. During the eighteenth century, for example, the Crown passed legislation in 1702, 1711, 1755, 1770, and 1795 ordering *sesmeiros* in Brazil to survey and register their holdings by a certain date, on penalty of losing their concessions. In each case, most *sesmeiros* ignored the order. As a result, each law made a new set of holdings illegal. All the while, however, the Crown continued to grant new *sesmarias* in areas already occupied, without declaring any of the existing concessions forfeited.

11. Thus, in some places and under some conditions but not others, legislation required city council approval of grants in 1713, prior land surveys in 1753, and size limitations in 1795. The principle that there are no gaps in the law is enshrined in the current Civil Code in its introduction, Article 4.

12. Costa (1985: 28) notes that in the course of the eighteenth century about seventeen hundred Brazilians received training at Coimbra.

13. With reference to land, *posse* signifies physical possession by various means, including occupation and cultivation, as distinct from property. Brazilian civil law has historically emphasized this distinction, based on Roman law and the theories of the German jurists Ihering and Savigny. In general terms, it considers property as a juridical power or bundle of rights including use, profit, alienation, and indemnity, which does not have to be exercised to continue valid. It views possession as a factual power that must be actively exercised. Property includes possession as its effect, but the cause of possession is not always property; e.g., a thief has possession but not property of stolen goods, a lessee has usufruct but not ownership, and so forth. In terms of its acquisition, the current Civil Code (art. 489) classifies possession as just when it is not "violent, clandestine, or precarious" and unjust when the contrary. It makes a further distinction, based on subjective criteria, between possessions acquired in good or bad faith. See Nascimento (1986), Levenhagen (1982), and Viana (1985) on these distinctions.

14. Such rights should not be confused with the customary law developing in African colonies at the same time as a residual category of indigenous legal practices not taken over by colonial governments (see Moore 1989). Rather, for Portugal and its colonies, custom was itself defined in legislation. As part of the legal reform of the Marquis of Pombal, the Law of Good Reason of 1769 defined customary rights by the following requisites: "conformity to the good reasons . . . that constitute the spirit of [the King's] laws," noncontradiction of these laws,

and age in excess of one hundred years (cited in Lima 1988: 54). Opinion was unanimous that the practice of seizing and occupying land for cultivation met the criteria of rationality and time but divided about its contradicting the rule that land in Brazil could only be acquired through the concession of *sesmarias*. On the Law of Good Reason, see Miranda (1928: 68–71) and França (1977: 518–21).

15. In 1845, the president of the province of Minas Gerais, one of the more populated regions, reported that 44 percent of its lands was claimed in *posses*, 36 percent in *sesmarias*, and 20 percent remained undistributed (cited in Dean 1971: 610). Dean makes the interesting point that the abolition of primogeniture in the 1830s may also have stimulated the expansion of land claims, as landholders mounted expeditions to obtain *posses* for each child.

16. Hirschman (1977) describes the development of this ethos for early modern Europe and Shklar (1991) for the American republic.

17. For example, A. C. Tavares Bastos published an exacting study in 1867 of U.S. immigration and land policy, which I discuss in this chapter.

18. Once again, Bonifácio appears socially progressive and politically conservative. While advocating radical land reform, he rewrote election laws (Instruction No. 57 of 1822) to deny political rights to nearly all wage laborers. See chapter 3.

19. Smallholding as a policy of national development attracted a number of steadfast advocates, whose passionate arguments had little effect until much later in the century.

20. Two such proposals were those of Carlos Augusto Taunay and Senator Nicolau Vergueiro, both discussed in Silva (1996: 105–7). Taunay observed in 1834 that projects of European colonization failed to solve the problem of labor on the plantations because immigrants with any resources bought slaves of their own. He recommended therefore importing free foreigners as "naked labor," without any resources other than their work, and, above all, not granting them free land. In the early 1840s, Vergueiro founded a private company to promote a new type of colonization that placed immigrants on plantations as sharecroppers. Over the next twenty years, this scheme created sixty-seven colonies and achieved marginal success in bringing new labor to the expanding coffee estates of São Paulo. It functioned as system of debt servitude. Poor European families signed contracts obliging them to work on the plantations until they repaid the subsidized costs of their passage and maintenance. The objective of Vergueiro's plan was to retain immigrants in the service of planters for as long as possible without recourse to a market in free labor. Ultimately, the many restrictions and contradictions built into the system to insure this goal caused it to collapse. See Costa's (1985: 94–124) analysis of this failure.

21. The most extensive account of the influence of Wakefield's theories in Brazil is Smith (1990). See also Dean (1971: 613–14), Carvalho (1981: 40), Lima (1988: 83–85), and Silva (1996: 99–105). Wakefield achieved renown in the 1830s and 1840s and was cited in John Stuart Mills's work as an authority on colonization. He was famously criticized by Marx, who devoted the last chapter of the first volume of *Capital* to debunking his theories about "the manufacture of wageworkers in the Colonies." Marx (1967a: 770) did not merely ridiculed Wakefield's motives: "Think of the horror! The excellent capitalist has imported bodily from

Europe, with his own good money, his own competitors! The end of the world has come!" He also shredded the argument and converted the remains to his own purpose: "It is the great merit of E. G. Wakefield to have discovered, not anything new about the Colonies, but to have discovered in the Colonies the truth as to the conditions of capitalist production in the mother-country. . . . Wakefield discovered that in the Colonies, property in money, means of subsistence, machines, and other means of production, does not as yet stamp a man as a capitalist if there be wanting the correlative—the wage-worker, the other man who is compelled to sell himself of his own free-will. He discovered that capital is not a thing, but a social relation between persons, established by the instrumentality of things" (766).

22. The Council's proposal clearly expresses Wakefield's influence: "One of the benefits of the precautionary measures that the Session has the honor to propose to Your Imperial Majesty is to make the acquisition of land more costly. . . . As the profusion of land concessions has, more than other causes, contributed to the difficulty that today is experienced in obtaining free workers, it is our evaluation that from now on land should be sold without exception. Increasing thus the value of land and, consequently, inhibiting its acquisition, it is to be expected that the poor immigrant would hire out his labor effectively for some time, before obtaining the means to become a landowner" (Bernardo de Vasconcellos and José Cesario de Miranda Ribeiro, cited in Lima 1988: 84).

23. My discussion of the 1842 bill and the subsequent Land Law of 1950 derives from from my reading of the original debates in the annals of Brazil's House of Deputies (1843 and 1850) and their description in Dean (1971), Lima (1988), and Silva (1996: 95–99, 141–65). Coffee planters of the rich Valley of Paraiba in Rio de Janeiro supported the measure because they were most in need of new labor. Planters in the decadent sugar-producing regions of the Northeast and those growing coffee in the frontier regions of São Paulo and Minas Gerais opposed it, as they needed new labor less and therefore believed that their monies would mostly benefit production in the Valley of Paraiba.

24. To be considered valid, existing *sesmarias* had to comply fully with their terms of concession, including legal survey and registration. Those that did not— almost all—required revalidation and incurred fines for not doing so within six months and forfeiture after six years. Moreover, uncultivated lands would be taxed. The bill acknowledged that encroachments on Crown lands (*posses*) could be validated without size restriction if occupied and cultivated before 1822 and only within strict size limits if more recent. However, it prohibited new concessions of *sesmarias*—except along Brazil's borders and for Indian reserves—and denied further validation of *posses*.

25. Records indicate that the number of African slaves imported to Brazil declined precipitously in just a few years before ceasing altogether: From approximately 54,000 in 1849, the number dropped to 23,000 the following year, 3,000 the next, and a mere 700 in 1852 (Graham 1968: 164).

26. For example, using population figures from the 1860 U.S. census, Tavares Bastos (1939a: 63–67) argued in 1867 that "spontaneous immigration [is not] incompatible with slavery but only with the slave trade."

27. Indeed, though later reversed, Parliament had passed a bill in 1830 prohibiting federal expenditures on foreign colonization. Handelmann (1982: 349)

illustrates the comparative disadvantage of Brazilian immigration by recounting the tribulations of the German settlers of São Pedro de Alcântara in the province of Santa Catarina. After settling on lands that the Crown donated, they were later forced to purchase them from local private parties, having concluded that it would be less costly, violent, and insecure to do so than to appeal to the central government for the legal protection of their grant.

28. Handelmann quotes an "official report" of 1850—but gives no attribution—that recommends smallholding "as the most powerful means to foment immigration." Dean (1971: 618) cites a revealing passage from the congressional debate on the revived reform bill in 1850. "The United States has to be taken as the model in this question," argues a deputy from Minas Gerais. "The introduction of free laborers in [Brazil], even if they do not come enslaved temporarily [a reference to the 1842 Wakefieldian model], is always useful; what we want is that our lands should have value, that there should be someone to cultivate them, and that our landowners should have an income . . . what we want is cultivated land and increased production."

29. The full text of the Land Law of 1850 I use is included as the appendix in Pereira (1932). The law made several new and important conciliations to landholders. *Sesmarias* qualified for validation if they had even incipient cultivation but met no other terms of their original concession. Productive *posses* could be legalized regardless of size. They were, moreover, rewarded with the addition of contiguous Crown land, up to a maximum of the largest *sesmaria* previously granted in the area. In perhaps the most significant placation of *posseiro* anxiety, the law permitted those who failed to meet the requirements of legalization to remain "in possession" of land productively used. However, they lost the unproductive areas of their claim and all property rights to the productive. In other words, the law clearly distinguished property from possession, yet recognized that productive possession without title generated limited rights of occupancy. Finally, much to the disappointment of those who wanted to use land reform to fund immigration, the law eliminated the annual land tax proposed in the earlier bill.

30. With regard to the national land survey and sale of public lands, legal historian Lima (1988: 67) observes that "in this aspect, the Law of 1850 is nothing more than a copy of the land laws adopted by the United States, whose leap in prosperity and civilization certainly dazzled our legislators." In his 1867 work on Brazilian immigration, Tavares Bastos (1939a: 78) cites a French study of the American case, in a pertinent example of comparative nation-state formulation: "'The American law of public lands became in essence a European law of emigration.' That is the model that the state-builders of Brazil adopted in the excellent [Land Law] of 1850."

31. He argued that "the maximum return for the state does not consist in the quantity [of land] sold, but in the increase of production and wealth through the appropriation and development of its lands." Moreover, "to think that by itself the system of selling national lands would be enough to attract to the United States the emigrants of the old world would be an incomplete and inexact appreciation, one that does not take into account the influence of individual liberties, local freedoms, decentralization, public education, [and]

all those things that constitute the mechanism of modern democracy" (1939a: 84–85, 59).

32. The 1850 Land Law established a minimum price of half a real and a maximum of two réis per square *braça* of public land, depending on location and quality. Tavares Bastos (1939a: 83–84) compared the price per acre in several countries. He found that at the time, the United States had a fixed price of $1.25 USD (about 2$500mil-réis) per acre of national land, whereas in Brazil an acre cost between 413 réis and 1$653mil-réis.

33. To qualify, settlers had to use the land productively for five years and pay a $26 fee. Foreign immigrants had to declare their intention to naturalize. The Homestead Act capped decades of debate between groups who disputed, as in Brazil, conceptions of land and labor in national development. It is a story well told in Robbins (1976: 92–298) about shifting regional and ideological alliances in the settlement of the American West, pitting Southern plantation interests against Eastern industrial ones, land speculators against independent small farmers, Know-Nothing nativists against immigration advocates, Dixie Democrats against new Republicans. The act was a triumph for those promoting "free land, free soil, and free labor" as the best means to consolidate American democracy. Yet, as Robbins analyzes, continuing government land grants of enormous size to corporate interests (e.g., railroad and timber) and to individual states steadily undercut its principle of land for the landless.

34. According to Tavares Bastos's research (1939a: 86–87), the American government sold nearly 147 million acres of national land between 1787 and 1858, 80 percent (118 million) during the years 1833 to 1858. The total sales revenue amounted to $185 million USD, approximately $2.6 million a year. By contrast, between 1859 and 1865, the Brazilian government had managed to sell a mere 210,600 acres, for a total revenue of $85,700 USD, about $12,200 a year. Whereas more than 2.6 million people had immigrated to the United States between 1850 and 1857 (about 377,500 a year), only 120,500 had gone to Brazil during the period 1855–62 (about 15,000 a year).

35. The federal government retained its authority over public land in federal territories (such as Acre) and Indian reserves although its control over land in "extinct" Indian villages was vigorously contested by the individual states. As Silva (1996: 295–300) documents, it reasserted its management of these lands by creating federal bureaucracies between 1906 and 1911 to sponsor new colonization and protect existing Indian settlements. The legislation authorizing these initiatives reproduced many problems of the 1850 Land Law. For example, definitive title to public land was only given to settlers who paid the entire costs up front. Although the lots were called "homesteads" (English in the original) and were inheritable, they could not be alienated or used as collateral. Such technical complications, financial limitations, and political conflicts practically nullified these federal initiatives.

36. This city-bound migration is clearly indicated by the number of foreign-born residents in the city of São Paulo and by the annual growth rate of its total population. Both peaked in the 1890s, when the growth rate was an extraordinary 14 percent a year due to the influx of foreign-born immigrants. Their

presence in the city reached its maximum of 55 percent of the population in 1893 (SEADE 2004: 9; Fausto 1984:10).

37. Tenurial ownership is associated with feudal services and allodial with modern commodity markets, in which land is freely owned without obligation to another vested with superior rights.

38. Cited in Lima (1988:76). Silva's (1996) discussion of the implementation of the 1850 Land Law is especially useful. She also traces the consequences of the 1891 Republican Constitution's transfer of public lands to state governments. Other discussions include Carvalho (1981), Porto (1965), and Pereira (1932).

39. Period reporting is replete with examples of such violence over land. See Silva 1996.

40. The use of *grilagem* and cognates to indicate land fraud is of uncertain etymology. Though this use is entirely contemporary, most Brazilians I have asked do not offer suggestions. On occasion, however, I have heard two possibilities. Both refer to the habits of the cricket (*grilo*) and to the development of the real estate market after 1850. The first is an analogy: although the claim swindler presents lots of documents to substantiate his claim to own a piece of land, his valid title is as hard to locate as it is difficult to find the cricket that you hear. The second is a technique: to make documents look old and bona fide, swindlers put them in a drawer with crickets. Their excrement is supposed to yellow the paper, though I have not yet tested this method.

41. American common law contrasts adverse possession with easement and, further, with prescriptive easement. These distinctions do not exist in Brazilian law. Whereas adverse possession (both in the United States and Brazil) results in complete title of ownership, easement only creates rights to certain use of land and has no effect on the underlying title. Moreover, an easement is created by express or implied agreement between owners of land for one owner to make use of the land of the other. Adverse possession is hostile.

42. Lima (1988: 91–112) covers debates through the 1930s. In 1931, a decree interpreted the 1916 Civil Code (Art. 67) to mean that *terras devolutas* were ineligible for *usucapião*. However, the 1934 Constitution contradicted this decree by not excluding public lands from its Article 125, which permits adverse possession of up to 10 hectares of productively used land for Brazilians without other property. This article was reproduced verbatim in the 1937 Constitution (Art. 148), with modifications in the 1946 Constitution (Art. 156), and in the 1964 Constitutional Amendment 10 (Art. 6). The 1946 Constitution added a paragraph that explicitly legitimates the possession of *terras devolutas* of up to 25 hectares. The 1964 amendment retained this paragraph and increased the maximum to 100. The fate of devolved lands remained in this state of possible contradiction until the 1988 Constitution (Art. 188) subsumed it—with different but no fewer ambiguities—under the principle that "the destiny of public and devolved lands will be rendered compatible with agrarian policy and with the national plan of agrarian reform."

43. This second sense was also complicated by the problem of Indian lands "rendered empty" by conquest and Indian villages "extinguished" for supposed lack of identifiable Indians. Although there was disagreement (see n.7), the dominant view held that these lands devolved to the Crown as proprietor of the

territory of Brazil. However debated, this sense that the state was the owner of *terras devolutas* by "original acquisition" got enshrined in the Consolidation of Civil Laws (1876, Art. 586), which served as the civil code until 1916. As the author of the Consolidation, Teixeira de Freitas, argued, "the State had acquired the devolved lands by original title, which has been called the right of conquest" (cited in Lima 1988: 91).

44. Every few decades, both state and central governments have tried to exercise greater control over private landed property by legislating new rules for the uniform registration, transcription, and issuance of titles. The next attempt was the Torrens Registry in 1890, created by the provisional federal government of the new republic. In deference to interests of rural landowners, however, it made registration voluntary for rural property (though, strangely, obligatory for urban) and, as a result, the Registry had no effect whatsoever. See Silva (1996: 233–36). Then came the Civil Code in 1916. It further clouded the problem of documenting real estate ownership by instituting the validity of both private contracts and public titles for property transactions, depending on their value. After that, the matter went through additional decrees and statutes, rather like the legal convolutions pertaining to devolved lands.

45. The term *bugreiro* comes from *bugre*, a generic and pejorative designation for wild Indian. It derives from the French *bougre*, which, according to *La Grande Larouse*, refers to an individual who is not respected or respectable and which can be used as an invective (from the Latin *Bulgarus*, Bulgare, and, by pejorative extension, "heretic" and "sodomite"). Vianna (1933: 114) contrasts the contemporary *bugreiro* with his predecessor, the *mameluco*, the half-breed who centuries earlier scoured the interior for Indian slaves and gold: "The old-time *mameluco* attacked to enslave; the one of today, crueler and more positive, is merely an exterminator: he sweeps and cleans the tropical forest of its American parasites."

46. At this point in the text, Vianna cites a passage from his contemporary, the renowned nationalist and author Monteiro Lobato: "[The *grileiro*] operates the greatest scams; he falsifies signatures, papers, seals; falsifies rivers and mountains; falsifies trees and boundaries; falsifies judges and registry offices; falsifies the pointer of Themis's balance [Justice]; falsifies the sky, the earth, and the waters; falsifies God and the Devil. But he triumphs. Subdividing the land into lots, the *grileiros* sell them to the legions of settlers who follow them like vultures by the smell of carrion. Five, ten years later, the flower of coffee whitens the region and incorporates it to the patrimony of national wealth."

Chapter 5: Segregating the City

1. Teresa Caldeira introduced me to Jardim das Camélias in 1987. She had conducted intensive fieldwork there from 1978 to 1982, which formed the basis of her pioneering 1984 ethnography. I first went to Lar Nacional a few years later with the president of Jardim das Camélias's neighborhood association, whom residents had invited for advice on legal and organizational aspects of their land conflict.

2. A municipal law in 1915 divided São Paulo into central, urban, suburban, and rural zones (see chapter 6). Influential studies in social science continued to use the latter two into the 1970s to describe the development of São Paulo. For example, although Langenbuch (1971) mentions *periferia* and *periurbano*, he mainly uses *subúrbios, rural,* and *arredores* (outskirts). However, by the middle of that decade, the term periphery and the concept of peripheral urbanization had become ubiquitous in significant academic and government studies. Examples include Camargo et al. (1976), Bonduki and Rolnik (1979), SEPLAN (1979), Kowarick (1980), and Caldeira (1984).

3. Historically, the most significant sign of that life was paved streets, and their existence neatly distinguished urban from rural for much of Brazilian history. Rural communities (i.e., *aldeias, povoadas, fazendas,* and *roças*) did not have streets. They had roads (*estradas*) and paths (*caminhos*). Only settlements classified as urban (*cidades* and *vilas*) had streets. However, the paving of modern transportation changed this physical and lexical distribution, and the core meanings of "urbanized" expanded to include additional infrastructure. Nevertheless, many neighborhoods in São Paulo's peripheries still have unpaved areas, and asphalting them remains a major aim of community mobilization.

4. Many studies ignore the juro-political conceptions of space and society in Brazil, even though the national census uses them to classify and analyze urban and rural populations.

5. The municipality of São Paulo (MSP) comprises ninety-six districts in an area of 1,509 square kilometers. Its population was 10.4 million in the 2000 census (map 5.1). The metropolitan region of São Paulo (MRSP) comprises thirty-nine municipalities in an area of 8,051 square kilometers and contained 17.8 million residents in 2000 (map 5.4). Its principal municipality is that of São Paulo, which is also the state capital. State and federal legislation (1973/75) created metropolitan regions for planning purposes.

6. These districts are Alto de Pinheiros, Campo Belo, Consolação, Itaim Bibi, Jardim Paulista, Moema, Morumbi, Perdizes, Pinheiros, Santo Amaro, Vila Andrade, and Vila Mariana (IGBE 2000) (map 5.1).

7. These twenty poorest districts are Anhanguera, Brasilândia, Capão Redondo, Cidade Tiradentes, Grajaú, Guaianases, Iguatemi, Itaim Paulista, Jaraguá, Jardim Ángela, Jardim Helena, Lajeado, Marsilac, Parelheiros, Pedreira, Perus, São Rafael, Sapopemba, Vila Curuçá, and Vila Jacuí (map 5.1).

8. There is universal agreement among urban historians that the condensed and the dispersed patterns best describe, in succession, São Paulo's growth from the late nineteenth century until at least the 1990s. In addition to references cited, my discussion here benefits from Caldeira 2000 and Rolnik 1997.

9. Morse (1970: 302) notes that between 1935 and 1939, 96 percent of the 285,000 migrants to the state of São Paulo were Brazilian.

10. The brutal distinctions of housing during this period were portrayed in an inventory of 200 domiciles conducted in 1942 by Donald Pierson, an American anthropologist on the staff of the Escola Livre de Política e Sociologia de São Paulo. He surveyed 100 domiciles in three wealthy neighborhoods (Higienópolis, Jardim América, and Pacaembú) and 100 in three impoverished ones (Bexiga, Canindé, and Moóca). Each domicile housed a single family. In the poor areas,

the 100 domiciles contained 447 people in 43 buildings. In the wealthy areas, the 100 domiciles were distributed among 100 houses, 1 family for each, housing 548 people. With regard to sanitary facilities, Pierson found a total of 48 toilets, many in outhouses, serving the 100 poor families, while 334 toilets accommodated the same number of wealthy families. He also found that the 100 wealthy homes had a total of 226 bathrooms for bathing, while the 100 poor homes had 12. Among the former, 190 had hot water; among the latter, 3. In Bexiga, 55% of the domiciles that lacked bathrooms also lacked basins for bathing. Home ownership varied as dramatically. In the wealthy neighborhoods, residents owned 86 of the 100 homes surveyed; in the poor, only 7 (Pierson 1942: 206, 223, and tables 16–17).

11. Key events were the First Congress on Housing (Institute of Engineering, 1931) and the Task Force on Economic Housing (IDORT, 1941). Both resulted in numerous publications, many of which appeared in the *Revista do Arquivo Municipal*. A special issue of that journal (IDORT 1942) published thirty-seven papers and lectures of the Task Force. IDORT also published its own journal, the *Revista de Organização Científica*, that featured many articles on housing (especially in numbers 125–136) and on other task forces it had organized, including one on the "scientific organization of work" and another on "the scientific organization of municipal administration." These stressed the need for fordism in production, modern management of labor, professional training, worker incentives, higher wages, and other means to improve the welfare and productivity of labor as the means of industrial expansion, national wealth, and social tranquility. I thank Ronaldo Romulo Machado de Almeida and Maria Teresa De Morais Pinto Furtado for their assistance in researching these institutions and their publications.

12. Two citations from IDORT articles demonstrate the tenor of attack: "The majority of the population lives in conditions that degrade human dignity and cause irreparable physical and moral damage. The statistics of mortality and morbidity demonstrate the biological danger of the contemporary anti-hygienic neighborhoods of the proletariat" (Oliveira 1943: 17); and "We have to eliminate, forever, the *cortiço*, which is the source of imperfection, the intoxicating and corrupting environment, and which is among us, nevertheless, the shelter of the poor. The *cortiços* are the creators of the bad elements for society, of the evils and vices that degenerate the poor classes; they are the centers of epidemics and contagious maladies" (Penteado 1943: 21).

13. The titles and citations here and below come from the two sources listed in note 11.

14. As one IDORT economist put it: "The world needs [household] consumers to balance large-scale production; the social ideal of the incorporation of the proletariat into modern society mixes thereby with the economic emergence of the masses" (Dodsworth 1942: 5).

15. For a finely illustrated study of the plan, see Toledo (1996). The plan did not appear de novo. The first intense urban reform occurred under mayor Antonio Prado (1899–1911). It dislocated people and activities from the center to its edge, transferring markets, widening streets, remodeling squares, and removing "services" like prostitution. Subsequent administrations continued this kind of redevelopment.

340

16. See Langenbuch (1971) for early land speculation in the hinterlands of São Paulo and Stiel (1984) for the history of transportation in the region.

17. Camargo et al. (1978: 54–55) reports that in the mid-1970s, 80% of loans granted by the National Housing Bank (BNH) went to middle-and upper-income applicants.

18. In all Brazil, the welfare institutes produced a total of only 124,024 units and the Popular Housing Foundation 16,964 during these years. See Azevedo and Andrade 1982; Bonduki 1998, 1994: 100–101; Grupo de Arquitetura e Planejamento 1985.

19. Given its obvious detrimental consequences on low-income housing, the motivation for issuing and renewing the Renter's Law is puzzling. In addition to the populist appeal of a supposed rent control, Bonduki (1998, 1994: 102–3) argues that the state wanted to encourage capital investments in industry. Hence, it schemed to discourage investments in rental property. He also suggests that it was intended as a means to reduce the costs to industry of reproducing the labor force (since rent was an item used in the calculation of wages) and thus increase the rate of private capital accumulation and profit. While it is difficult to prove this point, there is no doubt that much of the legislation designed to "help the poor" promoted by the Vargas and succeeding administrations had contradictory consequences that, in themselves, were not necessarily liabilities. To the contrary, they enabled the regimes both to fortify their popular legitimacy by claiming to champion workers and to consolidate their economic base by benefiting industrialists.

20. Much has been written on working-class organization and resistance during these decades. With regard to housing and rent, I have found particularly useful the articles in Kowarick (1994) and Paoli's (n.d.) unpublished doctoral dissertation.

21. An influential analysis of the relation between autoconstruction, exploitation, and capital accumulation is Oliveira (1972), though many observe that employers benefited with the development of autoconstruction as the "solution" to housing workers.

22. According to the 1950 census (IBGE 1950–2000; Sempla 1992), all neighborhoods in the historic center and the first industrial periphery either lost population or were stagnant between 1940 and 1950. In the former, for example, the annual population growth rate was –1% in Sé and Santa Ifigênia and –2% in Bom Retiro. In the latter, it was –2% in Brás and –1% in Moóca. At the same time, the expanding elite center gained population. Thus, Jardim Paulista and Pinheiros-Jardim Amèrica had annual growth rates of 6%. In what was then the distant periphery, however, growth was spectacular: Vila Maria registered 14% for the decade and Vila Prudente 12%. Even at the extremes of the municipality, in sparsely populated areas that would become dense with autoconstructed neighborhoods in later decades, growth was as high: 14% in Guaianazes and 12% in São Miguel Paulista. See map 5.3.

23. According to SEADE (2004c) this distribution remains unmistakeable even after sixty years of peripheral development. In the most outlying districts, 30%–33% of the population in 2004 was less than fifteen years old. In the next most peripheral ring of districts, this segment was 25%–29%. In the central districts, it was 12%–14%.

24. Camargo et al. (1976: 36) notes that in 1970 the average load per bus at the height of São Paulo's rush hour was 130 passagers, double the official maximum capacity.

25. On this aesthetics of autoconstruction, see Holston 1991a.

26. During the period of maximum sales in Lar Nacional, from 1967 to 1972, the minimum salary was readjusted six times by national law to keep pace with inflation.

27. It often occurred that buyers failed to make their payments. Residents in both neighborhoods told me that two options were common. In one, the developer reached an agreement with the delinquent buyer that he would pay off the arrears over time and with interest. Developers found this option preferable where the costs of resale were significant. If those costs were low or if no agreement could be reached, the developer expelled the buyer. To avoid a total loss, the latter tried to sell his stake in the lot to someone who would take over payments. In either case, developers reaped profits by selling the land again, charging transfer fees to a new buyer, or gaining interest payments.

28. In Lar Nacional, advertisements stated in bold that the "fixed price" of NCr $23,500 would not be readjusted. If so, then I calculate that diligent residents could have paid it off in seven years. However, the fine print of the contract included the qualification that the price could be readjusted for increases in the "wholesale costs of construction material (whenever that happens)," without specifying the rules of that determination.

29. It is hard to calculate this profit. I estimate that when the development company Lar Nacional vanished in 1974, it had received about NCr $17,000 (in 1969 values) for each 125 m^2 lot. No doubt, this constituted a handsome profit on the five hundred lots it developed.

30. The average home ownership rate in 2000 was 58% for districts of the central zone—69% in wealthy Jardim Paulista—and 71% for those in the eastern and the southern peripheries. It was 73% for districts in the western zone, which concentrates many of the wealthiest neighborhoods. In one of the poorest districts, Cidade Tiradentes, on the far eastern edge, it was 86%. In the districts of my fieldwork, home ownership was 69% in Vila Jacuí in 2000 (16% rented), 70% in 1991 (22% rented), and 60% in 1980. The last rate is for São Miguel Paulista, which then included much Vila Jacuí. In Sapopemba, it was 73% in 2000 (16% rented), 70% in 1991 (20% rented), and 52% in 1980. The last is for Vila Prudente, which then included Sapopemba (Censuses of 2000, 1991, 1980 in IBGE 1950–2000).

31. *Cortiço* residence has also increased. But it is notoriously difficult to measure, much more so than residence in *favelas*, because its existence is more easily hidden behind the façade of other sorts of dwelling. As a result, estimates vary widely. Nonetheless, there is agreement that the number of *cortiços* grew dramatically between 1991 and 2000 in both central and peripheral districts. The census estimated 24,168 domiciles "in rooms"—which indicates residence in a *cortiço*—in 1991 and 42,246 in 2000, a 75% increase.

32. IBGE 2000: vol. *São Paulo*, table 3.3.9.20.

33. Throughout the colonial and imperial periods, social assistance was provided privately through various kinds of associations, charities, and religious

brotherhoods. A legally defined socioeconomic component of citizenship did not exist. An exception was the right to a primary education for all Brazilians stipulated in the Imperial Constitution—a right, however, without substance. In any case, it was dropped from the Republican Constitution, which, in accordance with the orthodox liberalism of political elites, made no mention of social rights whatsoever. Studies of the Vargas period and its remaking of state and society are legion. In addition to the usual sources, I have benefitted from Maria Célia Paoli's (n.d.) unpublished doctoral dissertation. Let me note one precipitate of this period I do not discuss, namely, that the rise of the PT as a *labor* movement decades later depended in part on the legacy of Vargas's labor structures. I agree with French (1992), Keck (1989), and others who make this case. But this labor history is not my focus.

34. From 1888 to 1920, 73% of Italian immigrants went to São Paulo, 71% of Spanish, 35% of Portuguese, and 59% of all other nationalities (Vilela and Suzigan 1973: 268).

35. As Paoli (n.d.: 118) writes, the new state "recognized the rights to social and political participation only as an administrative and legal problem. Thus formulated, the social question under state aegis incorporates working-class demands, but eliminates any connotation of conquest and struggle; it incorporates employers' demands for limiting worker actions, but takes away their private power to discipline the labor force; and it incorporates parliamentary debate, but denies the existence of representative politics." See also Duarte 1999.

36. See Garcia (1982) for propaganda, censorship, and spectacle during the Vargas period. Weinstein (1996) examines the cultural and vocational training of workers in the 1940s. McCann (2004: 19–40) argues, however, that radio programming imposed by Vargas was ineffective in molding popular music and, through it, national popular culture.

37. See Dias (1962: chap. 3) for a discussion of these demands. The most significant labor laws include Two-Thirds (1930), Trade Unions (1931 and 1934), Female and Child Labor (1932), Eight-Hour Workday (1932), Collective Labor Agreements and Mixed Commissions of Reconciliation and Judgment (i.e., labor courts) (1932), Holidays (1934), Pension (1934), and Accidents (1934). The labor laws of the Vargas regimes were first decreed and then, often many years later, legislated.

38. Workers would also be denied a legal contract if they exercised a regulated profession, but their employer refused to classify them as such. Fischer (1999) makes the important point that many kinds of legal documents first became indexes of "worthy citizenship" among Brazil's urban population during the Vargas era. In addition to work passbooks, these included national identity cards, marriage and birth certificates, and rental contracts.

39. Paoli (n.d.), Weinstein (1996), and Wolfe (1993), among others, document many forms of resistance that independent unions and other organizations sponsored. For instance, the Communist Party of Brazil created a national front in 1935—the Aliança Nacional Libertadora—of neighborhood and occupational cells that proposed a new type of popular participation in urban issues (housing, sanitation, and transport), in addition to work, and that had a presence in the developing peripheries. In the mid–1940s, the Communist Party also created

Democratic and Popular Committees in the peripheries to provide a new base for organizing workers. The Vargas regime brutally repressed these popular and party actions at every turn and under the cover of law, particularly in the mid-1930s and during World War II. Paoli (n.d. 287–88) gives a compelling account of this violence, showing how unions were crushed and their records seized; newspapers censored and closed; hundreds of "undesirable" foreigners (mostly union leaders) expelled from the country; militant workers, intellectuals, military officers, and soldiers jailed and tortured; and members of parliament imprisoned. Under these conditions, an alternative formulation of citizenship did not materialize.

40. "Work is a social duty. Intellectual, technical, and manual work has the right to special protection and care of the state" (Art. 136). Article 139 further tied morality, legality, and citizenship to work: "the strike and the lockout are declared antisocial, harmful to labor and to capital and incompatible with the superior interests of national production."

41. The 1940 Census suggests the size of this sliver for the state of São Paulo. About 1.5 milion people had jobs in agriculture. Among the 853,339 economically active residents in nonagricultural occupations, about half had jobs in industry. The other half (424,852) subsisted "in conditions of inactivity or badly defined activity." Thus, at most 18% of the state's labor force might have had access to labor rights through their professions. The actual figure was in all likelihood considerably less, though in the city of São Paulo it was certainly more. In 2002, about 60% of Paulistanos who were economically active held work contracts in the formal sector with signed passbooks. However, that percentage plummets in the poorest, most outlying, and most populous districts of the peripheries, where it does not surpass 3% of the working population (map 5.5d).

42. Paoli (n.d.: 237-310) documents these abuses of law in detail. Two of my favorite absurdities are the law that allowed employers to specify what constituted a "just cause" for dismissal or loss of benefit and the one that required workers involved in a grievance to be suspended from work without pay during the entire trial period.

Chapter 6: Legalizing the Illegal

1. Similar examples of this sort of functional understanding of law appear across the theoretical and regional spectrum in classic anthropology, as an emphasis on maintaining social control through custom (Malinowski 1926; Radcliffe-Brown 1933), cleaning up social messes (Llewellyn and Hoebel 1941), producing social cohesion through conflict (Gluckman 1956), settling disputes (Gulliver 1963), and encouraging compromise and moderating ambiguity (Nader 1969). Even in an early study of "law as politically active," Barnes (1961: 193) concludes that although "jural institutions [where there are no courts] . . . in fact provide the rules by which [political] struggles are carried on . . . the law may nevertheless be regarded as an enduring consistent set of rules impartially applied." An exception is Leach's (1963) provocative but neglected paper in which he argues, against both Malinowskian and anti-Malinowskian functionalists, that in primitive society law serves to protect privilege.

2. See Nader 1965: 18–21 for samples from an older ethnography.

3. For example, essays in Starr and Collier (1989) suggest that legal systems create conflict; legislation is an arena of factional struggles (Vincent 1989); so-called customary law is an invention of colonialism (Cohn 1989 and Moore 1989); disputing may be used to promote harmony as a specific political strategy (Nader 1989); and legal discourse may introduce hierarchy in relations presumed equal (Greenhouse 1989; see also Santos 1988). My own work (1989 and 1991) stresses illegality as a source of law, a condition Coutin (2000) also finds in U.S. immigration law. Merry (1990) reveals how legal language and procedure alienate "legal consciousness" when they render social problems into case law. In short, legal anthropology has subverted its own origins. In addition, many of these studies emphasize that law is not only disruptive but also incoherent in practice. I argue a somewhat different point: far from being incoherent, the Brazilian legal system deploys technical complication and its chaos brilliantly for strategic ends.

4. For an ethnographic account of the significance of illegal residence in the peripheries of Brasília and their cycles of usurpation and legalization, see Holston 1989: 257–99.

5. See Rolnik (1997) for a discussion of this legislation.

6. The term *cartório* refers generically to all types of judicial offices that register and document transactions for the purpose of attributing authenticity and public faith to them. It includes notary offices, court clerk offices, and public registries and refers as well to the places where these services are performed and archived. The term may be used more narrowly to distinguish the complex system of public registries, including those for private individuals, corporations, real estate, and titles and documents. *Cartórios* are owned and operated by a notary public on the basis of a lifetime government grant. Each contains specialized officials who register transactions within their sphere of authority in legalized books and who authenticate copies of those transcriptions for use elsewhere. All acts and agreements must be so registered to have any legal significance—whence the notion of a social order of paper, sealing wax, and stamps. See Silva 1967 and França 1977 for terminological distinctions; Batalha 1984: 13–26 for a historical analysis of the system of public registries; and Batalha 1984: 455–66 and Rodrigues 1987: 400–409 for studies of the real estate registry specifically.

7. One significant problem was that each developer subdivided the land into different lot sizes, some 6 x 24 and some 6 x 20 meters, on top of the 1924 plan that parceled the land into lots of 10 x 40. These smaller lots cut through existing and planned streets, became superimposed on each other, nullified any correspondence between the 1924 plan and actual occupation, and therefore made regularization impossible. The government seemed oblivious to these developments, as it continued to assess property taxes on the basis of 10 x 40 lots. Needless to say, residents refused to pay taxes on 400 square meters when they only held 120 or 144.

8. The diligence of residents in making payments throughout this confused period follows not only from their lawyer's counsel on securing the status of buyers in good faith before the courts. It also follows from the importance these workers attach to the social and moral distinction of property ownership. They did not want to be accused of squatting.

9. The important exception to the generally alienated relation of the working classes to law is the labor law and courts instituted under Vargas. As I observed in the last chapter, however, this institutionalization of labor rights absorbed workers without autonomy or equality and left them, ultimately, with little more than frustration and division.

10. Telex from Feres Sabino, Attorney General of the State of São Paulo to Leonel João Carvalho de Castro, director of the Office of Federal Patrimony, August 1986. Author's archive.

11. Although some Brazilian anthropologists, especially Roberto DaMatta, have long argued for the importance of ambiguity in Brazilian social life, there is little research on systematic irresolution in other areas of law. An exception is Caldeira's (2000: 138–57) study of the legal ambivalence surrounding police violence. See especially DaMatta's 1979 classic study (English edition 1991). Although DaMatta stresses the significance of ambiguity, he generally presents it as that which fails to be one pole or the other of the clear-cut structural dichotomies that organize his analysis of social relations, such as house/street, personal/impersonal, private/public, and hierarchical/egalitarian. I view ambiguity and irresolution as productive aspects of social relations.

12. My own conception of law here is not reified, functionalist, or conspiratorial. In ascribing intentions, objectives, and motives to law, I am not invoking a supraindividual entity or collective historical subject as "law." Rather, I am referring to specific texts, procedures, practices, and institutions that are explicitly concerned with the regulation of social relations and to the people who use them. This regulation is, moreover, largely grounded in a consideration of intention. Thus, the intentions I speak of are neither free-floating nor hidden but attributable to specific actors, including legislators, judges, lawyers, litigants, swindlers, and criminals. Therefore, I stress intentional and not functionalist explanation, drawing this distinction between the two: the former accounts for behavior by focusing on its intended consequences while not neglecting the unintended; the latter explains individual actions by deriving them from the supposedly beneficial or self-regulating actual consequences of aggregate patterns of behavior.

13. The arguments I analyze are presented in various legal documents, such as titles, registrations, court records, notarized accords, and technical reports. They are also expressed by the people involved, with more passion but generally less precision. I am greatly indebted to Antônio Benedito Margarido for sharing his archive of these documents with me and for helping me to understand them. I have also consulted the records of the Neighborhood Association of Jardim das Camélias and local historical studies such as Bomtempi 1970.

14. The original letter of grant was written on 12 October 1580 by Jeronymo Leitão, "captain of the captaincy of São Vicente," and registered with the Municipal Council of São Paulo on 26 August 1622.

15. For example, the Crown issued a contradictory ruling in 1596 on the freedom of converted Indians that declared that "neither will the gentiles, in order not to fool themselves, think that by serving the residents they will be captives, nor will they serve them for more than two months." When the Jesuits protested the flagrant buying and selling of these Indians, the town council got the chief judge in 1612 to prohibit religious authorities "from taking legal action against

residents who sell free Indians because, even though this practice is criminal, its repression falls under the competence of the secular justice." This ruling did nothing other than establish justice's authority to do nothing—except perhaps marvel at the magic of legal language (cited in Bomtempi 1970: 46, 48).

16. The supposed genealogy of Adis's claim has become almost folkloric in Jardim das Camélias due to an open letter it circulated among residents in 1972 at the height of land violence. With no doubt unintended burlesque, it gave a detailed, legal-sounding history of its property rights and then lamented that it was being slandered by *grileiros* operating in the area. It alerted residents to the "false titles that the authentic *'grileiros'* exhibit" and urged them to verify the "origins" of its "legitimate rights" at the relevant *cartórios*.

17. An account of Medina's contract and some of the subsequent legal conflicts involving it may be found in Pereira (1932: 105–26). Pereira is of the opinion that neither Medina nor the bank had rights to one-half the lands. He argues that once having lost the concession for not constituting the first colony, the terms of recision did not apply.

18. The Supreme Court's decision is transcribed in Pereira (1932: 110–15).

19. In previous chapters, we observed that the voluminous production of law had become a strategy of rule in colonial times on both sides of the Atlantic. The Pernambucan social critic, Miguel do Sacramento Lopes Gama, noted the popularity of this strategy at the height of the empire: "The spirit of contentiousness and the love of bringing suit seem to be among the dominant passions of our Brazil; I cannot believe that in any other country there are as many lawsuits filed as there are among us." (*O Carapuceiro*, 1 July 1837; cited in Flory 1981: 37).

20. Two examples recently came to my attention. A man I know from Jardim das Camélias received by mail a traffic violation for speeding, recorded by a hidden camera. The photograph clearly showed, however, that the offending vehicle was not his: it was a different car with a different license plate. The innocent man appealed the fine, submitting to the Department of Motor Vehicles a photograph of the rear of his car for comparison and a copy of his ownership papers. His protest was denied without explanation. To appeal again, he had first to pay the fine. However, an agency that facilitates dealing with state bureaucracy suggested that a small "fee," properly applied, would resolve the problem. He confessed to me that the agency made him feel foolish that he had not offered cash initially and that he, the honest citizen, would now have to pay even more. The second example involves a middle-class group of eighteen friends who bought a parcel of land in an area of environmental protection near São Paulo, with the objective of constructing weekend homes. Wanting "to do the right thing," they followed all legal and environmental requisites in trying to get their land-development project approved. More than fifteen years later, however, their plans remain on paper, shelved in a variety of state offices. Nevertheless, on several sides of their property, housing condominiums have sprung up. When asked, these neighbors were forthcoming in suggesting two means to timely approval: bribe local officials or hire squatters to invade the land, build some shacks, and destroy enough vegetation to disqualify it from environmental protection. A resident of Lar Nacional explained this common sense to me in a discussion about obeying the law: "If you walk the straight and narrow, then they will say about you 'look: he does

everything correctly; he won't succeed at anything in life. Somebody speeding will crash into him because he stopped at a red light.'"

Chapter 7: Urban Citizens

1. That it is generally only the most active members of neighborhood organizations who exhibit the competence of law talk is beside the point for my arguments about new citizenship. Although the rank and file typically do not understand the complex legal reasoning involved and are unable to produce it, they refer problems to those who do—namely, their community leaders and attorneys—rather than express their frustrations violently. Neighborhood leaders and archives constitute a collective resource that residents as a group construct and utilize individually and collectively when necessary. Thus, law talk among them is publicized, generalized, and becomes public knowledge.

2. The electoral data for São Paulo are taken from Lamounier's (1980) detailed analysis of municipal elections in 1970, 1974, and 1978, particularly tables 4, 19, and 20. This study uses, as did most others during the 1980s, a subdivision of the municipality into eight "homogeneous areas," developed by state's Department of Economy and Planning to facilitate comparisons (SEPLAN 1977). This subdivision uses average family income as its basic criterion of classification, correlated with six other variables to establish sets of districts with the greatest similarity. These other variables are sanitary facilities, piped potable water, population density, population increase, infant mortality, and residential use. Their correlation with family income generated a total of eight "homogeneous areas," Area I having the best socioeconomic conditions and Area VIII the worst in the city.

3. See F. Cardoso (1980) on political parties during this period.

4. Several sources discuss the development of SABs until the 1970s. My discussion is drawn primarily from Singer (1980), Moisés (1978), and Moisés et al. (1981). See also Alvarez 1993. Afro-Brazilian organizations in São Paulo—including nineteenth-century black brotherhoods—have also consistently mobilized their members to fight for urban improvements (see Andrews 1991).

5. My emphasis here is on urban citizenship and neighborhood mobilization, not the new social movements per se, about which there is an extensive and well-known literature. On social movements in São Paulo, see Singer and Brant (1980), R. Cardoso (1983), and, in English, Kowarick (1994). For an overview and case studies in Latin America, see Oxhorn (1999) and Escobar and Alvarez (1992). I learned about the histories of the SABs and other collective activities in Lar Nacional and Jardim das Camélias from interviews with participants and original documents they retained. Additional and corroborating information about Jardim das Camélias comes from Caldeira 1984 (which briefly locates the SAB in the larger context of the district) and 1990 (which discusses the range of neighborhood activities and especially women's participation).

6. I base the neologism "revindicatory" on the Brazilian *reivindicar*, which means to make claims or demands and which the new working-class social movements ubiquitously used to means claims based on the recognition of rights. English has no concise equivalent in common usage. I take the liberty of anglicizing

the Brazilian word to convey this important concept succinctly. For the substantive form *reivindicação*, I sometimes use claim right, claim demand, and demand-action in addition to "revindication."

7. CEBs began to take root in Brazilian cities in the early 1970s, after influential clergy called for the creation of local ecclesiastical organizations that would be dedicated to the needs of the poor in the urban peripheries, use biblical exegesis to analyze their social problems, and become the foundation of a new "people's Catholicism" in Brazil. The CEBs provided an alternative social space, under the protection of the Church, for a variety of collective and politicized activities that developed in the idiom and under the cover of religious ones, including Mothers' Clubs, discussion groups, educational courses, collective purchases, and mobilizations for neighborhood causes. At their peek in the early 1980s, there were as many as eighty thousand CEBs throughout Brazil. The extent to which they politicized religion was a source of conflict for the Catholic Church. CEBs generally avoided explicit party identification. However, many in São Paulo openly identified with the PT, which in turn became known as the "party of the CEBs." For an overview of the CEBs, see Camargo, Muniz, and Pierucci 1980. A more comprehensive study is Azevedo 1987. A key partisan work in the debate about the politicization of the CEBs as a "church of the oppressed" is Frei Betto 1981.

8. See Heller (1976) for the theory of need in Marx—and related socialist political economy and revolutionary action—which she presents in terms of conflicts between the market needs of capital and the social needs of people (of "socially developed humanity") in determining questions of production, distribution, and welfare.

9. I know of no thorough history of the intellectual sources that account for the triumph of rights-based discourses in Brazil. Surely such a history would consider the global rise in the 1970s of rights discourse as the central component of democratization and, somewhat later, the internationally sponsored promotion of human rights directed at nations like Brazil under dictatorship. Additionally, it would investigate the influence of certain global currents on Brazilian leftist intellectuals with grassroots affiliations, particularly of the PT, and on intellectuals of the opposition to dictatorship generally. Important is the impact of the work of Antonio Gramsci on the Brazilian legitimation of democracy over revolution and the insistence that democracy must transform society and culture and not just the political system. For a discussion of the "Gramscian turn," see Dagnino 1998, though the Left in Brazil habitually distrusted "bourgeois rights" and had little to say about the foundation of rights in Marxist thought. Of greater importance for the "rights turn" in the urban social movements was the influence of Henri Lefebvre's (1968a, 1968b) work on "rights to the city" and "everyday life" as the arena of political struggle, Manuel Castells's (1972, 1983) on the "urban question and grassroots movements," and David Harvey's (1973) on "social justice and the city." These ideas captured the imaginations of planners, architects, lawyers, and social scientists, who promoted the urban social movements and who eventually became leaders of NGOs and local government. I would, moreover, point to the significance of classically liberal arguments for the rule of law and for the respect of rights to property and political citizenship. These also framed the broad

coalition against dictatorship and helped to legitimate rights as the currency of a national project of democratization.

10. Based on my investigation of court records, the land conflict in Lar Nacional appears to have the following origins. Some aspects of this genealogy remain inscrutable, which is not surprising given the nature of the overlapping frauds involved. Nevertheless, as a general account, it is not improbable. Four parties claimed to own large tracts of land in the region that include the subdivision of Lar Nacional: Lar Nacional Ltda., Pérola de Sá Franco, Humberto Reis Costa, and João Boaventura Fernandes Pereira. The first registered its acquisition of the land from José Thomaz de Sant'ana in 1967 at the 9th Cartório of Real Estate Registries. This transaction was based on Sant'ana's acquisition, registered in 1926 at the 3rd Cartório, from Benedito José de Assis. The latter held the oldest deed I could find, registered in archdiocese records of 1889. Sant'ana then sold a parcel of land in 1972 to Pérola de Sá Franco that appears to overlap with the one he sold to Lar Nacional Ltda., even though both transactions were registered at the same *cartório*. Reis Costa's claim is based on the "amicable division" of a gigantic parcel, registered at the 11th Cartório in 1952. As the property basis of this division is not apparent in the registry, such a friendly agreement immediately raises my suspicion as a common stratagem of *grileiros*. In any case, Reis Costa's part of the deal included the Estate of André de Jesus which seems to date from the 1880s and which includes the area of Lar Nacional. Finally, in 1966, Fernandes Pereira purchased the same Estate of André Jesus from Fausto Rodrigues Tavares, who claimed to have acquired the inheritance rights to these lands two years earlier and who was also a manager (and perhaps partner) of Lar Nacional Ltda. In 1966, Fernandes Pereira brought a possessory suit against Reis Costa, who countersued. Although the former won at the 6th Circuit Civil Court, an appellate court reversed the decision in 1972 and awarded possession to the latter. However, before Reis Costa could complete execution, the Federal Union and the State of São Paulo intervened. Each claimed to be rightful owner because the land lay within an extinct Indian village that each disputed. As a result, the case went to the Supreme Court in Brasília where it languished without further action for the next thirty years.

11. Dated 16 October 1972 (author's archive), this report is a court document that contains a list of the 210 houses the officials found. It specifies the names of 193 occupants and notes that ten were renters. The presumption is that the other 183 were owners. The report lists the remaining seventeen houses as unoccupied.

12. Lar Nacional Ltda. initially reacted to the possessory action between Fernandes Pereira and Reis Costa by filing a petition to exclude its holdings in the area, approximately 221,000 m². It argued that it was a third party to the dispute and therefore excluded from the judgment and, moreover, had legitimate ownership rights. The courts accepted this argument, but only partially granted the petition: although they excluded other areas that the company claimed, they refused to do so for the neighborhood called Lar Nacional. Rather, they decided that the company's ownership claim to this area of 96,478 m² was equivocal. Although it did not rule on which claims to this land were not dubious, its decision left the neighborhood subject to Reis Costa's writ of repossession.

13. Economically, Lar Nacional is a mixed working-class neighborhood, typical of the peripheries of São Paulo. In a 2004 survey of 121 houses (all owner occupied) in the principal area of the title dispute, I found the following profile of their heads of household: 51% engaged in some kind of economic activity and 49% did not. Among the former, 36% were legally registered in their economic activity, 10% were unregistered, 32% were regularly self-employed, and 14% did odd jobs. With regard to income, 77% made 5 minimum salaries or less, 47% made 3 or less, and 5% made more than 8. Almost all the households in Lar Nacional have several bread winners, although the number in each is rarely stable for long.

14. In the early 1980s, various factors combined to depoliticize the CEBs generally. These include Vatican promotion of religious orthodoxy and its rebuke of the "People's Church" and Liberation Theology in Brazil, poor performance of the PT in the 1982 elections, and continued local conflict about the nature of the evangelical mission. This depoliticization chilled CEB-SAB relations throughout São Paulo. See Della Cava (1989) for discussion.

15. In the 2004 survey of the 121 houses, I found the following levels of SAB participation and legal representation among heads of household: 96 are members, 20 are not, and 5 are uncategorized for one reason or another. Of the total, 107 (88%) claim to participate in SAB meetings. Participants thus included 11 nonmembers. To defend their property interests, 94 (78%) had hired a lawyer and 18 had not. On 9, I had no information. Of the 94 legally represented owner-residents, 91 had hired Margarido, the SAB's attorney. Of the 18 who said they had no lawyer, the reason given by almost half was inability to afford the legal expenses. One claimed to have legal title, 2 lacked any documentation for their lot, 2 claimed not to know about the dispute, and 2 to be too confused. I would only describe 1 of the 18 as a "free rider," because he considered the problem a collective one and felt that he would therefore benefit from the legal efforts of the others. The one claiming legal title was the only resident out of the 116 who responded definitively to have purchased from Reis Costa. The rest had either bought directly from the development firm Lar Nacional (81) or from those who had (34). Out of the entire 185 houses surveyed for tenure status in Lar Nacional, 87% were owner-occupied, 6% rented, 2% had commercial use, and the remaining 5% lacked information. There were no cases of squatting.

16. The SAB's mobilizations always insist on speaking with the highest-level official because, as a former president told me "we had already suffered so much because secretaries would stuff our petitions in a drawer; so, we ended up becoming shrewd."

17. Robert Gay (2006: 207–12) proposes "thick, thin, disguised, and denied exchanges" to refine the concept of clientelism. I agree with Gay that democratization in Brazil has created hybrid political forms and that "textbook definitions of clientelism tend to be simplistic and flawed" (197). It may be, as he argues, that in his case of a favela in Rio de Janeiro the neighborhood association's denial of clientelism only produced another form of clientelism disguised as democratic citizenship, which amounts to a "clientalization of democracy" (212). Yet it seems to me difficult to conceive of a politics of citizenship at all, much less one

freed from clientelism, if the criterion is that "public works [be] emptied of their political content" (211). Indeed, insofar as practices of citizenship concern rights and rights concern power, they are always tangled up with complex relations of exchange. I will show in the next section that Brazil's differentiated citizenship, with its special-treatment rights, systematically converts rights into privilege and duty into favor but that its insurgent citizenship counters this conversion.

18. On housing and urban administration movements, see Silva 1990; Bonduki 1992.

19. Two plenary organizations were largely responsible for the national coordination of popular constitutional initiatives: the National Movement for the Constitutional Assembly founded in Rio de Janeiro in early 1985 and the Pro-Popular Participation Plenums begun in São Paulo at the same time. The history of this popular participation in the assembly is related in Michiles et al. (1989). My discussion derives from this source and from the participation of the SABs in Jardim das Camélias and Lar Nacional.

20. The representativity of the 12,265,854 signatures may be viewed two ways. The rules established that each elector could sign a maximum of three popular amendments. That constraint suggests two interpretations. Either each signature represents one citizen-elector or each elector signed the maximum of three proposals. The first hypothesis yields 12 million citizen-signers or 18% of the electorate. The second yields 4 million signers, or 6%. As petition drives used both methods of gathering signatures, it is reasonable to split the difference and consider that the 12 million signatures represents 12% of the electorate.

21. On the new forms of democratic participation and association, see Avritzer 2002 (for a comparative analysis in Latin America) and 2004 (for essays on São Paulo). For a discussion of participatory budgeting, see Abers 1998 and Santos 1998; and for new democratic initiatives in urban planning, Caldeira and Holston 2005. In her moving work on death squad assassinations of street children, Scheper-Hughes (2006) discusses the mobilizations against this violence of those inspired by the new constitutional rights and legislation to protect children. See Fraser 1990 on the democratic vitality of multiple publics.

22. Essays in Stepan 1989 offer a good sample.

23. See discussion in chapter 5.

24. Barbosa's maxim is "Justice consists in treating the equal equally and the unequal unequally according to the measure of their inequality." See chapter 1 for discussion.

25. Typically, people justified affirmative action by arguing that "if there weren't a quota, the black would never enter university," as one resident said. However, two members of the SAB in Lar Nacional who strongly identify with being black were against it in any form.

26. See Caldeira 2000 for an analysis of the rejection of human rights for criminals and support for police violence. See also the next chapter.

27. As one resident of Jardim das Camélias explained, "I felt like a citizen. But I also felt afraid. To tell you the truth, I was shaking, because I never had to go to court before. I kept thinking that if I were a criminal, I would be calm, because the bad I would have already done. But if you are an honest citizen, you are afraid. It's true."

Chapter 8: Dangerous Spaces of Citizenship

1. Some of the work on these topics includes Adorno 1995; Arantes 2000; Caldeira 2000; Chevigny 1995; Fix 2001; Holston 1991b; Holston and Caldeira 1998; Paixão 1988; Paoli 1982; Pinheiro 1983; Scheper-Hughes 1992; Telles 2004; Zaluar 1985, 2004.

2. Let me remind the reader that by civil I refer not to the classic liberal separations of state and nonstate, political society and civil society, public and private, or to any dichotomies that typically derive from the state/nonstate divide. Rather, I use civil to specify the aspect of citizenship rights, practices, institutions, and values that concerns both individual liberty and security and justice as the means to all other rights. Thus, civil citizenship relates society and state ambiguously, not dichotomously: it differentiates society from the political system by defending the former from the abuses of the latter; however, it also integrates the two by utilizing state power to confront relations of inequality and domination within society itself and to shape people into certain kinds of citizens.

3. In 2005–2006, the following scandals befouled many in office, especially PT politicians and their allies in other parties. Huge bribes involved gaming, post office services, electoral propaganda, and school lunch programs, some with illegal payments to foreign bank accounts. However, these paled in comparison with two systematic corruptions of congress: the "big monthly" payments the PT apparently made with public funds to coalition members in congress to secure their votes, and the kickback scheme of the "mafia of bloodsuckers," in which federal deputies and senators attached riders to bills authorizing the purchase of overpriced ambulances for nearly five hundred municipalities. There have also been revelations of illegal abuse of power (one bringing down the all-powerful finance minister) and of vulgar corruptions (a PT operative caught at the airport with rolls of undeclared party money stuffed into his underpants — imagine the burlesque of fashion that ensued!). The best sources of information about these scandals are the newspapers and magazines (e.g., *Folha de S. Paulo* and *Veja*) and their online sites.

4. *Estado de S. Paulo*, 22 August 2006, A6. Initially, the PT's reaction to the accusations of corruption was to deny them and instead accuse "the elite" of attempting a coup. After the ambulance mafia was exposed, however, party faithful have increasingly justified corruption as natural to politics — an inherently dirty game of power at which elites have always excelled — and/or acceptable as PT practice because — as "the people" know — its ends are "noble." Populist and expedient justifications were abundant in the print media, for example, during the week of 21 August.

5. When the PCC leader, Marco Willians Herbas Camacho (aka Marcola) was asked during a congressional inquiry if the PCC finances the election of representatives, he replied: "No. It's easier to buy those already elected." *Caros Amigos* 10 (111)2006: 28.

6. This type of citizen conflict is especially apparent in democracies (often labeled liberal) where the state is committed to a constitution that provides citizens with formally equal rights but far less committed to providing them with equal means to realize those rights. As a result, the inequalities of class transform

the formal equalities of citizenship into substantive differences, as those who have the social and economic means to take advantage of their formal rights outperform those who do not. Thus, the unorganized poor in liberal democracies are typically formal citizens without much substantive citizenship. See Bendix (1977: 122–126) for more on these points.

7. The possible exhaustion of democracy I prefigure should not be confused with the current corruptions of the PT, which will surely affect its legitimacy as a political party. However, insurgent citizenship does not depend on the PT or, indeed, on parties as its only source of the political. It has a vitality and fatigue of its own. To understand these processes, an anthropological approach problematizes citizenship by expanding its study beyond narrow and totalizing conceptions of the political. I see this view as aligned with Rabinow's (2005: 41) proposal for an anthropology that "invent[s] means of observing and analyzing how various *logoi* are currently being assembled into contingent forms."

8. In his work on citizenship, civility, and violence, Balibar (2001:15) reminds us of the usefulness of the term "civility" to refer to conditions in which "politics as a collective participation in public affairs is possible." I use incivility to signify the nonviolent but still in-your-face assertion by the discriminated against that producing these conditions is both urgent and difficult. I use it to refer to the entanglement of citizenships at the moment when equality is an actual threat, when those who demand it threaten existing inequalities and those who are privileged by them feel threatened.

9. I discuss more comprehensively the realm of traffic and its relation to city planning and citizenship elsewhere (1989). See also O'Donnell (1988) for an insightful discussion of car traffic and the privatization of the public in São Paulo.

10. See Goldstein (2003) for an ethnographic account of the "aesthetics of domination" between middle-class employers and lower-class domestic workers in Rio de Janeiro.

11. I consider the development of this tripartite organization of domestic space and society elsewhere (1989: 174–82).

12. The reader may imagine that the percentage of middle- and upper-class residents in São Paulo who employ live-in help must be small and ever shrinking and that, as a result, the service quarters of their apartments are now used mostly as storage closets. Both assumptions would be false. Domestic day labor is universal in these households and live-in employees, especially nannies, remain fairly common. All middle-class dwellings have service quarters with small bedrooms for domestics. There is nothing past tense about this setup. They are never designed as closets. Even if some are used for storage, Brazilians never misrecognize them and the socioeconomic order of intimate distance they symbolize at the heart of the household.

13. Tagging has in recent years become ubiquitous in São Paulo. Taggers are invariably young men from the peripheries. They transcend their home neighborhoods by inscribing wall surfaces throughout the city with their names, in a repetitive verticalized script that most residents condemn as ugly, unintelligible, and criminal. They intrude in all types of space and especially target surfaces that seem least accessible. Their transgressions leave no cityscape unmarked, so that

citizens cannot avoid seeing them. By these means, taggers contest the security-driven privatization of São Paulo and create a new visual public of city surfaces that asserts the presence of the peripheries and their inequalities. This in-your-face demonstration is their objective, though most Paulistanos consider it proof of the deterioration of urban space and its public.

14. On middle-class consumer identities in São Paulo, see O'Dougherty 2002.

15. Related to the privatization I consider here is the sort generally associated with the neoliberalism that has also taken root in Brazil along with political democratization. I discuss its development in Caldeira and Holston (2005). It entails a new logic of social management and planning that replaces state-sponsored projects of modernization. In this regard, privatization signifies various things: It means selling off state-owned enterprises (including basic utilities) to private interests and cutting state subsidies to national production. It signifies undoing some social rights of corporatist labor legislation. It means contracting out to private enterprises social services that the state used to provide (from school lunches to prisons). It entails hiring NGOs with public funds to develop policy that government agencies used to produce. This kind of privatization undercuts the idea that the state is a direct producer of the national public sphere through state-owned and managed industry, public works, and welfare. It conditions the privatizations of the city described here by cutting public funds to municipal governments and requiring citizens to use private investments for urban development, both of which encourage people to rely on private security and fortification to deal with their fears of crime and violence.

16. See Paoli and Duarte (2004) on the problematic expression of diversity and Meyer (1991) on the ideology of progress in São Paulo.

17. On these conventions of ambiguity and subterfuge, see Meyer and Montes (1985) on *jeitinho*; Yudíce (1994) on *samba*; and DaMatta (1979) on *carnaval* and *malandragem*.

18. One owner in my building has not paid the monthly maintenance fees for almost ten years. With compounded fees, fines, and interest, he owes us — the rest who must support his use of the building — more than the apartment is worth. The building filed suit eight years ago. But he doesn't seem concerned. He is a pro at manipulating the justice system: he is a lawyer who has his own law firm to assist.

19. *Estado de S. Paulo*, 7 December 2005. The lawyer's rule of thumb is that litigation in Brazil takes on average fifteen years to work its way through the courts. Land disputes generally require, as in my cases, much more. It is, however, difficult to be precise about judicial statistics as they are rarely computerized or integrated.

20. Information about São Paulo's police ombudsman comes from Cunha (2000). I must add that there are many dedicated judges and prosecutors who struggle valiantly against entrenched corporate privileges and legalistic jurisprudence to bring greater justice to the justice system. The Public Ministry has also developed into a proactive and sometimes effective prosecutorial institution, charged with defending public interest. See essays in Vigliara and Macedo Júnior (1999) and Sadek (2000). The federal CPI on judicial corruption was convoked in 1997 with the ultimate objective of developing a comprehensive reform of the courts. Not surprisingly, many judges refused to testify or cooperate.

Nevertheless, the CPI uncovered a number of cases of such colossal corruption that it gained public legitimacy that even the judiciary could not deny.

21. With regard to urban crimes generally, of all incidents reported by the civil police for São Paulo in 1993 (389,178), only 20.4% resulted in the police fact-finding proceedings necessary for judicial action. For the last decade, that rate varied between 17% and 21%. In 1993, it was a low 73.8% for crimes of murder, though for drug dealing it reached 94.4% (SEADE, unpublished data). Although I do not have data on the number of conflicts that actually go to trial, it is widely thought to be low. Moreover, conviction does not necessarily mean jail and rarely does for police officers and middle-class defendants.

22. In the U.S. legal system of diffuse review, a ruling of unconstitutionality has *erga omnes* effects: it invalidates the legislative statute or administrative act in question and establishes a precedent, in addition to affecting the case at hand. In common law, a precedent may involve a novel question of law or an interpretation of an existing statute. In either case, under the doctrine of *stare decisis*, it will serve as the standard to decide future cases that rely on it or are distinguished from it, unless there are extremely compelling reasons to overturn it and establish a new precedent. Thus, this doctrine both allows judges to make law as a response to new legal and social questions and restrains them from using their powers to do so.

23. The movement of alternative law challenges Brazil's dominant legal positivism, contesting its focus on the state as the sole source of law and its view of legal norms as self-regulating. Alternative law has developed over the last two or three decades in some law schools, especially in the southern states and Brasília, and draws inspiration from international critical legal studies, legal pluralism, and urban social movements. It rejects the doctrinal position that there is only one unified law, that of the state, that this law has no gaps and contradictions, and that judges should apply statutes without seeking to accommodate social circumstances. Rather, the movement argues that to achieve justice, law must be based on and interpreted with reference to contemporary social relations as a vital source of rights. Thus, it stresses that legal norms can never be dissociated from social conflict and that new kinds of demand rights are always developing out of collective struggles. Usually waged in communities on the margins of the state, these struggles yield new norms of consensual behavior that are embodied in social practices traditionally excluded from formal legal considerations. Thus, alternative law proposes a dynamic relation between law and society, in which state law is continually reconceived in relation to social change. Affiliated jurists have created significant organizations of legal assistance. In São Paulo, these include the Center for Studies in Law and Study (at the University of São Paulo) and Pólis. Works that inspired the movement include Santos (1977) and Lyra Filho (1982). Three useful edited volumes are Falcão (1984), Sousa (1990), and Arruda (1991). See also Faria (1991).

24. For example, Article 7, paragraph XI provides urban and rural workers the rights to "participate in the profits [of their employers], or the results, not linked to remuneration, and, exceptionally, to participate in the administration of the enterprise, as defined by law." As this enabling legislation has never been enacted, the right is not exercisable, except voluntarily.

25. Most significant is legislation creating a new Public Ministry (1993), the City Statute (2001, see later in the chapter), a new Civil Code (2002/2003) and social security reform (2003/2005).

26. For example, among comments in English, Przewoski (1991: 84) calls it "temporizing" and Rosenn (1990) "transient."

27. Although the High Court retains powers of both diffuse and abstract review, the constitution made its job somewhat more manageable by limiting its jurisdiction as the court of last appeal only to cases that raise constitutional questions.

28. Articles 170 to 192 define an economic order that government policies often seem to contradict. An embodiment of new social rights, Article 170 establishes that "the economic order has as its objective to secure for all a dignified existence in accordance with the principles of social justice." Subsequent articles define these principles as "consumer protection, environmental protection, reduction of regional and individual inequalities, and the pursuit of full employment." Does the last render readjustment policies unconstitutional? Does the precept of a dignified existence invalidate the current minimum salary? Many jurists believe they do. The point is that only the judiciary can resolve such conflicts. Unless these provisions are eliminated from the constitution, the courts will eventually be forced to intervene in these questions of public policy and engage interpretations of law on the basis of ethical and not only technical merit.

29. See Caldeira and Holston (2005) for an analysis of the City Statute that space precludes here. We show that, predictably, its innovations in the democratization of urban development produce contradictions as well. As it requires citizen participation, it also allows for powerful corporations and real estate interests to engage these same innovations and to compete with the organized poor in shaping urban initiatives. The outcome is mixed. We show, by way of example, that the same instruments of the law are used to generate new forms of spatial equalization and segregation and, in these ways, both promote and undermine the expansion of democratic citizenship.

30. See chap. 7, and chap. 7, n. 10.

31. Teresa Caldeira and I developed the following analysis of violence and the perverse use of democratic discourses of rights together. See Caldeira (2006) for her interpretation of these issues.

32. The most important *comandos* are the PCC of São Paulo and the CV (Comando Vermelho) of Rio. In São Paulo, others include the Seta Satânica, CRBC (Comando Revolucionário Brasileiro da Criminalidade), and TCC (Terceiro Comando da Capital).

33. This and the other manifestoes I discuss were published in the major Brazilian newspapers (such as the *Estado de São Paulo*, the *Folha de São Paulo*, and the *Jornal do Brasil*) and may be consulted in their online archives. In my translations, I have retained original syntax as much as possible. The most useful work on the history and organization of the PCC I have found is a collection of articles and interviews published in an "extra edition" of the monthly magazine *Caros Amigos* (28 May 2006).

34. Following TV broadcast, the manifesto was published in the newspapers (14 August 2006). Parts repeat almost verbatim sections of a report on the RDD

issued in 2003 by the National Council of Criminal and Penitentiary Policy of the Ministry of Justice.

35. See note 1 for a sample of research. In São Paulo during this period, the homicide rate was around 65 per 100,000 inhabitants per year. However, among young men aged fifteen to twenty-four, it was an extraordinary 247 in 2002 (see map 5.5a)! For a discussion of police violence and its support in public policy and opinion, see Caldeira and Holston 1999 and especially Caldeira 2000 and 2002. The most lethal year of police action in metropolitan São Paulo was 1992, when military police killed 1,301 civilians, including 111 at the Casa de Detenção. In the same year, the Los Angeles police killed 23 and the New York police 27 (Chevigny 1995: 46, 67). After intense international pressure, the number killed dropped to 183 in 1996. But it rose again to over 500 by 2000, at which level it remains. The data below for 2006 are from Ibope (Instituto Brasileiro de Opinião Publica e Estatística), published in the Estado de S. Paulo (28 August 2006, A1, C1, C3).

36. Luiz Antonio Fleury Filho, Folha de São Paulo, 28 November 1989. Fleury was subsequently elected governor (1991–1995). Similar "tough talk" from the governor of Rio de Janeiro explicitly dehumanized citizens as criminal suspects. A few days after police killed thirteen suspected drug dealers in the favela of New Brasília, he issued the following statement: "These violent criminals have become animals. . . . They are animals. They can't be understood any other way. That's why encounters with them can't be civilized. These people don't have to be treated in a civilized way. They have to be treated like animals." (11 May 1995, cited in Cavallaro 1997: 10). It was never shown that those killed were drug dealers, and it was immediately established that some of the victims were not criminals of any sort.

37. The Comaroffs (2004) describe a different but related spectacle of reordering in postcolonial South Africa: not actual police violence, but dramatic enactments of crime and punishment by police, which aim to (re)establish plausible representations of social order and law in a world where the state seems incapable of ensuring either.

38. "Qualidade na Polícia Militar do Estado de São Paulo," Polícia Militar do Estado de São Paulo, http://www.polmil.sp.gov.br/qtotal/evolucao.asp.

39. In 1995, a founder of the PCC, Misael Aparecido da Silva, drafted a manifesto (the "Party of Crime") articulating the gang's identity. It became, along with the statute, required reading for gang initiation. The manifesto combines the rationalities of crime and revolution under the banner of justice, demonstrating a fusion of criminal gangs, anticapitalist politics, terrorist actions, and revolutionary parties found in subversive organizations worldwide—e.g., the ANC, IRA, Black Panthers, FARC, and jihad groups—though, as the PCC acknowledges, members joined as and remain criminals. The manifesto states: "The cowardly, capitalist, and corrupt . . . system itself created the Party [the PCC]. The Party is part of a dream of struggle; today we are strong where the enemy is weak. Our revolution . . . began in the penitentiary system and its objective is greater: to revolutionize the governmental system, to end this capitalist regime in which the rich grow and survive massacring the poorer class. As long as children die of hunger, sleep in the streets, have no opportunity for education and a dignified life,

the violence will only increase. Today's children who humiliate themselves begging will tomorrow, through crime, transform their dreams into reality, with all hatred, all revolt, for the oppressed of today will be the oppressor of tomorrow. What is not won with words will be won with violence and a gun in hand. Our goal is to affect the powerful, the owners of the world, and the unequal justice; we are not criminals by choice and yes we are subversives and idealists" (reproduced in *Caros Amigos*, 28 May 2006, 12).

40. International watchdog organizations use standard survey criteria of electoral procedure and political freedom to arrive at the number of electoral democracies in the world. As I have discussed elsewhere in greater detail (Holston 2006), I am critical of their electoral approach. However, I use their data to grasp both the importance of elections and their limitations in evaluating democracy. These surveys indicate that political democracy has taken root in remarkably varied ground since the mid-1970s. For example, based on research that Freedom House (1978–2001) has compiled since 1972 in annual world surveys of political rights and civil liberties, I calculate that during this quarter century, the number of electoral democracies more than doubled. If we exclude countries with a population of less than one million, it tripled. During this period, approximately 76 countries changed from nondemocratic to democratic political systems. In 1972, there were 52 electoral democracies, constituting 33% of the world's 160 sovereign nation-states. By 2000, the number had risen to 120 democracies out of 192 states, or 63% of the total, for a net gain of 68 democratic states. If it took 200 years of political change from the Age of Revolution to generate about 50 democratic states by 1970, it took only 20 more years to yield another 50.

41. For further discussion on the limitations of applying North Atlantic models of democracy to the postcolonial South, see Holston and Caldeira 1998 for Brazil; Comaroff and Comaroff 1997 for Southern Africa.

Bibliography

Abers, Rebecca. 1998. Learning democratic practice: Distributing government resources through popular participation in Porto Alegre, Brazil. In *Cities for Citizens: Planning and the Rise of Civil Society in a Global Age*, ed. Mike Douglass and John Friedmann, 39–65. Chichester: John Wiley & Sons.

Adorno, Sérgio. 1995. Discriminação racial e justiça criminal em São Paulo. *Novos Estudos* 43: 45–63.

Agamben, Giorgio. 1998. *Homo Sacer: Sovereign Power and Bare Life*. Stanford: Stanford University Press.

Alvarez, Sonia E. 1993. "Deepening" democracy: Popular movement networks, constitutional reform, and radical urban regimes in contemporary Brazil. In *Mobilizing the Community: Local Politics in the Era of the Global City*, ed. Robert Fisher and Joseph Kling, 191–219. Newbury Park: Sage Publications.

Anderson, Frank Maloy. 1908. *The Constitutions and Other Select Documents Illustrative of the History of France, 1789–1907*. 2nd ed. New York: Russell & Russell.

Andrade Sobrinho, J. M. 1942. A casa das setes peças. *Revista de Organização Científica* 11 (125): 10–19.

Andrews, George R. 1991. *Blacks and Whites in São Paulo, Brazil, 1888–1988*. Madison: University of Wisconsin Press.

Applewhite, Harriet Branson. 1993. *Political Alignment in the French National Assembly, 1789–1791*. Baton Rouge: Louisiana State University Press.

Arantes, Rogério Bastos. 2000. Ministério Público e corrupção política em São Paulo. In Sadek 2000, 39–156.

Arendt, Hannah. 1958. *The Human Condition*. Chicago: University of Chicago Press.

Aristotle. 1962. *Nicomachean Ethics*. Translated by Martin Ostwald. Indianapolis: Bobbs-Merrill Company.

————. 1978. *The Politics*. Translated by Ernest Barker. New York: Oxford University Press.

Arruda, Edmundo Lima de, Jr., ed. 1991. *Lições de Direito Alternativo*. São Paulo: Editora Académica.

Avritzer, Leonardo. 2002. *Democracy and the Public Sphere in Latin America*. Princeton: Princeton University Press.

————, ed. 2004. *A Participação em São Paulo*. São Paulo: Editora Unesp.

Azevedo, Marcello de, S.J. 1987. *Basic Ecclesial Communities: The Challenge of a New Way of Being Church*. Washington, D.C.: Georgetown University Press.

Azevedo, Sérgio, and Luiz Aureliano Andrade. 1982. *Habitação e Poder: Da Fundação da Casa Popular ao Banco Nacional da Habitação*. Rio de Janeiro: Zahar Editores.

Balibar, Etienne. 2001. Outlines of a topography of cruelty: Citizenship and civility in the era of global violence. *Constellations* 8 (1): 15–29.

Barnes, J. A. 1961. Law as politically active: An anthropological view. In *Studies in the Sociology of Law*, ed. Geoffry Sawer, 167–96. Canberra: Australian National University Press.

Bastos, Aureliano Cândido Tavares. 1939a. Memoria sobre Immigração. In *Os Males do Presente e as Esperanças do Futuro*, ed. C. Tavares Bastos, 56–127. São Paulo: Companhia Editora Nacional. Original publication, 1867.

————. 1939b. Reforma Eleitoral e Parlamentar e Constituição da Magistratura. In *Os Males do Presente e as Esperanças do Futuro*, ed. C. Tavares Bastos, 167–336. São Paulo: Companhia Editora Naciona. Original publication, 1873.

Batalha, Wilson de Souza Campos. 1984. *Comentários à Lei de Registros Públicos*, vols. 1 & 2. 3rd ed., rev. and exp. ed. Rio de Janeiro: Forense.

Bendix, Reinhard. 1977. *Nation-Building and Citizenship*. Berkeley: University of California Press.

Benhabib, Seyla. 2002. *The Claims of Culture: Equality and Diversity in the Global Era*. Princeton: Princeton University Press.

Berbel, Márcia Regina. 1999. *A Nação como Artefacto: Deputados do Brasil nas Cortes Portuguesas, 1821–1822*. São Paulo: Editora Hucitec/Fapesp.

Beviláqua, Clóvis. 1956. *Direito das Coisas*. 4th ed. Rio de Janeiro: Forense.

Bobbio, Norberto. 1989. *Democracy and Dictatorship: The Nature and Limits of State Power*. Minneapolis: University of Minnesota Press.

Bomtempi, Sylvio. 1970. *O Bairro de São Miguel Paulista: A Aldeia de São Miguel de Ururaí na História de São Paulo*. São Paulo: Prefeitura Municipal de São Paulo.

Bonduki, Nabil G. 1983. Habitação popular: Contribuição para o estudo da evolução urbana de São Paulo. In *Habitação em Questão*, ed. Lícia do Prado Valladares, 135–68. Rio de Janeiro: Zahar Editores.

————. 1992. *Habitação e Autogestão: Construindo Territórios de Utopia*. Rio de Janeiro: FASE.

————. 1994. The housing crisis in the postwar years. In Kowarick 1994b, 94–120.

———. 1998. *Origens da Habitação Social no Brasil: Arquitetura Moderna, Lei do Inquilinato e Difusão da Casa Própria*. São Paulo: Estação Liberdade: FAPESP.

Bonduki, Nabil G., and Raquel Rolnik. 1979. *Periferias: Ocupação do Espaço e Reprodução da Força do Trabalho*. São Paulo: FAUUSP–Fundação para Pesquisa Ambiental.

Bonifácio de Andrada e Silva, José. 2002. Apontamentos para a civilização dos índios bravos do Império do Brasil. In *José Bonifácio de Andrada e Silva*, ed. Jorge Caldeira, 183–99. *Coleção Formadores do Brasil*. São Paulo: Editora 34.

Boxer, Charles R. 1962. *The Golden Age of Brazil, 1685–1750: Growing Pains of a Colonial Society*. Berkeley: University of California Press.

Brubaker, Rogers. 1992. *Citizenship and Nationhood in France and Germany*. Cambridge: Harvard University Press.

Burns, E. Bradford. 1964. The Enlightenment in two colonial Brazilian libraries. *Journal of the History of Ideas* 25 (July–September): 430–38.

Caldeira, Teresa P. R. 1980. Para que serve o voto? As eleições e o cotidiano na periferia de São Paulo. In *Voto de Desconfiança: Eleições e Mudança Política no Brasil, 1970–1979*, ed. Bolivar Lamounier, 81–115. São Paulo: Editora Vozes/Cebrap.

———. 1984. *A Política dos Outros: O Cotidiano dos Moradores da Periferia e o que Pensam do Poder e dos Poderosos*. São Paulo: Editora Brasiliense.

———. 1988. The art of being indirect: Talking about politics in Brazil. *Cultural Anthropology* 3 (4): 444–54.

———. 1990. Women, daily life and politics. In *Women and Social Change in Latin America*, ed. Elizabeth Jelin, 47–78. London: UNRISD/Zed Books.

———. 2000. *City of Walls: Crime, Segregation, and Citizenship in São Paulo*. Berkeley: University of California Press.

———. 2002. The paradox of police violence in democratic Brazil. *Ethnography* 3 (3): 235–263.

———. 2006. "I came to sabotage your reasoning!" – violence and resignifications of justice in Brazil. In *Law and Disorder in the Postcolony*, ed. Jean Comaroff and John L. Comaroff, 102–49. Chicago: University of Chicago Press.

Caldeira, Teresa P. R., and James Holston. 1999. Democray and violence in Brazil. *Comparative Studies in Society and History* 41 (4): 691–729.

———. 2005. State and urban space in Brazil: From modernist planning to democratic interventions. In *Global Assemblages: Technology, Politics, and Ethics as Anthropological Problems*, ed. Aihwa Ong and Stephen J. Collier, 393–416. Malden, MA: Blackwell Publishing.

Camargo, Cândido Procopio F., et al. 1976. *São Paulo 1975: Crescimento e Pobreza*. São Paulo: Loyola.

———. 1978. *São Paulo: Growth and Poverty*. London: Bowerdean Press. Original edition, 1976.

Camargo, Cândido Procopio F., Beatriz Muniz de Souza, and Antônio Flávio de Oliveira Pierucci. 1980. Comunidades eclesiais de base. In Singer and Brant 1980, 59–81.

Campanhole, Adriano, and Hilton Lobo Campanhole, eds. 2000. *Constituições do Brasil*. 14th ed. São Paulo: Editora Atlas.

Cardoso, Fernando Henrique. 1980. Partidos políticos. In Singer and Brant 1980, 177–205.

Cardoso, Ruth Corrêa Leite. 1983. Movimentos sociais urbanos: balanço crítico. In *Sociedade e Política no Brasil pós-64*, ed. Bernardo Sorj and Maria Hermínia Tavares de Almeida, 215–39. São Paulo: Editora Brasiliense.

Carvalho, José Murilo de. 1981. Modernização frustrada: A política de terras no império. *Revista Brasileira de História*, March: 39–57.

———. 1988. *Teatro de Sombras: A Política Imperial*. Rio de Janeiro: Edições Vértice e IUPERJ.

———. 2001. *Cidadania no Brasil: O Longo Caminho*. Rio de Janeiro: Editora Civilização Brasileira.

Castells, Manuel, 1972. *La Question Urbaine*. Paris: Maspero.

———. 1983. *The City and the Grassroots*. Berkeley: University of California Press.

Cavallaro, James. 1997. *Police Brutality in Urban Brazil*. New York: Human Rights Watch.

Chalhoub, Sidney. 1990. *Visões da Liberdade: Uma História das Últimas Décadas da Escravidão na Corte*. São Paulo: Companhia das Letras.

Chevigny, Paul. 1995. *The Edge of the Knife: Police Violence and Accountability in Six Cities of the Americas*. New York: New Press.

Código Civil. 1990. *Código Civil*. 5th ed. São Paulo: Editora Saraiva.

Cohen, Felix S. 1982. *Handbook of Federal Indian Law*. Charlottesville, VA: Michie Company.

Cohn, Bernard S. 1989. Law and the colonial state in India. In Starr and Collier 1989, 131–52.

Comaroff, Jean, and John L. Comaroff. 2004. Criminal obsessions, after Foucault: Postcoloniality, policing, and the metaphysics of disorder. *Critical Inquiry* 30 (Summer): 800–824.

Comaroff, John L., and Jean Comaroff. 1997. Postcolonial politics and discourses of democracy in Southern Africa: An anthropological reflection on African political modernities. *Journal of Anthropological Research* 53 (2): 123–46.

Conrad, Robert Edgar. 1983. *Children of God's Fire: A Documentary History of Black Slavery in Brazil*. Princeton: Princeton University Press.

Cope, R. Douglas. 1994. *The Limits of Racial Domination: Plebeian Society in Colonial Mexico City, 1660–1720*. Madison: University of Wisconsin Press.

Costa, Emilia Viotti da. 1977. *Da Monarquia à República: Momentos Decisivos*. São Paulo: Editorial Grijalbo.

———. 1985. *The Brazilian Empire: Myths and Histories*. Chicago: University of Chicago Press.

Costa Porto, Walter. 2002. *O Voto no Brasil: Da Colônia à 6ª República*. 2th ed. Rio de Janeiro: Topbooks.

Coutin, Susan Bibler. 2000. *Legalizing Moves: Salvadoran Immigrants' Struggle for U.S. Residency*. Ann Arbor: University of Michigan Press.

Cunha, Luciana Gross. 2000. Ouvidoria de polícia em São Paulo. In Sadek 2000, 259–304.

Cunha, Manuela Carneiro da, ed. 1992. *Legislação Indigenista no Século XIX*. São Paulo: Edusp/Comissão Pró-Indio de São Paulo.

Dagnino, Evelina. 1998. Culture, citizenship, and democracy: Changing discourses and practices of the Latin American Left. In *Cultures of Politics, Politics of Cultures: Re-Visioning Latin American Social Movements*, ed. Sonia E. Alvarez, Evelina Dagnino, and Arturo Escobar, 33–63. Boulder: Westview Press.

DaMatta, Roberto. 1979. *Carnavais, Malandros e Heróis*. Rio de Janeiro: Zahar.

————.1991. "Do you know who you're talking to?" The distinction between individual and person in Brazil. In *Carnivals, Rogues, and Heroes: An Interpretation of the Brazilian Dilemma*, 137–97. Notre Dame: University of Notre Dame Press.

Dean, Warren. 1971. Latifundia and land policy in nineteenth-century Brazil. *Hispanic Historical American Review* 51 (4): 606–25.

de Certeau, Michel. 1984. *The Practice of Everyday Life*. Berkeley: University of California Press.

Degler, Carl N. 1971. *Neither Black nor White: Slavery and Race Relations in Brazil and the United States*. Madison: University of Wisconsin Press.

Della Cava, Ralph. 1989. The "People's Church," the Vatican, and abertura. In Stepan, 1989, 143–67.

Dias, Everardo. 1962. *História das Lutas Sociais no Brasil*. São Paulo: Edaglit.

Dodsworth, Luiz Martins. 1942. Casa e salário. *Revista de Organização Científica* 11 (126): 1–10.

Duarte, Adriano Luiz. 1999. *Cidadania e Exclusão: Brasil 1937–1945*. Florianópolis: Editora da UFSC.

Dubois, Laurent. 2004. *A Colony of Citizens: Revolution & Slave Emancipation in the French Caribbean, 1787–1804*. Chapell Hill: University of North Carolina Press.

Durham, Eunice Ribeiro. 1984. Movimentos sociais: A construção da cidadania. *Novos Estudos Cebrap* 10 (October): 24–30.

Escobar, Arturo, and Sonia Alvarez, ed. 1992. *The Making of Social Movements in Latin America: Identity, Strategy, and Democracy*. Boulder: Westview Press.

Falcão, Joaquim A., ed. 1984. *Confito de Direito de Propriedade: Invasões Urbanas*. Rio de Janeiro: Forense.

Faoro, Raymundo. 1975. *Os Donos do Poder: Formação do Patronato Político Brasileiro*. 2nd ed. São Paulo: Editora da Universidad de São Paulo.

Faria, José Eduardo. 1991. *Justiça e Conflito: Os Juízes em Face dos Novos Movimentos Sociais*. São Paulo: Editora Revista dos Tribunais.

Fausto, Boris. 1984. *Crime e Cotidiano: A Criminalidade em São Paulo, 1880–1924*. São Paulo: Editora Brasiliense.

————. 1986. *Trabalho Urbano e Conflito Social, 1890–1920*. São Paulo: Difel.

Fischer, Brodwyn. 1999. The poverty of law: Rio de Janeiro, 1930–1964. Ph.D. diss., Harvard University.

Fix, Mariana. 2001. *Parceiros da Exclusão*. São Paulo: Boitempo Editorial.

Flory, Thomas. 1981. *Judge and Jury in Imperial Brazil, 1808–1871: Social Control and Political Stability in the New State*. Austin: University of Texas Press.

Foucault, Michel. 1977. *Discipline and Punish: The Birth of the Prison*. New York: Pantheon.

365

————. 1978. *History of Sexuality, Volume I: An Introduction.* New York: Random House.

————. 1991. Governmentality. In *The Foucault Effect: Studies in Governmentality*, ed. Graham Burchell, Colin Gordon, and Peter Miller, 87–104. Chicago: University of Chicago Press.

França, Rubens L., ed. 1977. *Enciclopédia Saraiva do Direito.* São Paulo: Saraiva.

Fraser, Nancy. 1990. Rethinking the public sphere: A contribution to the critique of actually existing democracy. *Social Text* 25/26: 56–80.

Freedom House. 1978–2001. *Freedom in the World: The Annual Survey of Political Rights and Civil Liberties.* New Brunswick: Transaction Publishers.

Frei Betto [Carlos Alberto Libanio Christo]. 1981. *O Que É Comunidade Eclesial de Base.* São Paulo: Editora Brasiliense.

French, John D. 1992. *The Brazilian Workers' ABC: Class Conflict and Alliances in Modern São Paulo.* Chapel Hill: University of North Carolina Press.

Galeotti, Anna Elisabetta. 1993. Citizenship and equality: The place for toleration. *Political Theory* 21 (4): 585–605.

Garcia, Nelson Jahr. 1982. *Estado Novo: Ideologia e Propaganda Política.* São Paulo: Loyola.

Gay, Robert. 2006. The even more difficult transition from clientalism to citizenship: Lessons from Brazil. In *Out of the Shadows: Political Action and the Informal Economy in Latin America*, ed. Patricia Fernández-Kelly and Jon Shefner, 195–217. University Park: Pennsylvania State University Press.

Gluckman, Max. 1956. *Custom and Conflict in Africa.* Oxford: Basil Blackwell.

Goldstein, Donna M. 2003. *Laughter Out of Place: Race, Class, Violence, and Sexuality in a Rio Shantytown.* Berkeley: University of California Press.

Gomes, Mercio P. 2000. *The Indians and Brazil.* Gainesville: University of Florida Press.

Graham, Richard. 1968. *Britain and the Onset of Modernization in Brazil, 1850–1914.* Cambridge: Cambridge University Press.

————, ed. 1990. *The Idea of Race in Latin America, 1870–1940.* Austin: University of Texas Press.

Greenhouse, Carol J. 1989. Interpreting American litigiousness. In Starr and Collier 1989, 252–73.

Grupo de Arquitetura e Planejamento. 1985. *Habitação Popular: Inventário da Ação Governamental.* Rio de Janeiro: Finep.

Gulliver, Philip H. 1963. *Social Control in an African Society.* Boston: Boston University Press.

Guha, Ranajit. 1983. *Elementary Aspects of Peasant Insurgency in Colonial India.* Delhi: Oxford.

Gutwirth, Madelyn. 1993. *Citoyens, citoyennes*: Cultural regression and the subversion of female citizenship in the French Revolution. In *The French Revolution and the Meaning of Citizenship*, ed. Renée Waldinger, Philip Dawson, and Isser Woloch, 17–28. Westport: Greenwood Press.

Hale, Charles R. 2002. Does multiculturalism menace? Governance, cultural rights, and the politics of identity in Guatemala. *Journal of Latin American Studies* 34: 485–524.

Handelmann, Heinrich. 1982. *História do Brasil.* 4th ed. 2 vols. São Paulo: Ed. Itatiaia/Edusp. Original edition, 1860.

Harvey, David. 1973. *Social Justice and the City.* Baltimore: Johns Hopkins University Press.

Hegel, G.W.F. 1967. *The Philosophy of Right.* Translated by T. M. Knox. Oxford: Oxford University Press.

Heller, Agnes. 1976. *The Theory of Need in Marx.* New York: St. Martin's Press.

Hirschman, Albert O. 1977. *The Passions and the Interests: Political Arguments for Capitalism before Its Triumph.* Princeton: Princeton University Press.

Hohfeld, Wesley Newcomb. 1978. *Fundamental Legal Conceptions as Applied in Judicial Reasoning.* Edited by Walter Wheeler Cook. Westport: Greenwood Press.

Holston, James. 1989. *The Modernist City: An Anthropological Critique of Brasília.* Chicago: University of Chicago Press.

———. 1991a. Autoconstruction in working-class Brazil. *Cultural Anthropology* 6 (4): 447–65.

———. 1991b. The misrule of law: Land and usurpation in Brazil. *Comparative Studies in Society and History* 33 (4): 695–725.

———. 2001. Urban citizenship and globalization. In *Global City Regions*, ed. Alan J. Scott, 325–48. New York: Oxford University Press.

———, ed. 1999. *Cities and Citizenship.* Durham: Duke University Press.

———. 2006. Citizenship in disjunctive democracies. In *Citizenship in Latin America*, ed. Joseph S. Tulchin and Meg Rutherford, 75–94. Boulder: Lynne Rienner.

Holston, James, and Arjun Appadurai. 1999. Cities and citizenship. In Holston 1999, 1–18.

Holston, James, and Teresa P. R. Caldeira. 1998. Democracy, law, and violence: Disjunctions of Brazilian citizenship. In *Fault Lines of Democracy in Post-Transition Latin America*, ed. Felipe Agüero and Jeffrey Stark, 263–96. Miami: University of Miami North-South Center Press.

Human Rights Watch. 1991. *Rural Violence in Brazil: An Americas Watch Report.* New York: Human Rights Watch.

IBGE (Instituto Brasileiro de Geografia e Estatística). 1941. *Séries Estatísticas Retrospectivos: Quadros Retrospectivos*, no. 1. Rio de Janeiro: IBGE.

———. 1950–2000. *Censo Demográfico.* Rio de Janeiro: IBGE.

———. 1990. *Estatísticas Históricas do Brasil: Séries Econômicas Demográficas e Sociais de 1550 a 1988.* 2nd ed. Rio de Janeiro: IBGE.

———. 2001. *Anuário Estatístico do Brasil 2000.* Rio de Janeiro: IBGE.

IDORT (Instituto de Organização Racional do Trabalho). 1942. Jornada da habitação econômica. *Revista do Arquivo Municipal* 7 (82) (Março/Abril): 1–338.

Jaher, Frederic Cople. 2002. *The Jews and the Nation: Revolution, Emancipation, State Formation, and the Liberal Paradigm in America and France.* Princeton: Princeton University Press.

Jobim, Nelson, and Walter Costa Porto, ed. 1996. *Legislação Eleitoral no Brasil: Do Século XVI a Nossos Dias.* Brasília: Senado Federal.

Karasch, Mary C. 1987. *Slave Life in Rio de Janeiro: 1808–1850*. Princeton: Princeton University Press.

Keck, Margaret E. 1989. The new unionism in the Brazilian transition. In Stepan 1989, 252–96.

Kettner, James H. 1978. *The Development of American Citizenship, 1608–1870*. Chapel Hill: University of North Carolina Press.

Knight, Alan. 1990. Racism, revolution, and *indigenismo*: Mexico, 1910–1940. In Graham 1990, 71–102.

Kowarick, Lúcio. 1980. *A Espoliação Urbana*. Rio de Janeiro: Paz e Terra.

———, ed. 1994. *As Lutas Sociais e a Cidade—-São Paulo: Passado e Presente*. São Paulo: Editora Paz e Terra.

Kymlicka, Will. 1995. *Multicultural Citizenship*. Oxford: Oxford University Press.

Lamounier, Bolivar. 1980. O voto em São Paulo, 1970–1978. In *Voto de Desconfiança: Eleições e Mudança Política no Brasil: 1970–1979*, ed. Bolivar Lamounier, 15–80. Petrópolis: Editora Vozes Ltda.

Landes, Joan B. 1988. *Women and the Public Sphere in the Age of the French Revolution*. Ithaca: Cornell University Press.

Langenbuch, Juergen Richard. 1971. *A Estruturação da Grande São Paulo: Estudo de Geografia Urbana*. Rio de Janeiro: Instituto Brasileiro de Geografia.

Laxe, João Batista Cortines. [1868] 1962. Câmaras Municipais (Histórico). In *Regimento das Câmaras Municipais*, 3rd ed., 5–32. São Paulo: Editora Obelisco.

Leach, Edmund. 1963. Law as a condition of freedom. In *The Concept of Freedom in Anthropology*, ed. David Bidney, 74–90. The Hague: Mouton.

Lefebvre, Henri. 1968a. *La Vie Quotidienne dans le Monde Moderne*. Paris: Gallimard.

——— 1968b. *Le Droit à la Ville*. Paris: Anthropos.

Levenhagen, Antônio José de Souza. 1982. *Posse, Possessória e Usucapião*. São Paulo: Editora Atlas.

Lima, Ruy Cirne. 1988. *Pequena História Territorial do Brasil: Sesmarias e Terras Devolutas*. 4th ed. Brasília: Escola de Administração Fazendária. Original edition, 1933.

Llewellyn, Karl, and E. A. Hoebel. 1941. *The Cheyenne Way: Conflict and Case Law in Primitive Jurisprudence*. Norman: University of Oklahoma Press.

Locke, John. 1960. *Two Treatises of Government*. Edited by Peter Laslett. Cambridge: Cambridge University Press.

Lopes, Juarez Brandão. 1972. *Desenvolvimento e Mundança Social*. São Paulo: Editora Nacional.

Luz, Nícia Vilela. 1977. Inquietação revolucionária no Sul: a Conjuração Mineira. In *A Época Colonial: Administração, Economia, Sociedade*, 4th ed., ed. Sérgio Buarque de Holanda, 394–405. *História Geral da Civilização Brasileira*, vol. 1.2. Rio de Janeiro: Difel/Difusão Editorial.

Lyra Filho, Roberto. 1982. *O Que é Direito*. São Paulo: Editora Brasiliense.

Machado de Assis, Joaquim Maria. 1944. *Chronicas*. Vol. 4 (1878–1888). São Paulo: W. M. Jackson Editores.

Macpherson, C. B. 1962. *The Political Theory of Possessive Individualism: Hobbes to Locke*. Oxford: Oxford University Press.

Malinowski, Bronislaw. 1926. *Crime and Custom in Savage Society*. London: Kegan Paul.

Marshall, T.H. 1977. Citizenship and social class. In *Class, Citizenship, and Social Development*, 71–134. Chicago: University of Chicago Press.

Marx, Karl. 1967a. *Capital: A Critique of Political Economy*. Translated by Samuel Moore and Edward Aveling. Vol. 1. New York: International Publishers.

Marx, Karl. 1967b. On the Jewish question. In *Writings of the Young Marx on Philosophy and Society*, ed. Lloyd D. Easton and Kurt H. Guddat, 216–48. New York: Anchor Books.

Mattoso, Kátia M. de Queirós. 1986. *To Be a Slave in Brazil, 1550–1888*. New Brunswick: Rutgers University Press.

Maw, Henry Lister. 1829. *Journal of a Passage from the Pacific to the Atlantic: Crossing the Andes in the Northern Provinces of Peru, and Descending the River Marañon or Amazon*. London: J. Murray.

McCann, Bryan. 2004. *Hello, Hello Brazil: Popular Music in the Making of Modern Brazil*. Durham: Duke University Press.

Merry, Sally E. 1990. *Getting Justice and Getting Even: Legal Consciousness among Working-Class Americans*. Chicago: University of Chicago Press.

Merryman, John Henry. 1985. *The Civil Law Tradition: An Introduction to the Legal Systems of Western Europe and Latin America*. 2nd ed. Stanford: Stanford University Press.

Meyer, Marlyse, and Maria Lúcia Montes. 1985. *Redescobrindo o Brasil: A Festa na Política*. São Paulo: T. A. Queiroz.

Meyer, Regina Maria Prosperi. 1991. Metrópole e urbanismo: São Paulo anos 50. Ph.D. diss., Faculdade de Arquitetura e Urbanismo, Universidade de São Paulo, São Paulo.

Meyer, Regina Maria Prosperi, Marta Dora Grostein, and Ciro Biderman. 2004. *São Paulo Metrópole*. São Paulo: Edusp/Imprensa Official do Estado de São Paulo.

Michiles, Carlos, Emmanuel Gonçalves Vieira Filho, Francisco Whitaker Ferreira, João Gilberto Lucas Coelho, Maria da Glória Veiga Moura, and Regina de Paula Santos Prado. 1989. *Cidadão Constituinte: A Saga das Emendas Populares*. Rio de Janeiro: Editora Paz & Terra.

Minow, Martha. 1990. *Making All the Difference: Inclusion, Exclusion and American Law*. Ithaca: Cornell University Press.

Miranda, Pontes de. 1928. *Fontes e Evolução do Direito Civil Brasileiro*. Rio de Janeiro: Pimenta de Mello & C.

Moisés, José Álvaro. 1978. Classes populares e protesto urbano. Ph.D. diss., Department of Political Science, University of São Paulo, São Paulo.

Moisés, José Álvaro, Lúcio Kowarick, Lícia do Prado Valladares, Edison Nunes, Tilman Evers, Clarita Muller-Plantenberg, Stefanie Spessart, and Pedro Jacobi, eds. 1981. *Cidade, Povo e Poder*. São Paulo: CEDEC e Editora Paz & Terra.

Moore, Sally Falk. 1989. History and the redefinition of custom on Kilimanjaro. In Starr and Collier 1989, 277–301.

Morse, Richard M. 1970. *Formação Histórica de São Paulo*. São Paulo: Difel.

Nader, Laura. 1965. The anthropological study of law. *American Anthropologist* 67 (6, pt. 2): 3–32.

369

————. 1969. Styles of court procedure: To make the balance. In *Law in Culture and Society*, ed. Laura Nader, 69–91. Chicago: Aldine Publishing Company.

————. 1989. The crown, the colonists, and the course of Zapotec village law. In Starr and Collier, 1989, 320–44.

Nascimento, Tupinambá Miguel Castro do. 1986. *Posse e Propriedade*. Rio de Janeiro: Aide Editora.

Neiva, Venâncio de Figueiredo. 1938. *Rezumo Biográfico de Jozé Bonifácio de Andrada e Silva, o Patriarca da Independência do Brazil*. Rio de Janeiro: Irmãos Pongetti.

Neves, Lúcia Maria Bastos Pereira das, and Humberto Fernandes Machado. 1999. *O Império do Brasil*. Rio de Janeiro: Editora Nova Fronteira.

Nicolau, Jairo. 2002. *História do Voto no Brasil*. Rio de Janeiro: Jorge Zahar.

O'Donnell, Guillermo. 1988. Situações: Microcenas da privatização do público em São Paulo. *Novos Estudos Cebrap* 22: 45–52.

————. 1992. Transitions, continuities, and paradoxes. In *Issues in Democratic Consolidation: The New South American Democracies in Comparative Perspective*, ed. Scott Mainwaring, Guillermo O'Donnell, and J. Samuel Valenzuela, 17–56. Notre Dame: University of Notre Dame Press.

————. 1993. On the state, democratization and some conceptual problems: A Latin American view with glances at some post-communist countries. *World Development* 21 (8): 1355–69.

O'Dougherty, Maureen. 2002. *Consumption Intensified: The Politics of Middle-Class Daily Life in Brazil*. Durham: Duke University Press.

Okin, Susan Moller. 1992. Women, equality, and citizenship. *Queens's Quarterly* 99 (1): 56–71.

Oliveira, F. Batista de. 1943. Residência mínima. *Revista de Organização Científica* 12 (135): 15–23.

Oliveira, Francisco de. 1972. A economia brasileira: Crítica à razão dualista. *Estudos Cebrap* 2.

Ong, Aihwa. 2003. *Buddha Is Hiding: Refugees, Citizenship, the New America*. Berkeley: University of California Press.

Oxhorn, Philip. 1999. The ambiguous link: Social movements and democracy in Latin America. *Journal of Interamerican Studies and World Affairs* 41 (3): 129–46.

Paixão, Antonio Luiz. 1988. Crime, controle social e consolidação da democracia. In *A Democracia no Brasil: Dilemas e Perspectivas*, ed. Fabio Wanderley Reis and Guillermo O'Donnell, 168–99. São Paulo: Vértice.

Paoli, Maria Celia. 1982. Violência e espaço civil. In *Violência Brasileira*, ed. Roberto Da Matta et al., 45–55. São Paulo: Editora Brasiliense.

————. N.d. Labor law and the state in Brazil, 1930–1950. Ph.D. diss., University of London.

Paoli, Maria Celia, and Adriano Duarte. 2004. São Paulo no plural: espaço público e redes de sociabilidade. In *História da Cidade de São Paulo—A Cidade na Primeira Metade do Século XX*, ed. Paula Porta, 291–339. São Paulo: Editora Paz & Terra.

Pateman, Carole. 1989. *The Disorder of Women*. Stanford: Stanford University Press.

Penteado, Mário. 1943. Habitações populares. *Revista de Organização Científica* 12 (136): 21–28.

Pereira, J. O. de Lima. 1932. *Da Propriedade no Brasil*. São Paulo: Casa Duprat.

Pierson, Donald. 1942. Habitações de São Paulo: Estudo comparativo. *Revista do Arquivo Municipal* 7 (81) (Janeiro/Fevereiro): 199–238.

Pinheiro, Paulo Sérgio. 1983. Violencia sem controle e militarização da polícia. *Novos Estudos Cebrap* 2 (1): 8–12.

PNAD. 1983–2002. *Pesquisa Nacional por Amostra de Domicílios*. Rio de Janeiro: IBGE.

Porter, Kirk H. 1918. *A History of Suffrage in the United States*. Chicago: University of Chicago Press. Repr., Westport: Greenwood Press, 1969.

Porto, José da Costa. 1965. *Estudo sobre o Sistema Sesmarial*. Recife: Imprensa Universitária.

Postero, Nancy Grey. 2007. *Now We Are Citizens: Indigenous Politics in Post-Multicultural Bolivia*. Stanford: Stanford University Press.

Prado, Caio, Jr. 1967. *The Colonial Background of Modern Brazil*. Berkeley: University of California Press.

Przeworski, Adam. 1991. *Democracy and the Market: Political and Economic Reforms in Eastern Europe and Latin America*. New York: Cambridge University Press.

Rabinow, Paul. 2005. Midst anthropology's problems. In *Global Assemblages: Technology, Politics, and Ethics as Anthropological Problems*, ed. Aihwa Ong and Stephen J. Collier, 40–53. Malden, MA: Blackwell Publishing.

Radcliffe-Brown, A. R. 1933. Primitive law. In *Encyclopedia of the Social Sciences*, 9: 202–6. New York: Macmillian Company.

Reis, Arthur Cézar Ferreira. 1968. Os tratados de limites. In *A Época Colonial: Do Descobrimento à Expansão Territorial*, 3rd ed., ed. Sérgio Buarque de Holanda, 364–79. *História Geral da Civilização Brasileira*, vol. 1.1. São Paulo: Difusão Européia do Livro.

Resolo (Departamento de Regularização de Parcelamento do Solo). 2003. *Regularização de Loteamentos no Município de São Paulo*. São Paulo: Portela Boldarini Arquitetura e Urbanismo.

Robbins, Roy M. 1976. *Our Landed Heritage: The Public Domain, 1776–1970*. 2nd ed. Lincoln: University of Nebraska Press.

Rodrigues, Silvio. 1987. *Direito das Coisas*. Vol. 5, *Direito Civil* ed. São Paulo: Editora Saraiva.

Rolnik, Raquel. 1997. *A Cidade e a Lei: Legislação, Política Urbana e Territórios na Cidade de São Paulo*. São Paulo: Fapesp/Studio Nobel.

Rolnik, Raquel, Lúcio Kowarick, and Nadia Somekh, eds. N.d. *São Paulo: Crise e Mudança*. São Paulo: Editora Brasiliense.

Rosenn, Keith S. 1990. Brazil's new constitution: An exercise in transient constitutionalism for a transitional society. *American Journal of Comparative Law* 38 (4): 773–802.

Sadek, Maria Tereza, ed. 2000. *Justiça e Cidadania no Brasil*. São Paulo: Editora Sumaré/Idesp.

Salvador, Frei Vicente do. 1931. *História do Brasil, 1500–1627*. São Paulo: Cia. Melhoramentos.

Santos, Boaventura de Sousa. 1977. The law of the oppressed: The construction and reproduction of legality in Pasargada. *Law & Society Review* 12 (1): 5–126.

———. 1988. *O Discurso e o Poder: Ensaio sobre a Sociologia da Retórica Jurídica.* Porto Alegre: Editora Sergio Antonio Fabris.

———. 1998. Participatory budgeting in Porto Alegre: Towards a redistributive justice. *Politics & Society* 26 (4): 461–510.

Santos, Wanderley Guilherme dos. 1979. *Cidadania e Justiça.* Rio de Janeiro: Campus.

São Paulo Assemblea Constituinte. 1935. *Anais.* Vol. 2. São Paulo: Estado de São Paulo.

Schama, Simon. 1989. *Citizens: A Chronicle of the French Revolution.* New York: Alfred A. Knopf.

Schapera, Issac. 1955. *A Handbook of Tswana Law and Custom.* 2nd ed. London: Oxford University Press.

Scheper-Hughes, Nancy. 1992. *Death without Weeping: The Violence of Everyday Life in Brazil.* Berkeley: University of California Press.

———. 2006. Death squads and democracy in Northeast Brazil. In *Law and Disorder in the Postcolony,* ed. Jean Comaroff and John L. Comaroff, 150–87. Chicago: University of Chicago Press.

Scott, Joan W. 1992. Experience. In *Feminists Theorize the Political,* ed. Judith Butler and Joan W. Scott, 22–40. New York: Routledge.

———. 1996. *Only Paradox to Offer: French Feminists and the Rights of Man.* Cambridge: Harvard University Press.

SEADE (Fundação Sistema Estadual de Analise de Dados). 2000. *Memória das Estatísticas Demográficas.* São Paulo: SEADE.

———. 2004a. *Informações dos Municípios Paulistas.* São Paulo: SEADE.

———. 2004b. *Município de São Paulo.* São Paulo: SEADE.

———. 2004c. *São Paulo— Outrora e Agora: Informações sobre a População da Capital Paulista do Século XIX ao XXI.* São Paulo: SEADE.

SEMPLA (Secretaria Municipal de Planejamento—São Paulo). 1992. *Base de Dados para Planejamento.* São Paulo: SEMPLA.

———. 1995. *Dossiê São Paulo.* São Paulo: PMSP/SEMPLA.

SEPLAN (Secretaria de Economia e Planejamento, Estado de São Paulo). 1979. *Construção de Moradias na Periferia de São Paulo: Aspectos Sócio-Econômicos e Institucionais.* São Paulo: SEPLAN.

———. 1977. *Subdivisão do Município de São Paulo em Áreas Homogêneas.* Vol. Estudos e Pesquisas 13. Estado de São Paulo.

Sewell, William H., Jr. 1988. *Le citoyen / la citoyenne*: Activity, passivity, and the revolutionary concept of citizenship. In *The Political Culture of the French Revolution,* ed. Colin Lucas, 105–23. Oxford: Pergamon Press.

Shirley, Robert Weaver. 1987. *Antropologia Jurídica.* São Paulo: Editora Saraiva.

Shklar, Judith N. 1991. *American Citizenship: The Quest for Inclusion.* Cambridge: Harvard University Press.

Silva, Ana Amélia da. 1990. A luta pelos direitos urbanos: Novas representações de cidade e cidadania. *Espaço e Debates* 30: 29–41.

Silva, De Plácido e. 1967. *Vocabulário Jurídico,* 4 vols. 2nd ed. Rio de Janeiro: Forense.

372

Silva, José Afonso da. 1992. *Curso de Direito Constitucional Positivo*. 9th ed. São Paulo: Malheiros Editores.

Silva, Lígia Osório. 1996. *Terras Devolutas e Latifúndio: Efeitos da Lei de 1850*. Campinas: Editora da Unicamp.

Singer, Paul. 1980. Movimentos de bairro. In Singer and Brant 1980, 83–107.

Singer, Paul, and Vinícius Caldeira Brant, ed. 1980. *São Paulo: O Povo em Movimento*. Petrópolis: Editora Vozes.

Skidmore, Thomas E. 1990. Racial ideas and social policy in Brazil, 1870–1940. In Graham, 7–36.

———. 1993. *Black into White: Race and Nationality in Brazilian Thought*. Durham: Duke University Press.

Smith, Roberto. 1990. *Propriedade da Terra e Transição: Estudo da Formação da Propriedade Privada da Terra e Transição para o Capitalismo no Brasil*. São Paulo: Editora Brasiliense.

Smith, Rogers M. 1997. *Civic Ideals: Conflicting Visions of Citizenship in U.S. History*. New Haven: Yale University Press.

Soboul, Albert. 1974. *The French Revolution, 1787–1799: From the Storming of the Bastille to Napoleon*. New York: Random House.

Sousa, José Geraldo de, Jr., ed. 1990. *O Direito Achado na Rua*. 3rd ed. Brasília: Editora Universidade de Brasília.

Souza, Francisco Belisário Soares de. 1979. *O Sistema Eleitoral do Império*. Brasília: Senado Federal. Original publication, 1872.

Starr, June, and Jane F. Collier, eds. 1989. *History and Power in the Study of Law: New Directions in Legal Anthropology*. Ithaca: Cornell University Press.

Stepan, Alfred, editor. 1989. *Democratizing Brazil: Problems of Transition and Consolidation*. New York: Oxford University Press.

Stiel, Waldemar Corrêa. 1984. *História do Transporte Urbano no Brasil*. Brasília: Editora Pini Ltda.

Taylor, Charles. 1992. The politics of recognition. In *Multiculturalism and The Politics of Recognition*, 25–73. Princeton: Princeton University Press.

Telles, Edward E. 2004. *Race in Another America: The Significance of Skin Color in Brazil*. Princeton: Princeton University Press.

Thomas, Keith. 1963. History and anthropology. *Past & Present* 24 (April): 3–18.

Thompson, E. P. 1963. *The Making of the English Working Class*. New York: Vintage Books.

Toledo, Benedito Lima de. 1996. *Prestes Maia e as Origens do Urbanismo Moderno em São Paulo*. São Paulo: Empresa das Artes.

TSE (Tribunal Superior de Justiça Eleitoral). 1934. *Boletim Eleitoral—Suplemento ao N. 49*. Rio de Janeiro: TSE.

Viana, Marco Aurelio S. 1985. *Das Ações Possessórias*. São Paulo: Editora Saraiva.

Vianna, Francisco José de Oliveira. 1933. *Evolução do Povo Brasileiro*. 2nd ed. São Paulo: Companhia Editora Nacional.

Vigliara, José Marcelo Menezes, and Ronaldo Porto Macedo Júnior, eds. 1999. *Ministério Público II: Democracia*. São Paulo: Atlas.

Vilela, Anibal, and Wilson Suzigan. 1973. *Politica do Governo e Crescimento da Economia Brasileira, 1889–1945*. Rio de Janeiro: IPEA/INPES.

Vincent, Joan. 1989. Contours of change: agrarian law in colonial Uganda, 1895–1962. In Starr and Collier 1989, 153–67.

Wade, Peter. 1993. *Blackness and Race Mixture: The Dynamics of Racial Identity in Colombia.* Baltimore: Johns Hopkins University Press.

Wakefield, Edward Gibbon. 1829. *A Letter From Sydney, the Principal Town of Australasia; Outline of a Theory of Colonization.* London: Joseph Cross.

———. 1833. *England and America: A Comparison of the Social and Political State of Both Nations.* 2 vols. London: Richard Bentley.

Waldron, Jeremy. 1988. *The Right to Private Property.* Oxford: Oxford University Press.

Weinstein, Barbara. 1996. *For Social Peace in Brazil: Industrialists and the Remaking of the Working Class in São Paulo, 1920–1964.* Chapel Hill: University of North Carolina Press.

Wilkins, David E. 1997. *American Indian Sovereignty and the U.S. Supreme Court: The Making of Justice.* Austin: University of Texas Press.

Williamson, Chilton. 1960. *American Suffrage: From Property to Democracy, 1760–1860.* Princeton: Princeton University Press.

Wolfe, Joel. 1993. *Working Women, Working Men: São Paulo and the Rise of Brazil's Industrial Working Class, 1900–1955.* Durham: Duke University Press.

Yúdice, George. 1994. The funkification of Rio. In *Microphone Friends: Youth Music and Youth Culture,* ed. Andrew Ross and Tricia Rose, 193–217. New York: Routledge.

Zaluar, Alba. 1985. *A Máquina e a Revolta.* São Paulo: Editora Brasiliense.

———. 2004. *Integração Perversa: Pobreza e Tráfico de Drogas.* Rio de Janeiro: Editora FGV.

Index

Page references followed by *fig* indicate a photograph, followed by *t* indicate a table; followed by *m* indicate a map.

**FOR**MATION *Series*